*Monographs of the*
*Hebrew Union College*
*Number 22*

---

# *To Worship God Properly: Tensions Between Liturgical Custom and Halakhah in Judaism*

*An I. Edward Kiev*
*Library Foundation Book*

## *Monographs of the Hebrew Union College*

1. Lewis M. Barth, *An Analysis of Vatican 30*
2 Samson H. Levey, *The Messiah: An Aramaic Interpretation*
3 Ben Zion Wacholder, *Eupolemus: A Study of Judaeo-Greek Literature*
4 Richard Victor Bergren, *The Prophets and the Law*
5 Benny Kraut, *From Reform Judaism to Ethical Culture: The Religious Evolution of Felix Adler*
6 David B. Ruderman, *The World of a Renaissance Jew: The Life and Thought of Abraham ben Mordecai Farrisol*
7 Alan Mendelson, *Secular Education in Philo of Alexandria*
8 Ben Zion Wacholder, *The Dawn of Qumran: The Sectarian Torah and the Teacher of Righteousness*
9 Stephen M. Passamaneck, *The Traditional Jewish Law of Sale: Shulḥan Arukh, Ḥoshen Mishpat, Chapters 189-240*
10 Yael S. Feldman, *Modernism and Cultural Transfer: Gabriel Preil and the Tradition of Jewish Literary Bilingualism*
11 Raphael Jospe, *Torah and Sophia: The Life and Thought of Shem Tov ibn Falaquera*
12 Richard Kalmin, *The Redaction of the Babylonian Talmud: Amoraic or Saboraic?*
13 Shuly Rubin Schwartz, *The Emergence of Jewish Scholarship in America: The Publication of the Jewish Encyclopedia*
14 John C. Reeves, *Jewish Lore in Manichaean Cosmogony: Studies in the Book of Giants Traditions*
15 Robert Kirschner, *Baraita De Melekhet Ha-Mishkan: A Critical Edition with Introduction and Translation*
16 Philip E. Miller, *Karaite Separatism in Nineteenth-Century Russia: Joseph Solomon Lutski's Epistle of Israel's Deliverance*
17 Warren Bargad, "*To Write the Lips of Sleepers*": *The Poetry of Amir Gilboa*
18 Marc Saperstein, "*Your Voice Like a Ram's Horn*": *Themes and Texts in Traditional Jewish Preaching*
19 Emanuel Melzer, *No Way Out: The Politics of Polish Jewry, 1935-1939*
20 Eric L. Friedland, "*Were Our Mouths Filled with Song*": *Studies in Liberal Jewish Liturgy*
21 Edward Fram, *Ideals Face Reality: Jewish Law and Life in Poland 1550-1655*
22 Ruth Langer, *To Worship God Properly: Tensions Between Liturgical Custom and Halakhah in Judaism*

# To Worship God Properly

## Tensions Between Liturgical Custom and Halakhah in Judaism

Ruth Langer

HEBREW UNION COLLEGE PRESS
CINCINNATI

**Library of Congress Cataloging-in-Publication Data**

Langer, Ruth, 1960-
To worship God properly:tensions between liturgical custom and halakhah in Judaism / Ruth Langer.
p. cm.– (Monographs of the Hebrew Union College: no. 22)
ISBN 0–87820–421–0 (hardcover: alk.paper)
1.Judaism–Liturgy–History. 2.Prayer–Judaism. 3.Jewish Law.
4.Rabbinical literature–History and criticism. 5.Benedictions.
6.Piyutim–History and criticism. 7.Kedushah. I.Title. II.Series.
BM660.L26 1998
296.4'5'09–dc21 98-15069

Printed on acid free paper in the United States of America
Typeset by Posner & Sons Ltd, Jerusalem, Israel
Distributed by Wayne State University Press,
4809 Woodward Avenue, Detroit, MI 48201

The I. Edward Kiev Library Foundation

In September 1976 the family and friends of Dr. I. Edward Kiev, distinguished Rabbi, Chaplain, and Librarian of the Hebrew Union College-Jewish Institute of Religion in New York, established a Library Foundation in his memory to support and encourage the knowledge, understanding, and appreciation of scholarship in Judaica and Hebraica. In cooperation with the Hebrew Union College Press, the Foundation offers this work by Ruth Langer as an I. Edward Kiev Library Foundation Book.

# *Contents*

# *Preface*

Histories of Jewish liturgy generally have focused on reconstructing the origins of prayer texts, applying philological and form-critical methodologies to the limited evidence available from late antiquity. Significantly less attention has been paid to the development of the legal system that came to undergird these texts or to understanding their much better documented development in the medieval and modern worlds. This book addresses these lacunae, offering not a history of the specifics of the prayerbook itself, but rather an analysis of some of the dynamics that shaped Jewish liturgical law and determined the broader outlines of the prayer life of the Jews. While the focus here will be on the medieval period, later developments cannot be totally ignored.

Few thinking human beings would willingly participate in rituals they deemed meaningless, worthless, or even destructive. A potent force driving the early development of rabbinic prayer and its legal system was the need to establish that this innovative means of worship was indeed an acceptable, meaningful, constructive worship of God. Once the general outlines were established, Jewish communities and their leaders continually refined the details of this system to ensure its ongoing ability to please God, fulfill Israel's covenantal responsibilities of worship, and thus ensure God's continuing providential care for Israel. While the mechanics of acceptable liturgical prayer (as opposed to private, incidental prayer) have changed over the centuries as Jewish understandings of God have changed, this desire to offer and ensure acceptable worship has remained a constant overarching theme. The reshaping of these understandings by new intellectual and social currents has itself given form to the history of Jewish liturgy, generating rereadings and reinterpretations of the rabbinic legal traditions about prayer.

Such an immense topic is best approached through very specific case studies: the status of non-talmudic benedictions, the acceptability of added *piyyutim*, the necessity of community for reciting the *kedushah*. By way of introduction, Chapter One provides an analysis of the liturgical law presented by the corpus of Jewish writings from late antiquity as it was received in the medieval world. After a consideration of the rabbinic issues upon which the acceptability of prayer depends, I offer a basic list of the legal principles established by the Tannaim and Amoraim to ensure the proper functioning of their innovative system of worship. These principles came to form the authoritative guide for further developments in Jewish liturgy in later generations.

Central to these principles is the concept that acceptable liturgical prayer takes the form of blessings composed according to a specific pattern and invoking God in a very precise way. Chapter Two investigates the development and implementation of the corollary that invoking this blessing formula in ways that deviate from the specific directions of the Talmud constitutes precisely inefficacious and even dangerous prayer.

However, questions about appropriate prayer language go beyond the specifics of the blessing formula. Chapter Three traces and analyzes the battles fought over the legitimacy of inserting liturgical poetry into the fixed texts of the statutory prayers. Legal traditions ascribing efficacy to precise recitation of authoritative prayers found these creative additions to those texts extremely problematic.

The final chapter looks at a distinctly different aspect of the Jewish liturgical experience: the requirement of community for the proper recitation of certain prayers–specifically, for every prayer that includes the angelic liturgy. As in the preceding two chapters, though, the burning question is whether improper recitation of these prayers–in this case, in an improper setting–is dangerously unacceptable to God.

Underlying all three studies are additional dynamics, with implications for the general history of Jewish law. In none of these cases did rabbinic leaders have absolute control over the practices of their communities. In all of them, decisions based on legal theory had to interact with the active customs of given communities, with both the practitioners of the customs and the students of the legal theory often claiming to represent divine wishes. The resultant tension was sometimes resolved with the recognition that the implementation of the dictates of legal theory simply was not practical at that time. Under exceptional circumstances, a sage exerted his authority in efforts to eradicate a troublesome custom. More often, the two sides compromised by reinterpreting either the theory, the custom, or both, to bring them into harmony.

Active custom was not the only challenge to Jewish liturgical law. Persecutions uprooted individuals and communities, disrupting embedded customs and reshaping Jews' interactions with their God and with their greater world. Ways of understanding Judaism also shifted and such developments as the universal imposition of Babylonian talmudic law under the Geonim, the exposure to Greco-Arabic philosophy and poetics, and the emergence of the various schools of Jewish mysticism also challenged customary behavior.

We gain insights into these dynamics using the tools not only of historical scholarship, but also those of the anthropological study of ritual. Why is it necessary to have a single, fixed, blessing formula, and why is it so important to limit its application? What does the use of a specific unchanging liturgical formula express? What is the role of meaning in the language of ritual, and at what point does its performance move beyond specific dictionary definitions of the words? Such considerations also illumine the interactions of communal liturgy with rabbinic authority, as well as the variable levels of openness to liturgical change in historical Jewish communities.

While Jews have grappled with the problem of acceptable non-sacrificial worship of God for nearly two thousand years, their solutions have never been monolithic or simple. This book explores and seeks to explain some of those solutions.

I must express heartfelt thanks to numerous people and organizations who have aided me in this project. Prof. Samuel T. Lachs of Bryn Mawr College was the inspiring teacher who opened the doors of Jewish Studies and rabbinic literature for me. Prof. Jakob J. Petuchowski, of blessed memory, led me into the world of liturgy. Under his guidance I received my graduate training in the field and first conceived of the topic of my dissertation, now reshaped as this book. The initial studies that led to Chapters Two and Four were written under the guidance of Profs. Richard S. Sarason and Ben Zion Wacholder, respectively. Prof. Sarason and Prof. Mark Washofsky deserve additional thanks for their service as readers of my dissertation after Prof. Petuchowski's untimely death. To them and to all my professors at Hebrew Union College and Hebrew University, I owe a deep debt of gratitude.

Various others have offered invaluable suggestions along the way. Prof. Marvin Fox, of blessed memory, brought to my attention the theme of efficacious or acceptable prayer that underlies and unifies the various issues studied here. Prof. Reuven Kimelman read carefully and commented sagely on the original dissertation. Profs. Israel Ta-Shma and Ezra Fleischer read early versions of papers on which these chapters are based and pointed me towards more sophisticated research. I must also thank the various participants over the last few years in the Brandeis Seminar on Early Judaism and Christianity, especially Profs. Kimelman and Bernadette Brooten, for their detailed comments on and discussions of the introductory sections of Chapters One and Four. My colleague at Boston College, Prof. Anthony J. Saldarini, commented most helpfully on my interpretations of tannaitic-period history. Prof. Ithamar Gruenwald's comments on Chapter Four were also invaluable. My true gratitude goes also to my teacher, friend, and mentor, Prof. Michael A. Meyer, chair of the Publications Committee of Hebrew Union College, for indicating at the earliest appropriate moment his interest in this book, and to Barbara Selya, managing editor of the

HUC Press, for being such a wise and kind guide through the various stages of bringing the manuscript to publication. Any errors and omissions that remain are, of course, mine.

Institutions have also provided important support. Most significant has been my access to the excellent Judaica collection and friendly, helpful librarians at Brandeis University. Thanks are also due to the libraries and librarians of Hebrew College, Harvard University, and, especially, Hebrew Union College in Cincinnati. Fot references to Genizah manuscripts, I am grateful to Prof. Ezra Fleischer and his מפעל לחקר השירה והפיוט של האקדמיה הלאומית הישראלית למדעים. Research for my dissertation was supported by the National Foundation for Jewish Culture and the Memorial Foundation for Jewish Culture.

The wellspring of my life and my wellbeing is my family. From my parental home, I learned the values that enable me to pursue a career as a scholar–self-discipline, the drive for intellectual honesty, and a love of learning. From my husband's family, I have learned to pursue the highest standards of Jewish scholarship, and I thank my parents-in-law, Nahum M. and Helen H. Sarna, for all their help and support over the years, especially for their comments to the drafts of my dissertation, their encouragement, and their hours of babysitting. My children, Aaron and Leah, provide a critical diversion and balance to my life. It is a constant joy watching them grow and a particular joy watching them enter into the traditions of Jewish prayer and learning.

This book is dedicated in love to my husband, Jonathan D. Sarna, for his constant support, love, and encouragement. He is my best critic, my best friend, and a constant source of inspiration.

# *Abbreviations*

| | |
|---|---|
| *B.* | Babylonian Talmud |
| *HUCA* | *Hebrew Union College Annual* |
| *JAAR* | *Journal of the American Academy of Religion* |
| *JBL* | *Journal of Biblical Literature* |
| *JJLG* | *Jahrbuch der jüdisch-literarischen Gesellschaft* |
| *JJS* | *Journal of Jewish Studies* |
| *JQR* | *Jewish Quarterly Review* |
| *M.* | Mishnah |
| *MGWJ* | *Monatsschrift für Geschichte und Wissenschaft des Judenthums* |
| OH | Oraḥ Ḥayyim, first division of the Tur and Shulḥan Arukh |
| *P.* | Palestinian Talmud |
| *PAAJR* | *Proceedings of the American Academy for Jewish Research* |
| *REJ* | *Revue des études juives* |
| *SRHJ* | *Social and Religious History of the Jews* |
| *T.* | Tosefta |
| YD | Yoreh Deah, second division of the Tur and Shulḥan Arukh |

# 1

# The Creation of a Valid Non-Sacrificial Liturgy

In the concluding minutes of Yom Kippur, the most solemn day of the year, when Jews collectively and individually petition God to forgive their sins, one hears this cry:[1]

> פתח לנו שער בעת נעילת שער כי פנה יום. היום יפנה השמש יבוא ויפנה, נבואה שעריך.
> Open for us a gate even at the time of the locking of the gates, for the day is waning. The day is fading, the sun is beginning to set, let us enter Your gates!

While the theme of gates opening and closing is central to the poetry of this *neilah* or concluding service, the image itself is a multivalent symbol, rich in associations for the worshipers. On one level, the gate is the gate of mercy through which Jews seek to find atonement on this day. As the day ends, the astronomical "gates" of heaven close on the sun. But the "locking of the gates" also refers to the physical closing of the great gates that marked the end of any day's sacrifices in the Jerusalem Temple. Behind this prayer, then, is the profound consciousness that these particular gates are destroyed and may neither be opened nor shut. "Let us enter Your gates" thus is a prayer simultaneously for immediate forgiveness and for the future messianic redemption–when it will again be possible to seek atonement in the Jerusalem Temple.[2]

The author of this prayer and many of those reciting it were doubtless aware

1. This prayer (Davidson 243פ), likely a fragment of an otherwise lost poem, appears only in the rites of Germany and Poland. A few communities insert liturgical poetry in between the two lines. See: דניאל גולדשמידט, מחזור לימים נוראים, כרך ב, יום כפור (ירושלים: ח' קורן, תש"ל), 743–745.

2. This phrase, and indeed the entire prayer, is a literary allusion to Ps. 118:19-20, part of the Temple *hallel* liturgy taken over into the synagogue.

also of a set of traditions ascribed to Rabbi Elazar ben Pedat, who claimed: מיום שחרב בית המקדש נפסקה חומת ברזל בין ישראל לאביהם שבשמים (Ever since the Temple was destroyed, a wall of iron has separated Israel from her heavenly Father.) Any normal gates in this wall are sealed, for Rabbi Elazar also reported: מיום שחרב בית המקדש ננעלו שערי תפלה (Ever since the Temple was destroyed, the gates of prayer have been locked); but: אף על פי ששערי תפלה ננעלו, שערי דמעה לא ננעלו (even though the gates of prayer are locked, the gates of tears are not locked).[3] Without the Temple and its physically accessible entrance into God's earthly dwelling, Israel finds herself almost completely cut off. Only extraordinary means can enable her to find a "gate" into God's heavenly abode. The God who had been immanent and accessible in Jerusalem is now almost fully transcendent and inaccessible.

Not every early sage resorted to such bleak metaphors to describe the religious crisis facing Judaism after the Roman destruction of the Temple in 70 C.E. All, though, faced the reality that it was now impossible to perform the sacrificial acts of worship commanded in God's revealed Torah–acts that they understood as necessary to enable Israel to maintain her covenantal relationship with the Holy One. Even before the failure of the Bar Kokhba revolt in 135 demonstrated that the Temple would not be speedily rebuilt, sages began to search for other ways to stand in God's presence, to offer appropriate, acceptable worship, and to know that Israel was still under God's providential care. The result of this process was the system of Jewish worship still in effect today.

Although that basic system of rabbinic prayer[4] was well defined by the time of the codification of the Mishnah, it has constantly been subject to further refinements over the centuries. As these refinements have accumulated, they have been transmitted, along with the original system, as halakhah, which defines the legal boundaries of acceptable prayer. From an ideological standpoint, this law, as God's, should be timeless and unchanging. In actuality, however, its definition and implementation have been constantly shaped by the Jews' dispersal among the nations and by other historical changes, which have created diverse cultures within Judaism, each with customs it holds as sacred, or almost as

3. From *B. Berakhot* 32b.

4. Most discussions of Jewish liturgy refer to "synagogue prayer." This is a misnomer, developed perhaps because of an assumed parallel between the church and the synagogue. However, it is not at all clear, as we shall see below, to what extent early rabbinic prayer was tied to the synagogue structure. While one might claim that the synagogue came to be a sanctified gathering place for prayer, the liturgy has never been dependent on any dedicated or consecrated space. In addition, while the concept "church" applies not just to the building but even more to the community gathered in it, "synagogue" applies just to the building and not to the Jews who gather there.

sacred, as the legal tradition itself. At the same time, new intellectual currents have modified Jewish understandings of what exactly constitutes acceptable prayer and even how and why prayer may be efficacious. It is to the interactions of all these factors that we now turn.

Late first-century Israel was a society in chaos. Aside from the economic devastation occasioned by the war, the central structures of Second Temple-period Jewish political and religious life had been abolished, and the Roman conquerors had no real interest in replacing them. Internal rabbinic history reports that Rabban Gamliel, at least, was recognized by the Romans as spokesman for the Jews and was able to intervene successfully with the authorities on occasion. Gedaliah Alon suggests that this process of rabbinic ascension in Roman eyes was gradual. Beginning with Rabban Yoḥanan ben Zakkai's gathering of his students to his place of detention at Yavneh, it evolved, over at least a quarter of a century, into the regeneration of national organizations of civil and religious leadership that the Romans eventually recognized in a more formal way.[5] Seth Schwartz's reading of Josephus basically supports this understanding of the period, adding that the more prestigious priestly classes and the Herodian kings were actively maneuvering to receive Roman recognition at least until the mid-80s, when Rabban Gamliel provided political leadership to disparate groups and became the dominant interpreter of Torah in Palestine and even beyond.[6] Even so, Schwartz finds propaganda

5. *The Jews in their Land in the Talmudic Age (70-640 C.E.)*, trans. Gershon Levi (Cambridge, Massachusetts: Harvard University Press, 1989), chaps. 5-6.

6. *Josephus and Judaean Politics* (Leiden: E.J. Brill, 1990), Chapter V: AJ, The Pharisees, and Early Rabbinic Judaism, and Ch. VI: Conclusion. See too: Alon, *The Jews in their Land...*, 100ff., who discusses the probable opposition of the priestly classes to Rabban Yoḥanan ben Zakkai's leadership; and Tzvee Zahavy, *Studies in Jewish Prayer* (Lanham: University Press of America, 1990), particularly Chs. IV-V, who proposes that the influence of various competing groups, each promoting its form of prayer, contributed to the complex structure of what becomes rabbinic liturgy. Schwartz accepts the theory of Shaye J.D. Cohen, "The Significance of Yavneh: Pharisees, Rabbis, and the End of Jewish Sectarianism," *HUCA* 55 (1984): 27-53, that the pre-destruction sects themselves, without a Temple to define their issues, had already largely lost their identities in this period. (Compare also Cohen's *From the Maccabees to the Mishnah* [Philadelphia: Westminster Press, 1987], 132, 226f.) Another concurring perspective is that of David Goodblatt, *The Monarchic Principle: Studies in Jewish Self-Government in Antiquity* (Tübingen: J.C.B.Mohr (Paul Siebeck), 1994), who claims that the Romans continued their history of interference in Judean politics in their appointment of Rabban Gamliel to be the official Jewish leader of the nation, effectively ending the political leadership of the priests who, as active participants in the revolt, were no longer acceptable (217f.). Based on Josephus and rabbinic traditions about R. Gamliel (193f.), Goodblatt argues convincingly against those, like Fergus Millar, *The Roman Near East*

encouraging Jews to observe the law accurately in Josephus' *Antiquities*; he interprets this as evidence that the nation did not unanimously accept rabbinic leadership, even in the 90s.[7] If, as is increasingly being demonstrated, the Galilean rabbis of the second and third centuries had by no means achieved the level of religious authority that their literature (or its redaction by later generations) ascribed to them, it is also unlikely that their predecessors a century and more earlier, in even more unsettled times, had greater success.[8]

Even if their audience was limited, the rabbis gathering at Yavneh after the destruction of the Temple did consider themselves the legitimate leaders of the people, based on the authority of their received heritage of the Oral Torah.[9] Theirs was a dual challenge. Not only did they have to define the parameters of a new relationship with God that could function without reliance on the Temple and its sacrifices; they also had to convince the rest of the Jewish world that they taught God's authentic will and that their forms of worship were the only effective ways to maintain Israel's relationship with God, at least until the Temple could be rebuilt.

Before turning to an analysis of the liturgical system created by the rabbis and the legal principles they established to guarantee its efficacy, a methodological point is in order. Historians of the Jewish world of late antiquity and students of rabbinic literature have only relatively recently begun to identify the literary layers by which they might eventually gauge the historicity of rabbinic attributions and stories. Because the purpose of the present work is to pursue a limited set of themes into and through the medieval world, we will not engage in this modern problem, but rather encounter the classical rabbinic texts more in the

---

*31 BC - AD 337* (Cambridge, MA: Harvard University Press, 1993), 337, 383, who claim that the lack of any definitively confirming external evidence forces us to date the beginning of the patriarchate to the third, and even the fourth century.

7. *Josephus*..., 199, 216.

8. See Lee I. Levine, *The Rabbinic Class of Roman Palestine in Late Antiquity;* the articles in Part IV of his edited volume, *The Galilee in Late Antiquity*; and the study of Martin Goodman, *State and Society in Roman Galilee, A.D. 132-212* (Totowa, New Jersey: Rowman and Allanheld, 1983) chaps. 7 and 11. Much of the ability of these scholars and others to look critically at the rabbis' self-presentation in the talmudic literature is made possible by comparisons with other contemporary evidence. The question of real rabbinic influence during this period outside of the Land of Israel, especially in Babylonia, but even thorughout the diaspora, has not yet been sufficiently addressed. See the discusssion of Jacob Neusner, who also questions rabbinic authority, in his "Rabbis and Community in Third-Century Babylonia," in *Religions in Antiquity: Essays in Memory of Erwin Ramsdell Goodenough*, ed. Neusner (Leiden: E.J. Brill, 1968) 438-459; and the relevant sections of ישעיה גפני, יהודי בבל בתקופת התלמוד (ירושלים: מרכז זלמן שזר לתולדות ישראל, תשנ"א).

9. *Mishnah Avot* 1:1 presents this claim to authority.

way they have been read before the advent of modern academic scholarship. Although glossing over the multiplicity of communities, periods, and voices in the tannaitic and amoraic texts does not do them full justice, it does allow us to hear the voice of the final redacted traditions–the voice that, received and heard in the medieval world, affected the decisions made there.

### *Rabbinic Prayer in Dialogue with Temple Worship*

Any new system desiring to attract adherents must be designed in a careful dialectic between the old and the new, the accepted and the innovative. The rabbis did not have to wean anyone away from a previous mode of worship–the sacrificial system of the Torah and the Temple simply was suddenly unavailable–but they did need to develop their new form of worship in such a way that Jews would understand the necessity for participation. Therefore, they had to define their liturgical system in connection to and in opposition to the Temple, incorporating language and rituals with which the people already felt comfortable. Although there is no unambiguous evidence for widespread formal communal prayer on the rabbinic model before the destruction of the Temple, the concepts and rituals available to the rabbis almost certainly included the recitation of *shema*,[10] the ritual reading and exposition of Scripture, especially Torah, in the synagogue setting,[11] and probably an expectation that appropriate prayer language would be in Hebrew, largely derivative of the language of the Bible, especially Psalms, and structured as a series of blessings.[12]

10. Aside from rabbinic traditions placing this ritual in the Temple itself (*Mishnah Tamid* 4:3-5:1), the lack of any legend of institution in the literature suggests that its regular recitation was commonly assumed.

11. This is, indeed, the only synagogue ritual for which there exists independent evidence in this period in Israel or in the diaspora. Some claim that the designation of the synagogue in the Greek diaspora as "proseuche" indicates that the primary function of the building was for prayer. However, our only descriptions of activities in these buildings is of the reading and teaching of Scripture and of non-liturgical gatherings. See, for instance, Philo's Embassy to Gaius 132-134, 155-156, 311-313; Flaccus 47-48; Moses II, 215-216. See Martin Hengel's detailed study, "Proseuche und Synagogue: Jüdische Gemeinde, Gotteshaus und Gottesdienst in der Diaspora und in Palästina," in *Tradition und Glaube: Das frühe Christentum in seiner Umwelt, Festgabe für Karl Georg Kuhn*, ed. Gert Jeremias, Heinz-Wolfgang Kuhn, Hartmut Stegemann (Göttingen: Vandenhoeck & Ruprecht, 1971): 157-184; and Steven Fine's *This Holy Place: On the Sanctity of the Synagogue during the Greco-Roman Period* (Notre Dame University Press, 1997), chap. 1: "Sacred Places That They Call Synagogues: The Roots of Synagogue Holiness during the Second Temple Period."

12. This is the nature of the Temple-period liturgies recorded in rabbinic literature (for

The dominant model, though, was the Temple, deliberately chosen as the source of greatest continuity with the past, hope for the future, and connection with rituals of guaranteed efficacy.[13] The rabbinic traditions present most parts of the statutory liturgy as, at some level, substitutes for sacrifices, and the rabbinic texts frequently use the language of Temple rituals in their discussions of prayer. The *gemara* understands the primary statement linking the *amidah* to sacrifices, תפלות כנגד תמידין תקנום (they established prayers to correspond to the daily sacrifices),[14] as an expression of temporal equivalence rather than of substitution or replacement. However, earlier in the same discussion the comment תפלה במקום קרבן היא (prayer is in the place of sacrifice),[15] indicates that some, at least, found wider significance in the relationship. Similarly, the rabbinic texts record that the sacrifice of the heart (עבודה שבלב) is prayer (תפילה),[16] that prayer is greater than either good deeds or sacrifices,[17] and that one should invite someone to be the *sheliaḥ tzibbur*, not by asking him to "come and pray," but by requesting: בוא וקרב, עשה קרבנינו עשה צרכינו, עשה מלחמותינו פייס בעדינו (Come and draw near [to the ark], perform our sacrifices, petition for our needs, fight our battles, seek reconciliation for us).[18]

Most of the halakhic consequences of this direct linkage between liturgical

---

example: *Mishnah Tamid* 5:1; *Mishnah Yoma* 7:1; *Mishnah Taanit* 2) in some of the liturgical texts found at Qumran (as analyzed by Bilhah Nitzan, *Qumran Prayer and Religious Poetry*, trans. Jonathan Chipman [Leiden: E.J.Brill, 1994], Part I: Fixed Prayer in Qumran and in Mainstream Judaism) and in Ben Sira 51:12. Joseph Heinemann, in his *Prayer in the Talmud: Forms and Patterns*, trans. Richard Sarason (Berlin, New York: Walter de Gruyter, 1977), applies form-critical methodologies to uncover the various "grammars" of prayer available in late antiquity.

13. Compare the following discussion with Steven Fine's complementary treatment of what he terms the "templization" of synagogues in his *This Holy Place.*

14. *B. Berakhot* 26b; *P. Berakhot* 4:1, 7b reads תפלות מתמידין גמרו (they derived the prayers from the daily sacrifices).

15. *B. Berakhot* 26a.

16. *P. Berakhot* 4:1, 7a; a parallel comment is in the standard printed version of *B. Taanit* 2a, but not in most manuscripts or citations by the Rishonim. See the comment of Louis Ginzberg, פירושים וחידושים בירושלמי, כרך ג' (ניו־יורק: בית המדרש לרבנים באמריקה, תש"א–תשכ"א; ד"ח, תשל"א), 3; *Sifrei Devarim, Ekev* 41, Finkelstein ed., 87-88, preserves a variant.

17. *B. Berakhot* 32b. Note that the Munich manuscript version, as recorded in דיקדוקי סופרים, makes an even stronger statement: גדולה תפלה יותר מן הקרבנות כולן (prayer is greater than *all* of the sacrifices).

18. *P. Berakhot* 4:4, 8b. However, Louis Ginzberg points out that certain manuscripts read instead of קרבנינו (our sacrifices), קרבינו (our wars), creating a literary parallel with מלחמותינו (our battles). But the parallel in *Bereishit Raba* 49:8 (Theodor-Albeck, 506-507), although subject to variation in several manuscripts, consistently maintains a reference to the *amidah* as a sacrifice. See Ginzberg's ...פירושים וחידושים, III: 350.

prayer and the Temple sacrifices determine practical directives for prayer. Israel Knohl suggests that the rabbinic silent *amidah* echoes the absolute silence in which the priests performed the Temple sacrifices.[19] The appropriate times for the *amidah* are all defined in terms of the Temple sacrifices. The rabbis decree that *shaḥarit* may be recited through the fourth hour of the morning–based on Rabbi Yehudah ben Bava's testimony that he witnessed the performance of the Temple sacrifice at this time.[20] The Palestinian Talmud establishes that the time for *minḥah* corresponds, not to that of the regular, daily afternoon sacrifice (תמיד), but to that of the incense offering.[21] In both cases, these are times of Temple functions. Similarly, the Palestinian Talmud defines the time of *neilah* by the Temple precedent, rather than by natural time indicators.[22] The rabbis even couch some of the rulings about the appropriate times to recite *shema*, which no one claims replaces a Temple function, in terms of the Temple and priestly rituals. The Mishnah defines the earliest time for the evening recitation to be משעה שהכהנים נכנסים לאכול בתרומתן (from the time that the priests enter to eat their priestly portion). The redactor's decision to use this language instead of the functionally equivalent and more readily understood צאת הכוכבים (time that the stars come out) found in alternative traditions, reflects a conscious desire to cast as much liturgical discussion as possible in Temple terms.[23]

No less important than the issue of the time of prayer is the unquestioned assumption that one's physical orientation while reciting the *amidah* must always be towards the innermost sanctum of the Temple. In accordance with Solomon's prayer at the consecration of his Temple,[24] this holds wherever one is in the world. If one is unable physically to face or discern the right direction, one must at least direct one's heart properly.[25] Indeed, the vast majority of synagogues from late antiquity discovered in Israel are explicitly oriented towards Jerusalem, and by the fourth to sixth centuries, chancel screens begin to appear

19. "Between Voice and Silence: The Relationship Between Prayer and Temple Cult," *JBL* 115 (1996): 26-28.

20. *B. Berakhot* 26b-27a.

21. *P. Berakhot* 4:1, 7b. The Babylonian tradition apparently found both times acceptable, or was, in any case, less concerned about establishing an exact time for this service. See *B. Berakhot* 26b.

22. *P. Taanit* 4:1, 67c; note that the parallel in *P. Berakhot* 4:1, 7c does not resolve the question whether to define the time of *neilah* by Temple precedent or by the actual time of day.

23. *Mishnah Berakhot* 1:1; *Tosefta Berakhot* 1:1; *B. Berakhot* 2b-3a. For an extended exposition of these passages, see Carl M. Perkins, "The Evening *Shema*: A Study in Rabbinic Consolation," *Judaism* 43 (1994): 27-36.

24. I Kings 8:48ff.

25. *Mishnah Berakhot* 4:5-6; *Tosefta Berakhot* 3:16, 18; *B. Berakhot* 30a; *P. Berakhot* 4:5, 8b-c.

in some structures demarcating as especially holy the area of the Torah ark on the Jerusalem-facing wall. This screen may also recall the dividers between the inner and outer Temple courts.[26] Even if God's house has been destroyed, it is still המקום, "The Place," Israel's spiritual center and her most reliable locus of contact with the Divine.

Rabbinic prayers also consciously include certain direct references to or recreations of Temple rituals. Key to the *musaf* service is the recitation of the biblical verses about that day's additional sacrifice. Some medieval scholars deemed the correct repetition of these verses so critical that they limited their recitation on holidays to the *sheliaḥ tzibbur* who, perhaps because he had a written copy of the prayers, would be certain to recite them correctly.[27] *Mishnah Sotah* 7:6 records that the priestly benediction, clearly associated with the sacrifices, was already performed outside of the Temple precincts during Temple times, but with liturgical changes that indicated its lesser status. We have no evidence as to the context of this ritual. In the rabbinic period, this ritual was incorporated into the *amidah*, at its conclusion, and the liturgy then developed an additional prayerful response to its blessing of peace, now the concluding benediction of the service.[28] Beyond these, we can look to the incorporation into rabbinic prayer of such rituals as blowing the shofar, processions with the lulav, the counting of the omer, the priestly benediction, and the recitation of *hallel*, all of which had their original locus in the Temple.[29]

One striking passage develops the analogy between Temple worship and rabbinic prayer further:

> אמר עולא כל הקורא ק"ש בלא תפילין כאילו מעיד עדות שקר בעצמו. א"ר חייא בר אבא א"ר יוחנן כאילו הקריב עולה בלא מנחה וזבח בלא נסכים. ואמר רבי יוחנן הרוצה שיקבל עליו עול מלכות שמים שלמה יפנה ויטול ידיו ויניח תפילין ויקרא ק"ש ויתפלל וזו היא מלכות שמים שלמה. א"ר חייא בר אבא א"ר יוחנן כל הנפנה ונוטל ידיו ומניח תפילין וקורא ק"ש ומתפלל מעלה עליו

26. See Joan Branham, "Vicarious Sacrality: Temple Space in Ancient Synagogues," in *Ancient Synagogues: Historical Analysis and Archaeological Discovery*, ed. Dan Urman and Paul Flesher (Leiden: E.J.Brill, 1995), II: 328-329, 331-336.

27. See OH 591.

28. Reuven Kimelman suggests that the later addition of the priestly benediction to the *amidah* may explain why the Tannaim required bowing at the beginning and end of the preceding *hoda'ah* blessing to mark its status as the last of the series. See his "The Literary Structure of the Amidah and the Rhetoric of Redemption" (reference in bibliography).

29. Tradition presents many of these rituals as the subject of Rabban Yoḥanan ben Zakkai's ordinances in the first years after the destruction of the Temple. Determining their perpetuation, and in what form, was a crucial task. *Mishnah Rosh Hashanah* 4:1-4. See Jacob Neusner, *First Century Judaism in Crisis: Yoḥanan ben Zakkai and the Renaissance of Torah* (Nashville: Abingdon Press, 1975), 182ff.

הכתוב כאלו בנה מזבח והקריב עליו קרבן דכתיב ארחץ בנקיון כפי ואסובבה את מזבחך ה'.
Ulla said: If anyone recites *keriat shema* without [wearing] phylacteries, it is as if he bears false witness against himself. Rabbi Ḥiyya bar Abba cited Rabbi Yoḥanan: It is as if he sacrificed a burnt offering (*olah*) without a meal offering or a sacrifice (*zevaḥ*) without libations. Rabbi Yoḥanan also said: One who wishes to accept upon himself the complete yoke of the Kingdom of Heaven[30] should relieve himself, wash his hands, don phylacteries, recite *keriat shema*, and pray (the *amidah*). This is the complete (acceptance of the) Kingdom of Heaven. Rabbi Ḥiyya bar Abba said in the name of Rabbi Yoḥanan: Scripture considers all who relieve themselves, wash their hands, don phylacteries, recite *keriat shema*, and pray (the *amidah*) to be like those who build an altar and sacrifice upon it, for it is written, "I wash my hands in innocence, and walk around Your altar, O God."[31]

Rabbi Yoḥanan wants to impress upon the common people the importance of participating in the entire rabbinic ritual structure in its proper order. Therefore, he stresses that when one prays properly, the cosmic effect is equivalent to building an altar, i.e, to rebuilding the Temple, and offering a sacrifice. In other words, correct rabbinic prayer with its attendent rituals fulfills God's biblical commandments of worship.

That the rabbinic tradition as a whole treats this more as a rhetorical device of persuasion than a full-blown theological statement about the role of prayer is suggested by its failure to take this concept to its full logical conclusion. In their discussions of sacrifices, the rabbis stress the necessity of absolute precision in the performance of every detail of the ritual. If the elements of the rituals of Yom Kippur or even the daily *tamid* sacrifice are performed out of order, it is as if they had not been performed at all (לא עשה ולא כלום). The Tosafot, reflecting their medieval conceptions of fixed prayer, question why the *gemara* does not extend this concept to the order of the blessings of the *amidah*, as the Mishnah dictates the order of this liturgy in a fashion parallel to its discussions of the sacrificial rituals.[32] But the talmudic corpus does not take this step; one who prays improperly simply fails to fulfill his obligations (לא יצא ידי חובתו). While some of the shift in terminology here simply reflects the differences between the sacrifices performed to fulfill the obligations of all Israel as a community and the prayers recited to fulfill the obligations of the individual, it possibly also differentiates

30. This is a standard rabbinic term for the acceptance of one's status of fealty to God.

31. *B. Berakhot* 14b-15a, citing Ps. 26:6.

32. *B. Sanhedrin* 49b, citing *Mishnah Yoma* 5:7 and interpreting *Mishnah Tamid* 7:3(end). Tosafot, there, ד"ה אף סדר תמיד.

proper sacrifices, which have guaranteed heavenly impact, from proper prayer, which might have no more profound effect than merely to fulfill human responsibility to God.

While the integration of the Temple system into the rabbinic liturgical world was a crucial element in legitimating the rabbinic worship system, the rabbis themselves always considered their system a poor substitute. They looked forward to the speedy rebuilding of the Jerusalem Temple where God would again be worshiped properly and they certainly assumed that any sacrificial worship outside of the official Jerusalem Temple would be decidedly unpleasing to God.[33] Although, according to rabbinic sacred history, the original establishment of the rabbinic system could be traced to the Men of the Great Assembly or even the patriarchs,[34] it was then designed as a supplement to the Temple sacrifices, not as a substitution. Thus, while explicit and deliberate ties to the Temple and its rituals gave rabbinic prayer legitimacy and authority, it was equally crucial for the rabbis to differentiate the institutions, preserving intact the greater sanctity of the Temple itself. Anything less would have damaged the credibility of the rabbinic liturgy in the eyes of a community mourning for the loss of their Shrine. The rabbinic discussion of acceptable prayer, thus, had also to delimit the extent of permitted imitation of the Temple, a line which, as we shall see, was not always agreed upon.[35]

In at least the cases of the priestly benediction and the liturgy of the public fast day, the distinction between inside and outside the Temple[36] existed before the destruction of the Temple and was merely perpetuated afterwards. The rabbis

---

33. The very fact that we know of only a very few Jewish Temples erected in the diaspora, none of which postdate the Temple, only serves to prove this point. There is evidence of the use of incense altars outside the Temple, but no indication that animal sacrifices were offered in conjunction with this. See N.M. Sarna, "The Chirotonic Motif on the Lachish Altar," in Y. Aharoni, *Investigations at Lachish* (Tel Aviv, 1975), 44-46. Ruth Clements, Harvard dissertation (1997) on Origen's *Peri Pascha*, suggests that Philo's descriptions of Alexandrian Passover celebrations in Spec. II: 148-149 and Dec. 159 should be understood as attempts to justify the offering of this single animal sacrifice in Alexandria itself.

34. *B. Berakhot* 26b; *B. Megillah* 17b; *P. Berakhot* 4:1, 7b; *P. Pesaḥim* 5:1, 31d.

35. I disagree with Arnold Goldberg, "Service of the Heart: Liturgical Aspects of Synagogue Worship," in *Standing Before God: Studies on Prayer in Scriptures and in Traditions with Essays in Honor of John M. Oesterreicher*, ed. Asher Finkel and Lawrence Frizzell (New York: Ktav, 1981): 195-211, who claims that the rabbinic self-differentiation from the Temple indicates the non-liturgical status and degree of illegitimacy of rabbinic worship. Rather, one should be impressed by the pains taken by the rabbis to define themselves positively in terms of the Temple and understand the differentiations as imposed by necessity.

36. Contrary to the assumptions of many, a ritual performed "outside the Temple" does not mean it was necessarily performed in a synagogue.

record that the priests in the Temple recited the priestly benediction as a single blessing, raised their hands as high as their heads, and pronounced the Tetragrammaton. In all other places, however, they recited three separate blessings, raised their hands as high as their shoulders, and referred to God only by epithets.[37] Although blemished priests were completely forbidden from participating in the sacrifices and blessing the people in the Temple, the Talmud allows them to bless the people in the post-Temple setting if they are well known in the community so that their blemishes will not create a distraction. Thus, in the rabbinic liturgical setting, this issue of ritual purity never arises, and only practical concerns limit the participation of a blemished priest.[38]

Early second-century Tannaim rebuked Rabbis Ḥalafta and Ḥananiah ben Teradion for using Temple liturgical forms in the synagogue setting. These rabbis erred by using the Temple response, ברוך שם כבוד מלכותו לעולם ועד (Blessed be His name, whose glorious sovereignty is for ever and ever), instead of amen; they may have compounded their error by invoking this response after every blessing of the fast day liturgy.[39] In either case, the rabbinic sources assume that the Temple liturgy, or the liturgy of the Temple synagogue, not only employed this elaborate, doxological response to every blessing, but also used a blessing formula different from that in any other synagogue or prayer setting; this liturgy prefaced each blessing with ברוך ה׳ אלהינו אלהי ישראל מן העולם (ועד העולם) ברוך... (Blessed is the Lord our God, the God of Israel from eternity [unto eternity], blessed...). Jews may not recite these formulae outside the Temple and its Eastern Gate.[40] In the discussions of both the priestly blessing and the fast-day liturgy, the rabbinic traditions explicitly assign the most elevated, sanctified forms to the Temple rituals. This ensures that participants in parallel rituals elsewhere will be conscious of the lesser sanctity of their rites.

---

37. *Mishnah Sotah* 7:6; *B. Sotah* 38a.

38. *B. Megillah* 24b; *P. Taanit* 4:1, 67b. Compare also the issue of the priestly recitation of only a single blessing before *shema* in the morning in the Temple–apparently because it was too early to recite the *yotzer*. Without the excuse of the prior demands of the sacrificial cult, the rabbis carefully refused to perpetuate this custom of early recitation of *shema*. See *B. Yoma* 37b; *P. Berakhot* 1:1, 3a; 1:5, 3c; *B. Berakhot* 11b.

39. *Mishnah Taanit* 2:5; *B. Taanit* 16b.

40. *B. Taanit* 16b. This liturgical formula appears in the doxological conclusions to the five books of the Psalter, including the words given here in parentheses in Ps. 41:14 and 106:48. These words, according to rabbinic tradition, were added in response to sectarian denials of the existence of the world to come. (*Mishnah Berakhot* 9:5.) Heinemann, noting that this elaborate formula only appears explicitly in discussions of the fast day liturgy, questions whether it ever had a broader usage. He also indicates that we have no real evidence that *amen* was never recited in the Temple. See his *Prayer...*, 127. However, the appearance of these formulae in the Psalter suggests the possibility of their broader use.

But the story of Rabbis Ḥalafta and Ḥananiah ben Teradion also illustrates the spiritual tension engendered in the rabbinic system by the desire to perpetuate Temple forms. That tension would seem also to lie behind the rabbinic ruling that although the officiant at the seder must elevate the matzah and bitter herbs, the shankbone on the seder plate must be virtually ignored. It is only a symbol, not the real Passover offering, and even the appearance of eating sanctified food outside the Temple is to be avoided.[41] In this case, we can point to a plausible source for this reaction. S. Safrai cites evidence for the continuation of some forms of Passover offering, or at least the ritual eating of roasted kid, into the second century.[42] Rabbinic concern about the propriety of this attempt to preserve the Temple form of the seder could well have resulted in the dramatic deemphasizing of one of its central symbolic elements.

The rabbis differentiated between Temple and synagogue not only in rituals and prayers but also in their general attitude to the buildings themselves; while a need to establish the holiness of the place dictated similar rules of behavior in both places, one activity, spitting, was forbidden in the Temple but allowed in the synagogue.[43] Similarly, lepers were denied admission to the Temple, but they could enter the synagogue as long as a divider had been erected to separate them from the rest of the community.[44] Thus although the synagogue and rabbinic prayer substituted for the Temple in many ways, they remained at a separate and distinctly lower level of holiness.[45]

41. *B. Pesaḥim* 116b.

42. "הערות היסטוריות למשנת פסחים, פרק עשירי," המקרא ותולדות ישראל (מחקרים לזכרו של יעקב ליוור) (תל אביב: אוניברסיטת תל אביב, תשל"ב), 299–300.

43. *B. Berakhot* 62b-63a. Note that although the rabbis generally permitted expectoration in the synagogue, it was not considered a desirable behavior (it is like spitting before a king, according to *B. Berakhot* 24b), and they legislated exactly how one must perform this bodily function if it becomes necessary. See *B. Berakhot* 24b; *P. Berakhot* 3:5, 6d; *P. Megillah* 3:1, 73d.

44. *Mishnah Negaim* 13:12.

45. On the use of Temple symbols in the synagogue, see Fine's *This Holy Place.* The Temple menorah was widely depicted in the decorative arts of the early synagogue, and archaeological evidence points to its actual use for illumination, particularly in the ark area, both with seven branches and with other numbers. A *baraita* establishes that a menorah intended for use in one's home must be distinguished from the Temple candelabrum by having either fewer or more branches. This tradition of differentiation need not have begun only after the destruction of the Temple, but it certainly received added meaning then and did affect the form of the menorah as it came to be used in synagogue lighting. See *B. Menaḥot* 28b; *B. Arakhin* 6b; *B. Avodah Zara* 43a; *B. Rosh Hashanah* 24a-b; *Mishneh Torah, Hilkhot Beit Habeḥirah* 7:10; *Tur* YD 141. On the Palestinian tendency to consider the *ner tamid* of the synagogue to have a degree of sanctity that prohibited the use of its light for any practical purpose, see the discussion of Israel Ta-Shma, "'מקדש מעט' הסמל והממשות," בתוך כנסת

Legislative concern for ritual purity also derived from priestly precedents, which demanded a rigorous maintenance of standards for the Temple precinct itself, for the animals offered as sacrifices, for the officiants, and even for Israelites who wished to enter the Temple courts, let alone draw near to the inner sanctuary.[46] This system, established biblically, is premised on the idea that the Holy of Holies is the locus of God's indwelling on earth. As such, it is imbued with such a level of sanctity as to be dangerous to anyone unqualified to draw near, let alone enter. Only in a state of ritual purity could one penetrate the concentric circles of holiness to the limit decreed for one's lineage. The synagogue had no Holy of Holies, but the rabbis, without drawing explicit parallels with Temple procedures, understood God's presence to be invoked by the presence of a quorum of worshipers.[47] Even if most categories of ritual impurity no longer applied (especially because many could no longer be remedied), it was inconceivable to the rabbis that all such categories be abandoned and that one might stand in God's presence in just any state. They struggled to establish the appropriate degree of purity required for the verbal worship of God. One must distance oneself from any excrement, garbage, or bad odor by at least four cubits to recite *shema* or the *amidah*. This requirement is so serious that if one happens to enter such an impure area while reciting *shema*, one must stop the recitation, and if one notices in the middle of the *amidah* that one's location is unsuitable, one is required to remove oneself in the middle of the prayer.[48]

Thus the rabbis deliberately transferred Temple labels, rituals, and schedules to create a natural and comfortable setting with overtones of normalcy, sanctity, and continuity. Not only did the connection with the Temple help to legitimatize their revolutionary new system; it allowed them to justify changes as neces-

עזרא: ספרות וחיים בבית הכנסת, אסופת מאמרים מוגשת לעזרא פליישר, בעריכת שולמית אליצור, משה דוד הר, אביגדור שנאן, גרשון שקד (ירושלים: יד יצחק בן צבי ומכון בן־צבי לחקר קהילות ישראל במזרח, תשנ"ה): 351–364.

46. S. Safrai, *The Jewish People in the First Century: Historical Geography, Political History, Social, Cultural and Religious Life and Institutions*, (Philadelphia: Fortress Press, 1976), 873, 877; Menahem Haran, *Temples and Temple-Service in Ancient Israel: An Inquiry into Biblical Cult Phenomena and the Historical Setting of the Priestly School* (Winona Lake, Indiana: Eisenbrauns, 1985), especially chap. 9.

47. *B. Berakhot* 6a has edited the tannaitic tradition so that it refers to prayer. *Mekhilta*, Yitro 11 (Horowitz-Rabin, p. 243), commenting on Exodus 20:21, speaks only of ten men in the synagogue. *Mishnah Avot* 3:6 speaks of ten studying Torah together without specifying their location.

48. *B. Berakhot* 22b, 24b-25b; *P. Berakhot* 3:5, 6d; *P. Megillah* 3:1, 73d. Related issues debated include the protocol for praying while bathing–and hence immodestly clothed (*Mishnah Berakhot* 3:5; *B. Berakhot* 25b); and the status of a man who has had a seminal emission and has not yet ritually cleaned himself by immersion (*Mishnah Berakhot* 3:4-5; *Tosefta Berakhot* 2:12; *B. Berakhot* 20b-22b; *P. Berakhot* 3:4-5, 6c).

sary differentiations from rituals that were only permitted in Jerusalem. The rabbis could decree that only their own preferred practices were acceptable to God and hence permitted in the synagogue; they could relegate the customs of other groups or individuals to the currently nonfunctioning Temple. More frequently, though, they simply maintained a hierarchy of Jewish liturgical life, with the Temple and its strict requirements representing the highest rung and the rabbinic worship system, only slightly less strict on such matters as purity and order of ritual, just below it. Only slightly less efficacious than the biblically decreed sacrifices, it promised to fulfill Israel's covenantal obligations and guarantee access to God's ear.

### *Other Rabbinic Arguments for Efficacy*

In promulgating their worship system, however, the rabbis did not rely solely on connections to the Temple to establish their claims of efficacy. They asserted, in scattered comments, many of which are homiletical verging on the polemical, that certain types and attitudes of prayer contain the power to elicit divine response, to protect, to ensure long life, and to guarantee a place in the world to come. Their assertions make serious theological statements while impressing upon the people the value of assuming the rabbinical obligation to pray.

They maintained, for example, that in spite of the "wall of iron" separating the human and divine realms, certain parts of prayer do elicit a response from God. The Talmud records that when Israel responds, יהא שמיה הגדול מבורך (May His great name be blessed) in the synagogue or study hall, God nods His head and, while enjoying their praise, commiserates with them that they are in exile.[49] Another midrash assures Israel of the divine presence during the synagogue service, recording that when one stands to read Torah, it is as if God stands alongside.[50]

Although the rabbis conceived of the *amidah* as compensating for the unavailable communal daily perpetual and additional offerings, they did not decree

49. *B. Berakhot* 3a. It is unclear to what extent the *kaddish* was used at this period in the synagogue or if this passage even refers only to this prayer. This is our only specific talmudic reference to the use of this response in the synagogue. Heinemann characterizes it as a classic prayer of the study hall. See his *Prayer*..., chap. 10. The linguistic similarity between this response and the language of the known Hebrew doxological responses of the Temple raises the possibility that this passage alludes to some lost prayer. See Ismar Elbogen, *Jewish Liturgy: A Comprehensive History*, trans. Raymond P. Scheindlin (Philadelphia and New York: The Jewish Publication Society and the Jewish Theological Seminary of America, 1993; from 1913 German and 1972 Hebrew editions), 80ff.

50. *B. Megillah* 21a.

specific compensatory rituals for the guilt and sin offerings that individuals had brought to repair their status in the divine realm. This loss of ability to reconcile one's status with God must have been extremely difficult, at least for those who had the proximity or financial ability to frequent the Temple in person. On a day to day basis, rabbinic statutory prayer fulfilled this role in a sort of general, impersonal fashion with its inclusion of benedictions referring to repentance and forgiveness in the *amidah*. Other prayers, sometimes those composed for settings other than communal prayer, like the response to the kaddish, were also believed capable of tempering Divine judgment.[51] In the case of finding atonement for one's sins, the rabbis asserted that, at least to a certain extent, prayer would have the same efficacy. We find a strong statement of this in *B. Rosh Hashanah* 17b:

> ויעבור ה׳ על פניו ויקרא. א״ר יוחנן אלמלא מקרא כתוב אי אפשר לאומרו מלמד שנתעטף הקב״ה כשליח ציבור והראה לו למשה סדר תפלה.[52] אמר לו כל זמן שישראל חוטאין יעשה לפני כסדר הזה ואני מוחל להם. ה׳ ה׳ אני הוא קודם שיחטא האדם ואני הוא לאחר שיחטא האדם ויעשה תשובה.
>
> "The Eternal passed before him and proclaimed."[53] Rabbi Yoḥanan said: If it were not written in Scripture, it would be impossible to say this. [This passage] teaches that the Holy One, blessed be He, wrapped himself [in a tallit] like a *sheliaḥ tzibbur* and showed Moses the order of the prayers. [God] said to him, "Whenever Israel sins, they should follow this ritual, and I will forgive them." "The Eternal, the Eternal" implies: I am the Eternal before a person sins, and I remain the same after he sins and does penance.

Midrashic hyperbole aside, the essential point remains: God has promised that Israel does not need to rely on sacrifices; instead she has the option of using prayer to find expiation for her sins.

To bolster these claims for the efficacy of liturgical prayer, the rabbis maintained that correct performance of certain prayers would produce specific results: saying the evening *shema* would protect its reciter against the demons and

---

51. *B. Shabbat* 119b.

52. Note that the Munich manuscript reads, והראהו למשה רבינו ואמר לו, omitting סדר תפלה. Rabbinowitz finds no support for the version of the printed Talmud. See דיקדוקי סופרים. However, the reference to a *sheliaḥ tzibbur* places this squarely in the context of communal rabbinic prayer in any case.

53. Exodus 34:6. This midrashic interpretation arises from the similarity between the language of this biblical verse and the technical rabbinic term for the leader of the *amidah*, העובר לפני התיבה (the one who passes before the ark).

evil spirits of the night;[54] having a fixed place for prayer would protect against one's enemies;[55] reciting the *amidah* immediately after the *geulah* benediction of *keriat shema* would keep Satan from raising accusations all that day[56] and assure one a place in the world to come,[57] something also promised the one who recites Psalm 145 thrice daily.[58] A long life in this world is promised for those who pray in the synagogue morning and evening,[59] who do not deviate from the community's Torah cycle,[60] who prolong their enunciation of the "*d*" of *eḥad* in the *shema* properly,[61] who desist from reciting *shema* in an impure place,[62] who always make a blessing before reciting the priestly benediction,[63] and who prolong their prayer without expecting results.[64] Rabbi Meir cites the examples of two men who were on their deathbeds and another two who were tried in court for capital crimes. God answered the prayer of the one of each pair who prayed a "complete prayer"; he survived, but his counterpart died.[65] And in those cases where God seemingly has not answered Israel's prayers, the rabbis encourage praying more[66] or fasting.[67]

While certain of these claims are simply statements of rabbinic beliefs about

---

54. *B. Berakhot* 4b-5a; *P. Berakhot* 1:1, 2d.

55. *B. Berakhot* 7b.

56. *P. Berakhot* 1:1, 2d; phrased in *B. Berakhot* 9b as כל הסומך גאולה לתפלה אינו נזוק כל היום כולו (everyone who juxtaposes the *geulah* benediction and the *amidah* will not be harmed all day long).

57. *B. Berakhot* 4b, 9b.

58. *B. Berakhot* 4b.

59. *B. Berakhot* 8a.

60. *B. Berakhot* 8a.

61. *B. Berakhot* 13b; *P. Berakhot* 2:1, 4a.

62. *B. Berakhot* 24b.

63. *B. Sotah* 39a. Obviously, this only applies to priests.

64. *B. Berakhot* 54b-55a. Compare also *B. Berakhot* 32b, which claims that prolonged prayer is more likely to be answered when the worshiper is not trying to force God to respond to human will. The rabbis here, on the one hand, are trying to establish the efficacy of prayer and, on the other, are struggling with the theological difficulty inherent in claims of human abilities magically to bend the will of the Omnipotent.

65. *B. Rosh Hashanah* 18a.

66. *B. Berakhot* 32b; *P. Berakhot* 4:1, 7c; *P. Taanit* 4:1, 67c.

67. *P. Berakhot* 4:3, 8a. We can add here the reasoning given in *P. Taanit* 2:1, 65a, for locating the public fast day prayers in the public square instead of the Temple or synagogue. The rabbis assert that if prayers recited modestly have no effect, one should dramatize one's desperation by publicly denigrating the holiest object of Judaism, placing the Torah ark in the street with ashes on it, calling on God with the shofar like an animal, and going around in the cemetery like the dead–all designed to convince God of the sincerity of the worshiper and to elicit Divine concern.

the nature and efficacy of prayer, others clearly arose from rabbinic attempts to change existing customs. Promises of a long life or a share in the world to come (or threats of the opposite) were a typical rabbinic response to a situation in which they had no judicial power to enforce a particular practice, even in a community generally submitting to rabbinic leadership.[68]

One deliberate liturgical change that the rabbis buttressed with promises of benefits for those who complied occurred in the early tannaitic period, when only the superpious *vatikim* regularly combined their morning *shema* and *amidah*. Near the time of the codification of the Mishnah, some still considered it legitimate to separate and reverse the order of the prayers, at least under extenuating circumstances.[69] The Mishnah does not require the combination of these elements into a single service, and the talmudic traditions consider the various *baraitot* that do combine them to refer only to the customs of the *vatikim*.[70] But by the mid to late third century, the situation changed. Rav or R. Abba bar Yirmiah, both third-century Babylonian Amoraim, counted the principle of connecting the two prayers as one of the three mandatory תכיפות, conjunctions of rituals.[71] Although Rabbi Yoḥanan in Palestine still made a distinction between the required time for morning prayer for the common folk and for the superpious, he also encouraged and even expected that everyone would combine the two prayers, even in the evening. These statements about the beneficial effects of juxtaposing the prayers began to appear only in these early amoraic traditions, reflecting a period when stricter adherence to rabbinic norms was becoming more generally accepted and even expected.[72] Finally, only in the

68. For a survey of the punishments to which the rabbis condemn the speaker of *leshon hara*, an example of an area where the rabbinic courts were powerless, see my *Harm Through the Spoken Word:* לשון הרע and Related Concepts in Rabbinic Literature (Rabbinic Thesis, Hebrew Union College – Jewish Institute of Religion, Cincinnati, 1986), 38-52, 99-100, 118-120.

69. *B. Berakhot* 30a.

70. *Tosefta Berakhot* 1:2, 3:19; *B. Berakhot* 9b, 26a, 30a; *P. Berakhot* 1:2, 3a. On the technical difficulties of *Tosefta Berakhot* 3:19, see Lieberman, תוספתא כפשוטה, I:46.

71. *B. Berakhot* 42a; *P. Berakhot* 1:1, 2d. The other juxtapositions or conjunctions of rituals are the connecting of the laying-on of hands and the actual sacrifice, and an obscure connection between hand washing and a blessing. While both Rashi and Tosafot agree that the *B. Berakhot* passage refers to the hand washing after the meal and the grace after meals, in *B. Sotah* 39a, Tosafot understands it to refer to the requirement that priests wash their hands immediately before performing the priestly benediction. If that was the original intent, then this ruling also places rabbinic prayer in a Temple-like ritual structure.

72. *B. Berakhot* 4b, 9b, 26a. Note that *P. Berakhot* 1:5, 3c, records an incident in the time of Rabbi Yoḥanan where *shema* was recited late on a public fast day so that the *amidah* would be introduced by words of Torah.

name of the mid-fourth century Babylonian Abbaye does the Talmud record the first explicit requirement that everyone follow the full custom of the super-pious and recite *shema* at daybreak.[73] Thus in this case at least, it is likely that the rabbis made a concerted effort to change popular custom. To encourage first the combination of the two prayers and then their recitation at the correct time, they had to provide the incentive of divine protection in this world and a share in the world to come.

One might posit similar motivations for a number of the rabbinic statements about the efficacy of prayer. The rabbis frequently encouraged people to attend the synagogue and berated those who did not do so.[74] Rabbi Meir insisted on the benefits of a full *amidah* within a generation or so of the promulgation of the prayer at Yavneh. It is unlikely that many worshipers at that time could recite an abbreviated version properly, let alone the full text.[75] Similarly, the rabbis promised a long life for those who adhered to the community's cycle of Torah readings. We know from midrashic and poetic traditions that the triennial Palestinian Torah cycles were extremely flexible and may have varied even from one town to another. Without similar evidence, we cannot know for certain how the Babylonians arrived at their uniform annual cycle. Perhaps this promise of a long life is evidence of a transitional stage in the Babylonian tradition, a clash between the two customs,[76] or even of the development of the concept of a seriatum reading in general.[77]

Although we can posit specific reasons for the rabbis' decreeing rewards and

---

73. *B. Berakhot* 9b.

74. See, for example, *B. Berakhot* 4b, 7b-8a.

75. *B. Rosh Hashanah* 18a.

76. Rabbi Ami, to whom this statement is attributed in *B. Berakhot* 8a, was a Babylonian by birth but headed the Palestinian academy in Tiberias in the late third century. Ezra Fleischer posits that at this point, both the original annual cycle and the new triennial cycle coexisted in Palestine. He suggests that the triennial cycle developed in the tannaitic period as a practical response to the time pressures created by the introduction of prayer into the synagogue's rituals. The coexistence of such variant cycles must necessarily have been a source of tension among the Palestinian communities (especially as nothing suggests that there was necessarily uniformity in the calendars according to which the cycles were read). Fleischer suggests that the Babylonian communities, lacking the time-consuming Palestinian sermonic traditions, never felt compelled to drop their original annual cycle. See his "קריאה חד־שנתית ותלת־שנתית בתורה בבית הכנסת הקדום," תרביץ סא (תשנ"ב): 25–43.

77. Fleisher, in the same article, 29f.,suggests that early rabbinic texts preserve traces of a transition from readings devoted solely to the didactic needs of the moment (as in holiday readings) to the concept of a ritual reading of the entire Torah in order. See my "From Study of Scripture to a Reenactment of Sinai: The Emergence of the Synagogue Torah Service," *Worship* 72 (1998): 49.

punishments for some prayer behaviors, for others there are no such explanations. We do not know, for example, why *eḥad* should be lengthened[78] or why ceasing to recite *shema* when in an impure place should be more important than other concerns about ritual purity. What motivated the rabbis to make these statements is irrelevant, however, in terms of their impact. More crucial is that their system established that God hears, desires, and is pleased by prayer, and that the person who prays properly can expect certain rewards in this world and the next. This alone must have been a powerful argument, convincing Jews to follow rabbinic liturgical leadership.

### *The Principles of Talmudic Liturgical Halakhah*

Once the rabbis decreed that all Jews had an obligation, not just to pray, but to pray properly, they necessarily cast themselves in the role of teachers. The system they generated needed a set of relatively simple, accessible rules, a liturgical law that would enable them to promulgate their system and ensure its stability and acceptability.

The Tannaim and Amoraim generated hundreds of laws to distinguish between acceptable and unacceptable practices and define the nature of Jewish liturgy. Many were quite specific, regulating the wording or means of recitation of specific prayers under particular circumstances. A relatively smaller set are broader in scope, allowing for generalization between one specific instance of prayer and another, and can be regarded as the principles of Jewish liturgical law, guiding future generations and ensuring that official, communally ordained Jewish prayer remains acceptable to God. Because the ultimate source of authority for all later rabbinic Judaism was the Talmud, it is the primary source of these halakhic principles, which, at least in theory, govern all aspects of liturgical law for all time. Most of the principles are derived from the Babylonian Talmud, but because of complications created by Palestinian traditions, we cannot totally ignore the Palestinian Talmud either.

The resultant principles can be divided into three basic categories: laws that establish and regulate the communal nature of prayer; laws that generate the framework for the composition of prayers; and laws that define the parameters for the application of these various rules.

---

78. Those who theorize that this is to avoid saying *aḥer* forget that most people recited *shema* without a written text; the similarity between the two letters is visual, not oral. It is possible that this is a custom of some mystic origin, but I have no documentation. Lengthening a dental consonant is nearly impossible; those who claim to do so usually are prolonging an associated vowel sound.

### *A. The Communal Nature of Prayer*

1. **The communal setting is the ideal locus of worship**. Although the rabbis always recognized the legitimacy of–and the necessity of legitimating–the individual Jew's fulfillment of prayer obligations when alone, they consistently placed a higher value on prayer in the communal setting. The prayers of the individual must be the same as those of the congregation,[79] ideally recited at the same time.[80] However, the person praying alone must omit certain elevated, holier sections of the liturgy.[81] Although some rabbis were loathe to mix with the commoners in the synagogue, the Talmud carefully presents them as negative examples, recording the rebukes they received from their colleagues.[82] Participation in the synagogue and public identification as members of the community, then, was expected of Jews from all ranks of society. This egalitarianism can be seen as a "meta-principle" that underlies the entire category of general laws pertaining to the communal nature of prayer.

2. **Prayers must always be composed in the first person plural**, for one must always view oneself within the context of the community.[83]

3. **Any *davar shebikedushah* requires a quorum of ten.** *Mishnah Megillah* 4:3 decrees that certain rituals, *perisat shema*, the repetition of the *amidah*, the priestly benediction, the ritual reading of Scripture, various life cycle rituals, and the invocation of God's name in the *zimmun*, may not take place without the presence of a quorum of ten. The Babylonian Talmud states twice, once as a comment on this *mishnah* and once in a totally independent context, that כל דבר שבקדושה לא יהא פחות מעשרה (everything involving sanctity/sanctification of God, [*davar shebekidushah*], may not be recited in the presence of less than ten men).[84] There is no question that the Amoraim understood the rituals listed in *Mishnah*

79. *B. Taanit* 13b; *P. Berakhot* 5:2, 9b; *P. Taanit* 1:1, 63d.

80. *B. Berakhot* 7b-8a.

81. See A.3. below.

82. *B. Berakhot* 6b-8a; *P. Berakhot* 5:1, 8d.

83. *B. Berakhot* 29b-30a, discussing the traveler's prayer; *Mishnah Berakhot* 7:3; *B. Berakhot* 49b-50a; *P. Berakhot* 7:3, 11b-c, all with reference to the invitation to the grace after meals, and in *P. Berakhot*, with reference also to the *barekhu*, which, in the third person, excludes the leader. According to medieval authorities, Saadia Gaon resolved the challenge this presents to our principle by ruling that the leader includes himself by repeating the congregation's response. (*Otzar Hageonim, Berakhot, Perushim*, p. 84, #238.) Note the lack of objection to the singular phrasing of the bedtime and waking prayers discussed in *B. Berakhot* 60b. As Heinemann has demonstrated in his *Prayer*..., chap. 7, the more private a prayer, the more likely it is to be allowed to deviate from otherwise well-established laws of composition.

84. *B. Megillah* 23b; *B. Berakhot* 21b.

*Megillah* to be *devarim shebikedushah*, matters involving a higher degree of sanctification, but the talmudic texts do not directly address the meaning or the extent of this category. It is evident, though, that the greater sanctity invoked by the presence of the community of ten creates a more efficacious setting for prayer.[85] (For a fuller discussion of this issue, see Chapter Four.)

4. **Jews may fulfill the obligations of others so long as they themselves are obligated.** While communal prayer has an elevated level of sanctity, it also serves the more mundane function of creating a mechanism by which those who cannot themselves recite the prayers, from lack of education or lack of ability, can meet their prayer obligations. Already at Yavneh it was assumed that a prayer leader could function as the representative of another in performing a ritual or liturgical act, so long as he himself was obligated to that act.[86] Although the principle applies broadly to all prayer, including home rituals, it is particularly important for the *amidah* and its promulgation.[87]

Even when the prayers were generally known and, even more, once the availability of cheaply printed books made all prayer texts accessible to everybody, the institutions of the *kedushah* and *kaddish*, specifically designed to be recited only by the *sheliaḥ tzibbur* with congregational responses, helped to perpetuate–and add an additional purpose to–the institution of the prayer leader, whose function as repeater of the *amidah* came under attack from various corners of the medieval and modern worlds. The evolution of liturgical poetry, *piyyut*, as creative alternatives to the more standard prayer texts, also served to exalt and strengthen the role of the *sheliaḥ tzibbur*.

5. **Individuals may fulfill their obligations by responding *amen* or simply by listening.** What is required of those who rely on another to fulfill their

---

85. *B. Berakhot* 6a establishes that God's indwelling presence is found in the synagogue when a quorum of ten is present.

86. *Mishnah Rosh Hashanah* 3:8; *B. Berakhot* 20b; *P. Berakhot* 3:3, 6b; *P. Megillah* 2:1, 73a, 2:3, 73b limit this principle to those who are of full status in the community, i.e., free adult males with bodies and minds intact. Note that the mishnaic comment itself is unattributed and hence undatable, and none of these discussions explicitly apply this principle to the *amidah*. Under limited circumstances, women may fulfill the obligations of others, particularly other women. See Joel Wolowelsky, *Women, Jewish Law, and Modernity: New Opportunities in a Post-Feminist Age* (Ktav, 1997).

87. *B. Rosh Hashanah* 34b-35a; *P. Berakhot* 4:6, 8c; *P. Rosh Hashanah* 4:10, 59d, Goldman edition, p. 224. There is extensive debate already among the Amoraim about whether the educated could fulfill their obligations through this mechanism, and whether this leniency should be restricted just to Rosh Hashanah with its much more complex liturgy. For geonic discussions, see *Pirkoi ben Baboi* in *Ginzei Schechter*, II:548-549 and n. 23; and *Otzar Hageonim, Rosh Hashanah, Teshuvot*, pp. 68-70, #118-129. For a summary of the medieval discussions and references to other sources, see OH 124:1 and 591.

obligations? The Mishnah already presupposes–and hence does not discuss explicitly–the principle that people may fulfill their prayer obligations simply by responding *amen* to another's blessings; the tannaitic traditions see this response as minimally equal to or even more praiseworthy than offering the blessing oneself.[88] However, even active listening without a specific response is sufficient.[89]

6. ***Amen* is only a response to others.** The *amen* response was not part of the mandatory formulation of a blessing itself; rather, it was early designated specifically as the response of those hearing another pronounce a benediction. Tannaitic traditions term "boorish" or "reprehensible" the custom of responding to one's own blessing. Established exceptions to this probably reflect a different, Palestinian usage of the term as a marker for the end of a series of related blessings.[90]

7. **Prayers may be said in any language.** Although most rabbinic prayers were apparently composed in Hebrew, the vernaculars of the period were primarily Aramaic and Greek. To enable general participation in their liturgical system, the Tannaim decreed that the vast majority of prayers, with the exception of the priestly benediction, could legitimately be recited in any language.[91]

---

88. *B. Berakhot* 53b; *B. Nazir* 66b. See too the discussions of what sort of blessing appropriately receives the *amen* response: *Mishnah Berakhot* 8:8; *B. Berakhot* 53b; *P. Berakhot* 8:8, 12c; and of inappropriate modes of response: *Tosefta Megillah* 3:27; *B. Berakhot* 47a; *P. Berakhot* 8:8, 12c; *P. Sukkah* 3:10, 54a; *P. Megillah* 1:9, 72a. All these presuppose the basic efficacy of this response.

89. *P. Berakhot* 8:8, 12c. Compare the discussions, with regard to the recitation of the *hallel* Psalms in *B. Sukkah* 38b; *P. Sukkah* 3:10, 54a; and *P. Megillah* 4:1, 74c-d, regarding Scripture reading. Important also is the application of this principle in the medieval world to the issue of proper behavior of one who, in his personal prayer, is at a point where he may not interrupt himself when the *sheliaḥ tzibbur* is leading prayers like *kaddish* or *kedushah*, which require responses. For a summary of this complex discussion, see OH 104 and the supercommentaries on it.

90. *Tosefta Megillah* 3:27; *B. Berakhot* 45b; *P. Berakhot* 5:4, 9c. The most outstanding exception is the conclusion of the third blessing of the Grace After Meals. From the geonic period on, there were those who gave permission to interject *amen* after any similar series of blessings. See Saul Lieberman, תוספתא כפשוטה, V: 1207-1208 on *Tosefta Megillah* 3:27. *Amen*, as a biblical term, always had liturgical uses in prayers originating in less regulated settings, like those that Heinemann (*Prayer...*) labels private or study house prayers. Our discussion here pertains primarily, if not exclusively, to "synagogue-style" prayers.

91. *Mishnah Sotah* 7:1-2; *Tosefta Sotah* 7:7 (see Lieberman's תוספתא כפשוטה, VIII: 678, for discussion of the manuscript variants to this text); *Mishnah Megillah* 2:1 allows vernacular reading of Esther on Purim only by those who do not understand Hebrew. There was hesitation here and in the case of the *shema* about allowing liturgical recitation of translated biblical texts, based at least partly on concern lest the uneducated think that the text's orig-

Later generations basically continue this leniency, but the implications of the Babylonian tradition that, since angels only understand Hebrew, those praying in Aramaic forfeit angelic aid in bringing their prayers before God, complicated its application. However, public prayer, effective without this angelic mediation, may still be recited in the vernacular even though Hebrew remains the ideal.[92]

8. **Prayer requires intentionality.** The danger of creating a fixed, legally enshrined liturgy is that prayers might be recited with technical correctness, but quite mechanically and without concentration on their meaning and purpose. The rabbis establish that one should have *kavvanah* (intentionality and attention) to fulfill any commandment properly, including those involving prayer. However, they recognized the impossibility of universal achievement of this ideal, and consequently established minimum levels of concentration necessary for prayer to be acceptable.[93]

9. **Liturgical practices must preserve the honor of the community and not overburden it.** Formation of a liturgical system acceptable and accessible to the community must also ensure that, at an emotional level, people will react well to what is being promulgated. What otherwise might be permitted or de-

---

inal language was that of the translation. The Palestinian tradition maintained a clear preference for Hebrew for anyone who could understand it. See *P. Sotah* 7:1, 21b; *P. Megillah* 2:1, 73a.

92. *B. Sotah* 33a. The specific reference to Aramaic in this discussion enables various later authorities to allow private prayer in any other vernacular–a matter of particular importance to women, who were less frequently educated in Hebrew and often did not attend synagogue services. See the comments of the Rosh and Rabbenu Yonah to the beginning of chap. 2 of *Berakhot* and OH 101 and the commentaries there.

It is intriguing to speculate whether the preference for Hebrew prayer arises from the fact that Hebrew is the language of revelation, the language of God–hence prayer using God's own words has greater power than prayer in merely human speech.

93. *B. Berakhot* 13a, *B. Eruvin* 95b, and *B. Pesaḥim* 114b establish the principle. Debates over minimum requirements are found in *B. Berakhot* 13a-b, 16a, 30a-31a, 34b; *P. Berakhot* 1:2, 3b; 2:1, 4a; 4:1, 7a; *P. Shabbat* 1:2, 3a. The obligation is so significant that one who is unable to have *kavvanah* should not pray at all. See *Mishnah Berakhot* 2:5, 8; *B. Berakhot* 17b, 30b; *P. Berakhot* 2:5, 5a; 4:1, 7a; 5:1, 8d; *B. Eruvin* 64a.

For a fuller discussion of the nature of *kavvanah* in this literature, see Tzvee Zahavy, "*Kavvanah* for Prayer in the Mishnah and Talmud," in *New Perspectives on Ancient Judaism*, Vol. I: Religion, Literature and Society in Ancient Israel, Formative Christianity and Judaism, ed. J. Neusner et.al. (Atlanta: Scholars Press, 1990), 37-48; rpt. of *Studies in Judaism* (Lanham, MD, 1987); and H. G. Enelow, "Kawwana: the Struggle for Inwardness in Judaism," in *Studies in Jewish Literature Issued in Honor of Professor Kaufmann Kohler* (Berlin, 1913), 82-107. For a discussion of the medieval implications of this issue, see Joseph Tabory, "The Conflict of Halakhah and Prayer," *Tradition* 25 (1989): 17-30.

sired by individuals must be restrained in light of the honor of the congregation. This concept appears in two guises: the positive *kevod tzibbur*, the concern to establish or maintain the honored status of the assembled congregants;[94] and the negative *toraḥ tzibbur*, the desire not to overburden the congregants, especially to the point that they might be dissuaded from attempting to fulfill their own halakhic obligations.[95] This very broad-ranging and somewhat nebulous principle has potentially vast implications, although, as Petuchowski points out, over the generations it was most often honored in the breach.[96]

### *B. Blessings: The Structural Framework of Rabbinic Prayer*

The earliest rabbinic texts assume a liturgy composed of series of blessings. The Babylonian Talmud ascribes to the second-century Rabbi Meir the requirement that a Jew has a basic obligation to recite one hundred blessings daily.[97] But to what specifically did this obligation refer? To establish a unified system of guaranteed validity, the rabbis had to define the legitimate structure of the blessings and provide rules for their combination and incorporation into a liturgical format acceptable to God.[98]

1.a. **A liturgical blessing begins with the word *barukh*.** Although, as

---

94. By using only a ritually fit Torah scroll in the synagogue (*B. Gittin* 60a); by using a second scroll instead of making the community wait while rolling the first to the place of the second reading (*B. Yoma* 70a); by excluding people of lesser status, like women and men shabbily or immodestly dressed from reading from the Torah (*B. Megillah* 23a, 24b).

95. By distracting them by praying out loud (*B. Berakhot* 24b); by making requirements onerous by expanding the statutory liturgy (*B. Berakhot* 12b, *P. Berakhot* 1:5, 3c); by making everyone wait during one's prolonged or very physically active prayer (*Tosefta Berakhot* 3:5–see Lieberman's comments, תוספתא כפשוטה, I:29, *B. Berakhot* 31a); and by strictly requiring recompense for communal errors in liturgical procedures (*B. Berakhot* 27b).

96. Jakob J. Petuchowski, "Some Laws of Jewish Liturgical Development," *Judaism* 34 (1985): 318-320.

97. *B. Menaḥot* 43b. The historicity of this language may be questioned. Cf. the Palestinian traditions *Tosefta Berakhot* 6:24 and *P. Berakhot* 9:5, 14d, which both speak about performing (liturgical) *mitzvot* instead of reciting blessings, perhaps because the Tannaim had not yet formalized the specific blessing texts. The logical corollary to this statement was the definition of exactly which blessings are involved. The first such list preserved is that of Natronai Gaon in the ninth century, who includes many amoraic and geonic blessings. See Louis Ginzberg, *Geonica*, vol 2, Genizah Studies (New York: The Jewish Theological Seminary of America, 1909; rpt. n.d.), 114. My thanks to Reuven Kimelman for his insights on this matter.

98. Evidence suggests that the general concept of a blessing and the structuring of prayer as a combination of blessings was either an existing option or the obvious choice for the rabbis. See Heinemann, *Prayer*..., chap.3; and Bilhah Nitzan, *Qumran Prayer*..., 70-80.

Heinemann has demonstrated, many alternative invocations to blessings were used in the Second Temple world,[99] the tannaitic literature reflects an assumption that the halakhically preferred (and eventually required) liturgical blessing formula begins with the word *barukh*.[100]

1.b. **A liturgical blessing must mention God's name.** A tannaitic tradition establishes that use of the Tetragrammaton (or its derivatives) is preferred to reference to God as *Elohim* (or one of its derivatives) in a blessing.[101] The Talmud records in the name of the leading early third-century Babylonian Amora, Rav, that "any blessing that does not mention God's name is not a liturgical blessing."[102]

1.c. **A liturgical blessing must mention God's sovereignty.** In the same tradition, in the name either of Rav or of his Palestinian contemporary Rabbi Yoḥanan, we likewise find the requirement that "any blessing that does not mention the sovereignty (of God) is not a liturgical blessing."[103]

1.d. **A liturgical blessing addresses God in the second person.** The Palestinian Talmud also cites a dispute between Rav and Shmuel over whether the blessing must include the word "You."[104] In this case, in spite of the fact that the

99. *Prayer...*, chap. 3.

100. *Tosefta Berakhot* 1:9; *B. Berakhot* 46a; *B. Pesaḥim* 104b (see particularly the version of the Munich mss. in דקדוקי סופרים); *P. Berakhot* 1:5, 3d.

101. *Tosefta Berakhot* 6:20; *P. Berakhot* 9:1, 12d. Lieberman, תוספתא כפשוטה, I:122, suggests that this is a ruling against the usage of a sectarian group like that at Qumran. Such a blessing formula does appear in their texts. However, more recent decoding of the scrolls demonstrates a general lack of formal systematization in that collection of liturgical texts and a consistent tendency in at least some to use the same epithets to substitute for the Tetragrammaton as are common in rabbinic prayer. See Nitzan, *Qumran Prayer...*, 75.

102. *B. Berakhot* 40b.

103. *B. Berakhot* 40b; *P. Berakhot* 9:1, 12d. The possible reasons for this ruling and its origins do not really concern us here. For an extensive discussion, see the series of articles in the *Journal of Jewish Studies* 10 (1959): 169-172; 11 (1960): 173-176, 177-179; 15 (1964): 1-56, 149-154; and 17 (1966): 41-72, by J.G. Weiss, C. Roth, J. Heinemann, and E.J. Wiesenberg. These scholars attempt to determine whether this ruling was a polemic against sectarians or against temporal rulers. I favor Heinemann's theory that this amoraic ruling was primarily the codification of an existing situation; the literature records no disputations, and the existence of exceptions is a perfectly normal and expected characteristic of these statements of general principle.

The Rishonim, however, had to establish that the irregular beginning of the *amidah* (...our God and God of our ancestors, God of Abraham, God of Isaac, God of Jacob) is equivalent to mentioning God's sovereignty. They also clarified that the requirement refers to the entire phrase *melekh ha-olam* (sovereign of the universe) and not simply to the inclusion of the word *melekh* (sovereign). See, for example, the discussions of the Tosafot, *B. Berakhot* 40b, ד"ה אמר אביי, the *Rosh*, 6:23, on the same passage, and OH 214 and the commentaries on it.

104. *P. Berakhot* 9:1, 12d.

introduction of the normative blessing formula does come to include this word in its standard introductory phrase, Shmuel's opinion that the word "You" is dispensable prevailed. Perhaps because of their primary reliance on the Babylonian traditions, the standard medieval requirements for a normative blessing list only God's name and sovereignty (שם ומלכות),[105] and the occasional non-normative blessing retains "Blessed are You" while omitting these other crucial elements.[106]

2. **Every blessing begins and ends with a blessing formula**, but one-line blessings over foods, experiences, or for the performance of commandments need no concluding formula, and when more extended blessing texts form a series, only the first requires an opening formula.[107] According to this conception, two blessing formulae never follow one another in a single liturgical composition without some significant intervening text. Therefore individual brief blessings expressing a single thought, like the blessings before eating various kinds of food or performing commandments, cannot have a eulogy. Conversely, in a composition combining blessings that all begin and end with a blessing formula, all but the first drop their opening formula. The handful of exceptions to this more elaborate statement of our structural principle may well represent ancient traditions that predate the stricter formulation of the liturgy.[108]

3. **There must be a literary transition to the eulogy.** The body of the blessing must conclude with a literary transition echoing the language or ideas of the eulogy. For example, no matter how far the *yotzer* blessing has ranged from its original discussion of creation and the daily recreation of the morning light, it returns to this theme of light in the line(s) preceding its eulogy, "who creates the heavenly luminaries." This principle too is attributed to the third-century rabbi, Shmuel. The later Pumbeditan rabbis preferred to achieve an even tighter literary unity by requiring that this transition to the eulogy reflect the language

---

105. *Tur* and *Shulḥan Arukh*, OH 214; *Mishneh Torah*, *Hilkhot Berakhot* 1:5.

106. For example, the הנני prayer recited by the *sheliaḥ tzibbur* before beginning the *musaf* services of Rosh Hashanah and Yom Kippur.

107. See the citations in n. 100.

108. *Emet veyatziv*, the blessing following *shema* and lacking an opening formula, is, according to *Mishnah Tamid* 5:1, a blessing that was recited in the Temple. Fleischer suggests that this Mishnah's precise designation of the prayers is a secondary elaboration. The details of the later liturgy were added to the original statement that the priests merely recited three blessings. However, he fails to explain why these later sages would have designated this particular blessing in what otherwise is a setting corresponding to the *amidah*. See his "לקדמוניות תפילות החובה בישראל," תרביץ נט (תש"ן): 420–421. *P. Berakhot* 1:5, 3d discusses a series of other exceptions, many of which are parts of rituals that rabbinic traditions date to the Second Temple world.

with which the blessing began. Although only Babylonian traditions preserve this principle, the Palestinian *payyetanim*, at least in their more elaborate creations, followed strictly the ruling of Shmuel.[109]

Not only the form of the blessings needed to be regulated, but also the appropriate times to recite them. Various principles developed to govern the application of the blessing formula, both in its mandatory occasional uses and in the statutory prayers themselves.

4. **The concluding blessing (eulogy) of the prayer must be correct.** Both Talmuds agree that only the text of this concluding blessing is the ultimate determinant of whether or not one has fulfilled one's obligation to a specific prayer. Therefore if one erroneously uses a morning text in the evening or vice versa, as long as the eulogy demanded by the actual time of day is correct, one need not repeat the prayer.[110]

5. **One may not include multiple topics in one blessing.** *B. Sotah* 8a provides a long list of actions that may not be performed at the same time because of the principle, אין עושין מצות חבילות חבילות (one does not bundle together commandments). When one has two commandments to fulfill, they should be performed separately, so that each receives its full measure of *kavvanah*. In the realm of liturgy, the talmudic tradition teaches that the performance of each commandment requires a separate blessing.[111] The Babylonian tradition, particularly, insisted on a logical extension of this precept: that one may not include two distinct subjects in the eulogy of a single blessing.[112] The texts of the Palestinian rite found in the Cairo genizah demonstrate that this was not a significant concern in the Palestinian halakhic tradition. Where such blessings made their way into European rites, however, they served as flashpoints for dispute.[113]

---

109. *B. Pesaḥim* 104a. Shmuel's ruling has been preserved in two variants. One, that of the printed text and many versions of Alfasi, preserves the context of the passage and phrases the principle with reference to the *havdalah* benediction. However, the texts of several Talmud manuscripts, Rabbenu Ḥananel, and many Rishonim speak in terms of כל הברכות כולן (all of the blessings). See דיקדוקי סופרים on this passage.

110. *B. Berakhot* 12a; *P. Berakhot* 1:5, 3d; *P. Taanit* 2:3, 65c. This principle also allows for the institution of liturgical poetry, *piyyut*, which, at least in its Palestinian origins, replaced all but the concluding blessing of most of the statutory liturgy.

111. *B. Sukkah* 46a, with reference to the various rituals for Sukkot; *B. Pesaḥim* 102b forbids the sanctification of a single cup of wine for two purposes (see the commentaries on this passage that discuss the exceptions for *havdalah* and *kiddush* on the night of a festival).

112. *B. Berakhot* 49a. The statement of this principle is here followed by the *gemara*'s attempts to justify five pre-existing, well-established exceptions to the rule by finding intrinsic links between the separate subjects listed in the eulogies. However, these justifications are lame, particularly when one compares these texts to others the official tradition rejects.

113. For discussions of various blessings, see Zvi Groner, ברכות שנשתקעו (MA Thesis,

6. **One may not recite an unnecessary benediction.** Another important principle with roots in the Talmud, but whose significance is much greater to the medieval rabbis, is the prohibition against reciting a ברכה שאינה צריכה, an unnecessary benediction, lest one transgress the commandment לא תשא, the prohibition against improper use of the divine Name.[114] Blessings gain their power from their invocation of God; blessings used improperly are potentially blasphemous.[115] Originally, this principle would seem simply to prohibit a blessing that duplicates one already said or the recitation of a proper blessing at an improper time. In the medieval world, however, this concept was invoked against blessings the authorities considered unwarranted under any circumstances, either because none was called for, because the text was incorrect, or because a blessing was being used improperly. We will develop this concept in detail in Chapter Two.

7. **One may not change the established form of a benediction.** Just as the concern about unnecessary benedictions exerted a strong conservative force against expansion of the liturgy, so too did the principle first attributed to the second-century Tanna, Rabbi Yose, that, כל המשנה ממטבע שטבעו חכמים בברכה לא יצא (anyone who deviates from the rabbinically established form of the benediction does not fulfill his obligation).[116] The application of this rule extends beyond the

---

Hebrew University, 1964), 10, 50; Lawrence Hoffman, *The Canonization of the Synagogue Service* (Notre Dame and London: University of Notre Dame Press, 1979; rpt. 1986), 45ff. and notes; ישראל תא־שמע, "הפורס סוכת שלום – ברכה וגלגוליה," בתוך מנהג אשכנז הקדמון (ירושלים: מאגנס, תשנ"ב; מאסופות ב (תשמ"ח), קעז ואי'), 142–156. One resolution was often to rewrite the eulogy so that it had a single verb with multiple objects. Such an issue is evident in the various rewordings of the benediction of the *birkat betulim*, a blessing discussed extensively in the next chapter. On the variant texts of the blessing, see my article, "The Birkat Betulim: A Study of the Jewish Celebration of Bridal Virginity," *PAAJR* 61 (1995): 53-94.

114. This principle appears explicitly in two contexts: the question of whether one may, in effect, make *havdalah* twice, once in *maariv* and again over the cup of wine (*B. Berakhot* 33a); and as a possible reason for the High Priest's reciting the second part of his Yom Kippur Torah portion by heart instead of reading it from a second scroll (*B. Yoma* 70a; *B. Sotah* 41a). Many Rishonim are uncomfortable understanding this principle as a commandment of biblical origin, as may be implied by the *gemara*'s prooftext. They prefer to understand it as a rabbinic dictum (and hence a less serious transgression), buttressed by the biblical verse. See the sources listed in: "ברכה שאינה צריכה," אנציקלופדיה תלמודית כרך ד', עמ' 280, הע' 3–5.

115. Of course, one might inadvertently make the wrong blessing or say the same prayer twice. *P. Berakhot* 6:1, 10a, in discussing various food benedictions, provides a remedy for such a mistake: one can nullify a benediction by reciting the line: ברוך שם כבוד מלכותו לעולם ועד (Blessed is His name whose glorious kingdom is for ever and ever). See the Tosafot, *Berakhot* 39a, ד"ה בצר end, and the *Shulḥan Arukh* OH 206:6 for examples of the integration of this concept into the mainstream tradition.

116. *Tosefta Berakhot* 4:5; *B. Berakhot* 40b; *P. Berakhot* 6:2, 10b. This concept may have

general details of the blessing formula. Both Talmuds limit the right of the individual to alter the larger framework of the *amidah* and add blessings that deviate from the communal norm.[117] The Babylonian Talmud's citation of Rabbi Yoḥanan's explanation of the *baraita*, משום דקאמר ברכה דלא תקינו רבנן (because he recited a blessing that the sages did not establish), allows later generations to claim that only talmudically ordained blessings are legitimate. Most significant for future development of the principle, when the Palestinian Talmud records objections to prayer leaders who deviate from the established list of God's attributes for the *avot*, it paraphrases this *baraita*, saying: אין לך רשות להוסיף על מטבע שטבעו חכמים בברכות (You have no right to add to the formula that the sages established for the prayers).[118] This statement speaks not of changing, but of adding to the established format, enabling later rabbis to apply to this principle the tannaitic prohibitions of interchanging the forms of long and short blessings.[119] Not changing the established forms of benedictions becomes an increasingly powerful principle as the exact wording of liturgy becomes fixed. Medieval rabbis objected to any omission from these fixed texts, and many, especially those in the Babylonian and Spanish traditions, objected even to additions in the form of liturgical poetry, the topic of Chapter Three. Consequently, they eventually excluded it almost entirely from the codified prayers.

8. **One must bless before eating anything.** Tannaitic traditions established that deriving benefit from the world, especially through eating or drinking, must be preceded by a blessing. To omit the blessing is failure to acknowledge that all in this world is ultimately God's and is like the unauthorized partaking of goods dedicated to the Temple. The Babylonian Talmud elaborates even further, comparing failure to recite the proper blessing to consuming food consecrated to God, or theft from God and Israel. It stresses that uneducated people must find themselves a sage who can teach them the proper blessings.[120]

---

pre-rabbinic roots. As S. Talmon points out, Ben Sira 7:14 reads, "Do not enter into the meeting (conversation) of princes (Gk. elders), and do not repeat (Syriac: change) a word of (your) prayer." See his "The Emergence of Institutionalized Prayer in Israel in the Light of the Qumran Literature," *Qumran: Sa piété, sa théologie et son milieu*, ed. M. Delior (Paris: Duculot, 1978), 273.

117. *B. Taanit* 13b; *P. Berakhot* 5:2, 9b; *P. Taanit* 1:1, 63d, all referring to the people of Naveh or Nineveh who needed rain in the summer and wanted to alter their community's prayers accordingly.

118. *P. Berakhot* 9:1, 12d; *Midrash Tehillim* 19:2. It is interesting that in most forms of the Palestinian *piyyut* for the *amidah*, with the exception of the *me-ein shemoneh esreh*, these phrases of the *avot* were maintained as the standard liturgical introduction.

119. *Mishnah Berakhot* 1:4; *Tosefta Berakhot* 1:5-9.

120. *Tosefta Berakhot* 4:1; *B. Berakhot* 35a; *P. Berakhot* 6:1, 9d.

9. **One makes a blessing only over the essential food of a meal.** With such serious consequences for mistakes, whether intentional or not, one can easily envision a situation where anxiety or superpiety would develop, with people forestalling possible error by making individual blessings for every kind of food included in a meal or even for every bite. This would create two problems: the possibility of unnecessary blessings, with the consequent profanation of the divine Name;[121] and a system too demanding, time-consuming, and complex to be accessible and attractive to the commoner. Therefore the rabbis, at an early date, limited the obligation to recite blessings, establishing: זה הכלל כל שהוא עיקר ועמו טפלה מברך על העיקר ופוטר את הטפלה (This is the principle: whenever one has something essential to the meal and also something less essential, one recites the blessing over the essential [food] and this exempts the less essential [from requiring a blessing]).[122] With this general principle, all that remained was to establish the rules by which one could distinguish the principle food of the meal. Although the literature is filled with examples of theoretical borderline cases where the answers were not clear, for most people, especially those unable to afford sumptuous banquets, the procedures were straightforward.

10. **One must recite a blessing before fulfilling any commandment.** The third-century Amoraim established that not only eating, but performing *any* commandment–liturgical, ritual, or otherwise–requires a blessing preceding the action involved. Hence even in the case of the *megillah* reading, where the Mishnah specifically leaves the inclusion of a blessing to local custom,[123] these rabbis require a blessing preceding the ritual and make the blessing following it only optional.[124]

11. **Anything followed by a blessing must be preceded by one.**[125]

---

121. As discussed above, B.6.

122. *Mishnah Berakhot* 6:7. Cited in *B. Berakhot* 35b, 36a, 41a.

123. *Mishnah Megillah* 4:1.

124. *B. Megillah* 21b; *B. Sukkah* 39a (compare *B. Pesaḥim* 119b) treats the question of the blessings for *hallel*; *B. Menaḥot* 35b applies this principle to the blessings for donning the *tefillin*; *B. Pesaḥim* 7b applies it to the blessing for burning the ḥametz. *P. Berakhot* 9:3, 14a contains a dispute over whether the blessings should be said before or during the time of the performance of the commandment. Like the passage in *B. Pesaḥim* 7b, it contains a discussion of various cases that are or might be thought to be exceptions to the general principle. The only exception the Babylonian tradition allows to stand is ritual immersion, understood by the Tosafot there (ד"ה על הטבילה) to refer primarily to the immersion of a proselyte. The Tosafot also discuss the appropriateness of extending this precedent to any ritual immersion, and explain that postponing the blessing is appropriate lest fear of water or another factor keep one from immersing properly. Handwashing is a different case, they say, because of the necessity of touching bread only with dry hands.

125. *Mishnah Nidah* 6:10; *B. Berakhot* 44b; *B. Nidah* 51b-52a. Various rabbis and

12. **Statutory Jewish worship consists of a precise series of blessings, offered at specific times of day.** Chapters One and Four of *Mishnah Berakhot* and the talmudic commentaries directly on the Mishnah texts establish an obligatory framework for the daily Jewish liturgy: the recitation of *shema* and the blessings surrounding it in the morning and evening, and the recitation of the *amidah* in the morning, afternoon and evening. These two originally unrelated liturgical units must be juxtaposed in the morning and evening.[126] On the Sabbath and holidays, an additional *amidah*, the *musaf*, is recited, ideally between the morning and afternoon services. On Yom Kippur, a fifth *amidah* follows the afternoon service. The talmudic discussions define the precise times for these services, and at least the themes of the individual blessings of these components. They also define exactly when and with what procedures Scripture should be read, *hallel* should be recited, and so forth. This timetable was established to ensure the efficacy of the system meant to fulfill the role of the very precisely orchestrated rituals of the Jerusalem Temple sacrifices.

### *C. Application of the Principles*

An overly regulated system of prayers and blessings would preclude response to the needs of the moment or significant cultural change. At the same time, unrestrained variation would ultimately result in a loss of the basic unversal uniformity that undergirds rabbinic claims for the authority and ultimate holiness of the system. Thus the following principles developed to allow the liturgical text to incorporate appropriate timely themes into the regular cycle of holidays and to meet the needs of individuals or specific communities.

1. **Theological concerns dictate precise prayer texts.** Although there is no record that the rabbis dictated precise texts for most prayers (scholars may only *assume* the existence of such prayers, but have very little written evidence for them),[127] various factors necessarily influenced the creation of communal

---

communities have individual exceptions to this general principle, but no one refutes that in the majority of cases, no ritual or liturgical act will be merely followed by a blessing; a blessing must precede it, too, to establish the setting. Although there is surprisingly little discussion of this principle in the literature, the structure it establishes becomes a basic characteristic of Jewish prayer.

126. See above, p. 17, for a discussion of the development of this concept.

127. This may simply be a result of the early ruling that prayer texts, despite their contents, may not be saved from a fire on the Sabbath, and hence, כותבי ברכות כשורפי תורה (those who write benedictions are like those who burn the Torah). (*Tosefta Shabbat* 13:4; *B.Shabbat* 115b; *P. Shabbat* 16:1, 15c.) Fleischer, "קדמוניות...," 435 n. 96, however, suggests that prayer texts were indeed written down, and this *baraita* refers to blessings written using the name

norms and enforced conformity with them. Fleischer hypothesizes that anyone learning to pray, whether child or adult, needed to learn a fixed text.[128] At least within an individual family or community, then, even if not nationally, some standard wording for the daily statutory prayers was needed.

Because these local liturgies could be problematic, however, the rabbis attempted to forge more universal norms. The Tosefta records the statement, מברכות של אדם ניכר אם בור הוא אם תלמיד חכם הוא (One can recognize from a person's blessings whether he is a fool or a sage).[129] Whatever the Tosefta's original intent, the *gemara* cites this *baraita* as applying strictly to the proper wording of the Grace after Meals, where certain texts contained theological imprecisions that only an uneducated person would allow. In the process of denigrating certain phrases, the rabbis also suggested better ones, and these came to be considered proper and, ultimately, mandatory.[130]

This principle, though not invoked specifically, underlies much of the generation of fixed texts in the liturgy. For instance, when a third-century *sheliaḥ tzibbur* included an extensive listing of the attributes of God in the *avot*, leading rabbis rebuked him for theological imprecision: a long list implies comprehensiveness, an impossible task when applied to God, and the codified short list at least has biblical precedent.[131] This principle also underlies the listings of required themes to be included in certain blessings of the liturgy such as *emet veyatziv*[132] and the second and third blessings of *birkat hamazon*.[133] Thus, the desire of all to appear knowledgable, or, at the very least, to emulate the efficacious

of God with magical intent. But this still leaves us unable to account for the omission of prayer texts from the preserved tannaitic and amoraic literature.

128. "...לקדמוניות," 426, 430. However, even minimally educated Jews would have been familiar with the general linguistic culture of prayer and its vocabulary and syntax, and would have been able adequately to compose their own appropriate texts.

129. *Tosefta Berakhot* 1:6.

130. *B. Berakhot* 50a.

131. *B. Berakhot* 33b; *B. Megillah* 25a; *P. Berakhot* 9:1, 12d; *Midrash Tehillim* 19:2. The Babylonian and Palestinian traditions ascribe this incident to different rabbis. Both Palestinian texts add to the theological problems of these particular additions the comment, discussed above, B.7., אין לך רשות להוסיף על מטבע שטבעו חכמים בברכות (You do not have the right to add to the formula that the sages established for the benedictions). *B. Megillah* 18a states explicitly that excessive praise of God, beyond that established by the Men of the Great Assembly, is theologically unacceptable.

132. *Tosefta Berakhot* 2:1; *P. Berakhot* 1:6, 3d.

133. *B. Berakhot* 48b-49a; *P. Berakhot* 1:6, 3d. In the Babylonian version, Rabbi Abba labels one who concludes the second blessing with *manḥil aratzot* (who gives lands in inheritance) and the third blessing with *moshia et yisrael* (Redeemer of Israel) an ignoramus.

prayer of the sages, created a situation in which the language of the prayers and blessings was increasingly fixed.

2. **The more frequently said prayer or ritual precedes the less frequent.** How should the requirements of two overlapping systems, such as when a holiday falls on the Sabbath, be reconciled? A principle was established early by the School of Hillel: if two commanded actions coincide, the one more frequently required takes precedence. The Tosefta already accepts this as the halakhah, but only in the Babylonian Talmud do we find the generalization explicitly spelled out, formulated as the principle, תדיר ושאינו תדיר תדיר קודם ([When confronted with two rituals], one said frequently and the other not, the frequent [ritual] takes precedence).[134] This principle was apparently accepted early enough to govern the development of all standard combinations of themes, from the extended eulogies of the *kedushat hayom* benedictions for the Sabbath during a holiday, to the order of the incorporation of the Sabbath and festival insertions into *birkat hamazon*.

3. **Each *amidah* of the day contains the same references.** Systems with conflicting or differing requirements often overlap: the Sabbath of Ḥanukah, for example, where Ḥanukah does not require a *musaf* service but the Sabbath does, or a Yom Kippur on the Sabbath, where the Sabbath does not include a *neilah* service, but Yom Kippur does. Does the liturgy required by only one of the occasions still need to include references to both? Yes, the rabbis determined; each *amidah* of the day must include the same references. The only permitted differentiation among the various services is the *kedushat hayom* benediction specific to the *musaf* service.[135]

4. **Special rituals belong in the morning service.** The literature assumes (but never explicitly mandates in a liturgical context) that any ritual particular to a day should be performed as early as possible to demonstrate eagerness to

134. *Tosefta Berakhot* 5:25; *Tosefta Pesaḥim* 10:2-3; *P. Berakhot* 8:1, 11d; *P. Pesaḥim* 10:2, 37c; *B. Berakhot* 51b; *B. Pesaḥim* 114a; *B. Zevaḥim* 90b-91a. *B. Sukkah* 56a presents an exception to this principle, because logic requires that the less frequent blessing for sitting in the *sukkah* should precede *sheheḥiyanu*. See the *Tur* and *Bet Yosef* OH 643 and 661 for further debates over the issue.

135. *B. Shabbat* 24a-b; *B. Eruvin* 40a-b; *P. Berakhot* 4:1, 7c; *P. Taanit* 4:1, 67c. While the *musaf* service is always different, only the Sabbath liturgy distinguishes between the evening, morning, and afternoon *amidot*. However, the core paragraph of the *kedushat hayom* remains standard, and the differences are confined to poetic elaborations on it and the verses cited in that context. Ezra Fleischer discusses at length this unusual situation, and suggests evidence for an original text common to these three services and even to the *musaf*. See his תפילה ומנהגי תפילה ארץ־ישראליים בתקופת הגניזה (ירושלים: מאגנס, תשמ"ח), 24–44.

fulfill the relevant commandment.[136] The Talmud discusses the most obvious exception to this principle, the blowing of the shofar in the *musaf* service. The rabbis establish that logically even the ritual blowing of the shofar should occur in the morning service, but it was postponed because of persecutions, or, as the Palestinian Talmud suggests in an alternative reasoning, because at least two biblical sources indicate that the proper placement for the special ritual of Rosh Hashanah is in this additional service.[137] It is also possible that the Temple shofar blowing for Rosh Hashanah simply occurred later in the day.

5. **The placement of the *me-ein hameora* insertion depends on its content.** Tannaitic sources refer to liturgical acknowledgment of the history or particular topic of the day as *me-ein hameora* (about or embodying the event), applying the term to the regular additions to the liturgy for the holidays of Purim and Ḥanukah, for historical fast days, and, at least originally, for public fast days proclaimed because of communal need.[138] The Palestinian tradition, largely accepted by medieval Jewry, established that while any *me-ein hameora* referring to the future belongs in the *avodah* benediction, which anticipates the restoration of the Jerusalem Temple, one remembering the past should be placed in the *hodaah* benediction, which is a paean of praise and thanksgiving to God.[139]

6. **Personal petitions belong primarily in *shomea tefillah*, unless the topic is particularly appropriate elsewhere.** Confusion about personal petitions seems to have reigned from our earliest sources, probably because private incidental prayer had always been possible outside of any formal worship structure and required no legislation. The general understanding of later generations is

---

136. *B. Yoma* 28b and *B. Rosh Hashanah* 4a apply this concept to checking for ḥametz and circumcision.

137. *B. Rosh Hashanah* 32b; *P. Rosh Hashanah* 4:8, 59c, Goldman ed., 220-222. The precedent established in *Mishnah Megillah* 2:5 that the entire day is appropriate for various rituals does not change our principle. Once the ideal time has passed, the rituals for *megillah*, *hallel*, shofar, *lulav*, etc., must still be performed, for one is still obligated to fulfill these commandments. But their place in the liturgical structure of the day, with the exception of shofar, remains in the morning service.

138. See *Tosefta Berakhot* 3:10-11.

139. *P. Berakhot* 4:3, 8a; *P. Taanit* 2:2, 65c. The *Rif*, *Taanit* 10a, cites the Palestinian text more or less directly, but adds the comment that it is the universal custom to insert *naḥem* for the Ninth of Av in the benediction *boneh yerushalayim* instead, based on the lenient opinion in *B. Avodah Zarah* 8a that one's individual needs may be requested at the conclusion of any relevant benediction (of the intermediate thirteen). For further discussion of this issue, see the next principle. This exception was the topic of much discussion among the Rishonim, who were also troubled by the limitation of this prayer to the afternoon service, contradicting our previous principle. See the *Tur* and *Beit Yosef*, OH 557, and the literature to which they refer.

that personal petitions, while appropriate following the *amidah* in any case, may be inserted into *shomea tefillah*, the concluding blessing of the petitions of the weekday *amidah* that asks God in general terms to heed Israel's prayer. Exceptions to this, because the Talmud specifically mentions them, are individual petitions for health or sustenance, which may be inserted into the statutory petitions on these topics.[140]

7. **Variant customs may be combined to create a universal norm.** Just as the halakhah generated mechanisms for responding to the calendrical cycle or the particular needs of individuals, it also required a means to deal with established local customs. As the rabbinic system was spread and eventually standardized, it had to account for existing variations in custom and find ways either to integrate them as acceptable prayer or to reject them as errant. The Babylonian Talmud ascribes to Rav Papa, a late fourth-century Babylonian Amora, an integrative solution, calling for the combination of variant liturgical texts into a single, ultimately universal norm, even if the resultant text did not always fit absolutely into the talmudic norms for the composition of the liturgy.[141]

---

140. *B. Avodah Zarah* 7b-8a; *B. Berakhot* 31a; *P. Berakhot* 4:4, 8b; *Tosefta Berakhot* 3:6. *Mishneh Torah, Hilkhot Tefillah* 6:2-3; OH 119. The Babylonian tradition required the individual, on a fast-day, to insert his *me-ein hameora* into *shomea tefillah*, while the public prayer could include this replacement for the six extra blessings of the original fast-day liturgy as an extra full blessing. *P. Berakhot* 4:3, 8a distinguishes between the individual on a private fast-day, who may add the extra prayer, and the individual on a public fast-day, who may not. For a discussion of the parallel but corrupted *P. Taanit* 2:1, 65c, see my dissertation, *The Impact...*, p. 112, n. 109. Even communities living in climates that, unlike the eastern Mediterranean, required rain in summer had to confine their petitions for rain to *shomea tefillah*, lest it be confused with the standard winter request for rain in Palestine in the blessing for sustenance. See *B. Taanit* 14b, Malter ed., 51; *P. Berakhot* 5:2, 9b; *P. Taanit* 1:1, 63d; and the famous responsum of the Rosh, 4:10. See too the discussion of Daniel Sperber, מנהגי ישראל: מקורות ותולדות, כרך ג' (ירושלים: מוסד הרב קוק, תשנ"ד), 70 ואילך.

141. *B. Berakhot* 11b calls for the combination of different Torah blessings, even if, in a series of blessings, the second one maintains its independent form and still starts with the blessing formula. *B. Sotah* 40a calls for the combination of several Babylonian amoraic alternative texts for the congregation to say while the *sheliaḥ tzibbur* recites the *hodaah* benediction. In the Palestinian tradition, *P. Berakhot* 1:5, 3d, these alternative prayers each conclude with a eulogy, making their combination more problematic and less easily standardized; consequently, although combination was suggested, the option remained there to pick and choose.

In several cases, the most critical part of the blessing, the text of the eulogy, was at issue. The resultant combinations were problematic in that they transgressed the principle, discussed above, B.5., that eulogies may have only a single topic. See *B. Berakhot* 59b; *B. Taanit* 6b-7a, Malter ed., 18, on the blessing thanking for rain after a drought; *B. Megillah* 21b, on the blessing following the reading of the *megillah*; *B. Berakhot* 60b, on the blessing to be

The talmudic rabbis thus not only claimed that their liturgical system was efficacious; they established guidelines for its proper performance. Some of these guidelines guaranteed a proper atmosphere for the new system, one that would, within the limits of the possible, mimic and orient itself to the mourned Temple cult. Others taught Jews how to construct the language and syntax of the prayers themselves, and where to look for authoritative direction. It is impossible to know how broadly these rabbinic academic traditions affected actual Jewish liturgical life during the talmudic period. However, our earliest preserved liturgies largely conform to the basic system, and there is little internal evidence of serious opposition until the period of the Geonim.

Through geonic writings, we hear of developing resistance to rabbinic authority and the authority of the Babylonian Talmud, most notably from the Karaites and from communities that had looked to the Palestinian academies for guidance.[142] The Geonim attempted to quash any customs and legal traditions that did not conform to the Babylonian Talmud, which they accepted as the authentic redaction of the Oral Law. They were largely successful, and over the centuries the Talmud increasingly gained status and sanctity–to the point that, for many, it was the ultimate arbiter of liturgical legitimacy.

### *Changing Concepts of Acceptable Prayer*

The talmudic texts, however, never really question in any sophisticated fashion

---

recited after the elimination of bodily wastes; *B. Berakhot* 59a (compare *P. Berakhot* 9:2, 13d), on the blessing responding to the sighting of a rainbow.

Various other received liturgical texts, in their first preserved appearances, already show evidence of this sort of compromise, although we have no record of the process of combination. Examples just from the haggadah include the *geulah* benediction, which combines the texts of Rabbi Tarfon and Rabbi Akiva from *Mishnah Pesaḥim* 10:6; the structure of the *maggid*, which combines both Rav and Shmuel's suggestions (*B. Pesaḥim* 116a); and the *birkat hashir*, which combines Rabbi Yehudah and Rabbi Yoḥanan's suggestions from *B. Pesaḥim* 118a in various ways in various rites. From the daily liturgy, we can cite the incorporation of two versions each of the blessings surrounding *keriat shema* and the final blessing of the *amidah*, divided between the different services instead of combined.

142. Perhaps also from the early rabbinic traditions of Italy and the Rhineland, which were heavily reliant on their own received customs. It is also possible that the Karaite movement, which rejected rabbinic authority, developed from communities of Jews that had never been fully under rabbinic sway and resented geonic encroachment on their ways of life. See Zvi Ankori, *Karaites in Byzantium: The Formative Years 970-1100* (New York: Columbia University Press, 1959), Introduction; and Naftali Wieder, *The Judean Scrolls and Karaism* (London: East and West Library, 1962), 254f. On this topic in general, see Hoffman, *Canonization*... and Robert Brody, *The Geonim of Babylonia and the Shaping of Medieval Jewish Culture* (New Haven: Yale University Press, 1998), chaps. 6-8.

how prayer achieves its ends. In many ways, the rabbinic understanding is a continuation of that of Temple times, when God was physically present in the Holy of Holies and reliably accessible there, even if the Divine Presence could not be understood to be confined to any single spot. After the destruction, God was to be found in a heavenly Temple, a place to which the mystical adepts of the period could travel. There, they might gaze on the Divine throne, participate in the angelic liturgies, and at times, communicate directly with the Creator. In this conception, God, sitting in heaven, could choose to enjoy and respond to Israel's prayers, much as a human king might receive and respond to his subjects. Mystical texts of the period describe these angelic liturgies and their dependence on human prayer.[143] Michael Swartz claims that those mystics who composed *Ma'aseh Merkavah* "created prayer that assured them that their worship was being held in conjunction with the heavenly liturgy–that even in the absence of the Presence of God on earth, heaven and earth were in consonance when God is blessed both by angels and human beings."[144] Although the degree of rabbinic or even popular involvement in these early mystical traditions has yet to be satsifactorily determined, there is a basic consonance in this period between the mystical and nonmystical rabbinic literature about the nature of prayer.

As Jewish thinkers increasingly absorbed the sophistication of Greek philosophical thought, however, such a physical conception of God lost its appeal.[145] Pagan philosophical categories, when applied to monotheistic religions, led to the positing of God as ultimate perfection. In such a view, God cannot be affected by praise or respond to petition, for either one would require some change in God and compromise the Divine nature. A perfect God, then, must be unresponsive to prayer, totally inaccessible, and uninvolved in the world. This contradiction had the potential to precipitate a religious crisis, comparable in gravity to the earlier generation's loss of contact with God in His physical earthly dwelling. Some philosophers, indeed, abandoned the statutory prayers because of it.

In response, various twelfth-century mystical approaches radically altered

143. See Peter Schäfer, "The Aim and Purpose of Early Jewish Mysticism," in *Hekhalot Studien* (Tübingen: JCB Mohr (Paul Siebeck), 1988), 277-295.

144. *Mystical Prayer in Ancient Judaism: An Analysis of Ma'aseh Merkavah* (Tübingen: JCB Mohr (Paul Siebeck), 1992), 29.

145. For this discussion, I rely primarily on the most comprehensive study of the topic, Joseph Dan's article, "The Emergence of Mystical Prayer," in *Studies in Jewish Mysticism*, ed. Joseph Dan and Frank Talmadge (Cambridge, MA: Association for Jewish Studies, 1982), 85-120. In general, in spite of the centrality of prayer to the medieval mystical experience, all too little has been written on the subject.

rabbinic conceptions of prayer and the meaning of its efficacy. One solution appearing in mystic circles of the second half of the twelfth century, with roots that can be traced back at least to Saadia Gaon, was to posit emanations from this perfect God, known in the different traditions as *The Glory* (the most common term), *Greatness*, *Kingdom*, *Cherub*, etc. Those emanations with physical attributes served as the source of prophetic visions. In several of these conceptions, nonphysical emanations served as the appropriate object of prayer and the basis of the personal relationship with God craved by the pious Jew.

Communication and communion with such an emanation was dependent, according to the interpretations of the Ḥasidei Ashkenaz, on participation in the precisely defined details of the statutory liturgy, which they believed to have been deliberately developed so that its every nuance, including the order and number of its words and letters, would participate in the Divine harmony of which this emanation, along with the written Torah and creation itself, was but a part.[146] Thus by definition there could be only one correct version of the liturgy–that of the Rhineland mystics themselves. This conception only continued and, for some communities, finalized the process of canonization of the liturgy carried out under the Geonim, fixing every letter of the text. But more important for our purposes here, prayer's efficacy no longer depended upon direct communication with God–who was unreachable–or even upon communication with God's emanation through obvious meanings of words. True efficacy operated at a level beyond cognition, in the mystical and often mysterious significance of the relationships between the words and letters of which the prayers were composed.[147]

According to Joseph Dan's understanding, the mystics of this period in Provence and Spain, who laid the groundwork for what soon became known as *kabbalah*, were also responding to the challenge posed by philosophical specu-

146. According to one conception, prayer is even identified as one of the emanated divine powers. See Dan, pp. 113-115.

147. Dan, 91; and his "Prayer as Text and Prayer as Mystical Experience," in *Torah and Wisdom: Studies in Jewish Philosophy, Kabbalah, and Halacha, Essays in Honor of Arthur Hyman*, ed. Ruth Link-Salinger (New York: Shengold Publishers, Inc., 1992), 33-47, on the transformation of the prayerbook into a mystical text. See, too, the briefer discussion of Ivan G. Marcus, "The Devotional Ideals of Ashkenazic Pietism," in *Jewish Spirituality from the Bible through the Middle Ages*, ed. Arthur Green (New York: Crossroad, 1989), 359ff., who adds that these pietists insisted that those unable to concentrate on these esoteric meanings must indeed concentrate on the cognitive meanings of the prayers. Indeed, no mystical group ever exempted those who were uninitiated from some conventional level of *kavvanah*. See also his discussion in *Piety and Society: The Jewish Pietists of Medieval Germany* (Leiden: E.J. Brill, 1981), 97-100, which emphasizes, conversely, the special demands the pietists made on the communal synagogue, because they considered their own prayer more worthy.

lation. They too understood God to be ultimately unreachable and unaffected by human actions, but posited a realm of divine emanation with which the mystic adept could interact. The approach of these mystics differed from that of their northern brethren in the nature of this emanation and in the types of possible human interaction with it. Here is not the place to reproduce the various studies, many of them still in their infancy, of the kabbalistic thought of the different schools and periods in Provence, Catalonia, Castile, and the eastern Mediterranean.[148] But we can generalize and say that the among the primary goals of the kabbalist was the achievement of *devekut*, ecstatic adhesion to or absorption into the upper echelons of these emanations from God, generally referred to as the ten *sefirot*. Through the mystic's meditation on these *sefirot*, he would cause the upflow of energy that would repair the disunity characteristic of the heavenly realms since the creation of these *sefirot*–and precipitate a downflow of energy for the benefit of the lower realms, including that occupied by humans. General performance of the commandments, if done with the right intention, was an important part of this system. Yet the primary entrée to mystic participation in and repair of the sefirotic realm was prayer.[149]

Prayer, then, was one of the most powerful tools available to the kabbalist. It provided a primary means of access to the realm of the *sefirot*, enabling both their contemplation and their theurgic manipulation for divine and human benefit. A preferred mystic technique was to practice various meditations during the halakhically correct recitation of the statutory liturgy. Although various schools prescribed their own specific meditations and described their results in different terms, we see here, once again, a group moving significantly beyond the cogni-

---

148. Consult the various works of Gershom Scholem, Isaiah Tishby, Moshe Idel, and their students, many of which are available in English.

149. There has been remarkably little written on the kabbalistic understandings of prayer. Most comprehensive and persuasive is Seth Lance Brody, *Human Hands Dwell in Heavenly Heights: Worship and Mystical Experience in Thirteenth Century Kabbalah* (Ph.D. diss. University of Pennsylvania, 1991), especially chap. 4, "The Service of the Heart: Mystical Prayer in Thirteenth Century Kabbalah." See also Isaiah Tishby, *The Wisdom of the Zohar*, trans. David Goldstein (London: Oxford University Press, Littman Library, 1989; rpt., 1991), Vol. III, Part V, Section II, "Prayer and Devotion," Introduction, pp. 941-1016; the various references to prayer in Moshe Idel, *Kabbalah: New Perspectives* (New Haven: Yale University Press, 1988); Elliot Wolfson, "Mystical-Theurgical Dimensions of Prayer in *Sefer Ha-Rimmon*," in *Approaches to Judaism in Medieval Times*, Vol. III, ed. David R. Blumenthal (Atlanta: Scholars Press, 1988), 41-79; Mark Verman, "The Development of Yiḥudim in Spanish Kabbalah," *Jerusalem Studies in Jewish Thought* 8 (1989): 25*-41*; משה אידל, "התפילה בקבלת פרובנס," תרביץ סב (תשנ"ג), 265–286; and אפרים גוטליב, "משמעותה של התפילה בקבלה הספרדית," בתוך התפילה היהודית - המשך וחידוש, בעריכת גבריאל חיים כהן (ישראל: המכון ליהדות ולמחשבה בת זמננו, 1978), 168–189.

tive meaning of the words of the prayers, infusing the act of worship with new meanings, and, most importantly for our discussion, defining in relatively concrete terms how prayer achieves its efficacy, at least for the adept. These sorts of understandings remained powerful in the reinterpretations of kabbalah by the Safed school of the sixteenth century and among the Ḥasidim of the early modern world.[150]

Although the influences of new philosophical and theosophical systems led to revisions in Jewish understandings of the mechanisms of prayer and, hence, of the prerequisites for its efficacy, these same medieval thinkers were heirs to a tradition protected by the fences of the halakhah and the structures of prayer defined by the talmudic sages. The following chapters investigate specific issues of that halakhah to show how these realms merged their understandings of efficacious prayer, interacted with the ever-present and ever-changing realities of local Jewish custom, and were influenced by surrounding non-Jewish cultures and the vicissitudes of history. While the rabbis, in their rulings, were generally driven by their understandings of efficacious prayer, they also recognized the practical necessity of compromise with the customary practice of the community. In times of grave crisis, however, rabbinic authority was enhanced, and halakhah and the contemporary understandings of liturgical efficacy did succeed in changing actual communal custom.

150. See, for instance, ברכה ז"ק, "התפילה במשנתו של ר' משה קורדובירו," דעת 9 (תשמ"ב), 5–12; and the richer literature on Hasidism, including Louis Jacobs, *Hasidic Prayer* (London: The Littman Library of Jewish Civilization, 1972, rpt. 1993); and the relevant chapters in Rivka Schatz Uffenheimer, *Hasidism as Mysticism: Quietistic Elements in Eighteenth Century Hasidic Thought*, trans. Jonathan Chipman (Princeton: Princeton University Press; Jerusalem: Magnes, 1993).

# 2

# The Halakhic Status of Non-Talmudic Benedictions

The talmudic tradition establishes unequivocally that the basic building block of statutory Jewish prayer is the *berakhah*, the liturgical blessing formula, ברוך אתה ה' (אלהינו מלך העולם)... (Blessed are You, Eternal [our God, Ruler of the universe]...) and presents as normative Rav and Rabbi Yoḥanan's ruling that an acceptable blessing must mention both God's name and God's sovereignty.[1] The locus of the power of the formula lies precisely in these two elements, especially in the mention of God's name. Thus, within the worldview of a people for whom words in general have power, who understand divinity to be embodied in the writing or speaking of God's name, and who accept fully the prohibition of taking that name in vain, concern for the consequences of an uncalled-for tapping of the divine power led the rabbis to restrict casual use not only of the name, but also of the liturgical blessing that so powerfully invokes it.[2] While such restrictions have their source in the literature of the talmudic rabbis, they really only began to be applied consistently in the centuries of immense cultural upheaval following the expulsion from Spain, coinciding with the popularization and spread of Lurianic mysticism.

Although the halakhic principle that prohibits the recitation of non-talmudic blessings came to be more uniformly invoked in this period, the actual minhagim (customs) that incorporated such non-halakhic blessings were not so easily abandoned. Thus, the history of the application of this principle does not really show a straightforward triumph of halakhah over minhag, but rather a process of accommodation by which rabbinic authorities reinterpreted questionable liturgical customs and in so doing enabled them to conform to now dominant halakhic norms. This chapter documents and analyzes that process, focusing

1. *B. Berakhot* 40b. See Chapter 1, Principle B.1.
2. Oaths invoking God's name are a related issue.

primarily on the two most discussed illegitimate blessings in the writings of the post-expulsion rabbis, the *birkat betulim* (blessing over the tokens of virginity) and the priest's blessing at the *pidyon haben* (the redemption of the first-born son).

Anthropologists today generally agree that ritual language functions quite differently from everyday speech: its primary purpose is not to inform but to perform, to do something.[3] Performative language generally displays increased formality, invariance, and formulaic "'repeated word groups' that express an essential idea."[4] Invariant ritual language, such as that of the statutory Jewish prayers (by the medieval period at least),[5] by its very nature must be performative: it does not change in content from its last utterance and does not convey any information of which the participants, be they human or divine, were previously unaware. The repeated liturgical blessing formula, then, functions not just as a structuring device, but also as a signal of its performative nature.[6]

What does the performance of an invariant ritual convey? Roy Rappaport, in his article, "The Obvious Aspects of Ritual,"[7] notes that ritual incorporates canonical or fixed messages, ones that by definition have been said before; and that "the invariance of the liturgy may be an icon of the seeming changelessness of the canonical information that it incorporates or even an index of its actual changelessness..."[8] Not only is the liturgy pointing beyond itself to something

3. Richard Bauman, "Verbal Art as Performance," *American Anthropologist* 77 (1975): 292, observes that Plato and Sir Philip Sydney had implicitly recognized this in their respective denigrations of literature. Bauman and many others are applying to ritual language the linguistic understandings of J.L. Austin, *How To Do Things With Words* (New York: Oxford University Press, 1962).

4. Stanley Jeyaraja Tambiah, "A Performative Approach to Ritual," in *Culture, Thought and Social Action: An Anthropological Perspective* (Cambridge: Harvard University Press, 1985), 140-141.

5. On the tendency of Jewish prayer towards fixity, see Jakob J. Petuchowski, "The Liturgy of the Synagogue: History, Structure, and Contents," in *Approaches to Ancient Judaism, Vol. 4: Studies in Liturgy, Exegesis, and Talmudic Narrative*, William Scott Green, ed. (Chico, CA: Scholars Press, 1983), 41ff.

6. Fully aware of this feature of Jewish ritual language, the rabbis struggled with its implications. How can such an invariant prayer be effective communication with God and not mere mechanical recitation? This problem of *kavvanah* and the tensions between meaningful prayer and an invariant liturgy will be a focus of the next chapter.

7. In *Ecology, Meaning and Religion* (Richmond, CA: North Atlantic Books, 1979?): 173-221.

8. 179, 182. In anthropological discourse, while a "symbol" has a conventional meaning, linked by common agreement to its meaning, an "icon" has meaning because it formally resembles what it signifies, and an "index" is an expression contextually linked to its meaning. Rappaport develops his own, more specific definitions on p. 182.

timeless, but, Rappaport claims, the liturgical order has, on this account, an authority; and the act of performing this liturgy is a public act of acceptance or conformity to the canons of the liturgical order.[9]

In the case of rabbinic prayer, one can interpret participation as a public act of acceptance of the entire rabbinic system of Oral Torah. Early examples are the emphasis on the Pharisaic/rabbinic doctrine of resurrection of the dead in the *gevurot* blessing and the addition or elevation of the *birkat haminim*, both apparently composed so that those who did not conform to rabbinic ideology would have to exempt themselves from active participation in communal prayer. Most likely, adherance to the precise formula of the rabbinic liturgical blessing also signified submission to rabbinic authority.[10] As the Babylonian interpretation of Oral Torah became more absolute, Geonim demanded participation in its increasingly fixed liturgical system as an act of submission not only to the authority of the Babylonian ritual system, but also–and more importantly–to the Babylonian academies that promulgated it and to their understanding of Torah.[11] This unambiguous linking of invariant liturgy to the authority of the rabbinic Torah system (according to the norms of a particular rabbi or school of rabbis) became a significant dynamic of medieval Judaism. Particularly in Ashkenaz, however, that authority had its source not only in the Talmud and its interpretations, but also in ancestral custom. Conformity with minhag was not perceived as contradicting talmudically based authority, but as reliance on another authentic Torah tradition.[12]

---

9. 192-195.

10. We know, particularly from the liturgical texts found at Qumran, but also from Joseph Heinemann's analyses of rabbinic and Second Temple literature (*Prayer in the Talmud: Forms and Patterns*, trans. Richard S. Sarason (Berlin, New York: Walter de Gruyter, 1977), Ch. III.), that multiple blessing-type formulae were concurrent in the early rabbinic period, and it was not necessarily the case that one particular blessing should have triumphed over the others, or that there should be only one single form. We cannot know to what degree the rulings establishing the official blessing formula, recorded in the names of leading third-century rabbis, represent their codification of an existing situation or protest against these alternatives.

11. For the most detailed discussion of this process as it applies to liturgy, see Lawrence A. Hoffman, *The Canonization of the Synagogue Service* (Notre Dame and London: University of Notre Dame Press, 1979; rpt. 1986).

12. For the role of minhag in Jewish law, see Menachem Elon, *Jewish Law: History, Sources, Principles*, trans. Bernard Auerbach and Melvin J. Sykes (Philadelphia: Jewish Publication Society of America, 1994), II: 880-944. For detailed discussions of this issue specifically in Ashkenaz, see: ישראל תא־שמע, "הלכה מנהג ומסורת ביהדות אשכנז במאות הי"א–י"ב," בתוך מנהג ישראל הקדמון - חקר ועיון (ירושלים: מאגנס, תשמ"ז), 13–105; ידידיה דינרי, "המנהג וההלכה בתשובות חכמי אשכנז במאה הט"ו," בתוך ספר הזכרון לבנימין דה פריס, בעריכת א.צ. מלמד (ירושלים, 1968), 168–198; ידידיה דינרי, חכמי אשכנז בשלהי ימי הביניים (ירושלים: מוסד ביאליק, 1984), פרק שישי, חלק שביעי, "הבסיס העיוני של תוקף המנהג".

Rappaport's model, then, suggests that rabbinic authorities used the natural Jewish tendency towards liturgical fixity to their own political advantage to reinforce the greater system they were propounding. But fixity also reflects an important non-political aspect of the ritual. Drawing on the work of Anthony F.C. Wallace, Rappaport suggests that the invariant, performative nature of liturgical language itself conveys a sense of certainty: its unchanging nature points to that which is never changing in the cosmos. To the extent that its language remains unchanging, the ritual itself gains dimensions not just of authority, but also of efficacy and sanctity. Changes in language or other deviations from the liturgical norm, then, suggest the opposite: error, unorthodoxy, inefficacy, heresy, or blasphemy.[13]

Rappaport also suggests that invariance is tied to the perceived antiquity of ritual language. An element in the stability and efficacy of the entire system is that its very language seems never to have been invented and not to have changed from the time of its creation. This characteristic is only reinforced by invariance's freezing ritual language into archaic forms, rather than allowing it to evolve with the vernacular.[14] The deliberate literary archaism of Jewish ritual language lies in its composition in a Hebrew rich with biblical overtones, citations, and allusions–in a period when Hebrew was almost certainly not the vernacular. Nor is this characteristic limited to the language itself. As we shall see, the "discovery" or assumption of archaic roots for prayers is a standard device employed by rabbinic authorities since late antiquity to give authority to prayers and rituals that might otherwise be questioned.

Thus recitation of the liturgical blessing carries several layers of meaning, all of which contribute to the sense, developed early, that misuse of the formula, especially because it contains God's name, is not only erroneous and inefficacious (to use Rappaport's language) but even sacrilegious and dangerous. The parameters of such misuse broadened over time, so that by the sixteenth and seventeenth centuries, any blessing that could not be justified according to the rabbinic authority structures was suspected of total illegitimacy. By that time, the rabbinic authority structure rested primarily, at least in theory, on the primacy of talmudic law. Any blessing, any invocation of the sacrality it represented, that could not be understood to have its roots in talmudic or pre-talmudic antiquity,

13. Rappaport, 203, 208-9. In the continuation of his discussion, Rappaport derives the idea of the sacred, of God, from this human ritual experience. Because this social scientific perspective does not reflect the reality of the participants in a ritual system, it is irrelevant to our discussion. Once ritual exists in a community living in a relationship with the sacred or the divine, the ritual functions to enhance and reinforce this relationship.

14. On the archaism of ritual language, see, for instance, Bauman, "Verbal Art...," 295.

in the days of the great sages who knew God's will in such matters, was to be jettisoned–with the single controversial exception of changes made on the authority of new revelation received by R. Yitzḥak Luria. Thus, the archaism of Jewish liturgy came to extend not only to its language, but also to its content. It is to this process that we now turn.

## *Unnecessary Blessings and Blessings Recited in Vain*

The redacted Talmud inherited by medieval Jews specifically or implicitly indicated the instances in which pious Jews must acknowledge God's involvement in their lives by reciting a liturgical blessing according to the rabbinically defined ritual format.[15] Especially for occasional prayers like the wedding benedictions[16] or blessings to be made for unusual occurrences,[17] the *gemara* quite explicitly dictated wording, deeming inappropriate and ineffective certain possible phrasings of accepted benedictions and, in a few instances, rejecting entire benedictions.[18] Even in those cases where the Talmud dictated only the general theme of the blessing, it nevertheless left no doubt that a blessing was to be said. Hence, by early in the geonic period, the theoretical claim arose that the Babylonian Talmud's authority was absolute; it had established every possible instance in which one could legitimately recite a liturgical benediction. Any use of the rabbinically authorized blessing formula outside of the ordained instances would fall under an extension of the talmudic proscription against reciting a ברכה שאינה צריכה, an unnecessary blessing or a ברכה לבטלה (a blessing recited in vain)–both of which constitute a profanation of the divine Name, a transgression of the commandment לא תשא (You shall not take the name of the Eternal your God in vain).[19] To legitimately ritualize occasions not indicated in the Talmud, one may only invoke some alternative formula that avoids the specific combination of words by which the rabbis defined the official liturgical *berakhah*.[20]

15. See chap.1, Principle B.

16. *B. Ketubot* 7b-8a.

17. See chap.9 of *Berakhot.*

18. See chap.1, Principle C.1., above. Blessings that the Talmud explicitly rejects as being of incorrect content include "שלא עשאני בור" (who has not made me an ignoramus) (*B. Menaḥot* 43b) and the priest's recitation of any benediction at the ceremony for the redemption of a first born son (*B. Pesaḥim* 121b).

19. See chap.1, Principle B.6.

20. Such alternative formulae used throughout the history of rabbinic prayer include: simple omission of God's name from the blessing, alternative addresses to God as הרחמן (the Merciful One), or המקום (the Place), and versions of ...יהי רצון מלפניך ה' אלהינו (may it be Your

In this conception, the ways by which such blasphemous invocation of the blessing formula occurs fall esentially into three categories:[21]

(1)The first and simplest category involves using an established blessing for its original function, but at a time when one is not obligated to recite it, most frequently because one already has,[22] because one has recited a separate blessing that is more comprehensive,[23] or because some other requirement for its recitation is not being met–such as the presence of a quorum or the correct time of day.[24]

(2)The second category contains more egregious transgressions than the first and includes reciting an established blessing for a purpose other than that ordained by the sages. Rabbis raise this concern when discussing such questions as whether one should recite a blessing before performing a ritual whose authority is minhag rather than halakhah, such as over the abbreviated *hallel* on Rosh Ḥodesh,[25] or over women's performance of commandments to which they are not obligated;[26] or whether the officiant at a life cycle ceremony who has recited

---

will, Eternal our God...). For discussion of the origins and early use of these various formulae, see Joseph Heinemann, *Prayer in the Talmud...*, especially the final chapter.

21. See: אנציקלופדיה התלמודית ,"ברכה שאינה צריכה" for a detailed discussion of both of these interrelated concepts.

22. *B. Berakhot* 33a, with reference to the *havdalah* blessing over the wine. Compare *Otzar Hageonim, Rosh Hashanah*, pp. 55-56, #100, regarding the *shofar* blessing.

23. See chap. 1, Principle B.9. In a very different context, Ezra Fleischer suggests that this growing Babylonian (geonic) concern about unnecessary benedictions may lie behind the evolution of the late Palestinian rite. When the Palestinians first added the Babylonian *pesukei d'zimra* to their existing ritual for reciting psalms before the main service, they apparently maintained the framework of blessings that had developed independently in each rite. The subsequent dropping of their indigenous blessings can be understood as a response to a superimposed Babylonian concern about unnecessary blessings. See his תפילה ומנהגי תפילה ארץ־ישראליים בתקופת הגניזה (ירושלים: מאגנס, תשמ"ח), 242.

24. *Beit Yosef* OH 89, ד"ה ואם עבר והתפלל אחר ד' שעות, in regard to the *amidah*. See also the responsum ascribed to Hai Gaon, ספר שערי תשובה סי' קטו, regarding *kiddush*.

25. תשובות רש"י, מהדורת אלפנביין, סי' שמ"ז, עמ' 351; *Tosafot Sukkah* 44b, ד"ה כאן במקדש כאן בגבולין.

26. An early discussion of the issue, attributed to Hai Gaon, debates whether women may recite the blessings over circumcision, Torah, and discernment etc., in which they do not participate. See ספר שערי תשובה, סי' שמה. General Ashkenazi opinion follows Rabbenu Tam who permits women to recite the blessings (*Tosafot Rosh Hashanah* 33a, ד"ה הא רבי יהודה הא רבי יוסי). See too, the *Rosh, Rosh Hashanah* 4:7, *Kiddushin* 1:49. For contrary opinions, see Rashi to *B. Eruvin* 96a and *B. Rosh Hashanah* 33a; and Maimonides, *Mishneh Torah, Hilkhot Tzitzit* 3:9. See the discussions in Moshe Meiselman, *Jewish Women in Jewish Law* (New York: Ktav Publishing House, Yeshiva University Press, 1978), 47-48; and Eliezer Berkovits, *Jewish Women in Time and Torah* (Hoboken, New Jersey: Ktav Publishing House, 1990), 70-74.

a blessing over the wine must taste it;[27] or whether the *birkhot hashaḥar*, the benedictions originally tied to the actions of an individual rising in the morning, can properly be recited communally at the beginning of the morning service.[28]

(3) Although the practical halakhic literature concerns itself at great length with the first two categories, the third and historically most interesting–and the one that concerns us here–involves blessings for which there exists absolutely no talmudic precedent, thus calling into question the legitimacy of their invocation of the divine Name under any circumstances. We shall refer to these blessings as *non-talmudic* rather than *post-talmudic* simply because, while many are of later origin, some are blessings rejected by the Talmud, some appear in some versions of the Talmud but not in others, and some may well have already existed during the talmudic period as local customs not known in the centers of talmudic activity or not deemed worthy of comment.

In as diverse a religious community as Judaism had become by the post-talmudic period, the successful dissemination of an authoritative halakhic prohibition of any non-talmudic blessing could not have been simple. Because there are lacunae in the list of blessings included in the Babylonian Talmud, various ritual responses likely existed during the talmudic period–even in the Babylonian academies–that for one reason or another do not appear in the corpus of literature that emerged from that world. Not only do we lack a single comprehensive liturgical text from this period, but we know from the materials found in the Cairo genizah that additional prayers and alternative formulations were concurrently developing in the Palestinian rite. Other non-Babylonian diaspora communities likely also developed their own liturgical traditions. Are these variants all to be deemed non-talmudic and hence illegitimate, or do they have a valid status as local minhag? Aside from concurrent variants, time and the vicissitudes of history exposed Jews to new ideas and led them to desire to incorporate new means of liturgical expression into their ritual practices. Did post-talmudic Jews have the right to compose new blessings using the official formula that the talmudic rabbis had deemed most effective and sacred? Did such compositions constitute a basic failure to accept the authority of God's law and guarantee inefficacious, even dangerous results? Granted, new prayers could always be phrased with alternative formulae, but their level of ritual sanc-

27. See ש. אסף, תשובות הגאונים, סי' לט, עמ' נד, and the parallel responsa he lists there. On the ongoing debate throughout the medieval period on how to handle a circumcision ceremony on a fast day when the officiant may not taste the wine, see: ישראל תא־שמע, "ברכות המילה על הכוס בט' באב – כיצד?" בתוך מנהג אשכנז הקדמון - חקר ועיון (ירושלים: מאגנס, תשנ"ב; מ"הברכה על היין בטכס ברית המילה," אסופות ד (תש"ן), מט–נו), 327–335.

28. משנה תורה, הלכות תפילה ז:ז–ט; תשובות רבנו אברהם בן הרמב"ם, סי' פג.

tity would thereby be diminished. Jews wished to ritualize additional aspects of life and naturally wanted to legitimatize these rituals by invoking God with the well-established liturgical *berakhah*.

As we shall see, even in the sixteenth and seventeenth centuries, when absolute prohibition of the non-talmudic liturgical blessing became widespread, rabbinic authorities had to contend with the reality of popular custom, which included rituals obviously dating to the geonic period or perhaps even earlier. Indeed, the popular natural desire to incorporate liturgical blessings into rituals is evident even within the talmudic literature.

A prime example are the blessings for the *hallel* psalms. Although the Mishnah clearly presupposes the recitation of these psalms outside the Temple context, it leaves the option of including a concluding blessing on Sukkot to local custom[29] and dictates this blessing at the Passover seder.[30] There is no formal initial blessing in either case, although in the case of the seder, the Mishnah does prescribe a prayer that forms a transition to the recitation of *hallel* and functions literarily as a blessing. However, perhaps because of its antiquity, this prayer lacks what later became the formulaic words that would make it a proper *berakhah*.[31] But by the time of the fourth-century Babylonian Amora, Abbaye, several additional liturgical principles had been formulated, and the pattern of encapsulating ritual elements with opening and closing blessings was well established. Commenting on the passage from *Mishnah Sukkah*, he ruled that one can derive the obligation to recite a blessing preceding the *hallel* from the principle of the third-century Amora, Shmuel, that one must recite a blessing before fulfilling any commandment.[32] Perhaps because of the variations in local customs regarding the blessing following the *hallel*, he does not invoke the principle that anything followed by a blessing must be preceded by one.[33]

When we look at the liturgy of the geonic period, this tendency to sacralize and ritualize liturgical expression by the addition of formal blessings is quite marked. The Talmud establishes only very generally that Jews should prepare

---

29. *Mishnah Sukkah* 3:11 reads: מקום שנהגו . . . לברך אחריו יברך אחריו, הכל כמנהג המדינה (in a place where they were accustomed to recite a blessing after it, they may do so; it all depends on the local custom). The *gemara*'s edition omits the word אחריו (after it) both times, but clearly presupposes it in its comment.

30. *Mishnah Pesaḥim* 10:7 reads: רביעי גומר עליו את ההלל ואומר עליו את ברכת השיר (Over the fourth cup of wine, one completes the *hallel* and recites the *birkat hashir*).

31. *Mishnah Pesaḥim* 10:5. The prayer beginning לפיכך contains all the content (and more) that one would expect in a blessing at this point, including an acknowledgement of obligation.

32. *B. Sukkah* 39a. See chap. 1, Principle B.10.

33. See chap. 1, Principle B.11.

themselves mentally for prayer and that daily recitation of certain psalms is an ideal for which one should strive.[34] However, in the earliest extant geonic treatises on prayer, the *pesukei d'zimra*, complete with a framework of blessings, are an established part of the morning service. *Halakhot Gedolot*, from the late ninth century, records an earlier ruling that the latecomer trying to catch up should abbreviate the psalms recited but not the blessings themselves, which clearly are already more essential liturgically than the psalms they came to frame.[35] Natronai Gaon's famous responsum detailing the hundred blessings one is required to recite daily simply lists *barukh she-amar*, assuming that his readers will know it.[36] Although no geonic traditions attempted to hide the post-talmudic nature of the opening blessing particularly, none made excuses for its existence either. Most Rishonim did not question the legitimacy of this blessing and referred to its origins only vaguely as an enactment of the rabbis.[37]

---

34. *Mishnah Berakhot* 5:1 and the *gemara*'s commentary on it; *B. Shabbat* 118b.

35. Ed. Hildesheimer, I: 14-15, records this responsum of R. Moshe Gaon, who was the Gaon in Sura from 829 to 839 (Brody's dating), making it plausible that this responsum was original to R. Shimon Kayyara's text, especially if we follow the dating of Neil Danzig, who dates *Halakhot Gedolot* to the last quarter of the ninth century. See his: מבוא לספר הלכות פסוקות עם תשלום הלכות פסוקות (ניו יורק וירושלים: בית המדרש לרבנים באמריקה, תשמ"ג), 184–186, 271. See also Robert Brody, *The Geonim of Babylonia and the Shaping of Medieval Jewish Culture* (New Haven: Yale University Press, 1998), 228, 344. It is also possible that this is a later interpolation into the text, especially as *Halakhot Gedolot* itself includes no direct discussion of this part of the service. However, this responsum appears too in the contemporary *Seder Rav Amram Gaon* which grants it even greater antiquity by indicating that R. Moshe Gaon was transmitting the opinion of his teachers. In spite of the difficulties involved in validating the authenticity of Amram's prayer texts, there can be little doubt that these blessings are integral to the *Seder Rav Amram Gaon*, as he included a lengthy discussion of the exact wording appropriate for the concluding eulogy of *barukh she-amar.* (Goldschmidt ed., #9, p. 8.) Saadia presents this entire section of the service as a voluntary offering of Israel and specifically describes the blessings as enacted by the sages. (*Siddur Rav Saadia Gaon*, 32.)

36. Louis Ginzberg, *Geonica* (New York: The Jewish Theological Seminary of America, 1909), II:116.

37. See, for instance, the *Rif*, *Berakhot* 23a, cited by the Rosh, *Berakhot* 5:5; *Sefer HaItim*, 249; Maimonides, *Mishneh Torah*, *Hilkhot Tefillah* 7:12; *Abudarham Hashalem*, 64. While the *Tur* OH 51 seems to follow in this same line, he introduces the idea found in the *Sefer Hapardes* ascribed to Rashi (321), which understands the ruling of Rabbi Simlai in *B. Berakhot* 32a, that one must always praise God before beginning to pray, to be the legal enactment of the institution of *pesukei d'zimra*. Some Aḥaronim, like R. Yoel Sirkes, the *Baḥ*, then can say that if reciting these psalms is a rabbinically decreed mitzvah, and, if one must make a blessing before performing a mitzvah, there can then be no real questions about the legitimacy of this blessing. However, a significant weakness in this argument is that *barukh she-amar* does not take the form of a blessing for a mitzvah (which would require the formula: בא"ה אמ"ה אשר קדשנו במצותיו וציונו..., "...who has sanctified us by His commandments

*Barukh she-amar* is only the most obvious example of the easily legitimated geonic additions to the corpus of liturgical blessings. Other new blessings went beyond giving added structure to established liturgical situations and granted increased sanctity to entire rituals or sections thereof: the blessing over the sabbath candles, the blessing concluding the *vidui* (the confessional prayer), the blessing concluding the *hoshanot* poems on Sukkot, the blessing for the priest to say at the ceremony of the redemption of the first-born son, and the blessing for the bridegroom to recite when displaying the tokens of his bride's virginity. Still others first appeared in the geonic period and became accepted parts of the standard liturgy, but they are most likely accretions from other liturgical contexts and difficult to explain as logical additions to the liturgy. This group includes the *birkat hapesukim*, the selection of verses forming a third blessing after *shema* in the evening, and the series of paragraphs included in the morning benedictions that concludes with the blessing מקדש את שמך ברבים (who sanctifies Your name publicly).[38]

Thus the basic human tendency to ritual invariance, seen here in the growing rabbinic insistence on fixed liturgy, existed in significant tension with the drive toward the legitimation of new rituals through the invocation of conventional formulas. Complicating this dynamic was the fact that the Talmud itself directly insists on invariance only in the opening formula of the liturgical blessing and in the basic structure of the prayers, leaving most of the rest of the liturgy and its specific texts to the realm of custom. Only in the medieval world, when rabbinic traditions claimed invariance for their specific regional customs, was the

---

and commanded us to…"). Note, too, the discomfort with the status of this blessing that appears in attempts to justify it based on parallels with the *hallel* blessings. See, for example, *Orḥot Ḥayyim*, *Hilkhot Meah Berakhot* 21; *Shibbolei Haleket*, ed. Mirsky, 147.

38. On the origins of the *birkat hapesukim* and the rabbinic debates over it, see below, p. 90f. The second prayer may have its origins in a Palestinian custom modelled on that of Rabbi Yehudah Hanasi in *B. Berakhot* 13b, that ensured the recitation of at least the first line of *shema* early enough in the morning; and in a desire to find a way to fulfill the Shammaite custom of standing for *shema* in the morning without transgressing the Hillelite halakhah that applied to the full recitation with the blessings. See: – ישראל תא־שמע, "קריאת שמע 'על המיטה' מה היא?" בתוך מנהג אשכנז הקדמון..., 326, and his suggestion that this morning liturgy, complete with blessings, evolved, at least in Ashkenaz, as a parallel to the elevation of the bedtime *shema* there. The variations among current Ashkenazi rites in the exact wording of this concluding blessing are also evidence for its late origins. Compare, for example, the wording cited above from Baer's סדר עבודת ישראל, to that of the Israeli סדור רנת ישראל, which reads more felicitously, המקדש את שמו ברבים, (who sanctifies His name publicly). Sefardim have eliminated the liturgical blessing formula from this prayer, and in most cases, have dropped the *birkat hapesukim* entirely.

fixity of the blessing formula consistently extended to the specific content of the texts with which it was associated.

Before the sixteenth century, requirements for *kavvanah* in prayer, the sheer variety of extant rites, and the pious desire to elevate and ritualize additional occasions all encouraged the application of the invariant, efficacious blessing formula to new content and contexts. Assertions of rabbinic authority and seemingly principled objection to non-talmudic benedictions did arise earlier, but these were largely secondary claims, buttressing objections to the specific content of the custom involved or part of political attempts to assert greater general leadership over a given community. In those days, invocation of the liturgical blessing formula in "new," non-talmudic situations was usually accepted benignly, i.e., without comment, as an appropriate means of Jewish ritualization. By the sixteenth century, however, the gradual growth in the theoretical authority of the Talmud, the increasingly influential mystical interpretations requiring fixed prayer texts, the upheavals that altered local customs, and the invention of printing all contributed to a more rigid insistence on invariance in application of the blessing formula as dictated by the Talmud or, if necessary, by some alternative authority of equal or greater antiquity.

### *Discussions of the Issue in the Geonic Literature*

The earliest preserved explicit ruling against non-talmudic blessings is from the geonic period, more or less contemporaneous with the first appearance of the most significant corpus of blessings that contradict the principle. This coincidence alone suggests that rabbinic reservations about such benedictions were heretofore confined largely to the realm of halakhic theory and never energetically applied to practice in the community.

Pirkoi ben Baboi cites Rav Yehudai Gaon in his letter addressed to the Jews of Kairouan, sometime around the year 800:[39]

> וכן א'ר' יהודאי זכ' אד' וג' לברכה, כל ברכה שאינה בתלמוד אסור לברך אותה ואסור להוסיף אות אחת.
>
> This is what R. Yehudai said, may our master's memory be a blessing: It

39. Scholars now disagree with Ginzberg's assumption (*Ginzei Schechter*, 504-508) that Pirkoi ben Baboi directed this *book* (not a letter, but a more formal composition) to the Jews of Palestine, and agree that the actual addressees were the Jews of Kairouan who had not been under Babylonian influence at all until the Arab conquest. See: ב.מ. לוין, "משרידי הגניזה," תרביץ ב (תרצ"א), 385; שלום שפייגל, "לפרשת הפולמוס של פירקוי בן באבוי," ספר היובל לכבוד צבי וולפסון (ירושלים: *AAJR*, תשכ"ה), רמו ואילך.; Moshe Gil, "The Babylonian Yeshivot and the Maghrib in the Early Middle Ages," *PAAJR* 57 (1990/91): 69; and Brody, *The Geonim*..., 113f.

is forbidden to recite any blessing that is not in the Talmud or even to add a single letter.[40]

The specifics with which Pirkoi ben Baboi or R. Yehudai Gaon buttressed this generalization might indicate that it applied narrowly to unauthorized variants of accepted blessings rather than to all unauthorized blessings, but Pirkoi ben Baboi had already earlier argued extensively against changing the wording of established benedictions. He emphasized the care with which the sages established wordings of benedictions to illustrate the exhaustive nature of amoraic concern for prayer texts in general, to the point that no new ones were allowed.[41] In addition, in his preceding arguments, Pirkoi ben Baboi stated explicitly that one must place under a ban anyone overheard reciting an unnecessary benediction or oath, that he considered it praiseworthy to refrain from reciting benedictions when there was any doubt about their necessity, and that he considered blasphemous any invocation of the divine Name in unauthorized situations.[42] A fragment published separately (and out of context) by Shraga Abramson includes a responsum of Yehudai Gaon forbidding the non-talmudic ceremony of *hatarat nedarim* (the release of vows), because it involved an unnecessary blessing, the speaking of falsehood, and an attempt by common people to take on the responsibilities of the academy and its sages.[43] In that case, while the non-talmudic nature of the blessing was an important factor in the theoretical ruling against the ceremony, its popular, unlearned origins, its challenge of rabbinic authority, and the basic question of whether vows can be annulled also militated against it.[44] Very clearly, issues of liturgical efficacy, use of the blessing formula, and submission to rabbinic authority all

---

40. *Ginzei Schechter*, 550.

41. Implied in this is his argument for the absolute, definitive authority of the Babylonian Talmud.

42. 544, 546.

43. שרגא אברמסון, "על ברכת התרת נדרים ושבועות," סיני נ (תשכ"ב), קפה.

44. שרגא אברמסון, "פסקים קדומים, א. ברכה על התרת נדרים ושבועות," סיני מט (תשכ"א), רי–ריד and the follow-up in *Sinai* 50. Abramson's location of the origin of this ceremony in Palestine may be questioned. It and the Kol Nidrei ceremony, another ritual release from vows, may well have their origins in the popular culture of Babylonia itself. See especially: שלמה דשן, "חידת 'כל נדרי': בירור אנתרופולוגי והיסטורי," פרקים בתולדות החברה היהודית בימי הביניים ובעת החדשה מוקדשים לפרופסור יעקב כ"ץ... (ירושלים: מאגנס, תש"ם), 144–146; and the criticism of Abramson's articles in Zvi Groner's M.A. Thesis, ברכות שנשתקעו, Hebrew University, 1964. Neil Danzig suggests that the Geonim of this period generally avoided the entire issue of the release of vows. *Masekhet Nedarim* was not taught in the official study sessions of the academies, and its subject matter was omitted from many of the early geonic halakhic works. See his ...מבוא להלכות פסוקות, 91, 195-197, 426-427. This supports Deshen's arguments that the Geonim purposefully avoided this element of popular, syncretistic culture.

intertwine here.

The extent to which the school of Yehudai Gaon actually implemented this strict stance against non-talmudic benedictions is questionable. *Halakhot Gedolot* basically summarizes the talmudic discussions and does not provide many additional prayer texts; its data pertinent to our question is limited. However, as we have received it, it does require the recitation of the post-talmudic *birkat betulim*, the blessing by which the bridegroom ceremonially acknowledges that his bride was indeed a virgin,[45] and it includes the blessing *magbiah shefalim* (who raises up the lowly) in its list of the morning benedictions.[46] Because the possibility exists that our received text of *Halakhot Gedolot* reflects later interpolations, the text of Pirkoi ben Baboi is our sole evidence that, by the early ninth century C.E., the Babylonian academy (or elements thereof) considered only talmudic blessings to be legitimate.

Roughly a century after Yehudai Gaon, Natronai Gaon also voiced opposition to specific non-talmudic benedictions. He was asked about a ceremony that officially begins the seven days of mourning upon return from the cemetery with a blessing recited over a cup of wine. His response leaves no room for doubt:

> וכי קביעת אבילות בשתיית כוס תלוי?...וברכה זו שכתבתם לא שמענו מעולם ואין לה זכרון בתלמוד ולא שמענו בשתי ישיבות שיש מי שאומר ברכה זו ולא שמענו מרבותינו.
>
> Is the formal beginning of mourning dependent on the drinking of a cup of wine?... As to this blessing that you wrote about, we have never heard of it, there is no trace of it in the Talmud, and we in the two academies have never heard of anyone saying this blessing or heard of it from our teachers.[47]

Three significant arguments form the basis of R. Natronai's ruling here: the talmudic traditions mark the formal beginning of mourning by other rituals; the Babylonian Geonim have no received oral tradition justifying the ceremony in question; and the blessing itself has no talmudic basis. To these we may possibly

---

45. Ed. Hildesheimer, II: 226.

46. Ed. Hildesheimer, I:152. On the history of this blessing, see: משה חלמיש, "ברכת המגביה שפלים - ברכה שנשתכחה," אסופות ב (תשמ"ח), קצא-ר. We will discuss this blessing in greater detail below.

47. *Otzar Hageonim*, *Mashkin*, p. 43, #126, *Ketubot*, pp. 32-33, #107; Zvi Groner, ברכות שנשתקעו, 29; E.E. Urbach, *Arugat Habosem*, IV:66-76. Compare to this the statement of the Gaon, Sar Shalom, Natronai's predecessor, who objects to any change in the circumcision blessings, claiming that because they appear in the *gemara*, no one has the right to change them. (*Seder Rav Amram Gaon*, ed. Goldschmidt, 180.) Someone's alternative text, either an innovation or simply a variant custom, must have elicited this comment.

add a fourth, that the non-Babylonian nature of this ceremony made it *ab initio* objectionable.[48]

In another context, Natronai Gaon also expressed forcefully his vision of the Talmud as the only legitimate halakhic authority in liturgical matters. In criticizing those who include the *shema* in every *kedushah* instead of restricting it to the *musaf* service, R. Natronai Gaon says:

> ואלו שיש ביניכם שנראים כמדקדקים וגורעין ומוסיפים ומשנין, לא יפה הם עושים שמשנים ממנהג שתי ישיבות. ומנהג שלנו אין אנו משנים ממה שאמרו חכמים בתלמוד בין בשבתות בין בימים טובים, ואי מתקלעינן למקום ואמר חזן מאי דלא דמי מסלקינן ליה.
>
> Those among you who seem to be punctilious, but really delete, add, and change, are not acting appropriately in deviating from the custom of the two academies. Our custom does not deviate from that dictated by the sages of the Talmud, whether for Sabbaths or festivals, and if we happen to be somewhere where the *ḥazzan* recites inappropriate [prayers], we remove him.[49]

Ironically, the talmudic literature contains no discussion of Natronai's precise subject, the formulation of the *kedushah*. Nevertheless, his message is clear. The custom of the academies is to have universal authority. As heirs to the talmudic traditions, they now embody the living authority of the Talmud itself and as such, are the guarantors of acceptable, efficacious prayer.

---

48. The entire question of the tannaitic *birkat avelim* and its understanding in amoraic and geonic Babylonia is quite complicated. The Babylonian Amoraim seem to have inherited terminology for ceremonies that never quite fit their practice. Thus while various requirements for blessings surrounding burial and the formal mourning process appear in the Talmud, their application is ambiguous. What is certain is that there is no *birkat avelim* in the Talmud that corresponds to the ceremony described by Natronai's questioner, or to that described in a similar question posed to his Pumbeditan colleague, Paltoi Gaon. Paltoi ruled more leniently than Natronai, saying that although this blessing is not customary anywhere in Babylonia, those whose sages have established it for them may recite it. (*Otzar Hageonim*, *Mashkin*, p. 44, #127.) This blessing appears in the *Seder* of Natronai's contemporary, Rav Amram Gaon, (ed. Goldschmidt, 187) without any comment. Goldschmidt apparently did not consider it a gloss, although it could well represent one of the many customs of early Ashkenaz which crept into our manuscripts. One late geonic source of unclear provenance does include this blessing in its description of funeral and mourning customs, the *Sefer Hamiktzo'ot*, as cited by Rabbi Ephraim of Bonn (Urbach, *Arugat Habosem*, IV:66-76; שמחה אסף, ספר המקצועות (ירושלים: מוסד הרב קוק, תש"ז), 7–10.) For further discussion of the talmudic mourning blessings, see Lieberman's תוספתא כפשוטה, I:47-50 to *Berakhot* 3:23-24; the entry "ברכת אבלים" in the אנציקלופדיה התלמודית; and Nissan Rubin, "Birkat Avelim - The Blessing of Mourners," *Approaches to Ancient Judaism*, N.S., Vol. 5, ed. Herbert W. Basser, Simcha Fishbane (Atlanta: Scholars Press, 1993), 119-141.

49. *Seder Rav Amram Gaon*, ed. Goldschmidt, 32.

These claims of close reliance on talmudic tradition are clearly hyperbolic vis-à-vis not only the *kedushah* but other blessings too. In clarifying what specifically fulfills Rabbi Meir's requirement that a Jew recite one hundred blessings daily,[50] R. Natronai listed ...ב'..גביה שפל (*magbiah shefalim*), as well as the blessings framing *pesukei d'zimra* and the third blessing after *shema* in the evening,[51] which he, in another responsum, justified as the enactment of רבנן בתראי (later rabbis).[52] A separate responsum requires the blessing over the Sabbath lights, and even justifies it in spite of its non-talmudic status.[53]

Given that Natronai consistently asserted talmudically grounded authenticity in tandem with claims for the authority of the Babylonian academies and their customs, it is likely that he considered them to be equivalent. The authority of the academy grew from its status as the heir to the talmudic traditions. The boundaries of the Talmud could thus be stretched to include various additional oral saboraic and geonic traditions, and to exclude non-Babylonian traditions too.[54] Nonetheless, Natronai Gaon does require, in certain cases, strict adherence to the wording of the talmudic liturgy. Whatever his intentions, later sages could find in them, if they so desired, precedents for their own claims.

Although these various statements of R. Amram Gaon's immediate predecessors and contemporaries appear in our received version of his *Seder*, there is no evidence in the work itself that he personally took such an intransigent stance.[55] Amram may simply have ignored most variant customs as inappropriate for inclusion in an authoritative liturgical guide. Although he occasionally fulminates against what we now recognize as Palestinian ritual practice, not once in

50. *B. Menahot* 43b; *P. Berakhot* 9:5, 14d. See the discussion of these texts in chap.1, Principle B., n. 97.

51. *Geonica*, II:115-117.

52. *Seder Rav Amram Gaon*, ed. Goldschmidt, 62.

53. *Otzar Hageonim*, *Shabbat*, p. 27, #83. This may also be the source of the parallel comment in *Seder Rav Amram Gaon*, ed. Goldschmidt, 61, although it is not attributed to Natronai there.

54. See Neil Danzig, ...מבוא להלכות פסוקות, 13-16, and the other materials listed in his index, for the impact of the saboraic traditions on geonic halakhah.

55. Scholars agree that the *Seder*, as we know it today, is the work of sages in the generations following R. Amram. It includes many citations of Natronai Gaon, with whom R. Amram was not on the best of terms, citations of Amram himself in the third person, and citations of later Geonim. For a brief summary of the literature, see Goldschmidt's introduction to his edition, 7-11. See also: ירחמיאל ברודי, "לחידת עריכתו של סדר רב עמרם גאון," בתוך כנסת עזרא: ספרות וחיים בבית הכנסת, אסופת מאמרים מוגשת לעזרא פליישר, בעריכת שולמית אליצור, משה דוד הר, אביגדור שנאן, גרשון שקד (ירושלים: יד יצחק בן־צבי ומכון בן־צבי לחקר קהילות ישראל במזרח, 1994), 30, who, following Ginzberg, argues that these are almost certainly additions since Geonim almost never cite one another in their responsa.

these passages does he raise the argument that a particular blessing is non-talmudic. His closest argument is his rejection of the talmudic blessing, *matir asurim*, as unnecessary because it duplicates another talmudic blessing, *zokef kefufim*. But this is an argument based on logic, not authority, and the more accurate version may well be the responsum in *Shibbolei Haleket*, which records that R. Amram removed the blessing *magbiah shefalim*.[56] Amram is aware of and cites the question posed, probably to Natronai Gaon, about the authority for requiring the blessing over the Sabbath candles,[57] and he repeats Natronai's discussion of the late but still legitimate origins of the third blessing after the evening *shema*.[58] Aside from these, the original version of R. Amram's prayerbook, to the extent that it can be determined, may well have contained no non-talmudic benedictions. In our editions, as Goldschmidt points out, the blessing before the bedtime *shema* is very likely an interpolation of the Franco-German copyist(s) whose custom this was.[59] The *Halakhot Gedolot* ruling requiring *birkat betulim*, the blessing over the tokens of virginity, is also a late interpolation into Amram's *Seder*, as it appears only in a manuscript of Franco-German origin.[60] Moreover, although Goldschmidt does not voice any doubts about the originality of the text, Amram's mourning blessing might fall into this category too.[61] Louis Ginzberg's observation that the non-talmudic status of benedictions was not of concern to R. Amram thus can neither be verified nor refuted based on the evidence available.[62]

Ginzberg's assertion, in this same discussion, that Saadia Gaon objected specifically to non-talmudic benedictions rests on equally shaky ground, especially as Ginzberg's source for Saadia's specific comment is a citation in the fourteenth-century *Orḥot Ḥayyim*.[63] No earlier citations of Saadia's criticism of the special poetic blessing for the conclusion of the Torah reading on Simḥat

---

56. Ed. Goldschmidt, 3. *Shibbolei Haleket*, ed. Mirsky, 136, #4. See too the responsum (and the editor's notes to it) that is likely *Shibbolei Haleket*'s source: תשובות הגאונים החדשות ועמן תשובות, פסקים ופירושים מאת חכמי פרובאנס הראשונים, מהדורת שמחה עמנואל (ירושלים: מכון אופק, ספריית פרידברג, תשנ"ה), סי' ל, עמ' 28–29.

57. p. 61.

58. p. 62.

59. p. 54. See too: ישראל תא־שמע, "קריאת שמע 'על המיטה' – מה היא?," 317.

60. p. 182.

61. p. 187. However, note that Amram simply records the texts of the various mourning prayers and gives no context at all to the problematic *birkat avelim*. Is this all an addition to the prayerbook? See the discussion above, n. 48.

62. *Ginzei Schechter*, II:517.

63. קריאת ספר תורה, סוף נ"ח. Ginzberg repeats this assertion in his article, "Saadia's Siddur," *JQR* 33 (1942): 331-332, where he reads an objection to the non-talmudic use of a blessing formula into Saadia's objection to the priest's reciting any blessing at the *pidyon haben*.

Torah, including the fragments of Saadia's *Siddur* unknown to Ginzberg, make reference to the non-talmudic status of the blessing. Robert Brody[64] maintains that there is absolutely no evidence that Saadia Gaon ever invoked our principle in order to establish or buttress his objections to a particular blessing. He criticizes Joseph Heinemann's assertion to the contrary, claiming that had Heinemann examined more closely his assumption that our principle was operative for Saadia, he would not have had to try so hard to justify the long list of non-talmudic benedictions that appear in Saadia's *Siddur.* This list includes at least two instances where Saadia concluded his own original prayers with a liturgical *berakhah*, something he would not have done were he to have accepted the theoretical ruling that only talmudically decreed blessings are legitimate.[65] Thus, says Brody, Saadia Gaon, whose principled objections to various prayer texts are famous, did not consider the Talmud to be the definitive source for all possible applications of the rabbinic blessing formula.

Brody, though, has probably interpreted Saadia's words a little too narrowly. He claims that Saadia's objections a) to the individual's concluding his Yom Kippur confessional with a formal eulogy because "this is not the place for a benediction" and b) to the priest's blessing at the *pidyon haben* as "without basis,"[66] do not reflect a principled objection to non-talmudic benedictions. However, Brody is making an argument from silence, as Saadia does not give detailed reasons for either of these objections. Saadia does not call on the custom of the Babylonian academies or give specific objection to the content of the blessings,

64. Robert Brody, "Saadya Gaon on the Limits of Liturgical Flexibility," in *Geniza Research after Ninety Years: The Case of Judaeo-Arabic*, ed. Joshua Blau and Stefan C. Reif (Cambridge: University Press, 1992), 40-42.

65. יוסף היינימן, "יחסו של רס"ג לשינוי מטבע התפלה," בתוך עיוני תפילה, בעריכת אביגדור שנאן (ירושלים: מאגנס, תשמ"א; מבר אילן א (תשכ"ג), 220–233), 111–116. Heinemann tries to justify these two supposed exceptions by understanding them to fit the known, if not officially sanctioned, model of prayers written for private recitation. These, having only concluding blessings but not the officially sanctioned opening formula, contradict the talmudic principles of prayer structure. This may help us to understand why Saadia only concluded his prayers with blessing formulas; it does not justify his use of a liturgical blessing to begin with.

Naphtali Wieder points out that even the seeming deletion of the divine Name from the conclusion of *hashkiveinu*, which corresponds to the later compromise that effectively combined the second and third blessings after *shema* in the evening (see below, p. 90f.), almost certainly reflects a scribal emendation to Saadia's *Siddur*, since not a single source justifies the later change based on Saadia's precedent, and parallel fragments do not support the text of the manuscript on which our printed *Siddur Rav Saadia Gaon* is based. See his: "פרקים בתולדות התפילה והברכות," סיני עז (תשל"ה), קכז–קלג.

66. In this case, Brody is following Assaf in retrojecting into Saadia's world later arguments explaining why the priest may not recite a blessing here.

making it likely that his authority for the proper use of benedictions must have been the Talmud. Like his predecessors, Brody is looking for a consistent application of our principle. However, like Natronai, Saadia knew the principle forbidding non-talmudic benedictions, but applied it inconsistently. Other factors probably determined Saadia's actual ruling, and talmudic authorization or lack thereof was a convenient support.[67]

Beyond this, there is little discussion of non-talmudic blessings in the surviving geonic literature. R. Sherira Gaon and his son Hai were questioned whether recitation of the non-talmudic blessing for the Sabbath candles was grounded in minhag or halakhah, and if its basis was halakhic, what the talmudic source was. While the question here indicates concern for the talmudic authority supposedly underlying all blessings, the geonic answer reflects a much more flexible approach: they reply that if the obligation to light the candles is halakhically well-established, then one may infer the obligation to make a blessing.[68] This logic would lead easily to permission to recite a blessing over the performance of any commandment and to a nullification of any notion that the Talmud specifically decrees where blessings are justified or not. Indeed, Hai Gaon seems to have operated in this way. The authority for one of the non-talmudic blessings current in medieval Spain, the priest's blessing at the ceremony for the redemption of the firstborn son, is indicated in one source to be Hai Gaon,[69] and Hai Gaon specifically justifies the blessing over the tokens of virginity as a received tradition among the sages.[70]

However, Hai Gaon imposed some limits; he objected to a custom of concluding the *hoshanot* poems on Sukkot with the blessing established for the conclusion of the *megillah* reading on Purim, ברוך אתה ה' האל המושיע (Blessed are You, Eternal, the God who saves). Such a custom is an excellent example of a community's

---

67. In the case of the blessing after the confessional prayer, Saadia is probably objecting to a Palestinian custom, although this cannot be proven. As Zvi Groner has shown in his article, "הברכה על הווידוי וגלגוליה," בר אילן יג (תשל"ו), 168–158, the blessing is authorized by tannaitic sources, but there is no discussion of it in amoraic sources in either Talmud, and the Babylonian Geonim seem not to know even the tannaitic sources. The blessing appears in early Ashkenazi sources and in one genizah text that Wieder identified as Babylonian but strangely so (to the point that one might assert that the blessing appears there from Palestinian influences). It was apparently never recited in Spain and Provence. Thus, it seems never to have been a Babylonian custom; it seems to have all the typical markings of a Palestinian custom that became current in Ashkenaz. See the various sources cited by Groner. On the priest's blessing at the *pidyon haben*, see below.

68. *Otzar Hageonim, Shabbat*, pp. 27-28, #85.

69. *Otzar Hageonim, Pesaḥim*, pp. 130-132, #361-362. See below for a discussion of the reliability of this attribution.

70. *Teshuvot Hageonim*, Harkavy, p. 230, #438.

elevation of an established ritual by the addition of an otherwise invariant and well-established blessing. According to the version recorded by Yitzḥak ibn Ghayyat, R. Hai's objection is only that this is an unnecessary blessing, and there are sages here (in Babylonia) who would prevent its being said.[71] The version recorded in the *Manhig* specifically calls such a *ḥazzan* errant, הוא מוציא מפיו ברכה לבטלה שלא תיקנוה חכמי' כי אם במגילה (for he utters a blessing in vain that the sages had ordained only for the *megillah* reading).[72] Is this viewed as a non-talmudic benediction, or merely the misuse of an established benediction? Part of the answer hinges on whether the author of the *Manhig* had received a fuller, more authentic version of Hai's responsum, or whether the added explanation was Hai's, some intermediate copyist's, or the *Manhig*'s attempt to clarify the text. But given the nature of the situation described, this is not a simple transferral of the Purim blessing to an analogous situation on Sukkot, since only the eulogy of the blessing is involved, and its meaning is radically altered by its new reference to the general cries for salvation in the *hoshanot* instead of the specific historical events of Purim. It now functions as a new blessing, and Hai is probably objecting to the non-talmudically/rabbinically justified addition of a liturgical *berakhah* to the ancient poetry of this ritual.

In the geonic period, then, the leading Babylonian sages formulated the concept that the authority of the Talmud, as interpreted by their academies, extended to determining legitimate applications of the rabbinic blessing formula. From Yehudai Gaon on, we have evidence that rulings were made based on this principle. However, we can identify no individual authorities who applied it consistently and insisted upon uprooting post-talmudic blessings that had become implanted in their own customary liturgy. Geonim like Saadia, who themselves composed new blessings, still invoked the principle when convenient. In actuality, then, it was primarily called upon to buttress other agenda, spoken or unspoken, that had led the Geonim to try to overthrow a particular liturgical custom. These agenda generally involved the imposition of Babylonian rabbinic authority over groups inside and outside Babylonia resistant to the geonic claims of superior knowledge of God's will. The understanding of the liturgical blessing as an absolute reflection of the authority of Torah had not yet fully come into its own.

---

71. *Shaarei Simḥah*, I:114-115; *Otzar Hageonim*, *Sukkot*, p. 58, #144.

72. ed. Raphael, 405.

### *The History of Selected Non-Talmudic Benedictions*

In the wealth of post-geonic halakhic literature, we find relatively few direct discussions of the non-talmudic benediction. Those authorities who do focus on the concept usually do so in the context of a very few specific blessings. Therefore, before attempting a synthetic, comparative statement, it is useful to trace the history of the two blessings that engendered the most comment and became exemplary of the problem.

#### *1. The* Birkat Betulim*: The Blessing Over the Tokens of Virginity*[73]

We read in *Halakhot Gedolot*, following its description of the wedding ceremony:

> וכד מפיק לסודרא מחייבינן לברוכי אי איכא כסא ואסא מברך עלייהו בורא פרי הגפן ובורא עצי בשמים והדר מברך אשר צג אגוז בגן עדן שושנת העמקים בל ימשול זר במעין חתום על כן אילת אהבים [זרע קדש][74] שמרה בטהרה חק לא הפרה בא״י הבוחר בזרעו של אברהם.
>
> When he brings out the sheet [stained with the blood of virginity], we require him to recite a blessing. If wine and spices are available, he recites over them, "who creates the fruit of the vine" and "who creates fragrant trees." Then he recites the benediction, "who placed the walnut in the Garden of Eden, the lily of the valley, so that no stranger shall have dominion over the sealed spring; therefore, the loving doe preserved her [holy seed in][74] purity and did not break the law. Blessed are You, Eternal One, who chooses the descendents of Abraham.[75]

---

73. For a more detailed analysis of this blessing, its meaning and its history, see my article, "The Birkat Betulim: A Study of the Jewish Celebration of Bridal Virginity," *PAAJR* LXI (1995): 53-94.

74. These two words do not appear in any version of *Halakhot Gedolot* or in any text citing it, but they do appear consistently in almost every liturgical manuscript of the prayer from every period. See below, p. 62.

75. ed. Hildesheimer, II: 226. Early Ashkenazi sources cite *Halakhot Gedolot* as their primary authority for this ceremony (See the discussion of ישראל תא־שמע, "תשובת הרמב"ם בענין ברכת־בתולים," in *Maimonidean Studies*, Vol. 2, ed. Arthur Hyman [New York: The Michael Scharf Publication Trust of Yeshiva University Press, 1991], 10-11), but the fact that Hildesheimer offers no variants on this text leaves some room to question whether it is a later, Ashkenazi interpolation of their own custom. Roth (אברהם נפתלי צבי רות, "מבית מדרשם של הגאונים ב'גנזי קויפמן," סורא ב (תשט"ז), 282–283), however, published a manuscript fragment of *Halakhot Gedolot* that does include a variant of our blessing, beginning "אשר צר זוג בג"ע...", a text with similarities to that of Hai Gaon, our only other Babylonian source for the prayer. (On variant versions of this line from other sources, see my "The *Birkat Betulim*...") *Halakhot Gedolot* is clearly the origin of the verbatim interpolation of this passage in the Oxford manuscript of the *Seder Rav Amram Gaon*.

An integral and mandatory part of this wedding celebration, then, is the public ceremony that occurs when the groom emerges from the marriage chamber bearing the cloth stained with the tokens of his bride's virginity. This moment is sanctified by the recitation of a special blessing, known most commonly as the *birkat betulim*, the blessing over the tokens of virginity. This ceremony receives ritual weight comparable to that of other life-cycle celebrations (and *havdalah*); blessings over wine and spices (if they are available) precede and establish the ritual context of the ceremony. Indeed, in the genizah, we find the title *kiddush betulim* and many of the variants of the blessing's concluding eulogy include the term מקדש (sanctifies), reflecting this ritual setting.[76]

The actual text of the *birkat betulim* is similar in literary form and style to the blessing said at the circumcision ceremony, אשר קידש ידיד מבטן (who sanctified the beloved one from the womb). However, unlike the circumcision prayer, which appears already in tannaitic sources,[77] there is no trace of our ceremony in pre-geonic literature. This omission is strange, given the biblical origins of the concern for the bride's virginity,[78] the economic significance of the bride's virginity in determining the amount of the *ketubah*, and the great detail in which the talmudic tradition describes the rest of the wedding ceremony (in the Babylonian Talmud, at least)[79] and discusses protocol for claims that the bride lacked virginity (טענת בתולים).[80] It is highly likely, then, that this ceremony, with its blessing, either did not exist or was not normative in the mainstream talmudic world.[81]

---

76. *Birkat betulim* is the most common title for the blessing in the writings of the Rishonim and their successors. In the genizah, it appears also with the titles: קידוש דם בתולים (Ms. Cambridge Or. 1080 1/2, p. 9); קדוש בתולים (Ms. TS NS 110.20, p. 6 verso and Bodleian ms. Heb. e. 25, Oxford 2701/9); and ברכת דם בתולים (TS H.11/78, p. 5).

77. *Tosefta Berakhot* 6:13; *B. Shabbat* 137b; *P. Berakhot* 9:4, 14a. Both blessings use allusive, poetic language beyond the level normally found in prayer texts. One notes here particularly the classical payyetanic form, צג, derived from the root יצג, which appears biblically only in the הפעיל and הופעל. See יוסף יהלום, שפת השיר של הפיוט הארץ־ישראלי הקדום (ירושלים: מאגנס, תשמ"ה), פרק ח, תאוריה ומעשה בצורות הפועל, 86–96, on the payyetanic tendency to create two-letter rooted verbs. Not once does this blessing mention the virgin bride directly, but rather it alludes to her with the expressions: *walnut*, *lily of the valley*, *sealed spring*, and *loving doe.*

78. Deuteronomy 22:13-21.

79. *B. Ketubot* 7b-8a.

80. See, for example, *B. Ketubot* 9af., 36af., 44af. See, too, the article "טענת בתולים," אנציקלופדיה תלמודית.

81. Ta-Shma suggests that there may be a hint of this ceremony in *P. Berakhot* 9:4, 14a, where *kiddushin* by intercourse is among the three cases for which one makes a blessing after performing the mitzvah instead of before. ("תשובת הרמב"ם...", 11, n. 6.) However, if our ceremony were a blessing for בעילת מצוה, the obligatory intercourse that consummates the marriage, it could not be phrased as an exclusive acknowledgment of the bride's virginity. One would then require an entirely different blessing for the wedding of a non-virgin bride. A

The blessing itself is a paean to the virgin bride and is composed of a series of poetic allusions to biblical verses that can be applied to her. Before her wedding night, she was the newly created Eve, a walnut, with the multiple layers of shell guarding the meat, a lily of the valley hedged about by thorns; her womb was a sealed spring, reserved for her husband and his children.[82] Most versions not directly based on *Halakhot Gedolot*–including essentially every prayerbook I have examined in which it appears at all–add, in connection with her preserving her purity, a variation on the phrase זרע קדש (sanctified seed), an allusion to Numbers 5:28: אם לא נטמאה האשה וטהרה היא ונקתה ונזרעה זרע (But if the woman has not defiled herself and is pure, she shall be unharmed and able to retain seed), which, in its original context, describes the fertility due to the wife who has been cleared from her husband's accusations that she was adulterous by the trial of drinking the bitter waters of the *sotah.* The final phrase of the blessing, then, refers also to the bride's preservation of her virginity, especially between the time of her engagement and the consummation of her marriage when sexual relations with a man other than her betrothed would have been adulterous. She has not broken this law, she shall be blessed with fertility, and, perhaps most important to the groom, any children are guaranteed to be his and to be the "seed of Abraham." Thus, although the obvious biblical origin of this ceremony lies in Deuteronomy 22, the rabbinic ceremony developed in a different exegetical context, one more appropriate for a festive response by the groom, and one where the fertility theme so appropriate to celebrating a marriage's consummation was intrinsic.[83]

The *birkat betulim* is a full-blown non-talmudic benediction, receiving apparent authorization from one of the most influential texts to emerge from the geonic world. Its allusive poetic language, its appearance among the genizah texts, and indications that Palestinian Jews placed a higher emphasis on bridal virginity than did their Babylonian kindred all point to a probable Palestinian origin for the blessing. However, from the late geonic period on, its usage can be documented in most corners of the Christian and Muslim worlds, with the possible exception of Muslim Spain. The norms of the surrounding non-Jewish society seem to have influenced greatly its actual implementation. It retained its public

blessing referring to the man's mitzvah of performing the act of intercourse would also logically make some reference to his actions. Ta-Shma's suggestion may derive from the discussions of the generation(s) following the Maharshal, who try to make this connection as a means of justifying this benediction. See below, pp. 69-71.

82. Note the allusions to Song of Songs 6:11, 2:1-2, 7:3, 4:12, Proverbs 5:16-19 (more of which is cited in some versions).

83. For a detailed explication of language of the blessing, see my "The *Birkat Betulim*...," 57-65.

nature in many Arab lands, but increasingly became a private ceremony in Christian realms as the earlier medieval emphasis there on celebrating bridal virginity diminished.[84] However, evidence for its mode of performance is limited, as many of the Rishonim merely reproduce the text of *Halakhot Gedolot* or even just the blessing alone, adding little or no new comment.[85] The eventual fate of this blessing, then, was determined not only by theoretical halakhic concerns about non-talmudic benedictions, but also by changing norms in the worlds in which Jews lived. As the popular culture became less invested in the custom itself, the halakhic criticisms of it began to affect actual practice.

The only other preserved geonic response to this ceremony continues the permissive view taken by *Halakhot Gedolot*, while directly confronting and dismissing the non-talmudic nature of the blessing. Hai Gaon responded to Rav Yehudah bar Yosef, Resh Kalah in Kairouan:

> וברכת בת' שאמרת אשר נטע גנת אגוז בגן עדן ליתא בתלמוד אלא קבלה היא בפי חכמ'. ואנן הכין שמענה הכין אמרין לה אשר צג זוג בגן עדן...
>
> The *birkat betulim* that you cited, "who planted a walnut garden in the Garden of Eden," is not in the Talmud, but it is a received tradition among the sages. This is how we have heard it and how we recite it: Who placed a couple in the Garden of Eden...[86]

In his missing query, Rav Yehudah of Kairouan must have wanted to know

84. For elaboration on all these points, ibid., 66-85.

85. Explicit citations of *Halakhot Gedolot* are found in the *Rokeah*, 239, #352 (note that our blessing appears only in his citation of *Halakhot Gedolot*, with a blessing over wine but no spices, but it does not appear in his subsequent description of actual wedding festivities); *Sefer Or Zarua* of R. Yitzhak b'R. Moshe of Vienna, I:46a, #341 (citing the *Sheiltot*, but his language is that of *Halakhot Gedolot*, and the *Sheiltot*, as we know it, contains no such material; he eliminates both the wine and the spices, but preserves the public setting of the blessing); and Rabbenu Yeruḥam, ספר תולדות אדם וחוה, נתיב כב, חלק ב who cites Rabbenu Nissim that this ceremony requires a cup of wine. Many other texts simply rule, without specific attribution, "הרואה דם בתולים אומר..." (One who sees the blood of virginity says...). This itself clearly became a literary tradition, and it is quite reasonable to suppose that its origin lies in a slight rewording of *Halakhot Gedolot* to reflect the now private nature of the ceremony. See, for instance, *Maḥzor Vitry*, 586; *Sefer HaOrah*, 178; *Sefer Orḥot Ḥayyim*, *Hilkhot Nidah* 8; and *Sefer Kol Bo*, 53a.

86. *Teshuvot Hageonim*, Harkavy, p. 230, #435. Our blessing appears in the *Seder Rav Amram Gaon*, p. 182, and the *Siddur Rav Saadia Gaon*, p. 98 (variants to line 3), only as glosses to the text. The insertion into Amram is the text of *Halakhot Gedolot*, while the gloss to Saadia, written by someone rather unfamiliar with the text, is more similar to the version of Hai Gaon here, reading זוב which the editors of the printed text have corrected to זוג. But these glosses give us no evidence for geonic usage. On the textual variants noted here, see my "The *Birkat Betulim*...," 58-59, 86.

under what authority this blessing exists, since it does not appear in the Talmud. Hai Gaon acknowledges this problem, but considers the received tradition of the sages to be a sufficient source of authority. Thus, in spite of any theoretical necessity for all blessings to originate in the Talmud, for Hai Gaon, the minhag of the sages, at least in this case, is adequate justification.

Within two centuries of Hai Gaon's responsum, Maimonides took quite a different tack. His responsum is valuable historically, not only for his legal response, but also because the query itself constitutes one of the fullest extant descriptions of the performance of the *birkat betulim*. Maimonides was asked:

> ...וכן יורנו הדרתו ג"כ ענין הברכה הנקראת ברכת בתולים והיא אשר צג אגוז בגן עדן, וזה שבעת שבא הקהל בבית החתן ביום השבת להתפלל או לברכ[ו] נוטל המברך בידו כוס ומברך על הגפן ו[על] הבשמים ומברך זאת הברכה אשר צג ופותח בה בשם ובמלכות וחותם בשם כשאר הברכות. היש לזאת הברכה עיקר או היא מנהג. יורנו הדרתו. וכן מברך אחריה ג"כ השבע ברכות המפורסמות בלא שתהיה שם סעודה. האם מברך אלו הברכות עובר בזה או לאו? או זה מותר משום שיש שם אנשים שלא באו ביום הקדושין? יבאר לנו הדרתו, המותר לומר זאת הברכה הנזכרת אם לאו, ושכרו כפול.
>
> ...And would His Honor also instruct us in the matter of the blessing called the *birkat betulim*, which is "who placed a walnut in the Garden of Eden." (This ceremony takes place) when the congregation comes to the house of the bridegroom on the Sabbath to pray or to bless him. The celebrant picks up the cup, recites the blessings over the wine and the spices, and recites this blessing, "who placed," beginning and ending it with the liturgical blessing formulae like all the rest of the blessings. Does this blessing have a (halakhic) basis, or is it (simply) customary? Instruct us, Your Honor. Also, he recites after it the well-known seven (wedding) benedictions without there being a meal. Does the one who recites these blessings transgress or not? Or is it permitted because there are people there who did not come on the day of the wedding? Clarify this for us, Your Honor, whether it is permissable to say the mentioned blessing or not, and your (heavenly) reward will be double.[87]

There is little in this query to indicate its geographical origin. It could have come from any community that performed weddings on Friday afternoon, making the consummation of the wedding occur on the Sabbath night. This was the case,

87. תשובות הרמב"ם, II:364-365, #207.

we know, in Italy[88] and in Yemen,[89] and likely in other communities too. Indeed, Maimonides' response suggests personal familiarity with the custom, making it likely that it was current in Egypt, or perhaps one that he had encountered during his migration from Spain. Maimonides replied as follows:

> ומעניין אותה [הברכה] הנקראת ברכת בתולים הרי הוא ברכה לבטלה בלא ספק, נוסף להיותה מנהג מגונה מאד, שיש בו מחוסר הצניעות ומזניחת קדושת הדת וטהרתה, מה שאין למעלה ממנו, ר"ל אותה התקהלות מגונה שקוראים קידוש הבתולים. ואסור למי שיש בו יראת שמים או צניעות לבוא אליו בשום פנים. וכתב משה.
>
> Regarding that blessing called the *birkat betulim*, it is undoubtedly a blessing in vain, in addition to its being a very despicable custom that involves a lack of modesty and befouls the holiness and purity of the law to the highest degree. I mean that despicable assemblage that they call the sanctification of the tokens of virginity. It is forbidden for anyone who has fear of Heaven or modesty to attend it under any circumstances. Signed, Moshe.[90]

Offended by the blessing and especially by the ceremony surrounding it, Maimonides forbade it absolutely. He never even commented on the use of the seven wedding benedictions in this context, for once the gathering itself does not exist, there will be no occasion to recite the blessings.

How do we understand this response? Evidence from the genizah suggests that not simply the blessing itself but the full *kiddush betulim*, with wine and spices, and occasional poetic elaboration, was being recited in Egypt.[91] We also know from later periods that the custom among the Muslims in Cairo was to parade the tokens of virginity through the streets of the city.[92] Maimonides, however, came from Spain, where this celebration of bridal virginity, if performed at all, was private. No pre-Maimonidean Spanish text mentions the *birkat*

---

88. As demonstrated by a detail in a wedding *piyyut* of Amitai bar Shefatia, discussed by Ezra Fleischer, "בחינות בשירת פייטני איטליה," הספרות 30–31 (1981): 141; and Ta-Shma, "תשובת הרמב"ם...", 13. Amitai's ceremony delays the signing of the *ketubah* until after the display of the tokens of virginity. There is no evidence for a similar delay here.

89. The Yemenite Jews apparently developed this custom in reaction to the Karaite prohibition of intercourse on the Sabbath. See Erich Bauer, *Ethnologie der jemenitischen Juden* (Heidelberg, 1934), 162-163. The responsum of Abraham Maimonides to the Yemenite Jews, which criticizes this blessing, also gives indirect evidence for the Yemenite use of the blessing during this period. However, it is unlikely that this community would have so blatantly ignored the ruling of Maimonides himself had they been his correspondents. See: שו"ת תשובות רבנו אברהם בן הרמב"ם, מהדורת פריימן, עמ' 134, צ.

90. p. 366.

91. For these genizah texts, see my "The *Birkat Betulim*...," 87-93.

92. Hilma Granqvist, *Marriage Conditions in a Palestinian Village* (Helsingfors, 1935), II: 127ff.

*betulim*, and none do after him until the Rosh; hence there is no evidence at all for the practice of the Jews of Muslim Spain. There is also no evidence that Spanish Jews ever held a public ceremony like that of the east. It was thus probably not part of Maimonides' tradition. He may well have seen it as an imitation of the gentile world and personally found it offensive. As a result, it was natural for him to begin his criticism by invoking the non-talmudic status of this blessing, calling it a ברכה לבטלה, an improper use of the blessing formula, and, only after that, listing the more subjective and probably more substantial grounds for his objections to it as a breach of modesty.

Israel Ta-Shma holds Maimonides' responsum directly responsible for the eventual elimination of the *birkat betulim* in the east.[93] However, there is little evidence to buttress his claim, and, as we shall see, the blessing's widespread elimination can be better attributed to other factors. The writings of Maimonides' son Abraham establish that his father apparently did succeed in abolishing the custom in Egypt, but that it was still practiced in Yemen.[94] Ta-Shma points out that Maimonides' student from Aleppo, R. Yosef ben Yehudah, while not abolishing the blessing itself, ruled quite specifically that it must be recited privately, כדי שלא להוציא לעז על הבתולות (so as not to speak ill of the young women). This concern for preserving modesty may well stem from Maimonides' ruling, but R. Yosef ben Yehudah could not or did not want to eliminate the blessing altogether. Considering its geonic acceptance as a received tradition to be a sufficient source of authority, its non-talmudic origin was not an issue for him.[95]

The only other rabbinic authority obviously influenced by Maimonides in this matter was his son Abraham. But Abraham's stance was more dictated by his hard-line theoretical objections to all non-talmudic benedictions or misuse of the blessing formula. We find no trace of his father's objections to breaches of modesty–perhaps because, at least in his immediate world, these were no longer occurring among Jews. Abraham Maimonides, in his essay *Sefer Hamaspik Leovdei Hashem*, rules explicitly against any use of the blessing formula not established by the "men of tradition," such as the *birkat betulim*, which was established by "errant people."[96] And in his responsum, he labels it "a blessing without foundation, which it is forbidden to recite," and attributes its origins to *ḥazzanim* too ignorant to differentiate between the permitted and forbidden.[97] Beyond

93. "תשובת הרמב"ם...", 10.

94. תשובות רבנו אברהם בן הרמב"ם, מהדורת פריימן, עמ' 134, שו"ת צ.

95. Ta-Shma, "תשובת הרמב"ם...", 12, citing from the commentary of R. Yehuda Almadari to *Ketubot*.

96. ספר המספיק לעובדי השם, הוא כתאב כפאיה אלעאבדין, מהדורת נסים דנה, 232.

97. סי' צ.

these, I have located not a single citation, direct or indirect, of Moses Maimonides' responsum on this blessing. Thus it is difficult to prove that he had any widespread influence on its future recitation beyond the Egyptian community.

Indeed, although not every discussion of wedding customs in the post-Maimonidean medieval Jewish literature mentions the *birkat betulim*, most of the major authorities do. Not a single one mentions concerns about modesty, most likely because of the increasingly private nature of the ceremony, and relatively few even confront the blessing's lack of talmudic origins.[98] Of these few, the most influential is the Rosh, who cites *Halakhot Gedolot* but is clearly concerned about the legitimacy of this blessing. His comment, ואפשר שברכה זו תקנוה הגאונים ז"ל ומסתבר לברכה אחר שמצא בתולים (It is possible that this blessing is a geonic enactment, and it seems reasonable to assume that one may recite it after [the groom] has found the proof of virginity),[99] is a grudging permission, based on geonic authority, to continue the existing custom. We can infer a similar turning to ancient authority in *Tzedah Laderekh*, which begins ברכת בתולים הכתובה בתיקון הקדמונים (the blessing of virginity which is written in the enactment of the earliest rabbis).[100] Abudarham elaborates:

> וברכה זו אינה במשנה ולא בגמרא ולא בתוספתא ואפשר שתיקנוהו [הגאונים כמו שתקנוהו][101] ברכת פדיון [הבן] שכתבנו למעלה וכתב הרא"ש ומסתבר...
>
> This blessing is not in the Mishnah or in the Gemara or in the Tosefta, and it is possible that the Geonim established it like they established the blessing for the redemption of the first born, as we wrote above,[102] and the Rosh wrote, 'it seems reasonable...'[103]

Although Abudarham acknowledges most specifically the non-talmudic nature of this blessing, for him its geonic origins and the authority of the Rosh overcome this problem. Similar acknowledgment and justification are expressed by his contemporary Rabbenu Yeruḥam[104] and by the fifteenth-

---

98. In the context of a more general discussion of non-talmudic blessings, Rabbenu Tam alludes in a responsum to the non-talmudic nature of the *birkat betulim*. His conclusions are difficult, suggesting a distinction between various types of non-talmudic blessings, maintaining those established for definite commanded actions, and preferring the elimination of others, including the *birkat betulim*. We will treat this responsum in detail below, p. 86.

99. *Ketubot* 1:15.

100. מאמר שלישי, כלל שני, פרק ראשון.

101. In the Warsaw, 1877 edition, p.198. This seems to be a simple scribal or printer's error in the Jerusalem, 1963 edition of *Abudarham Hashalem*.

102. See below, p. 83 in this chapter.

103. *Abudarham Hashalem*, 365.

104. ספר תולדות אדם וחוה, נתיב כב, חלק ב.

century *Leket Yosher* of R. Yosef b"R. Moshe of Augsburg.[105] In the early sixteenth century, R. Meir ibn Gabbai begins his extensive commentary by excusing himself for explicating a blessing found neither in the Mishnah nor in the Talmud, כי הגאונים תקנוה בדוגמא עליונה (for the Geonim, in establishing it, patterned themselves on a heavenly model).[106]

Why, after relative silence among earlier sages, including almost all of the northern-European sages, is there this flurry of interest in the origins of this blessing in the fourteenth century? One explanation may simply be the literary convention that led sages to cite their predecessors. More likely, the ceremony itself was becoming more prominent in these circles because of kabbalistic interest in it. The allusive language of the blessing, especially its opening image, the walnut tree, made it particularly amenable to mystical interpretation.[107] The blessing is explicated in the prayerbook commentary of the early kabbalist and teacher of Naḥmanides, Rabbenu Yehudah b"R. Yakar,[108] which is cited without attribution and expanded upon by Abudarham,[109] and in the extensive early sixteenth-century kabbalistic commentary of R. Meir ibn Gabbai in his *Sefer Tolaat Yaakov.*[110] In the halakhic sources of this same period, we find a similar hint of an awakening of interest in the actual performance of the ceremony. Now, however, Rabbenu Yeruḥam, whose citation tradition derived from *Halakhot Gedolot* no longer contains reference to any larger ceremony, follows Rabbenu Nissim's directive that this blessing must be said over a cup of wine.[111] While both modern scholars and earlier rabbinic authorities doubt that Rabbenu Nissim ever discussed the *birkat betulim*, Ta-Shma points out that Rabbenu Yeruḥam, in any case, understood this as the appropriate way to perform the ceremony.[112] This "new" understanding was strengthened when R. Moshe Isserles cited it in his glosses to the *Shulḥan Arukh.*[113]

This increased interest in the meaning and performance of the *birkat betulim*

---

105. p. 64.

106. *Sefer Tolaat Yaakov*, 93.

107. On mystical uses of the symbolism of the walnut, see Alexander Altmann, "Eleazar of Worms' *Ḥokhmath Ha-'Egoz*," *JJS* 11 (1960): 111; and J. Dan, "Ḥokhmath Ha-'Egoz, Its Origin and Development," *JJS* 17 (1966): 73-76. Dan places the origins of this symbolism much earlier.

108. פירוש התפלות והברכות, מהדורת שמואל ירושלמי (ירושלים: מאורי ישראל, תשכ"ט), חלק ב', עמ' מד. Note that this commentary does not contain overtly mystical content.

109. *Abudarham Hashalem*, 365.

110. pp. 93-94.

111. ספר תולדות אדם וחוה, נתיב כב, חלק ב.

112. "תשובת הרמב"ם...", 12. He cites: שרגא אברמסון, רב נסים גאון (ירושלים, תשכ"ה), 240; and the *Perishah*, EH 63.

113. EH 63:2.

ceremony coincided with or perhaps elicited renewed questions about its legitimacy as a non-talmudic benediction. In the fourteenth century, these concerns were satisfactorally addressed by assertions of geonic composition or claims that the Geonim had accepted and promulgated the blessing. The Geonim were, after all, the heirs of the talmudic academies. As such, they were authoritative interpreters of the Oral Law and provided a voice from antiquity. Since the earliest known prayerbooks and detailed writings about liturgical matters came from them, acceptability and efficacy were necessarily ascribed to the prayers they had established. But by the late sixteenth to early seventeenth centuries, even this attribution of geonic authority was not sufficient. R. Yissachar Baer Eilenburg, in his seventeenth-century *Sefer Beer Sheva*, understands the Rosh's hesitant statement that "it is possible that the Geonim established it," as implying that the blessing may actually be a composition of the more ancient and authoritative Amoraim.[114] This same assumption of talmudic origins appears later in the seventeenth century in the *Turei Zahav* of R. David Halevi,[115] but is disputed as illogical by his younger Turkish contemporary, R. Ḥaim Benveniste.[116] By this time, as we shall see below, these authorities understood the halakhic prohibition of non-talmudic blessings to be absolute and excluded even geonic traditions from legitimacy. The only way they could justify the Rosh's stance on the *birkat betulim* and preserve the legitimacy of their custom was to read this possibility of amoraic origins into his words.

Discomfort with the non-talmudic status of this blessing also led to attempts to conform with rabbinic norms by altering either the ceremony itself or its significance. One of the principles by which non-talmudic blessings were legitimated was the requirement that the performance of any positive commandment be accompanied by a blessing. Therefore, if the Talmud had not specifically dictated a blessing, but had clearly established the commandment–as in the case of lighting candles for the Sabbath–it is legitimate to recite a blessing and even to consider the blessing obligatory.[117] A marriage does involve the groom's performance of a talmudically recognized positive commandment for which there is no blessing–the בעילת מצוה, his consummation of the marriage through inter-

114. חלק באר מים חיים, סי' טז. On the appearance of this passage in the *Derishah*, EH 63:2, of R. Yehoshua Falk Katz, Eilenburg's teacher, see: שרגא אברמסון, "להקים שם," קרית ספר סא (תשמ"ו–תשמ"ז), 173.

115. OH 46:6.

116. *Sefer Kenesset Hagedolah*, YD 305.

117. For a rather extreme statement of this, see: פירושי רבנו אליהו מלונדריש ופסקיו, לב. See also below, pp. 87ff.

course.[118] Some authorities consider the *birkat betulim* to be the blessing for the performance of this mitzvah, included among those few to be recited after the deed, lest the intercourse not be completed or the bride not be found a virgin. This novel interpretation–novel because the blessing text does not acknowledge any commandment and takes the form of a blessing of praise, not a blessing for a mitzvah–appears primarily in later texts, written at a time when all non-talmudic blessings were regarded as illegitimate and when new ways were sought to justify extant customs.

Only possible hints of such a transformation of meaning appear in the writings of the Rishonim. The *Likutei Hapardes* of Rashi records, ברכת בתולים לברך החתן בליל זווגו עם הכלה (the groom should recite the *birkat betulim* on the night of the consummation of his marriage).[119] The omission of any instruction that this blessing should be said afterwards, in connection with seeing the virgin blood, is very strange and possibly significant. More telling is the statement of R. Yehudah b"R. Yakar: ...יש חתנים שמברכים קודם ביאה (there are bridegrooms who, before intercourse, recite the blessing...).[120] Such a custom may lie behind the Rosh's comment, ומסתבר לברכה אחר שמצא בתולים, which we now might better translate, "It is reasonable to assume that he should recite the blessing *after* he has found the tokens of virginity," as a protest against an improper use of the blessing.[121]

The more explicit connection of our blessing with the groom's performance of his commandment may in fact be an inadvertent consequence of the organization of the *Tur*, EH 63, which includes this blessing at the conclusion of a very abbreviated discussion of the laws of marriage consummation. The *Tur* does not introduce this blessing as a new topic or explicitly connect it to the confirmation of virginity–allowing later authorities to apply the blessing to the act of consummation, combining the two discussions. Eilenburg, in a lengthy discussion in his *Sefer Beer Sheva*, understands the *birkat betulim* to be connected to the act of intercourse and not to the bride's virginity. However, he eventually rules that this act of intercourse does not constitute the type of mitzvah that requires a blessing, as it is only a preparation for the real mitzvah of procreation, and (folk wisdom holds that) no bride conceives on her wedding night.[122] In the next

118. See the tannaitic and amoraic sources listed in the article, "בעילת מצוה," אנציקלופדיה תלמודית, ד:סו–סט.

119. p. 67.

120. פירוש התפלות והברכות, חלק שני, מד.

121. This is the understanding of the *Derishah* EH 63, although he has no evidence of anyone's actually reciting the blessing before the consummation of the marriage.

122. ספר באר מים חיים, סי' טז. *Derishah*, EH 63. Note that Eilenburg does not need to rely on this means of justifying this blessing. He has already suggested that it has talmudic status, based on the Rosh's language, as discussed above.

generation of Polish and Lithuanian commentators on the *Tur* and *Shulḥan Arukh*, we find comments like those of R. Yoel Sirkes:

> ...אם כן ברכת בתולים שמצוה מן המובחר הוא ונקראת גם כן בעילת מצוה משום דמאותו ביאה ואילך יקיים מצות פרו ורבו...
>
> ...in this case, the *birkat betulim*, which is one of the choicest commandments, and is also called "the mitzvah of consummation" because from that act of intercourse on, he will fulfill the commandment to procreate...

However, he concludes, the timing of this blessing is not critical because it is ultimately a blessing of praise, not a blessing for the performance of a commandment.[123]

Such a transformation in the understanding of the blessing was necessary because, in eastern Europe at least, the ritual acknowledgment of virginity was itself no longer culturally important. In addition, by the time of these Aḥaronim, strong criticism had been voiced there by R. Shlomo Luria (Maharshal) against the recitation of any non-talmudic blessing. In his *Yam Shel Shlomo*, he explicitly ruled that one should not recite the *birkat betulim* using the liturgical blessing formula,[124] and later authorities cite him as flatly ruling against the recitation of this blessing.[125] By the the early twentieth century, we can see in the ruling of the *Arukh Hashulḥan* of Yeḥiel Mikhal Epstein that both these criteria became operative. He comments that some say that one should not recite this non-talmudic benediction; some say that one should recite it without the liturgical blessing formula and without a cup of wine; and (in any case), we are now not concerned with this blessing.[126] But in the generations immediately following the Maharshal, there was clearly some opposition to this overthrow of a custom explicitly justified by such important authorities as the Rosh, the *Tur*, and the *Shulḥan Arukh*, including the Ashkenazi emendations of Moshe Isserles.[127] Although the redefinition of the *birkat betulim* as a blessing for the commandment of consummating the marriage did not ultimately justify its recitation, it provides an excellent example of the persistence of minhag in the face of halakhic challenge.

There is only limited evidence that the *birkat betulim* survived into the modern age. The prayer never became a standard inclusion in the prayerbooks of most

---

123. קונטרס אחרון מהב"ח לאה"ע סג. Compare too the comments of the טורי זהב and the חלקת מחוקק. Note that the אנציקלופדיה תלמודית discusses the *birkat betulim* only in its article on "בעילת מצוה".

124. כתובות, פרק א, דין כג.

125. חלקת מחוקק, באר היטב וטורי זהב לשולחן ערוך, אה"ע סג:ב; ב"ח על הטור, שם.

126. *EH* 63, #10.

127. Note that not a single one of these authorities cites the responsum of Maimonides!

rites, so its non-appearance in a manuscript or printed edition is probably meaningless. But in the microfilms of the Jewish Theological Seminary's liturgy collection, it does continue to appear in the seventeenth and eighteenth century in some, but not all, manuscripts of Yemenite prayerbooks,[128] in one siddur identified simply as seventeeth-century Sefardi with kabbalistic commentary,[129] and in a seventeenth-century Italian handbook for life cycle events.[130] The most unusual appearance of the ceremony is in a nineteenth–century text from Bombay, where the bridegroom is specifically directed to omit שם ומלכות, the halakhically critical terms of the liturgical blessing formula.[131] However, in the vast majority of this collection, even in those texts that include marriage ceremonies, the *birkat betulim* does not appear.

Various other references to the blessing in halakhic sources represent literary or legal traditions rather than living custom. Many sources continue simply to mention it when citing the *Shulḥan Arukh*, with no additional comment. Others discuss the blessing, as we shall see below, in pilpulistic attempts to resolve internal contradictions in the Rosh. Still other references are simply vague. But in addition to the sources otherwise cited here, we can add the testimony of the *Sefer Kenesset Hagedolah*[132] from seventeenth–century Turkey, which, at the end of its reference to the *Sefer Beer Sheva* citing the Maharshal's opposition, adds words not found in our editions of the *Sefer Beer Sheva*: ומנהג עכשיו לברכה (it is the custom now to recite this blessing). In the eighteenth century, Johann Christoph Georg Bodenschatz, a German Christian, at the end of his description of a Jewish wedding, wrote:

> Noch dieses muss erinnern, dass bey den Juden gebräuchlich, wenn der Bräutigam bey seiner Braut das *Signum virginitatis* findet, er folgenden Segen zu machen pflegt; בא"י אמ"ה אשר צו אגוז...
> One must also remember this, that it is customary among the Jews that when the bridegroom finds his bride's tokens of virginity, he must recite the following blessing: Blessed are You, Eternal our God, Ruler of the Universe, who commanded a walnut...

128. In the Jewish Theological Seminary's microfilmed liturgy collection, it appears in #4500, p. 72a; #4753, ENA 20, p. 15b; #4760, ENA 79, n.p.; #4846, Acc. 0292 p. 127a; #8091, Acc. 03206, n.p.; #8431, n.p.

129. #4192, p. 202b. I have found it in two other Sefardi siddurim of this period: the *Seder Berakhot, Order de Bendiciones y los Acaziones en que fe deven dir* (Amsterdam, 1687); and Ms. Heikhal Shlomo, Jerusalem 433 74/38 (Bayonne, France, 1707).

130. #4329, Acc. 10820, p. 10.

131. #4679, ENA 1646.

132. EH 63.

Bodenschatz's reliability, however, is to be questioned. He admits that Christians are not allowed at Jewish weddings, and he himself has only once seen the wedding dances. He has clearly depended heavily on the *Mishneh Torah* and *Shulḥan Arukh* for his details; and his Hebrew and transliteration (or the printer's) are full of errors.[133]

The existence of a long-standing minhag gives it immense status within the world of actual practice. Halakhic objections can be raised effectively only after the custom has lost significant elements of its original meaning. In the case of the *birkat betulim*, the halakhically questionable ceremony had received the explicit approval of leading earlier authorities. Later rabbis, then, confronted with a conflict between the custom and their now authoritative legal theory, sought to upgrade its halakhic status by transforming the blessing's meaning (to a blessing for *beilat mitzvah)* or its history (to origins in the talmudic world), rather than try to decree its abolition. Others attempted a relatively minor transformation, such as the removal of the halakhically crucial elements of the blessing formula, to maintain the custom in conformity with their understanding of halakhah. Although the blessing did persist in some corners of the Jewish world, in general, it fell prey to a loss of interest in celebrating bridal virginity (particularly in Europe) and even more so, to a general clamor to rid the liturgy of every questionable use of the liturgical blessing.

## *2. The Priest's Blessing at the Redemption of the First Born*[134]

When discussing the *birkat betulim*, the Rosh had merely acknowledged its lack of talmudic origins, indicating that the blessing could nonetheless be recited. However, when confronting another blessing of geonic origins, a blessing recited by the priest at the *pidyon haben*, the ceremony for the redemption of a first born son,[135] he reacted quite differently, saying:

ונהגו לברך ברכה זו בארצות הללו. ובצרפת ובאשכנז לא נהגו לברך ברכה זו ולא מצינו שמברכין

---

133. *Kirchliche Verfassung der heutigen Juden, sonderlich derer in Deutschland* (Erlangen, Coburg, 1748-49; 2nd ed. with corrected transliterations, Frankfort, 1756), IV: 129.

134. I am indebted for much of this material to Prof. Israel Ta-Shma and his addendum to מרדכי מרגליות, הלכות ארץ ישראל מן הגניזה (ירושלים: מוסד הרב קוק, תשל"ד), לב–לז. I especially thank him for sharing his personal copy with his added notes.

135. The concept that all first-born males, whether human or animal, are consecrated to God derives from God's saving of the Israelite first born during the tenth plague. The priests are commanded to allow the human first born to be redeemed after one month for five shekels. See Exodus 13:1-2, 11-15 and Numbers 18:15-16.

שום ברכה שלא הוזכרה במשנה או בתוספתא או בגמרא. כי אחרי סידור רב אשי ורבינא לא מצינו שנתחדשה ברכה. וגם ראשית הברכה איני מבין אשר קידש עובר במעי אמו אי קדושת בכור קאמר בפטר רחם תלה רחמנא. ומותר להטיל מום בבכור קודם שיצא רובו.

...they are accustomed to recite this blessing in these lands (Spain), but in France and Germany, it is not their custom to recite it, and we have not found that one should recite any blessing that was not mentioned in the Mishnah, Tosefta, or Gemara, for after Rav Ashi and Ravina's compiling (of the Talmud), we have not found that any new blessings were created. In addition, I do not understand the beginning of the blessing, "who sanctified the fetus in its mother's womb." Did not the Merciful One make the sanctification of the first born dependent on its vaginal birth? It is (even) permitted to create a blemish on a firstborn (animal) before most of it has emerged.[136]

The contrast between the Rosh's reactions to these two blessings and the comment his inconsistency arouses among the early Aḥaronim is a vital key to understanding the developing halakhic category of the non-talmudic blessing in rabbinic thought.

What is this blessing? Most of the references to it by the Rishonim, including the Rosh, indicate that its origins lie in a geonic enactment. The earliest preserved mention of it is by Saadia Gaon in his *Siddur*, where he too objects to it, saying:

ויש שחידשו בברכת פדיון הבן דברים שאין להם עיקר ואינם שום כלום, כמו אשר יצר את הילד במעי אמו ועוד, אבל אין רשות לכהן לברך כלום בשעת פדיון הבן.

And there are those who make innovations in the blessing [i.e., the ceremony] for the *pidyon haben* that have no basis and are worthless, like "who formed the child in its mother's womb," and more, but the priest has no right to recite any blessings at the time of the *pidyon haben*.[137]

Saadia objects to this blessing because the Talmud, in its discussion of the ceremony for redemption of the firstborn, decides that the two established blessings of the ceremony, בא"י אמ"ה אקב"ו על פדיון הבן ושהחיינו ("Blessed...who has sanctified us with His commandments and commanded us concerning the redemption of the firstborn son" and "...who has given us life..."), are to be

136. Rosh, *Kiddushin* 1:41; compare the parallel passages at the end of *Bekhorot*, *Hilkhot Pidyon Bekhor* 1 and *Shut Harosh*, 49:1. In these he raises the additional objection: ועוד למה יברך הכהן אינו עושה שום מצוה אלא מקבל מתנות כהונה (In addition, why should the priest recite a blessing when he is not performing any commandment but only receiving his priestly due)?

137. p. 100.

recited by the baby's father and not by the priest.[138] This tradition, then, according to Saadia's reading, eliminates any possibility of the priest's legitimately reciting any blessing at the time of the ceremony, for such a blessing would have no (talmudic) basis.[139] Saadia's is clearly not the geonic enactment known by later authorities!

The earliest positive reference to this blessing is a responsum, usually ascribed to Hai Gaon, found in the collection *Shaarei Teshuvah*. This volume, as we know it today, however, is a reworking of earlier geonic collection(s) by R. Moshe de Leon, who did not hesitate to tamper with the texts, change their attributions, and otherwise create forgeries to support the world of his Zohar. While this responsum does appear in the manuscripts from which modern scholars believe de Leon worked, it is clear that he also made some minor alterations in the text, and we cannot be certain that the attribution, based on the heading he placed several responsa earlier, is accurate, especially as no other medieval text gives a specific attribution at all.[140] However, while de Leon's changes affected parts of the stylized dialogue of the greater ceremony, they apparently left our blessing intact. As the majority of medieval texts vary only slightly from this, we can use the blessing as found in *Shaarei Teshuvah*[141] as the basis of our discussion. It reads:

...ואמרו רז"ל שחייב האב לברך בשעה שנותנם לכהן שתי ברכות אקב"ו על פדיון הבן ושהחיינו.[142]

ונהגו רבותי' ראשי הישיבות ומקיימי' מצות כהונה והזריזים בהם כשהם פודים בכור פטר רחם מביאין כוס של יין והדס ומברכי' בורא פרי הגפן ובורא עצי בשמים.
ואח"כ אומר הכהן בא"ה אמ"ה אשר קדש עובר במעי אמו ומ' יום חלק רמ"ח איברים ואח"כ נפח בו נשמה דכתיב ויפח באפיו נשמת חיים ויהי האדם לנפש חיה.[143] עור ובשר הלבישו ובעצמות וגידים סככו דכתי' עור ובשר תלבישני ובעצמות וגידים תסוככני.[144] והאכילו בנס נפלאותיו מאכל ומשתה דבש וחלב להתענג בו וזימן מלאכיו לשמרו במעי אמו דכתיב חיים וחסד עשית עמדי וגו'.[145] (ואח"כ) [אביו][146] אומר זו בני בכורי וזהו ראשית אוני ופי שנים ראוי לתת לו שכן כתוב בתורת משה לתת לו פי ב'. אמו אומר' זהו בני בכו' שבו פתח הקב"ה דלתי בטני חמש סלעי'

138. *B. Pesaḥim* 121b.

139. See the discussion of this comment above, p. 57.

140. See the article by Neil Danzig, "תשובות הגאונים 'שערי תשובה' ושו"ת מן השמים," תרביץ נח (תשמ"ט), 21–48, especially the last page. I thank Prof. Israel Ta-Shma for the reference.

141. ed. Wolf Leiter, #47.

142. *B. Pesaḥim* 121b.

143. בראשית ב:ז.

144. איוב י:יא.

145. איוב י:יב.

146. לפי כל הגרסאות האחרות.

נתחייבנו לתת לכהן לפדותו ממנו שכך היא גזרת מלך שנא' אך פדה תפדה[147] ואומר ופדויו מבן חדש תפדה[148] ונא' ולקחת חמשת חמשת שקלים לגלגלת[149] יהי רצון מלפני אלהינו שכשם שהכניסו אביו לפדיון זה כך יכניסהו לתורה לחופה ולמעשים טובים בא"ה מקדש ישראל בבכוריהם ופדיונם.
ואח"כ מגביה הכהן שתי ידיו וסומך על ראשו ואומר לאביו איזה חביב עליך יותר בנך או חמש סלעים הללו והאב אומר בני חביב עלי ואני פודהו...

...and the sages said that the father, when he gives [the money] to the priest, must recite two blessings: "who has sanctified us with His commandments and commanded us regarding the redemption of the firstborn son," and "who has given us life [and sustained us and brought us to this day]."[150]

It was the custom of our teachers, the heads of the academies, who uphold punctiliously the priestly commandments, that when they redeem a firstborn, the first to emerge vaginally from the womb, they bring a cup of wine and myrtle and recite "who has created the fruit of the vine" and "who has created fragrant branches."

Then the priest says: Blessed are You, Eternal our God, Ruler of the universe, who sanctified the fetus in its mother's womb. After forty days You distributed [his] 248 bones and then infused his soul into him, as it is written, "He blew into his nostrils the breath of life, and the man became a living being."[151] He clothed him with skin and flesh and wove him bones and sinews, for it is written, "You clothed me with skin and flesh and wove me of bones and sinews."[152] He fed him through His miraculous deeds, food and drink, honey and milk for his enjoyment, and appointed His angels to guard him in his mother's womb, for it is written, "You bestowed on me life and care; [Your providence watched over my spirit]."[153] Afterwards, [the father] says, "This is my firstborn son, this is the beginning of my strength, and it is appropriate to give him a double portion [of my estate], for so it is written in the Law of Moses to give him a double portion." His mother says, "This is my firstborn son with whom the Holy One, blessed be He, opened the doors of my womb. We are obligated to give five *selaim* to the priest to redeem [our son] from him, for such is the ruling of the King, as it is said, "...but you shall have [the firstborn of man] re-

147. במדבר יח:טו.
148. במדבר יח:טז.
149. במדבר ג:מז.
150. *B. Pesaḥim* 121b.
151. Genesis 2:7.
152. Job 10:11.
153. Job 10:12.

> deemed,"[154] and it says, "Take as their redemption price, from the age of one month up,"[155] and it says, "Take five shekels per head."[156] May it be pleasing before our God, that just as his father has brought [the baby] for this redemption, so may he bring him to Torah, to the marriage canopy, and to good deeds. Blessed are You, Lord, who sanctifies Israel through their firstborn and their redemption.
>
> Then the priest raises both his hands and places them on [the baby's] head and says to the father, "Which do you prefer, your son or these five *selaim*?" The father replies, "I prefer my son, and I redeem him"...

We also have early evidence for this blessing in the commentary of Rabbenu Ḥananel to Deuteronomy 18:3;[157] it is otherwise found exclusively in Provençal and Sefardi sources.[158] This tradition inserts a series of blessings to be recited by

---

154. Numbers 18:15.

155. Numbers 18:16.

156. Numbers 3:47.

157. *Migdal Chananel ueber Leben und Schriften R. Chananel's in Kairuan*, Festschrift for Azriel Hildesheimer (Leipzig, 1876), 42. The authors of this Festschrift, Hildesheimer's colleagues, do not document their sources adequately. It is possible that they have culled this directly from the responsa of the Rashba, where it is cited (I:#200, #758). This text does not include the mother's declaration or any issues of inheritance, and cites prooftexts for the redemption only from Exodus.

158. The blessing appears with minor variants in the following sources: הלכות בכורות להרמב"ן, פרק שמיני, לדף מט עמ' א; בית הבחירה על מסכת פסחים לר' מנחם ב"ר שלמה לבית מאיר המכונה המאירי, מהדורת יוסף הכהן קליין, רנז; ספר שאלות ותשובות שחבר...ר' שלמה בן אדרת, א:ר, תשנ"ח; ספר ארחות חיים לר' אהרן הכהן מלוניל, מהדורת משה בן אליקים שלעזינגער, חלק שני, פרק ב', סי' ג', עמ' 19–20; הרא"ש, קדושין א:מא, הלכות פדיון בכור א (סוף מס' בכורות); שאלות ותשובות להרב רבינו אשר ז"ל, כלל מט:א; טור, יו"ד שה; אשתורי הפרחי, כפתור ופרח, מהדורת אברהם משה לונץ, כרך ב', פרק ששה עשר, עמ' תכה–תכו; אבודרהם השלם, שנה–שנו; מנחם בן אהרן בן זרח, צדה לדרך, מאמר ראשון, הכלל החמישי, עמ' מג.; ספר מנורת המאור לרבי ישראל בן יוסף בן אלנקאוה, מהדורת ענעלאו, ג:488; שאלות ותשובות ריב"ש, סי' קלא. Finally, mention should be made of the collection of texts published from an otherwise unidentified Oxford manuscript which apparently contained a random collection of medieval responsa and other materials, by מנשה גראסבערג, ספר גבול מנשה (פראנקפורט דמין, תרנ"ט). Pages 20-22 contain a parallel text to ours; 22-24 record three alternative prayers, which we will discuss below.

I have located the blessing in the the following prayerbook manuscripts: Ms. Sassoon College 24 (229) (14th c. Sefardi maḥzor); in the Jewish Theological Seminary's microfilmed liturgical manuscript collection, #4783 (14-15th c. Provençal or Catalonian); #4674 ENA 1596 (15th c. Sefardi); #4602 (catalogued as 14-15th c. Sefardi, noted on the microfilm as Italian-Ashkenazi–the state of the manuscript makes identification difficult); #4797 ENA 2608 (19th c. North African or Yemenite–as an addition to the manuscript).

The single non-Sefardi text I have located that includes this blessing apparently bases itself on literary tradition and not active custom. The Yaavetz cites "early great sages" and R. Yitzhak Trani, and indicates that the blessing is *reshut* (permitted but not required). See his: בית מגדל עוז..., חלק א' (בולוגנא, תק"ח), חלק ברכת חורי.

the priest into the normative talmudic/geonic ceremony for the *pidyon haben*, transforming the entire ceremony into an elaborate *kiddush* or sanctification. As in the geonic period *kiddush betulim*, the blessings are now recited over wine and aromatic myrtle. Similarly, the opening language of its eulogy, ...מקדש ישראל (who sanctifies Israel...) also marks its status as a ritual of sanctification. The parallelism extends to the nature of the blessing too, as it is also a blessing of praise, describing God's actions. Its opening language, אשר קדש עובר במעי אמו (who sanctified the fetus in its mother's womb) is practically synonymous on a simple non-allusive level with the opening language of the tannaitic circumcision blessing, also recited over a cup of wine, אשר קדש ידיד מבטן (who sanctified the beloved one from the womb). But here the formal similarities end, for, as is obvious, this blessing is quite lengthy, not particularly allusive in its language, and where it might be allusive, assumes that the listener needs explanation and inserts prooftexts.

As many, most famously, the Rosh,[159] have indicated, the content of this blessing is strange. The first section describes God's role in forming and guarding the fetus from its conception until birth. The language here, if the constant prooftexts were eliminated, is almost poetic and fits liturgical style for such a setting. However, the divine acts described are irrelevant in this context; they apply to every fetus, not just the son who will be firstborn vaginally as the result of his mother's first pregnancy. Abruptly, the prayer moves to a description of the normative *pidyon haben* ceremony, listing the parents' declarations that this child does indeed fulfill the criteria that make his redemption necessary. But as Naḥmanides indicates in his discussion of the text, the father's declaration that this child, as the firstborn, qualifies to inherit a double portion of his estate, is also irrelevant to this ceremony. In the case where the baby's mother is not the father's first wife, this might even be untrue.[160] Following Naḥmanides' suggestion, most later sources omit this line.[161] These declarations move smoothly into a description of the parental obligation to redeem their son, complete with the appropriate prooftexts. However, it is not at all clear who the speakers are, as this section follows the mother's declaration, but it is phrased in the first person plural. Has the father been quoting his wife, and does she not speak at all? It seems unlikely that she would be the one to make the detailed statement about

159. See above, pp. 73-74.

160. הלכות בכורות להרמב"ן, פרק שמיני, לדף מט עמ' א.

161. *תא־שמע, הלכות ארץ ישראל מן הגניזה*, לג; I find no basis for Ta-Shma's claim here that Naḥmanides, like the Rosh, rejects this blessing as having no talmudic basis. Note, too, that his references to Naḥmanides in the second half of this paragraph all should read "the Rosh."

these obligations; but it is equally strange that she be included in the "we," for the obligation to redeem the son falls quite squarely on the father, or secondarily, if he fails to do so, on the son himself when he is older. The mother is in no way obligated by halakhah.[162] Finally, without any real transition, the blessing concludes with the prayer recited at the conclusion of the circumcision ceremony–but there outside the context of a formal blessing–that the baby grow up to a life filled with the basics of a Jewish existence. From here, again without the requisite literary transition, we have the concluding eulogy. I know of no parallel to this formal hodgepodge in all of Jewish liturgy.

Its pervasive appearance in Spanish literature, however, vouches for the authenticity of the responsum ascribed to Hai Gaon. As the Rosh indicates, this blessing was not part of the minhag of French and German Jews, and indeed, I have not found it in any of their early halakhic or liturgical works. However, our knowledge of the Franco-German rituals for the redemption of the firstborn is limited by their omission from *Mahzor Vitry* and all texts modeled on it.[163] It seems likely, though, that the Spanish Jews learned this blessing more or less directly from the Babylonian Geonim, and that there can be little basis for assigning it to the Palestinian halakhic and liturgical heritage received by the Jews of central and northern Europe. The very fact that Saadia Gaon, an immigrant from Egypt via Palestine to Babylonia, reacted so strongly against it suggests that it was an unfamiliar, most likely Babylonian, custom that he first encountered after leaving his birthplace.

We can reconstruct a bit of the prehistory of this blessing from clues embedded in the Palestinian ceremony of redemption found in the genizah and published by Margulies. Here, not bound by the Babylonian halakhah, the priest is the one to recite the blessing for the act of redemption instead of the father, and, in one of the versions of the ceremony, the priest precedes this blessing with words reminiscent of our text:

כשיהייתא במעי אמך הייתה ברשות [בוראך ועכשיו] <אתה> ברשותינו וקודש אתה כמה שאמרה התורה קדש לי כל בכור פטר כל רחם גו'...

When you were in your mother's womb, you were under the authority of your Creator, but now you are under our authority, and you are holy, as

162. For additional commentary on this blessing and especially for discussion of the mother's role here, see Lawrence A. Hoffman, *Covenant of Blood: Circumcision and Gender in Rabbinic Judaism* (Chicago: University of Chicago Press, 1996), 179ff.

163. One early Ashkenazi ceremony for the *pidyon haben*, found in the *Likutei Hapardes Me-Rashi*, 121-122, contains no reference to this blessing.

the Torah says, "Consecrate to Me every firstborn, the first issue of every womb...[164]

He then continues with a discussion of the technicalities of the act of redemption, which, while different in its focus than our prayer, still reflects the same desire to rehearse the halakhic aspects of the ceremony during its performance.[165]

The halakhic authority of the Babylonian Talmud was such that it was not easy to ignore its direct ruling that only the father may recite the two blessings it specifies for the ceremony of redemption of the firstborn. Indeed, as Ta-Shma points out, in Italy, which adopted the Palestinian ceremony, the father did so, not the priest.[166] But this left the priest, who to the popular mind must have seemed to be the officiant at this ceremony, without any prayers to say. His words might be nice formulae, but they lacked the level of sanctity and official authority conferred by the liturgical *berakhah*. It was a natural move, then, to create a third blessing, in addition to those discussed in the Talmud. To compose this blessing, it was also natural to look to a functional parallel, the liturgy for the *mohel* at the circumcision. Hence, this blessing begins and ends with words reminiscent of those beginning and ending the formal post-circumcision liturgy.

This blessing, then, represents one of the ways that Jews attempted to elevate the ritual sanctity of the priest's participation in the *pidyon haben*, by creating for him a blessing combining the formula which in Palestine preceded the blessing with themes appropriate to a life cycle ceremony for a baby boy. This particular solution probably originated in Babylonia, where it was known as early as the time of Saadia Gaon. The text of our particular blessing has not appeared among the genizah manuscripts,[167] and it lacks the poetic language characteristic of Palestinian prayer texts. Its literary awkwardness may point to an origin outside of the more sophisticated cultural centers of the academies–and may also account for Saadia's objection and his giving no indication that this was a custom of the Geonim themselves. However, the introduction of the responsum in

---

164. Exodus 13:2.

165. מרדכי מרגליות, הלכות ארץ ישראל מן הגניזה, כט–ל. As Margulies points out in his introductory discussion about the two versions of the ceremony he publishes here, the Palestinian ceremony was the one adopted in Italy, although not in France and Germany, and he lists several manuscripts of Italian *mahzorim* that include the ceremony. Indeed, this is the origin of the ceremony recorded in ספר תניא רבתי, סי' צח. Ta-Shma, in his discussion of this text (p. 36), seems to indicate that, in spite of its similarities to the Palestinian ceremony, the roots of the Italian ceremony are still in our prayer. I fail to understand the basis of his claim.

166. p. 37.

167. According to the catalogue of the מפעל לחקר השירה והפיוט של האקדמיה הלאומית הישראלית למדעים. My thanks to Professor Ezra Fleischer for providing this information.

*Shaarei Teshuvah* identifies it explicitly as "the custom of our teachers, the heads of the academies, who uphold punctiliously the priestly commandments." Since the received responsum is attributed to Hai Gaon, this may represent the late geonic academy's acceptance and integration of this ritual.

The text of the geonic responsum preserved in *Shaarei Teshuvah* and the Palestinian ritual found in the genizah apparently were not the only attempts made to elevate the priest's role. At least three additional blessings have been preserved, two of which maintain the beginning and eulogy of our blessing. All three are more literarily unified, with fewer disparate themes. None contains the declarations of the parents or the concluding wishes for the future of the child, neither of which really belongs in a sanctification blessing for this ceremony. However, all contain explicit references to the plague on the Egyptian firstborn, the biblical origin of the notion of the sanctity of the firstborn, and all discuss the consequent responsibilities of the redeemed nation. This theme is eminently appropriate to a blessing that might have been titled קדוש פדיון הבכור (the sanctification of the redemption of the firstborn). There is no evidence as to who actually recited these other blessings. One appears in *Orḥot Ḥayyim* as an alternative version,[168] and the Rivash[169] is aware of versions of this blessing that mention explicitly the Egyptian plague and the redemption from Egypt. That our blessing was the one to receive prominence seems to be an unfortunate fluke of history, which perhaps can be attributed to its written authorization in the geonic responsum and in the works of Rabbenu Ḥananel.

In addition, almost every discussion of this ceremony indicates that the priest concludes by reciting biblical verses of blessing for the child, including, of course, the priestly benediction. This too can be seen as an attempt to invest the participation of the priest with ritual importance and sanctity in a way that could not be halakhically objectionable. Apparently, though, these verses were not sufficiently specific to the redemption ceremony, and, although a nice addition, did not fully elevate the role of the priest. The introduction of a blessing that could be said in full ceremony over wine and aromatic herbs, like the blessings of so many other rituals, was more satisfactory.

Saadia Gaon's objections seem to have had no impact on actual practice, at least in Spain, North Africa, or Babylonia, the areas where we know the blessing continued to be said. From his time until that of Naḥmanides, we have no evidence of anyone having questioned its validity. Even Naḥmanides challenged

---

168. Ed. Schlesinger, II, Chapter 2, #3, pp. 19-20. R. Aharon Hakohen of Lunel, as we know, recorded in his book the many customs he observed in the course of his wanderings. He does not indicate who says which version of this blessing.

169. שאלות ותשובות ריב"ש, סי' קלא.

only the appropriateness of any discussion of the future inheritance of the baby, and not the halakhic status of the blessing as a whole.[170] The Rashba, in discussing the difference between Rabbenu Ḥananel's text and the more common Spanish version, explicitly acknowledged the blessing's non-talmudic status; considering that as justification for allowing flexibility in its language, not a reason to disqualify it, he allowed people to choose whichever version they preferred.[171]

The first post-geonic challenge to the legitimacy of the blessing by a person of consequence occurred only when the great German refugee rabbi, the Rosh, came to Provence and Spain and learned of a custom, new to him, that flatly contradicted his understanding of the *gemara.* Fully aware of the geonic basis of the custom, he raised a series of objections to it.[172] As we saw above, he begins by noting that the blessing is customary only in Spain and not in France and Germany. He then continues:

> ולא מצינו שמברכין (שום) ברכה שלא הוזכרה במשנה או בתוספתא או בגמרא כי אחרי סדור רב אשי ורבינא לא (מצינו ש)נתחדשה ברכה.
>
> For we have not found that they recite/one recites any blessing that is not mentioned either in the Mishnah or in the Tosefta or in the Gemara, for after Rav Ashi and Ravina arranged [the Talmud], we have not found any new blessings introduced.

The subject of this sentence is ambiguous. He says either that the Franco-German Jews do not recite any post-talmudic blessings, or that in all cases, post-talmudic blessings are to be considered illegitimate. It seems somewhat unlikely that he could make the first distinction, based on regional custom, since the Franco-German rites certainly contained their share of non-talmudic blessings.[173] The more general reading, then, objecting to all non-talmudic benedictions, was more likely his intent. He next observes that one cannot argue that the priest is here reciting a blessing for the performance of a positive commandment, for the priest does not fulfill any mitzvah in this ceremony; he only receives his due as a priest.[174] Finally, he objects to the opening subject of the blessing as not only irrelevant, but wrong: it implies that

---

170. הלכות בכורות להרמב"ן, פרק שמיני, לדף מט עמ' א.

171. ספר שאלות ותשובות שחבר...ר' שלמה בן אדרת א: ר, תשנ"ח.

172. The Rosh's response appears in three separate places in his printed works, each slightly different. See his commentary to the *Alfas, Hilkhot Pidyon Bekhor* 1 and *Kiddushin* 1:41, and his responsum, 49:1.

173. See below, p. 86.

174. This comment appears only in the Rosh's responsum and in his discussion of *Hilkhot Pidyon Bekhor,* not in his commentary to *Kiddushin.* The omission is probably an error, as the three texts seem to have the same source.

the holiness attached to the firstborn begins while the fetus is still *in utero*, rather than at the moment of birth. These last two objections can be seen as straws grasped by a man intent upon overthrowing an established minhag. The blessing makes no claim to accompany the performance of a commandment; it is clearly a blessing of praise. And to a certain extent, the sanctity of the firstborn does apply to the yet unborn child: for if the mother miscarries, her next child will not have to be redeemed.[175] The Rosh's most substantial argument, then, is the blessing's lack of talmudic basis and explicit contradiction of talmudic halakhah. However, he clearly does not feel this to be sufficient in the face of actual custom or common perception of talmudic authority. Thus, like his predecessors, he must add further arguments.

Did the strong objections of this immigrant sage to a minhag unfamiliar to him have any impact? The *Tur*[176] and Abudarham[177] essentially cite the Rosh, in that they, like him, begin with the geonic responsum, including the blessing in question and conclude by citing his objections. Abudarham even goes so far as to suggest that Saadia's opening line would solve the Rosh's objections to its wording. However, he is careful to point out that Saadia too objected to the priest's making any blessing during this ceremony. Did these fourteenth-century rabbis rule against the blessing themselves? The implication is yes, but it is done so gently and inexplicitly that one can infer that they are only half-heartedly supporting the overthrow of the still common Spanish custom. This supposition receives support from the halakhic manual, *Tzedah Laderekh*,[178] written for the guidance of a Spanish Jewish courtier, which makes no reference at all to the Rosh's objections.

The Rivash,[179] in fact, writing somewhat later, clearly works hard to justify the blessing. He argues that, although the priest does not fulfill any explicit mitzvah in the *pidyon haben* ceremony, he does take an active role, which distinguishes his participation here from the receipt of any other priestly due. In addition, he identifies the *berakhah* as a blessing of praise that alludes to the exodus from Egypt, the plague on the Egyptian firstborn, and the saving of the Israelite firstborn, and he indicates that some versions make this theme explicit. Only after all this does he cite the Rosh, but without additional comment. Does

175. A child born by caesarean section also does not need to be redeemed, for it is not considered פטר רחם (an opener of the womb). However, this is more a modern problem, as, in the pre-modern world, caesareans were too dangerous to the mother to be performed frequently.

176. YD 305.

177. *Abudarham Hashalem*, 355-356.

178. מאמר ראשון, כלל החמישי, עמ' מג.

179. שאלות ותשובות ריב"ש, סי' קלא.

he feel compelled to include this halakhic ruling but uncomfortable about disputing it openly? He has already answered the Rosh's major objections to the specific blessing and justified its recitation. Most likely he understands the objection to non-talmudic blessings either to be insubstantial or to refer only to the Franco-German and not the Spanish Jews, for he neither acknowledges nor disputes the Rosh's stance. In his eyes, understanding this one as a blessing of praise justifies its recitation.

Prayerbook manuscripts from this period indicate that the custom persisted, particularly in Spain.[180] There is evidence, though, that the Spanish exiles, at least in the east, discontinued it. In Joseph Karo's world, the blessing was evidently not recited, for his *Beit Yosef*[181] cites the Rosh's objections twice, and comments briefly on the wording of the blessing as found in the *Tur.* The blessing does not appear in the *Shulḥan Arukh* or the *Kesef Mishneh.*

A more extensive discussion appears in the query of R. Yisrael Najara and the response of R. Yom Tov Tzahalon. In the course of his query, Najara describes various customs known to him for the *pidyon haben* ceremony. The only one that includes our blessing is one he identifies as a geonic enactment, rather than as a living custom of a particular community. However, having mentioned the blessing, he discusses the Rosh's objections to it, including only the issue that the priest is making a blessing when he is not fulfilling a mitzvah, an objection Najara refutes as irrelevant since this is a blessing of praise. Tzahalon, in his response, indicates that he checked other versions of the Rosh's comment; in the *Kiddushin* version, the Rosh does not object on this basis at all–and hence probably never actually voiced this objection, just the other ones listed there.[182] Tzahalon's response is further indirect evidence that this blessing was not part of his living minhag: he never discusses the blessing's non-talmudic status or its difficult content, questions he could not easily have ignored were the blessing recited in Palestine in the late sixteenth to early seventeenth centuries. Thus the concern of both rabbis here was the theoretical problem of understanding the intent of a great rabbi, the Rosh; they were not discussing practical halakhah.[183]

A few generations later, R. Ḥaim Benveniste, in his *Kenesset Hagedolah,*[184] in-

180. See above, p. 77, n. 158.

181. YD 305.

182. Tzahalon seems not to know the Rosh's responsum, which also includes this criticism of the blessing and which might have led him to different conclusions here.

183. שאלות ותשובות מהרי"ט צהלון החדשות, מהדורת יוסף בוקסבוים, מסעוד בן שמעון, ומשה רובינשטיין, סי' א. Najara claims that, as a blessing of praise, the blessing is suitable for the priest to recite, to which Tzahalon adds, anyone could say it. Again, these are more reactions to the Rosh's error in considering this a blessing for a mitzvah than rulings about actual practice.

184. YD 305.

dicates that the Jews of Constantinople and Tirya (near Izmir, Turkey) do not recite this blessing. However, he reports that a pious sage, R. Yosef Kohen, one of R. Yosef Trani's most important students, was accustomed to recite it on the basis of his teacher's approval. This, though, seems to be the unique custom of an individual. Benveniste does not object to it but apparently knows no one who has reinstated the blessing based on Trani's probably theoretical ruling.[185] Scattered evidence does exist for the persistence of the custom in some form. A manuscript identified as nineteenth-century, either from North Africa or Yemen, includes our full blessing.[186] A description of the customs of the Jews of Djerba indicates that the priests there continued to recite it over wine and spices, but omitted the critical elements of the liturgical blessing formula, שם ומלכות, thus neutralizing the halakhic problem.[187] Gedalia Oberlander's recent study of traditions for the *pidyon haben* claims that our custom survives in some Sefardi communities. However, his sources cannot be verified as his citations point only to a limited reintroduction of the blessing by some Hasidic Jews, i.e., Ashkenazim, based on Yaakov Emden's labeling it permitted based on Trani's precedent.[188]

Well established among the Jews in Spain, the *pidyon haben* blessing seems to have survived the expulsion only in isolated instances. The abandonment of customs and the intensification of halakhic concerns about illegitimate blessings led to a serious consideration of the Rosh's specific objection to this blessing. We can fully understand its fate only in the in the context of increasing objection to blessings of this sort.

### *Direct Discussions of the Issue*

As we have seen, most of the Geonim and Rishonim applied the geonic concept that the Talmud was the only source of legitimate blessings inconsistently, if at all. These rabbis almost always invoked the concept accompanied by other, more substantive objections, implying that, in the real world, this theoretical

---

185. I have located no direct literary evidence of Trani's discussion.

186. Jewish Theological Seminary, Liturgical Manuscript Microfilm Collection, #4797, ENA 2608, p. 79.

187. ספר קול יעקב ובני יעקב (ג'רבה: עידאן כהן צבאן הדאד, תש"ה), חלק שני, עמ' יז.

188. גדלי' אבערלאנדער, ספר פדיון־הבן כהלכתו (ירושלים, תשנ"ג), פרק ח, סימן יז, עמ' רמד–רמה. Emden's comment, cited above, p. 77, n. 158, is cited in the commentary to the Hasidic work, ספר משמרת שלום (ווארשא, n.d.), סימן יט:ו. The twentieth-century Yaakov Werdiger in his commentary "שירותא דצלותא" בתוך סדור תפלה צלותא דאברהם, מהדורה שניה (ישראל: וועד להוצאת הסידור צלותא דאברהם, ?198), תשז–תשח, mentions that Emden is the only one among the Aḥaronim to mention this blessing. He claims that in actuality, no one recites it, whether Ashkenazi or Sefardi. This siddur itself includes the blessing, but only as the custom of the Geonim and Rishonim.

halakhic criterion standing alone carried insufficient authority to prevail over the regnant minhag. The most strongly voiced objections to non-talmudic benedictions came from the pens of immigrant rabbis who were affronted by an unfamiliar custom in their new community. Their personal lack of investment in the community's custom induced them to criticize it more harshly than native sages did. Over time, though, and especially into the period of the early Aḥaronim, the chorus of voices making a principled objection to non-talmudic benedictions and using this principle as a yardstick by which to measure the legitimacy of actual practice grew, to the point that extant non-talmudic blessings, even in the daily liturgy, required justification and reinterpretation.

Over the hundreds of years under study here, isolated voices stand out, making theoretical declarations about the nature of blessings and the source of authority for their recitation. Listening to these voices, one hears a growing concern for the absolute authority of the Talmud as the arbiter of liturgical efficacy. One also notices increasing attempts to differentiate between kinds of blessing situations so as to harmonize theoretical halakhah and actual practice. The consistent question posed is whether a means exists to justify certain types of blessings that do not explicitly appear in the talmudic text. Although the answers become stricter, in most cases rabbinic authorities struggled to legitimate regnant custom and find a way to ensure conformance with halakhic sensitivities without undermining either minhag or halakhah.

Evidence from the world of the Tosafists in northern Europe indicates a relatively lenient approach to our question. Rabbenu Tam, in a responsum criticizing Rabbi Meshullam bar Nathan of Narbonne's elimination of the non-talmudic blessing over the Sabbath lights, establishes three sources of authority for recitation of additional blessings. First, he legitimates the recitation of a blessing for the performance of an halakhic obligation if the motivation for the blessing arises from חיבת מצוה, a desire to show esteem for the performance of the commandment and to enhance other aspects of the greater obligation. Second, he considers aggadic materials to be legitimate sources of this obligation. Finally, he lists geonic precedents, not only for the blessing over the Sabbath candles, but for the recitation of many other non-talmudic blessings, including the *birkat betulim.* However, while the entire responsum up to this point seems to imply that any one of these three justifications is sufficient, the last line of our received text indicates significant ambivalence. He says, השומע ישחק לו וכל העוקרה יעקר (Anyone who hears [such blessings] might be derisive, and anyone who uproots one [i.e., eliminates one] may do so). If this statement refers to all non-talmudic blessings, including the blessing over the Sabbath candles, it fully undermines the entire responsum, formulated as an objection to the elimination of this blessing. It is therefore extremely difficult to draw any conclusions from this, most likely, corrupted text.[189]

Another Tosafist, Rabbenu Eliahu of London, elaborated on an aspect of the view expressed by Rabbenu Tam. R. Eliahu warns that if one is in any doubt as to whether the invocation of the liturgical blessing formula is justified, one should omit it, for one must always be wary of reciting an unnecessary blessing. He continues, though, to say that one should recite as many justified blessings as possible; this means that one must recite a blessing for the performance of every positive commandment. Thus, he is "sometimes in the habit" of making blessings for the more ethical commandments, like rising in the presence of a old man and showing honor to his elders.[190] Although this precedent creates opportunities for many non-talmudic blessings, it is not a license to invoke God's name in a liturgical blessing at will. Leniency only applies to positive commandments, to actions whose performance is divinely sanctioned or required.[191]

More or less at this same period, though, among the Ḥasidei Ashkenaz, we find a very free use of a sort of blessing formula, using God's name but omitting reference to divine sovereignty. This formula characteristically introduces the concluding eulogy of a long benediction, but in these texts it appears as the opening formula. *Sefer Ḥasidim* records the custom of one pietist to make a blessing

---

189. ספר הישר לרבנו תם, חלק השאלות והתשובות, מהדורת שרגא ראזענטהאל, סי' מה:ד, עמ' 81–82; *Tosafot Shabbat* 25b, ד"ה חובה. All citations of this responsum that I have seen omit this difficult final part. See, for example: חיד"א, ספר עין זוכר בתוך ספר יעיר אזן (למבורג, תרכ"ה), מערכת ב אות לז, דף עט עמ' ב; עובדיה יוסף, שו"ת יביע אומר חלק ו, או"ח, סי' כט. Many other sources refer to Rabbenu Tam's responsum without citing it directly.

It is a geonic conception that lighting Sabbath lights requires a benediction because it is a talmudic obligation. See *Otzar Hageonim, Shabbat*, 27-28, #83-85. Note that the examples Rabbenu Tam cites of geonic non-talmudic blessings are not blessings for the fulfillment of any talmudic obligation, but rather what become known as blessings of praise. He seems not to make this distinction.

190. פירושי רבנו אליהו מלונדריש ופסקיו, מהדורת מרדכי יהודה ליב זק"ש, לב.

191. Examples of such blessings are: the various versions of the blessing for *yibum*, the performance of a levirate marriage, which seems to be a Sefardi/Provençal custom (see the אנציקלופדיה תלמודית, "יבום", which cites as its earliest literary source for the blessing the *Sefer HaItur*, which in turn cites by title only an earlier sage, perhaps R. Yehudah Barzilai of Barcelona. Note also the *Baḥ*'s characteristic objections to this custom in his commentary to *Tur* EH 166); and the Ashkenazi custom requiring women to bless "לשמוע מגילה" (to hear the *megillah*) instead of "על מקרא מגילה" (concerning the reading of the *megillah*) based on *Halakhot Gedolot*'s assertion of a woman's different and lesser obligation to this mitzvah (*Mordekhai, Megillah* 779, citing the Raviah; *Rema,* OH 689:2 and *Mishnah Berurah*; note that Rav Ovadiah Yosef, *Shut Yabia Omer* I:44:1, characteristically objects to this as a deviation from the blessings established by the Talmud). My thanks to Prof. Nahum M. Sarna and Rabbi Benjamin Samuels, who brought these examples to my attention.

over each limb of his body,[192] and Malachi Beit-Arie discovered at the end of a western Ashkenazi siddur manuscript, written around 1326/7, a series of prayers, mostly reflecting the traditions of the Ḥasidei Ashkenaz, that includes "blessings over the limbs." This seems to be a *piyyut*, written to be incorporated into the *birkhot hashaḥar*, consisting of a short introductory passage that paraphrases the standard liturgy (using just isolated words of a standard blessing formula, but not in any halakhically questionable manner), followed by thirty-eight blessings for the parts of the body. Each line begins, ...ברוך אתה ה' על (Blessed are You, Eternal One, for...) followed by a short list of body parts, each with a first-person singular possessive suffix and another word describing that part's function. This descriptive word consistently ends with the third-person plural possessive suffix תם–, thereby unifying the entire work with a simple rhyme. Following these thirty- eight blessings is a concluding blessing, also beginning with the same liturgical formula, which in turn is followed by a series of thirteen rhymed pairs of generalized blessings, all beginning ברוך אתה ה'.[193] The passage from *Sefer Ḥasidim* implies that these German pietists did indeed consider these to be blessings.

But did the Ḥasidei Ashkenaz consider them *liturgical* blessings, similar to others? It should be noted that a similar formula appears in the *Rokeaḥ* as an invocation to the discussion of the laws of menstrual purity. This strange blessing begins, ...בא"י אלהי ישראל מן העולם ועד העולם אשר קדשנו במצותיו וצונו (Blessed are You, Eternal One, God of Israel, from everlasting to everlasting, who has sanctified us by His commandments and commanded us...).[194] This unusual hybrid replaces the standard formulaic reference to God's sovereignty, required for a talmudic liturgical *berakhah*, with part of the Temple blessing formula.[195] The reference to divine sovereignty is exactly the part missing from the "blessings over the limbs." For the Ḥasidei Ashkenaz, it seems, an opening blessing that omitted *malkhut* was not a liturgical *berakhah*, and hence could not fall into the category of an unnecessary blessing and run the risk of invoking God's name improperly. Use of the biblical ברוך אתה ה'[196] as an opening formula, despite its

192. מהדורת ראובן מרגליות, קנה–קנו, סי' קנה.

193. מלאכי בית־אריה, "ברכות האיברים," תרביץ נו (תשמ"ז), 272–265. He cites Ms. Oxford, Bod. Opp. 758 (Neubauer 1105), pp. 436b-438b.

194. ספר הרוקח הגדול..., מהדורת שניאורסון, עמ' קצה, סי' שיז.

195. *Mishnah Berakhot* 9:5. The *Rokeaḥ* itself explicitly recognizes the standard rabbinic blessing formula, 252, #363. See the discussion of the Temple blessing formula above, chap. 1, p. 11.

196. Ps. 119:12. Note that recitation of this verse in full is a standard means of avoiding an improper blessing with its consequent improper use of God's name if one has inadvertently begun to recite the first three words of the liturgical blessing. Hence it carries no liturgical weight on its own except in a concluding benediction.

similarities to the statutory *berakhah*, despite its restricted liturgical use in other positions, and despite its inclusion of God's name (which does appear in other non-liturgical blessing formulae, like ...יהי רצון מלפניך ה' אלהינו, "May it be acceptable to You, Eternal our God..."), was to them a permitted means of sanctifying additional ritual actions beyond those halakhically specified.

In contrast to this very liberal approach of the northern European Jews, Maimonides and his son Abraham taught a very strict interpretation of the appropriate usage of the liturgical *berakhah*. As Jose Faur has documented,[197] Maimonides developed a principle that, while broader in its impact, eventually very much influenced the rabbinic attitude toward the non-talmudic blessing. This principle, ספק ברכות להקל, means that in any situation where one has the slightest doubt as to whether a blessing is required, one should avoid the possibility of unnecessarily invoking God's name and be lenient about the obligation to recite a blessing. As Maimonides states most strictly in his responsum to the sages of Lunel,[198] the only blessings with unquestionable legitimacy are those specified by the talmudic sages. Where the sages did not establish a blessing explicitly, none may be recited, even for biblical commandments. This goes well beyond Maimonides' earlier discussion in his *Mishneh Torah*[199]where he says that one is obligated to recite the blessing over the Sabbath candles "just as one is obligated to make a blessing over anything for which one is obligated rabbinically (מדברי סופרים)." The Lunel responsum comports better with Maimonides' ruling in his *Hilkhot Berakhot*[200] that there can be no legitimate blessing over a minhag (however ancient its authority) or in any circumstance in which one perceives doubt as to the legitimacy of the blessing. But as Faur indicates, Maimonides actually applied this principle of restricting the recitation of blessings to blessings for the performance of commandments, where lack of a blessing will not detract from the actual mitzvah involved. It does not apply to blessings of praise where the mitzvah itself consists of the recitation of the blessing and where, consequently, if doubt exists, one can recite the blessing. As would be expected, succeeding generations struggled to determine the exact application of this restrictive principle, particularly, as Faur indicates, the Sefardi Aḥaronim, for whom Maimonides' ruling became a key principle of liturgical law.

For our purposes here, it is most significant that Maimonides explicitly ruled against the recitation of any non-talmudic blessing, and that, implicitly, he made

---

197. יוסף פאור, "ספק ברכות להקל – כלל שטבעו הרמב"ם," אסופות א (תשמ"ז), שמג–שנט.
198. תשובות הרמב"ם, II: 604-606, #333.
199. *Hilkhot Shabbat* 5:1.
200. 11:16.

a distinction in cases of doubt between the halakhic status of blessings for mitzvot and blessings of praise. He never discussed these two points concurrently; hence, we have no reasoned theoretical statement of his stance regarding the use of the liturgical blessing formula in a non-talmudic blessing of praise. Nor do his statements about liturgical issues directly related to our problem fully illuminate us on this point. As we saw above, he referred to the *birkat betulim* as a ברכה לבטלה בלא ספק (undoubtedly a blessing in vain). By eliminating even the possibility of doubt as to this blessing's status, he clearly condemned it as illegitimate. However, it is unclear whether he regarded it as a blessing for something that should not be considered a mitzvah or as an undoubtedly improper blessing of praise. As we have seen, it was considered by some to be a blessing of praise, and by others to mark liturgically the performance of a mitzvah, either the consummation of the marriage, or, perhaps, the confirmation of the bride's virginity itself.

Another clue to Maimonides' stance appears in his treatment of the fifth blessing of the evening *keriat shema*, referred to variously as ברכת הפסוקים, the blessing of verses, or by its opening line, ברוך ה' לעולם אמן ואמן, or by the opening line of its final section, יראו עינינו.[201] This blessing blatantly deviates from both the mishnaic scheme for the structure of this section of the liturgy, which specifies only two blessings after *shema* in the evening,[202] and from the early amoraic requirement that there be no interruption between these blessings and the *amidah*.[203] This additional blessing surfaces first in the geonic literature, where Natronai attributes it to the "later rabbis."[204] From then on, it seems to have provided an ongoing halakhic challenge: Naphtali Wieder documents several of the attempts to bring it into line with talmudic liturgical law. Maimonides and his followers simply omit God's name from the concluding benediction of the second blessing after *shema*, *hashkiveinu*. With no liturgical *berakhah* to mark the end of the prayer, they effectively combine *hashkiveinu* and *birkat hapesukim* into a single blessing, eliminating the problem. Obviously, Maimonides accepted the validity of the non-talmudic *birkat hapesukim* and its concluding blessing and was not among those who called for its total omission[205]–whether because of its antiquity or its

201. For discussion of this blessing, see: נפתלי וידר, "פרקים בתולדות התפילה והברכות," סיני עז (תשל"ה), קכז–קלג. The halakhic history of this blessing deserves more study.

202. *Mishnah Berakhot* 1:4.

203. *B. Berakhot* 4b, 9b.

204. *Seder Rav Amram Gaon*, 62, and various citations of this in later literature. See Wieder, "...פרקים", 127, nn. 60-61.

205. *Abudarham Hashalem*, 141, cites R. Yitzḥak ibn Ghayyat and Maimonides as calling for the abolition of this blessing. As Wieder points out, this should read, not Maimonides, but Naḥmanides, whose objection was well known and cited by such sources as the *Talmidei*

nature as pure praise of God. Maimonides' primary concern was to preserve the mishnaic structure of the service, as his son, Abraham verifies.[206] Interestingly, Maimonides' student, R. Yosef ben Yehudah, had originally solved the problem by omitting the troublesome blessing for the *birkat hapesukim*–the more logical response to a concern about its non-talmudic nature. Upon receipt of the Rambam's siddur, however, he changed his custom to follow Maimonides'–effectively adjusting his halakhic priorities.[207]

Maimonides' strong theoretical stance against the recitation of any unnecessary blessing, including, particularly, the non-talmudic blessing, echoes also in the works of his son, who states explicitly in the surviving and published section of his *Sefer Hamaspik Leovdei Hashem* that no one is permitted to create new blessings using the official formula of the liturgical *berakhah* and that any such blessing or any established blessing recited inappropriately is unnecessary and an abuse of the divine Name. In apparent contrast to his father, R. Abraham is especially strict regarding blessings of praise, the category into which he apparently casts the *birkat betulim*. Acknowledging the human need to respond ritually to new situations, he suggests that the God-fearing person can, if he has immense spiritual concentration, very occasionally recite an appropriate biblical verse or something similar, so long as it does not include a liturgical blessing.[208] Thus, aside from the few non-talmudic benedictions ingrained in the liturgy at least since the early geonic period and inoffensive in their content, the Maimonides family allowed no non-talmudic uses of the liturgical *berakhah*.

Why were the Maimonideans the first to take such an uncompromising stance towards non-talmudic blessings? Several reasons may be suggested. Both father and son applied rigorous philosophical principles to religious matters. For them, compromising ideal law with actual custom detracted from their logical and elitist ideals. In addition, they were an immigrant family confronting the customs of the east as outsiders, allowing them to respond with serious criticism to certain customs that seemed normal to Egyptian Jews. Concurrently, as Naphtali Wieder has documented, they did not hesitate to try to introduce new

*Rabbenu Yonah* to *Berakhot*, 2b; *Orḥot Ḥayyim*, *Din Tefillat Arvit* 4; and the *Tzror Haḥayyim*, p. 8.

206. Wieder, 131, cites from what is probably a lost section of R. Abraham's ספר המספיק לעובדי השם, preserved in Hebrew translation in the "חידושי הרמב"ם" at the beginning of the מעשה רוקח לר' מסעוד חי רוקח (ויניציה, תק"ב) and reprinted elsewhere from there. This passage does not appear in Dana's recent edition.

207. Wieder, 132, identifies his source as coming from R. Yosef's book, בסתאן אלאזהאר (גן הפרחים), which has been lost, but this section was preserved, thanks to R. Yaḥya Tzalaḥ, who copied it in its original Arabic from R. Yaḥya Bashiri's marginal notes to the Tikhlal.

208. pp. 232-236.

customs.[209] In other words, for them ancestral custom was not a powerful determinant of appropriate ritual, especially in the face of halakhic logic.

There is no evidence that this exacting stance had immediate influence on European Jewry. Maimonides' contemporary and critic, R. Abraham ben David of Posquieres, the Ravad, took essentially an opposite position, allowing any blessing for the performance of a mitzvah, and suggesting that in the case of permitted but inconsistently invoked blessings, it is better simply to omit God's name, on the model of the blessings upon arising listed in the ninth chapter of *Berakhot*. In any case, if one uses the full blessing formula, no damage is done.[210] Similarly, approximately a century after Maimonides, the Provençal commentator on the *Mishneh Torah* Rabbenu Manoaḥ of Narbonne states explicitly that in reciting the post-talmudic blessing, *birkat hapesukim*, one does not improperly invoke God's name in an unnecessary benediction:

> דהא רבנן בתראי תקנוה, והרשות נתונה לכל גדול שבכל דור ודור לתקן ברכה לפי המתחדש לאנשי דורו, דקיימא לן יפתח בדורו כשמואל בדורו.
>
> For the later rabbis (Saboraim) established this, and each great sage in every generation is permitted to establish (new) blessings according to the new needs of his generation, for we have a tradition, "Jepthah was to his generation as Samuel was to his."[211]

R. Manoaḥ continues, positing that this was (Hai) Gaon's justification in establishing(!) the priest's blessing at the *pidyon haben*, even though it has no talmudic basis. To what then does the talmudic prohibition of unnecessary benedictions apply? To the improper use of established benedictions either for other than their intended purpose or when one has already fulfilled the obligation to recite them. He concludes this section by reiterating his main point:

> אבל אם יחדשו ברכה על עניין שנתחדש לו אל שייך ביה למימר שעובר משום לא תשא, והרשות בידו לברך.
>
> But if he creates a new blessing for a new situation, it is not appropriate to say that he transgresses the commandment of not taking God's name in vain, and he has every right to recite the blessing.[212]

R. Manoaḥ's intention is to ensure that non-talmudic customs current in his

---

209. השפעות אסלאמיות על הפולחן היהודי (אוקספורד: ספרית־מזרח ומערב, תש"ז).

210. השגות הראב"ד על הרז"ה, סוף ברכות, עמ' מד.

211. *B. Rosh Hashanah* 25b.

212. ספר המנוחה, הוא פירוש רבינו מנוח מנרבונה על הרמב"ם, מהדורת אלעזר הורביץ, חלק א: הלכות קריאת שמע תפלה וברכות, הלכות ברכות א:טו, עמ' רלו–ז.

world receive halakhic justification. He responds here not only to Maimonides and his stringent approach, but also, clearly, to those in southern France and in the nearby schools of northern Spain–many of whom are cited by R. Aharon Hakohen of Lunel in his *Orḥot Ḥayyim*–who were questioning the legitimacy of the *birkat hapesukim*.[213] Perhaps it is for this reason that R. Manoaḥ mentions here the priest's blessing at the *pidyon haben*, for this was an unquestioned part of the ceremony in Provence and Spain, at least until the advent of the Rosh. The implication is that if one can accept one blessing, one should be able to accept the other and the theoretical basis for the authority on which both are based. One might wonder, though, whether R. Manoaḥ's leniency in the matter of non-talmudic blessings extended to the acceptance of new blessings created by a contemporary: the Meiri basically echoes R. Manoaḥ, but presents his extremely lenient view as the position of "a few sages."[214] We have no evidence that R. Manoaḥ's understanding had a broader impact.

Be that as it may, it is evident that objections to the *birkat hapesukim* were overcome. The *Tur* and its supercommentators all accept that, although the blessing appeared later than the Mishnah, its origins are still very early, in a time when Jews were still praying their evening prayers in the fields and the evening *amidah* was optional. Rather than endanger themselves by staying out of the town until after dark, they substituted this shorter prayer containing eighteen mentions of God's name.[215] As we have seen and will see again, such an ascription of origins enables Jews to maintain a minhag and overrule halakhic objections to it. Antiquity constitutes a solid source of authority and validation.[216]

With the persecutions, expulsions, and consequent migrations of the fourteenth century, we begin to find a mixing of traditions and the voicing of stronger criticisms of non-talmudic blessings, especially when they appear only in a minhag of others. We have already seen the most historically important example: the Rosh's condemnation of the priest's blessing for the *pidyon haben* while allowing the *birkat betulim*. However, before analyzing the theoretical discussions gener-

---

213. הלכות תפלת ערבית, סי' ד.

214. בית הבחירה על מסכת ברכות..., מהדורת שמואל דיקמן, מהדורה שניה, עמ' 13. Although the Meiri seems a bit hesitant about agreeing fully with R. Manoaḥ, he clearly makes reference to this same tradition, as he combines justification of the *birkat hapesukim* with the geonic innovations such as the priest's blessing at the *pidyon haben* and blessings for the widow and widower.

215. OH 236.

216. On the human tendency to create history to authenticize current practice or ideology, see Bernard Lewis, *History Remembered, Recovered, Invented* (Princeton, N.J.: Princeton University Press, 1975; rpt., New York: Touchstone Books, 1987).

ated by that internal contradiction, it is necessary to consider another locus of rabbinic concern–non-talmudic morning blessings.

The *gemara*, in *B. Berakhot* 60b, presents a long series of blessings to accompany the various activities involved in beginning one's day: waking, rising, washing, and dressing. The original intent was that these blessings were to accompany actions; if one omitted a step, one omitted its blessing. The talmudic text itself does not assume the list to be necessarily comprehensive, and the Geonim seem to have assumed it was flexible. As we saw above,[217] Natronai Gaon, in his enumeration of the hundred blessings one must recite daily, includes the blessing *magbiah shefalim* (who raises the lowly), which appears in no known Talmud manuscript. Indeed, as Moshe Ḥalamish notes, many siddurim include other individual blessings that do not appear in the Talmud, a combined result of a non-absolutist approach to the *Berakhot* passage and the original nature of this liturgy as the private prayer of the individual.[218] The geonic readiness to remove talmudically ordained morning blessings that were no longer relevant also points to their non-fundamentalist approach to the passage.[219] Indeed, this section of the liturgy only gradually became part of the public prayer service; Maimonides' objection to the blessings' formal incorporation into the communally recited liturgy indicates that the new custom was by no means adopted universally.[220]

Consistent with our general findings, in spite of the variation in extant customs for this part of the daily prayer, there is relatively little discussion of its legitimacy among the Rishonim. As should be expected, R. Abraham, the son of Maimonides, called *magbiah shefalim* (and other blessings listed in the query posed to him, which is no longer extant), blessings for which he knows no basis

---

217. p. 55.

218. משה חלמיש, "ברכת 'מגביה שפלים' – ברכה שנשתכחה," אסופות ב (תשמ"ח), קצא. Non-talmudic blessings that no longer appear in our liturgy include "מעורר ישנים" (who arouses the slumbering), "מחיה המתים" (who resurrects the dead–in this context), and "מקיץ רדומים" (who wakes the sleeping). The Munich manuscript of this passage of *Berakhot*, as recorded in דקדוקי סופרים, includes the blessing "עוטה אור כשלמה" (who wraps Himself in light like a garment).

219. See Amram Gaon's comment, above, p. 56. A different version of it appears in *Shibbolei Haleket*, ed. Mirsky, 136-7, #4, where Amram removes "מגביה שפלים" (who raises the lowly) instead of "מתיר אסורים" (who frees the captives). He and Natronai Gaon remove "עוטה ישראל בתפארה" (who wraps Israel in a crown of glory) as not relevant where men do not wear turbans.

220. *Mishneh Torah*, *Hilkhot Berakhot* 7:9. The earliest attestation to this custom may go back to Natronai Gaon, as cited in Raphael's edition of *Sefer Hamanhig*, 33-34. However, Raphael's reconstructed text has no support from other manuscript editions. Elbogen's citation of Amram is not supported by Goldschmidt's critical edition. (*Jewish Liturgy*..., 76, Heb., 68.; *Seder Rav Amram Gaon*, ed. Goldschmidt, #1, p. 2.)

or appropriate time, that are not mentioned in the Talmud, and that, if they appear in the siddur, must be there because of the error of the scribe or some rabbi or cantor. Neither they nor any similarly innovative blessings beyond those mentioned in the Talmud should be recited.[221] It is significant that *Shibbolei Haleket* cites only geonic sources and no discussions of the Rishonim on the question of the content of these blessings, adding no original comment.[222] Even the *Tur* still fully accepts variations in custom, simply noting that the Ashkenazim add a blessing, *hanoten layaef koaḥ* (who gives strength to the weary), and commenting that, although the blessings referring to the general ordering of the world must be recited by everyone without exception, the blessings referring to the various human acts of rising in the morning should be recited only if they are relevant.[223] Ḥalamish suggests that much of the opposition to *magbiah shefalim* was unvoiced, for despite widespread evidence for its inclusion in rites from all corners of the medieval Jewish world, various important sages simply omitted it, even from their citations of Natronai Gaon's enumeration of the mandatory hundred daily blessings. He posits that this silent elimination was a direct consequence of the voiced opposition to the blessing by those who found its content problematic or who objected in general to the addition of non-talmudic benedictions.[224] Arguments based on omissions are problematic, especially when they pertain to a custom with as much documented variation as the *birkhot hashaḥar*. Much more significant is the paucity of specific opposition to the non-talmudic additions to this part of the liturgy. For the most part, it seems that the Rishonim did not consider the talmudic list of morning blessings to be prescriptive.

However, as we move into the fifteenth and sixteenth centuries, this situation changes, perhaps driven in part by a need to respond to the theoretical issues raised by the Rosh's internal contradictions. Ḥalamish cites a comment written in a fifteenth-century Sefardi siddur manuscript: הגהה. מגביה שפלים אינה נזכרת בגמ' ועל כן לא כתבתיה. ריב"ץ [=ר' יוסף בן צדיק] ז"ל (Comment. *Magbiah shefalim* is not mentioned in the *gemara*; hence, I did not copy it. R. Yosef ben Tzaddik of blessed memory).[225] The Ashkenazi R. Yaakov Barukh Landau in his *Sefer HaAgur* first

221. תשובות רבנו אברהם בן הרמב"ם, סי' פג, עמ' 123.

222. ed. Mirsky, #4, 136-137.

223. OH 46.

224. "ברכת 'מגביה שפלים'...", קצד–קצה; citing Maimonides; *Sefer HaEshkol*, Albeck ed., 10; *Manhig*, ed. Raphael, 33ff.; *Tur*, סמ"ג, מצות עשה, הלכות ברכות, קיד.; and many other sources from Provence and Spain especially, including kabbalistic works. See his comments.

225. "ברכת מגביה שפלים...", קצה. Citing Ms. British Library (sic) Or. 11564, p. 28b. The identity of the departed R. Yosef ben Tzaddik (who was obviously not the scribe), and hence the original date of this comment, cannot be established based on information available.

cites the *Tur*'s neutral comment about the Ashkenazi addition, *hanoten layaef koaḥ,* and then adds:

> ואני המחבר קבלתי מרבותי שאין להוסיף עוד על אילו ברכות שנתקנו רק כמו שנזכרים בגמרא ועליהן אין להוסיף ומהן אין לגרוע. ואפילו על הברכה מהנותן ליעף כח ראיתי מקטרגים מאחר שאינה נזכרת בגמרא. ובסדר ברכות של בעל סמ"ק אינה נזכרת ברכת ליעף כח, וכן ברוקח בסדר של ברכות מ"מ המנהג מצרפת ואשכנז לאומרה, אכן ראיתי בסדורי טלייני וקטאלנ"י וספרדים הרבה ברכות שלא הוזכרו לא בגמרא ולא בפוסקים ואין להם ראיה ומנין.
>
> ...and I the author received (the tradition) from my teachers that one should not add anything to the established blessings, but only (recite them) as they are mentioned in the *gemara*; one should not add or delete from them. I even saw some people criticizing the blessing *hanoten layaef koaḥ* because it is not mentioned in the *gemara.* The list of blessings by the author of the *Sefer Mitzvot Katon* does not include the blessing *layaef koaḥ,* and similarly the list of blessings in the *Rokeaḥ.* In any case, it is the custom in France and Germany to recite it. Also, I have seen in Italian, Catalonian, and Spanish siddurim many blessings that were not mentioned in the *gemara* or the medieval halakhic works and therefore have no standing in the (talmudic) enumeration of the benedictions.[226]

Although Landau stops short of suggesting any change in minhag[227] and even, somewhat polemically, justifies the Ashkenazi one on the basis of Italian and Spanish transgressions of the same halakhic principle, he still states that principle rather unequivocally. We may question whether his first general comment refers to the halakhic authority of the Talmud in determining all legitimate blessings, or whether it only applies to the *birkhot hashaḥar.* Given the nature of his transition to the specific discussion of *hanoten layaef koaḥ,* saying that he has "even" seen some applying the principle to this blessing, he probably intended it as a general statement. Most likely, then, he is referring to the comment of the Rosh in his criticism of the priest's blessing at the *pidyon haben.* Although that comment was acknowledged more explicitly as a statement of principle in the *Leket Yosher*'s discussion of the *birkat betulim,* written by Landau's Ashkenazi contemporary, R. Yosef b"R. Moshe, it was similarly rejected as a determinant of actual custom.[228] Another fifteenth-century Ashkenazi

---

226. ספר האגור השלם לרבינו יעקב ברוך בן יהודה לנדא, מהדורת משה הרשלר, הלכות ברכות, סי' פז, עמ' לא.

227. On the high value placed on minhag in his world, see: ידידיה דינרי, חכמי אשכנז בשלהי ימי־הביניים: דרכיהם וכתביהם בהלכה (ירושלים: מוסד ביאליק, תשמ"ד), פרק שישי, "היחס בין המנהג וההלכה במאה החמש־עשרה."

228. ספר לקט יושר לרבנו יוסף ב"ר משה, מהדורת יעקב פריימאנן, עמ' 46, discussed above, p. 68.

In the case of the concluding eulogy of the confessional prayer, Landau does rule that Ashkenazi minhag should not persist, because in this instance, there is a clear disagreement

authority, R. Moshe Mintz, also explicitly cites it as a halakhic principle, but he uses it to invalidate some form of special candle blessing being recited on returning home from the synagogue on Friday night.[229]

In the sixteenth and, even more markedly, in the seventeenth century, the principle that non-talmudic blessings lacked authorization for invocation of the divine Name emerged as a theoretical concept worthy of direct rabbinic discussion and demanding a more consistent application. Discussions of one questionable blessing now tended to include others as well, and authorities resolved these problems by advocating one of four possible solutions: eliminating the entire passage; eliminating just the liturgical blessing formula (or a crucial element thereof); reinterpreting the prayer itself to obviate the halakhic concerns; or "discovering" some myth of origins that justified the continued recitation of the prayer. Such solutions resulted not in a radically transformed minhag, but in one undergirded by a more consistent halakhic approach.

This process was still in transition in the thought of Karo. In his *Beit Yosef*, he, like R. Meir ibn Gabbai,[230] accepts the recitation of the *birkat betulim* because of its geonic authorization, and in the *Shulḥan Arukh*, he simply indicates, without even raising the spectre of the blessing's halakhically questionable status, that some do recite it.[231] He seems not to know the priest's blessing for the *pidyon haben* as a living custom, so it was not an issue. But when he discusses the *birkhot hashaḥar*, he invokes our principle in criticizing the Ashkenazi custom of including *hanoten layaef koaḥ:*

> אע"פ שיש סמך יפה לברך ברכה זו מאחר שלא נזכרה בתלמוד איני יודע איך היה רשות לשום אדם לתקנה ומצאתי שכתב האגור שראה מקטרגים עליה מטעם זה והרמב"ם וסמ"ג והרוקח לא הזכיר' והכי נקטינן.
>
> Even though there is good support for reciting this blessing, since it is not mentioned in the Talmud, I do not know how anyone had the right to

---

between Rav Amram, who wrote that reciting this blessing is an error, and Rashi, who allowed it, and a corresponding difference between Sefardi and Ashkenazi custom. Here, his reasoning is that the doubt cast by the halakhic disagreement makes the status of the blessing too questionable to justify its recitation. (*Sefer HaAgur Hashalem*, #929, p. 149.) Is he here relying on Maimonides' principle of ספק ברכות להקל? In any case, as Zvi Groner has demonstrated, this blessing is only quasi-non-talmudic, as it is based on a baraita which the Babylonian geonic and Spanish literary traditions seem not to have known. See: צבי גרונר, "הברכה על הווידוי וגלגוליה," ספר השנה בר אילן יג (תשל"ו), 158–168, and above, p. 58, n. 67.

229. שאלות ותשובות רבינו משה מינץ, מהדורת יונתן שרגא דומב (ירושלים: מפעל תורת חכמי אשכנז, תשנ"א), חלק ב, סימן פז.

230. See above, p. 68.

231. EH 63:2.

> establish it. I found that the *Agur* wrote that he saw people criticizing it for this reason, and Maimonides, the *Sefer Mitzvot Gadol*,[232] and the *Rokeaḥ* do not mention it. This is our conclusion.

Karo rules similarly against *magbiah shefalim* and *somekh noflim* (who supports the falling) as also lacking talmudic authorization, and then returns to the conclusion of the comment of the *Agur*, which he reads as a general condemnation of all the non-talmudic blessings found in the Italian, Catalonian, and Spanish rites.[233] However, he omits the key phrase of the *Agur*, מ"מ המנהג מצרפת ואשכנז לאומרה (in any case, it is customary in France and Germany to recite [*hanoten layaef koaḥ*]). This selective citation and consequent twisting of the *Agur*'s point is significant, for as a rabbi of the Spanish school, Karo gives minhag and halakhah very different weights than his fifteenth-century German colleagues did. He is also not ruling here, it seems, against any minhag common in his own community.

The Ashkenazi response to Karo's ruling was mixed. R. Moshe Isserles' comment to the *Shulḥan Arukh* seems to be a strong rebuttal, affirming the conventional Ashkenazi precedence given to minhag over theoretical halakhah. He says: אך מנהג פשוט בבני אשכנז לאומרה (however, it is a widespread custom among German Jews to recite it.) Since he offers no similar comment in his *Darkhei Moshe*, however, his *Shulḥan Arukh* comment should not be understood as a refutation of the halakhic principle Karo espouses, but a descriptive statement–like Landau's in his *Agur*–that in spite of halakhic concerns, Ashkenazi practice remains unchanged. Thus, for Isserles, custom alone is still a sufficient source of authority from antiquity and he feels no compulsion to justify these blessings.

In his *Yam Shel Shlomo*, R. Shlomo Luria, the Maharshal, in describing an incident that occurred in his academy, takes quite a different approach. After he had ruled that the *birkat betulim* should be recited without a full liturgical blessing because of its lack of talmudic authorization, others challenged him, questioning his justification for reciting the blessing *hanoten layaef koaḥ,* which has only midrashic basis and not even geonic support. He responded that perhaps one should not recite that blessing either–a ruling that had support in the works of the Aḥaronim (here meaning rabbis since the Rosh)–and that the case was even stronger against the recitation of *magbiah shefalim*.[234] A later responsum, in which the Maharshal describes his personal prayer customs, confirms that he did indeed eliminate these two blessings from his prayers and expresses surprise

---

232. Note that our text of the *Agur*, cited above, reads *Sefer Mitzvot Katon.*
233. OH 46:6-7; *Beit Yosef*, ד"ה עוד ברכה אחת; בקצת סדורים; כתב האגור.
234. שלמה לוריא, ספר ים של שלמה, כתובות פרק א, דין כג.

at the *Tur*'s neutral attitude to *hanoten layaef koaḥ* in light of the Rosh's statement of principle in *Bekhorot* that no post-talmudic blessings may be recited.[235] There is no evidence from this account that the Maharshal was responding to Karo, but the question posed to him might possibly have been evoked by Karo's ruling. In any case, we find here that a leading Ashkenazi rabbi consistently ruled against the recitation of non-talmudic benedictions, and in the case of the *birkat betulim* ruling, influenced others.[236]

As Moshe Ḥalamish has demonstrated, debate over the recitation of *hanoten layaef koaḥ* shifted signficantly in the second half of the sixteenth century after students and colleagues of the leading mystic, the Ari, R. Yitzḥak Luria Ashkenazi, spread the word that the Ari himself recited this blessing.[237] Consequently, we begin to find kabbalistic interpretations of its meaning, and the growing assumption that if the Ari himself was contradicting the ruling of the *Shulḥan Arukh*, he must have received divine revelation that permitted the blessing. A tradition also spread that when, at the end of his life, Karo became aware of the custom of the Ari, he reversed his own ruling. That reversal lies behind the rebuke of the seventeenth-century R. Ḥaim Benveniste to those in his Turkish town, Tirya, who, upon hearing of Karo's change of mind, began to recite *hanoten layaef koaḥ* with a full liturgical *berakhah*. He says:

> וגערתי בהם שלא מפני עדות המעיד ששמע על פי השמועה נניח מה שכת' כאן ונבא לידי ברכה לבטל' ועוד שהטענה שכתב רבינו ז"ל שמאחר שלא נזכרה בג' אין לנו רשות לאמרה טענה יפה היא...
>
> I rebuked them, for we should not, based on people's witness and rumors, abandon what is written here [by Karo], lest we begin to recite a *berakhah levatalah*. Additionally, the argument that our rabbi (of blessed memory) recorded is appropriate: since it is not mentioned in the *gemara*, we have no right to recite it...[238]

Apparently, that "rumor" was already known and accepted as evidence for Karo's change of mind by the seventeenth-century Ashkenazi *Magen Avraham*[239]

---

235. ספר שאלות ותשובות מהרש"ל, סי' סד, עמ' קפו–קפז.

236. It is intriguing to ask to what extent Luria's hardline position was influenced by the upheavals of the greater world around him–i.e., the struggles between the Protestants and Catholics for religious and political control of Europe. These wars did affect the Jews' physical and economic security. Was the Maharshal influenced by a climate of extreme religious conservatism in his greater world?

237. See, for example, Ḥaim Vital's *Shaar Hakavvanot*, on this blessing.

238. *Kenesset Hagedolah* OH, (Jerusalem, 1965), p. 25 on the *Beit Yosef* OH 46.

239. To OH 46:6.

and the eighteenth-century Ḥida.[240] Slowly the influence and authority of Lurianic custom overcame most halakhic objections to this blessing–not without opposition, especially by those who rejected mystical revelation as a source of halakhah.[241]

Not every authority used the traditions of the Ari as a mechanism to permit this blessing. Most fascinating from our perspective is the remark of R. Yoel Sirkes (sixteenth to seventeenth centuries), in his supercommentary *Bayit Ḥadash* to the *Tur*, who solves the problem of the Maharshal by asserting that this blessing must have come from earlier versions of the Talmud, especially those known to the rabbis who established the custom of early Ashkenaz. Thus any omission of *hanoten layaef koaḥ* or even *magbiah shefalim* on the claim that they are not talmudically authorized is a transgression, he said, for which one will ultimately be brought to judgment. Similarly, R. Yaakov Emden, in his commentary to the siddur, considered *hanoten layaef koaḥ* a geonic enactment.[242]

For many jurists, the simple force of minhag or the extra authority of Lurianic minhag was sufficient to justify the recitation of non-talmudic blessings in the *birkhot hashaḥar.* Others, like these Ashkenazi rabbis, could not so easily ignore the theoretical claims of halakhah and the authoritative status of the talmudic text as the source of all acceptable uses of the liturgical *berakhah.* Like Sirkes, some bridged the gap between minhag and halakhah by assuming that the written authority must once have existed, either in a lost Talmud variant or in a geonic tradition. In the case of the *birkat betulim,* we saw above the assumption of the *Sefer Beer Sheva* and others that the blessing may have had its origins among the Amoraim.[243] This mythological authenticization allowed these questionable blessings to acquire the authority and guarantee of liturgical efficacy that antiquity implies within the rabbinic system.

A fascinating example of this process occurs in the interpretations of the blessing *barukh she-amar.* Until the fourteenth century, most rabbinic discussions of its origins assumed the existence of some vague rabbinic enactment, the exact nature of which was of no great concern. The *Tur*[244] mentions in passing that the

---

240. שו"ת טוב עין סי' ז; ברכי יוסף, או"ח מו:יא

241. For a detailed summary of the sources and a contemporary contribution to the dispute over the halakhic authority of mystical revelation, see: עובדיה יוסף, שו"ת יביע אומר, חלק א, או"ח סימן מא; חלק ב, או"ח, סימן כה: יב–יג. See also the various relevant studies in Jacob Katz's הלכה וקבלה: מחקרים בתולדות דת ישראל על מדוריה וזיקתה החברתית (ירושלים: מאגנס, תשמ"ו).

242. משה חלמיש, "ברכת 'הנותן ליעף כח'," אסופות א (תשמ"ז), שסא–שעו. See the sources he has cited here for the usage of this blessing in various times, and the rulings and commentaries concerning it.

243. See above, p. 69.

244. OH 51.

blessing appears in *Sefer Heikhalot.* R. David ben Yehudah Ḥasid, in his influential kabbalistic prayer commentary, *Or Zarua*, states that *barukh she-amar* was *not* established by the men of the Great Assembly. Instead, scholars and men of wisdom received it directly from "the tradition of the covenant" when a note fell from heaven.[245] R. David was no doubt rebutting a theory suggested by some unidentified group or person in his world. Obviously it was not a mainstream theory, judging from the literature of the period. However, in the sixteenth century, R. Meir ibn Gabbai, in his commentary *Sefer Tolaat Yaakov*, miscites the *Or Zarua*, stating that it ascribes *barukh she-amar* specifically to the men of the Great Assembly, who established the prayer on the basis of a note that fell from heaven.[246] This clever ascription removed all doubt about the legitimate origins of *barukh she-amar* by placing its provenance in the same mythical pre-talmudic antiquity as the *amidah*, the paradigmatic Jewish prayer. This explanation eventually became standard in noncritical prayer commentaries.

The impetus to generate and accept such "origins" for this single prayer must have come from the continuing need to justify its recitation. Before Ibn Gabbai's solution was widely accepted, Ḥizkiah da Silva, in his *Peri Ḥadash*, a late seventeenth-century Sefardi commentary on the *Shulḥan Arukh*, challenged the geonic right to establish new blessings, basing his argument on the Rosh's objections to the priest's blessing at the *pidyon haben*.[247] Da Silva was either unaware of, or, more likely, unconvinced by, the kabbalists' solution, which had already been cited by the *Turei Zahav*, and which would again be cited to refute Da Silva's objections, by the eighteenth-century commentators, the *Peri Megadim*[248] and the *Beer Heitev*.[249] The *Beer Heitev*, like his Sefardi contemporary, the Ḥida,[250] also points to the *Tur*'s identification of the source of the blessing in the *Sefer Heikhalot* as proof of its pre-talmudic origins. Da Silva's resistance to kabbalistic influence on the liturgy is also evident in his pointed opposition to

245. Ms. JTS 2203, 15b. See Gershom Scholem's discussion of this work in: "פרקים מתולדות ספרות הקבלה," קרית ספר ד (1928), 302, 321, where he describes it as highly dependent on the writings of Moshe de Leon and the main expression of the kabbalist understanding of prayer until the sixteenth-century emergence of the new center in Tzefat. In the introduction to this commentary (Ms. JTS 2203, 8b), cited by Scholem, 321, David ben Yehudah Ḥasid specifically points to the definitive authority of the men of the Great Assembly in the final establishment of the liturgy. This makes his acknowledgment of *barukh she-amar* as a later prayer all the more significant.

246. p. 21.

247. To OH 51.

248. פתיחה להלכות ברכות השחר; משבצות זהב, או"ח, נא:א.

249. OH 51:1.

250. עין זוכר, מערכת ב, אות לז.

the recitation of *hanoten layaef koaḥ*. He indicates that the custom to recite it had spread in Jerusalem, but a few individuals, including himself, refused to do so.[251]

Da Silva was by no means the first to confront the implications of the Rosh's inconsistency for the status of other non-talmudic blessings. The earliest published text directly to juxtapose and attempt to resolve the Rosh's contradictory stances towards the two geonic blessings is that of the Ashkenazi R. Yissakhar Baer Eilenburg in his *Sefer Beer Sheva*.[252] Eilenburg reads the Rosh very closely, establishing that he had sufficiently serious reasons for objecting to the priest's blessing that he could have casually added its lack of talmudic basis to the list. Instead, the Rosh stated as a general principle of liturgical law that one may recite no blessing, שום ברכה, that is not mentioned in the Talmud. This, according to Eilenburg's reading of the Rosh, indicates that even if there were no other grounds on which to object to a blessing, if it is non-talmudic, one may not recite it. The Rosh's prefacing the rest of his objections with וגם (and also) indicates that these other reasons are all secondary. Why did he not object to the *birkat betulim*? Because, as discussed above, implied in his statement that "it is possible" that it is a geonic enactment, is the equal possibility that the Amoraim enacted it. If so, it is "talmudic" even if not mentioned there. Having accepted the halakhic principle that only talmudically ordained blessings are legitimate, Eilenburg then adopts one of the standard ways to justify a non-talmudic benediction; he finds an origin for it that obviates the problem.

R. Ḥaim Benveniste, the seventeenth-century Sefardi author of *Sefer Kenesset Hagedolah*, cites Eilenburg in his commentary to *Even Haezer* 63 and basically agrees with him. However, in his commentary to *Yoreh Deah* 305, he differs, claiming that the Rosh could not have objected to the priest's blessing at the *pidyon haben* primarily or solely on the basis of its non-talmudic status, or he would not have accepted the *birkat betulim*. Even if this were his primary objection, the Rosh had greater grounds for objecting to the priest's blessing at the *pidyon haben* than to the *birkat betulim* because in the former case, the father is already reciting a blessing for the occasion and no mitzvah is incumbent upon the priest. In the case of the *birkat betulim*, there is no other blessing ritualizing the occasion, so it is preferable to recite it even though it does not appear in the Talmud. He also finds Eilenburg's assumption of talmudic origins for the *birkat betulim* unconvincing and reports, without judgment, the individual custom of R. Yosef Kohen to perpetuate the Sefardi recitation of the priest's blessing at the

251. *Peri Ḥadash* OH 46:6.

252. ספר באר שבע, חלק באר מים חיים, סי' טז. On the history of this passage in the *Derishah*, see p. 69, n. 114, above.

*pidyon haben*.[253] However, Benveniste also condemns outright non-talmudic additions to the *birkhot hashaḥar* on the basis of the Rosh's ruling regarding the priest's blessing.[254]

How can we understand Benveniste's inconsistencies?[255] Obviously he accepts the principle of talmudic authority for legitimate blessings but seems to believe that actual and rabinically legitimated minhag determines practice. He notes that, in spite of the Maharshal's objections, it is the custom to recite the *birkat betulim*. The individual priest can recite his blessing because he does so as a Sefardi Jew extrapolating from his influential and authoritative teacher R. Yosef Trani's interpretation of the Rosh. But those adding blessings in the morning not only contradict Karo's written works, which are authoritative; they are also acting only on the basis of rumors, not rabbinic authority. Would Benveniste have ruled otherwise about the *birkat betulim* had Karo specifically objected to it, or about the priest's benediction had Karo mentioned it at all? Would he have supported changes to the *birkhot hashaḥar* had the authority cited been within the halakhic and not the mystical tradition?

Benveniste's various statements illustrate the complexity of decision making on our question in this period. Not only does each rabbinic authority take a stand on the specific halakhic tradition, but this stance is necessarily influenced by a) his position vis-à-vis the halakhic authority of the Zohar and kabbalistically derived practices, many based on the customs and private revelations of the Ari; and b) the degree of automatic validity ascribed to minhag, both in that rabbi's halakhic community and in his own particular hierarchy of values.

For instance, typical of many Ashkenazi authorities (but not the Maharshal), R. David Halevi, in his *Turei Zahav*,[256] relies entirely on the authority of minhag in this issue. Although he explicitly acknowledges the opinion that only talmudic blessings are legitimate, he then asserts that one relies on the authority of minhag to determine which blessings one actually recites. Having stated the latter as an absolute, he must then find a way to reconcile the contradictory rulings of the Rosh. His interpretation begins with the Rosh's wording regarding the *birkat betulim*, where the Rosh states that "it is possible that the Geonim established it." To him, as to Eilenburg, "it is possible" indicates the possibility

253. See above, p. 85.

254. See above, p. 99.

255. Which raised problems for his successors. See the Ḥida, עין זוכר, מערכת ב', אות לז.

256. OH 46:6. His view conforms with that of the *Leket Yosher*, p. 46, which essentially ignores the implications of the Rosh's ruling against non-talmudic blessings as irrelevant in the face of actual minhag.

of amoraic origins. Thus, the custom to recite a particular blessing, even if non-talmudic, should be allowed to persist, for it is possible that the Geonim who established the blessing had some talmudic basis. In his view, then, the Rosh's statement was not intended as a principle of liturgical law, and those already reciting the priest's benediction at the *pidyon haben* need not eliminate it. The Rosh was simply communicating the Franco-German reason for not including it in their minhag. In the case of the *birkat betulim*, which was a universal custom, there was no need to raise the issue of its non-talmudic origins. And this understanding, claims the *Turei Zahav*, applies equally to the non-talmudic additions to the *birkhot hashaḥar*. Minhag is a fully valid authenticator of blessings, and talmudic origins or lack thereof play a role only in the analysis of the customs of others or in cases where the minhag is not clear. Thus, by rereading the Rosh, the *Turei Zahav* maintains the principle of requiring talmudic origins for blessings, but by assuming that established customs must obviously also have roots of sufficient antiquity, he creates a mechanism that legitimates almost any established practice.[257] The theoretical halakhic category has significance but little real impact. The *Turei Zahav*, though, almost certainly would not countenance the creation of new blessings. For him, the liturgy remains invariant and authoritative–but it actually has two sources of guaranteed efficacy, the literary traditions of the Talmud and received ancestral custom.

Another work of this same period, the *Sefer Halakhot Ketanot* of R. Yaakov Ḥagiz,[258] contains a brief answer to a question posed by one of the students in his Jerusalem academy: Can one recite a blessing not mentioned in the *gemara*? He responds that the Rosh was relying on the authority of *Halakhot Gedolot* in permitting the *birkat betulim*, and in the case of the priest's blessing, he was only giving the view of the Ashkenazi Jews and not his own; but it is best to recite it without a full liturgical blessing formula, omitting reference to divine sovereignty.[259] He continues with a more general statement, that the entire concept of an unnecessary blessing applies only to making a blessing at an inappropriate occasion, not to the question of the legitimacy of the form of the blessing itself. In addition, the (Maimonidean) concept that, in cases of doubt, one should not

---

257. Thus he transmits Ibn Gabbai's tradition about the origins of *barukh she-amar*–which only adds credence to his claims of ancient roots for all customs.

258. I:#224.

259. This passage lacks clear antecedents for its pronouns and could be read any of several ways. After recapitulating the two traditions of the Rosh, first about the priest's blessing and then about the *birkat betulim*, he says: י"ל משום דדברי ה"ג הן דברי קבלה א"נ יהיב טעמא לבני אשכנז וליה לא סבירא ליה וטוב לברכה בלא מלכות. Aside from the other ambiguities, does he really mean to suggest elimination only of mention of God's sovereignty from the blessing formula, maintaining God's name?

recite the blessing, refers to cases where one is unsure whether it is appropriate to recite an established benediction; and in general, it is best to praise God as much as possible. Indeed, in another responsum, he acknowledges that he follows local custom and recites *hanoten layaef koaḥ*.[260] In other words, he too acknowledges the concept of non- talmudic benedictions but rejects its application in the face of regnant minhag.

These discussions increasingly enter the realm of *pilpul*, and the fate of the blessings we have been following was ultimately determined in the reality of the synagogue. Between the objections of the Rosh and the disintegration of the Spanish community that recited it, the priest's blessing at the *pidyon haben* has largely faded out of existence. The *birkat betulim* continues to appear in a few scattered rites by virtue of reinterpretations of its origins or meaning, but has also largely fallen victim to rabbinic concerns about improper invocation of the liturgical blessing formula. Origins in authoritative periods of antiquity have been identified for *barukh she-amar*–with the men of the Great Assembly–and for the *birkat hapesukim*, before the evening *amidah* became firmly part of the (amoraic) public synagogue service. The private revelation of the great kabbalist, the Ari, authorized the recitation of *hanoten layaef koaḥ*.

While much of the ongoing discussion of these issues recapitulates and nuances the pronouncements of earlier authorities, some aspects re-emerge with vigor in the modern responsa of R. Ovadiah Yosef, a leading Sefardi authority in Israel. He guides a community of uprooted immigrants whose native customs, having been disrupted, are subject to questioning and open to change. Ovadiah Yosef devotes significant energy to establishing that women may not use a full liturgical blessing when reciting *she-asani kirtzono* (who has made me according to His will) as their substitution for the talmudic but inappropriate *shelo asani ishah* (who has not made me a woman).[261] This women's blessing appears first in the halakhic literature in the fourteenth century in the *Tur*[262] and Abudarham,[263] with no discussion of its origins or novelty, and Karo includes it in his *Shulḥan Arukh*.[264] As we have seen above, the fourteenth-century rabbis, and to a certain

260. I: #184. Ḥagiz does not specify where he is writing this responsum. It may be Jerusalem, where he founded a yeshiva, for the language of the *Peri Ḥadash* (OH 46:6) echoes and inverts Hagiz's, and Da Silva was explicitly responding to the Jerusalem custom.

261. שו"ת יחווה דעת, חלק ד, סימן ד.

262. OH 46.

263. אבודרהם השלם, עמ' מב.

264. OH 46:4. Note that a variant שעשיתני אשה ולא איש (who has made me a woman and not a man) appears in an Italian siddur written in 1471 by Abraham Farissol (Ms. JTS 8255). See the forthcoming article on this blessing by Joseph Tabory, who documents other variants from this period.

extent, Karo too, were still inconsistent in rejecting blessings that lacked clear talmudic origins. Thus many supercommentators say nothing at all about the woman's *berakhah*; of those printed with the *Shulḥan Arukh*, only the Ashkenazi *Turei Zahav* and the *Eshel Avraham* specifically support its recitation. The *Peri Ḥadash* objects to its lack of talmudic authorization, as had the Radbaz,[265] and as do two leading eighteenth-century Sefardi rabbis, Yisrael Yaakov Algazi in Israel[266] and Yehudah Ayash in Algiers.[267] The Ḥida calls for its recitation without a full liturgical blessing.[268] Similar voices come from the Ashkenazi world, especially as we move toward and into the twentieth century. Seligmann Baer, in his *Seder Avodat Yisrael*, abbreviates the blessing formula, citing the Ḥida.[269] Barukh Halevi Epstein of Pinsk calls for its recitation without a full liturgical blessing,[270] and the *Arukh Hashulḥan* is of the opinion that even though it appears in a few prayerbooks, current custom is not to recite it at all, and it should be expunged.[271]

However, in almost every current Ashkenazi prayerbook, the blessing does appear in full and receives no attention in the major contemporary prayerbook commentaries. It does not appear in most Hasidic prayerbooks, perhaps due to the assumption that these books were just for men. In Israeli prayerbooks, only the most recent Sefardi rites follow R. Ovadiah Yosef's ruling. We must assume, especially for those commenting directly on the *Tur*, the *Shulḥan Arukh*, or the prayerbook itself, that silence means approval of the full blessing. It is too early to know whether Sefardi women will follow Ovadiah Yosef's ruling and if, and to what extent, it will penetrate into the Ashkenazi world. As we have seen, and will continue to see in the coming chapters, rabbinic determinations of what constitutes efficacious prayer do not easily or automatically affect popular minhag.

* * *

From the earliest levels of talmudic legislation about prayer, the rabbis concerned themselves with the possible ill effects of improper recitation of blessings, whether worded wrongly or invoked at an improper occasion: blessings involve the use of God's name; therefore they are inherently powerful

265. ספר מצודת דוד, טעמי המצות לרדב"ז (זאלקווא, תרכ"ב; ד"ח ישראל, תשכ"ד), מצוה ע"ד.

266. ספר שלמי צבור (שאלוניקי, תרנ"ה; ד"ח, ישראל, n.d.), דף נ"ד, עמ' ב.

267. ספר מטה יהודה (ליוורנו, תקמ"ג; ד"ח, ירושלים תשל"א), או"ח, מו:י.

268. ספר עבודת הקדש (בני ברק: הוצאת ספרים "מישור," תשמ"ו), קשר גודל, סימן ה, אות כ"ג.

269. Rödelheim, 1868; rpt. Tel Aviv, 1957, p. 41.

270. ברוך שאמר (תל אביב: הוצאת עם עולם, תשכ"ח), עמ' ל; מקור ברוך (ניו־יורק: חייל, תשי"ד), חלק ג', עמ' תתקפ"א.

271. OH 46:11.

and potentially dangerous. The logical result of such concern was to seek definitions of exactly what Jews should say and when. This process underlies the gradual "canonization" of growing segments of Jewish prayer and the composition, beginning in the geonic period, of the first officially sanctioned Jewish prayerbooks. But such a formalization of ritual required a source of authority. For the wording and structure of the rabbinic liturgy, the Bible provided few sources of direct legitimation. Like most of Jewish life, then, the theoretical authority for prayer and its blessings came to be the Oral Law, embodied in the Talmud. From Yehudai Gaon on, we have literary evidence for the concept that only blessings sanctioned by talmudic tradition were reliably justified invocations of God's name.

From the earliest periods, too, we know that halakhic theory and actual minhag did not always mesh. Halakhic authorities, confronted with a blessing not recorded in the Talmud, had to devise a means either to abolish that minhag or, more frequently, to interpret it so that it could be understood as standing within the bounds of the theoretical halakhah. In the case of non-talmudic blessings, minhag rarely overruled halakhah; more often, rabbis devised interpretations of either one or the other, stretched the boundaries of the theoretical halakhah, reinterpreted the minhag, or found new origins for it, so as to remove the conflict.

Conversely, only rarely were strong stances taken against active customs based on the theoretical authority of the Talmud. This occurred only when the sages were personally involved in culture conflicts; most were themselves refugees confronted with a world of customs new to them, some of which they found objectionable. Yehudai Gaon was attempting to establish the authority of the Babylonian academies and their Talmud over those parts of the world still dominated by Palestinian or non-rabbinic traditions. The Maimonideans brought Spanish norms with them to Egypt and the eastern Mediterranean. The Asherides, i.e.–the Rosh and the Baal Haturim–imported German values to Spain. Karo was attempting to preserve and reconstruct the Sefardi world after the final expulsion from Spain. The shock waves of that disaster, as well as the transfer of the northern European centers of Jewish learning from Germany to Poland and Lithuania–coinciding with the post-Reformation religious wars–may well have contributed to the harshness of R. Shlomo Luria's stance (although he himself was not a refugee). The rabbis of the seventeenth century faced the challenges of integrating the now popular kabbalah of the Lurianic school, confronting the upheavals of European wars and Sabbateanism, and developing or continuing to develop the traditions of the many new centers of Jewish learning. All of these shifts created confrontations between different minhagim, forcing sages to analyze and justify their own traditions and to apply the same tools of judgment to new customs that presented themselves.

Why is it only in the centuries following the expulsion from Spain that we find this increased emphasis on the measurement of customs against theoretical halakhic standards? As we have seen, although the problematic nature of non-talmudic blessings had been recognized for three-quarters of a millennium, few if any rabbis had applied our legal principle with any consistency. In earlier periods, generally those who did invoke it did so only in cases where they had other objections to a given blessing; in doing so, they almost never made reference to other questionable blessings. Non-talmudic blessings, as a category, were of minimal or no concern.

Several factors explain this shift in rabbinic focus. First, the traditions of learning gradually included more criticisms of questionable blessings by influential rabbis–criticisms that had to be acknowledged and dealt with in any later work. The greatest post-geonic critics of non-talmudic blessings were, as we have seen, among those rabbis on whom Joseph Karo relied as his "pillars of halakhah," to whom he turned first in generating the rulings of his great halakhic works. This only heightened the attention paid to them. Second, the invention of printing enabled rabbis to study diverse halakhic traditions, allowed the speedy spread of new works, and placed a prayerbook in the hands of increasing numbers of Jews. The effects of printing also facilitated the development of regional rather than local minhagim, encouraged the spread of popular mystical works, and forced rabbinic leaders to scrutinize the contents of siddurim. Finally, the growing role of *pilpul* as an academic methodology demanded that internal contradictions, even in the *posekim*, be resolved. Once individual scholars began to address non- talmudic blessings as a category, those who dealt with related topics were forced to confront the principle and, if they did not accept its universal application, to justify exceptions to it.

The status of minhag in Jewish liturgy is such that no rabbinic authority could possibly nullify all non-talmudic blessings. Every rabbi had to make exceptions, at least in practice, for the universally accepted blessings for *pesukei d'zimra*. As we have seen, strategies for broadening the range of other acceptable blessings and resolving the halakhah/minhag conflict fell into many categories. Some rabbis simply accepted geonic authority as equivalent to that of the Talmud or assumed that geonic authorization must be based on their knowledge of amoraic traditions. More creative solutions included "discovering" histories of blessings that gave them pre-geonic antiquity, positing variant talmudic texts on which ancestors must have based their customs, or accepting as authoritative mystically received divine revelation. Some authorities attempted to redefine the nature of particular blessings to allow them to fall into what they considered less regulated categories, such as blessings for the performance of a mitzvah or, conversely, blessings of praise. Finally, especially in Ashkenaz, we find those who claimed that minhag was the major determinant of legitimate prayer on the assumption that those who originated the custom acted on proper authority; considerations of talmudic status only become operative when the details of the minhag itself were unclear.

The upheavals of Jewish history, however, have often blurred the mandates of minhag. Most frequently, changing intellectual trends and large-scale migrations have challenged the culture of communities and subjected their customs to rabbinic scrutiny. With the weakening of minhagim, the rabbis gradually turned to the Talmud as the timeless, absolute, operative authority by which to judge the efficacy of liturgical customs. Although no generation has yet applied with total consistency the principle that non-talmudic blessings are automatically illegitimate and hence potentially dangerous invocations of the divine Name, this concept grew to be an accepted halakhic principle whose exceptions had to be justified.

# 3

# The Language of Prayer: The Challenge of *Piyyut*

רבי אליעזר אומר: העושה תפלתו קבע אין תפלתו תחנונים

Rabbi Eliezer said: If one makes one's prayer fixed, it is not true supplication.[1]

רבי שמעון אומר: הוי זהיר בקרית שמע ובתפלה; וכשאתה מתפלל, אל תעש תפלתך קבע, אלא רחמים ותחנונים לפני המקום ברוך הוא, שנאמר: כי אל חנון ורחום הוא ארך אפים ורב חסד ונחם על הרעה.

Rabbi Shimon said: Be careful in reciting the *shema* and in the *amidah*; and when you pray, do not make your prayer fixed, but rather pleas for mercy and supplications before the blessed God, as it is written, "For He is gracious and compassionate, slow to anger, abounding in kindness, and renouncing punishment."[2]

Chapter One described the various rabbinic claims for the legitimacy of their verbal, Temple-less system of worship, and then the halakhic principles that developed to ensure the integrity and continuity of the new system. Chapter Two explored the functioning of a set of halakhic principles that pertain to the *berakhah* formula. We turn now from the question of the application of this liturgical blessing formula to issues affecting the body of the prayer texts themselves.

Mere mechanical recitation of the proper words at the proper time neither inspires the worshiper nor, the rabbis assert, pleases God. In order for prayer to be acceptable, it must be recited with intentionality, with attention to its meaning, with *kavvanah*.[3]

In the two mishnaic passages above, the Tannaim warn against making one's

1. *Mishnah Berakhot* 4:4.
2. *Mishnah Avot* 2:13, citing Joel 2:13.
3. See chap. 1, Principle A.8.

prayer קבע, fixed. Even the Amoraim were not quite sure how to understand this admonition; the redactors of the talmudic traditions listed a variety of interpretations, ranging from the existential to the practical. One group understood the Mishnah's warning to pertain only to the attitude in which the worshiper recites a standard set of prayer texts, ensuring that the prayers do not seem burdensome or routine and are recited in a truly supplicatory fashion. Another group, in contrast, heard a requirement that the worshiper actually modify and add to these standard prayers regularly.[4] Although this second understanding would seem to be the logical means of ensuring *kavvanah*, those concerned with the correctness of the wording of their prayers found any changes threatening. Thus both Talmuds immediately counter this suggestion of required innovation, citing R. Zeira's statement that his attempts to innovate caused him to err in the rest of his prayer.[5] As discussed in the previous chapter, modern readers can understand the words of R. Zeira–and of all who understand the mishnaic dictum to refer only to the manner in which one recites fixed texts–as an example of the natural human tendency towards invariance and rigidity in ritual behavior, which, hopefully, guarantees the liturgy's efficacy. The tension between this tendency to fixity and the requirement that prayer, to be acceptable, must be recited with *kavvanah* is the essential dynamic underlying the historical debates to be explored in this chapter.

Anthropologists studying ritual language have been puzzled by the degree to which the words of the ritual often have meaning, in the conventional, semantic sense, only to the ritual experts of the society (and sometimes not even to them), yet the ritual functions, serves a purpose, and has value for the society as a whole. In its inception the ritual language is fully understood–i.e., it can be recited and heard with *kavvanah* by all participants in the ritual. Over time, the language itself achieves a level of sanctity and becomes fixed. Because it does not reflect developments within the living culture, however, the unchanging sanctified language becomes archaic in both content and form; without delib-

4. *B. Berakhot* 29b; *P. Berakhot* 4:4, 8a.

5. Note that although the Palestinian Talmud seems to conclude from R. Zeira's statement that the proper interpretation of the Mishnah is its first one, that one should not recite prayer like one is reading a letter, it then continues on, recording that: רבי אליעזר היה מתפלל תפלה חדשה בכל יום. רבי אבהו היה מברך ברכה חדשה בכל יום (Rabbi Eliezer used to recite a new prayer every day. Rabbi Abbahu used to recite a new blessing every day). We cannot know for sure what this text means by a "new prayer" or a "new blessing," especially as these are the two sages upon whose tradition R. Zeira relies in support of his hesitancy to innovate. The Palestinian tradition is multivocal on this issue. Compare, too, the ambivalence over the issue of *iyyun tefillah* (contemplation on prayer), as discussed by Israel Ta-Shma, "'עיון תפילה' וראשית מעשה הפיוט," תרביץ נג (תשמ"ד), 285–288.

erate study, most worshipers can no longer understand the ritual's semantic meaning, which remains the domain of the elite. For the majority of the worshiping community, the power and meaning of the ritual must exist at the performative and/or illocutionary levels, where language functions not to convey information but to create situations and to inculcate and perpetuate social norms. As with the blessing formula, the very invariance of the entire liturgy comes to be an icon or index of the unchanging authority it represents–which helps guarantee the efficacy of the rite. This trend is reversed only by revival, reform, or revolution, any of which reinvest the ritual with language that is readily understood and meaningful to the entire community involved.[6]

This anthropological understanding of the ritual process may be applied, with certain qualifications, to Jewish liturgy. As we have seen, halakhah requires both semantic meaning and fixity in prayer texts. Because a minimum intentionality is always necessary, Jewish prayer could never legitimately become completely obscure. Although it was generally recited in a language other than the vernacular, it was assumed that all (men) would learn sufficient Hebrew for minimal comprehension. (Provision existed for vernacular prayer too, when necessary.[7]) Even when the liturgy became totally fixed, those worshipers who could not understand Hebrew knew that focused concentration on the words was necessary for the prayer to be acceptable. Thus the requirement of *kavvanah*, designed to counteract the effects of fixity, preserved at least elements of meaningfulness in Jewish prayer. Nevertheless, the tendency to ossification existed. Jakob Petuchowski has pointed out that what one generation created spontaneously, as an expression of their devotion and *kavvanah*, following generations adopted as fixed and mandatory parts of their liturgies.[8] Indeed, vast masses of Jews over

---

6. I have derived this understanding of the dynamics of ritual language from Maurice Bloch, "Symbols, Song, Dance and Features of Articulation: Is Religion an Extreme Form of Traditional Authority?," *Archives of European Sociology* 15 (1974): 55-81; Roy A. Rappaport, "The Obvious Aspects of Ritual," *Ecology, Meaning, and Religion* (Richmond, California: North Atlantic Books, c. 1979), 182; Stanley Jeyaraja Tambiah, "A Performative Approach to Ritual," *Culture, Thought and Social Action: An Anthropological Perspective* (Cambridge, MA and London, England: Harvard University Press, 1985), 123-166; and Wade T. Wheelock, "The Problem of Ritual Language: From Information to Situation," *JAAR* 50 (1982): 49-71.

7. This seems to have been especially true for women, who are obligated to pray at least the *amidah*. The commentary recorded by the students of Rabbenu Yonah of Gerona to the beginning of chap. 2 of the *Rif* on *Berakhot*, 7a, indicates that it was a universal custom for women to pray in vernacular tongues.

8. Jakob J. Petuchowski, "The Liturgy of the Synagogue: History, Structure and Contents," in *Approaches to Ancient Judaism*, vol. 4: *Studies in Liturgy, Exegesis, and Talmudic Narrative*, William Scott Green, ed. (Chico, California: Scholars Press, 1983), 41ff.

the course of the centuries have recited prayers without understanding them at all.

One issue that epitomizes the struggles to define an efficacious resolution of these tensions between *keva* and *kavvanah*, between fixity and spontaneity, between sanctified archaic prayer and meaningful language, and between halakhah and minhag, is the question of the inclusion of liturgical poetry in the statutory blessings of *keriat shema* and *amidah*.[9] This poetry, known as *piyyut*, developed in Palestine sometime during the talmudic period, and came into full flower in the late Byzantine world and the early years of the Arab conquest. Although some of it was designed to augment the standard liturgy, its most important early genres were created as alternatives to the standard texts of the prayers, to be presented by the *sheliaḥ tzibbur* as the public prayer of the synagogue on particular days. Thus, instead of a fixed and totally predictable liturgy, the Palestinian synagogue had a vehicle that allowed for change and artistic expression through the modes of poetry and, especially in later periods, choral music.[10]

This creativity, however, did not go unchecked. Wanting to preserve enough variety to alleviate boredom and ensure fervor in prayer, the community still needed to believe these innovative prayers would meet their obligations to the Divine. Hence, at least by the time for which we have evidence, elaborate sets of unwritten rules governed the language, content, structure, and general aesthetics of the payyetanic endeavor. While these rules and expectations changed slowly over the generations, they always channeled the creativity of the *payyetanim* and ensured that certain basic expectations of rabbinic liturgical halakhah would be met.[11] It is also likely that many individual congregations early

---

9. Much poetry exists for other liturgical stations, but almost all of these others filled spots where minhag dictated the prayers much more than halakhah, especially talmudic halakhah. As we shall see, Sefardi rabbis in the early-modern and modern periods extended this concern to *piyyut* inserted into *pesukei d'zimra* and its blessings.

10. See the description of this institution in, among other places: עזרא פליישר, "בין ארעי לקבע בתפילת הרבים בארץ־ישראל הקדומה," ספר הזכרון להרב יצחק נסים גאון...חלק השירה והפיוט, בעריכת מאיר בניהו, (ירושלים: יד הרב נסים, תשמ"ה), 7–15. For fuller descriptions of the early history of piyyut, see the relevant sections in Aharon Mirsky's books: הפיוט: התפתחותו בארץ־ישראל ובגולה (ירושלים: מאגנס, תש"ן); ראשית הפיוט (ירושלים: הסוכנות היהודית לארץ־ישראל, תשכ"ה). The best concise English description is Jakob J. Petuchowski, *Theology and Poetry: Studies in the Medieval Piyyut*, The Littman Library of Jewish Civilization (London, Henley and Boston: Routledge & Kegan Paul, 1978), 11-15.

11. The most complete description of these rules in each historical period is to be found in the relevant sections of Ezra Fleischer's books: שירת־הקודש העברית בימי־הביניים (ירושלים: כתר, 1975); היוצרות בהתהוותם והתפתחותם (ירושלים: מאגנס, תשמ"ד).

A critical question continues to be the degree to which the average Jew even understood

established fixed cycles of *piyyut*, so that the same poetry was always recited on particular occasions. These specific cycles account, at least in part, for the tendency of later *payyetanim* to write new genres of *piyyut*; existing stations within the liturgy of their congregations were filled. At the same time, any change in this cycle would constitute a liturgical revolution, a breaking of the invariance, and a drawing of attention anew to the meaning of the prayers.

Early *piyyut* had value not only as a source of *kavvanah*, controlled variation, and additional meaning in the liturgy. It also served an important symbolic function. As explained in Chapter One, after the Romans, by destroying the Temple, halted the sole biblically sanctioned means of covenantal worship of God, the creators of the rabbinic system of prayer drew on Temple themes and symbols to give authority and legitimacy to the new ritual structure. Ever mindful that the synagogue and rabbinic liturgy were not the Temple and its sacrifices, the rabbis were careful to preserve distinctions between the two realms. The only remaining irrefutable link between Israel and God was Torah, especially in its written form, but also, to the rabbinic mind, in its oral interpretations. Thus, although the orientation of the synagogue building was almost always towards Jerusalem, the internal focal point of the building became the Torah ark and its scroll(s). This ark, the only ritual object of the synagogue not confined to special holiday use, began to appear in the archaeological record as a fixed architectural feature by the fourth century, located on or near the wall facing Jerusalem.[12] Thus, by the period in which we can posit the pre-history of *piyyut* as an increasingly important part of synagogue liturgy in Palestine, the Temple orientation of synagogue prayer was symbolically and physically mediated by the Torah.[13]

It is safe to assume that language drawn from and alluding to Scripture permeated and validated any standardized rabbinic liturgy from the earliest times. Hebrew, the language of prayer, was first and foremost the language of Scripture, and its liturgical use gave all prayer sanctity and a sense of efficacy. But *piyyut* took this relationship much further. Our earliest known works integrate

---

the difficult language and embedded allusions that constituted much of the payyetanic corpus. Shulamit Elizur has recently suggested that the various segments of the *kedushta* were written with differing degrees of difficulty precisely so as to give the less educated of the community access to the content of the poetry. See her "קהל המתפלל והקדושתא הקדומה," בתוך כנסת עזרא: ספרות וחיים בבית הכנסת, אסופת מאמרים מוגשת לעזרא פליישר, בעריכת שולמית אליצור, משה דוד הר, אביגדור שנאן, גרשון שקד (ירושלים: יד יצחק בן־צבי ומכון בן־צבי לחקר קהילות ישראל במזרח, תשנ"ה), 190–171.

12. See chap. 1, pp. 7-8.

13. By the time of *piyyut*, we can also assume that rabbinic ritual had become the ritual of the synagogue.

direct citations of biblical verses and learned allusions to Oral Torah into their substitutions for the standard liturgy, and, by the late Byzantine period, *piyyutim* often devote their main theme to that day's scriptural lection. Torah, both written and oral, became the mediator for the Jew's prayer to God, not only as the physical focus of the synagogue setting, but also as the very substance of the prayers themselves.[14] Although it would be hard to prove that Jews were always conscious of this aspect of *piyyut*, recognition of it certainly lies behind the arguments of those attributing the origins of *piyyut* to a "period of persecution" when, because Torah study was officially forbidden, the sages substituted poetic versions of rabbinic traditions for the statutory public prayers.[15] Whatever the historicity of this tradition, it clearly recognizes that a central symbolic function of *piyyut* was to integrate the Torah and its study into prayer.

If this is the case, then, not only does prayer replace sacrifices, but, through *piyyut*, it encompasses another route to God, that of revelation itself. Lacking explicit support in canonized rabbinic sources, it is a supreme example of a minhag developed in response to needs perceived to be unmet by the halakhic system. Integrated widely into Jewish worship, it was a means of ensuring *kavvanah*, of creating meaningful prayer, and of increasing the efficacy of that prayer by making revealed knowledge its medium.

This is not to say that *piyyut* existed outside the parameters established by the principles of liturgical halakhah. An institution like *piyyut* relies on the assumption that the prayer of the *sheliaḥ tzibbur* can legitimately fulfill the obligations of others,[16] and that individuals can meet their own obligations by listening and responding "amen."[17] Although the language of most *piyyut* was Hebrew, some was composed in other languages.[18] No matter what might become the text of

---

14. An extreme form of this incorporation of Scripture into prayer was of course the early Karaite liturgy. Anan called for the exclusive use of biblical language. See: אברהם אליהו הרכבי, ספר המצות לענן: לתולדות הקראים וספרותה (ס"ט פטרסבורג, 1903; הדפסה שנית בתוך מספרי המצות הראשונים לבני מקרא (ירושלים: מקור, תשכ"ט)), 158. The later Karaite prayerbooks incorporated vast quantities of *piyyut*, differing from its rabbanite kindred primarily in its relative avoidance of midrashic and talmudic allusions.

15. See below, pp. 122-123, for a discussion of these traditions.

16. See chap. 1, Principle A.4.

17. See chap. 1, Principle A.5.

18. See chap. 1, Principle A.7. Most *piyyut* that we know of in the vernacular, particularly in Aramaic, was not written as a replacement for prayers, or even for insertion into the statutory liturgy. Rather, it was an addition to the Torah reading, or an elaborated mandatory translation (*targum*). See, for example Michael L. Klein, *Genizah Manuscripts of Palestinian Targum to the Pentateuch* (Cincinnati: Hebrew Union College Press, 1986); and יוסף היינימן, "שרידים מיצירתם הפיוטית של המתורגמנים הקדומים," בתוך עיוני תפילה, בעריכת אביגדור שנאן (ירושלים: מאגנס, תשמ"א; מהספרות ד (תשל"ג), 362–375), 148–167. But we have some evidence for vernacular

the blessing itself, however, *piyyut* always maintained a proper eulogy,[19] and, as discussed above, *kavvanah*, at least at a minimal level, was always a requirement for effective prayer–and thus, for *piyyut* as well.[20]

However, other halakhic principles became grounds for disputes over the legitimacy of the payyetanic endeavor. Some authorities considered it to be a burden that detracted from the community's honor.[21] At times, the contents of the poems were questionable.[22] Some *piyyut* created situations where all *amidot* of the day no longer contained the same references.[23] Others made reference to the special events of the day or added petitionary language in inappropriate places.[24] According to some understandings, *piyyut* was particularly problematic because it changed the established form of the benediction.[25] As we shall see, medieval detractors of *piyyut* also extended the meanings of additional talmudic laws in their attempts to create firm halakhic objections to the integration of liturgical poetry within the blessings of the statutory liturgy.

However, none of the halakhic arguments ever categorically denied the validity of all liturgical poetry. *Piyyutim* have been written for almost every part of every synagogue service of any significance and for many home and life cycle rituals as well. Many of these genres of *piyyut* raise no halakhic issues because they fill places whose liturgy is fully a matter of minhag, like the prayers introducing and concluding the synagogue service, surrounding the reading of the Torah, or at a festive meal or life cycle celebration. At issue in the medieval world were only those *piyyutim* written for inclusion in the blessings of *keriat shema* and *amidah*. These two essential parts of the daily statutory prayer were well defined by the Mishnah and the Talmud, and any alteration to them became potential halakhic issues. Indeed, until the early modern period, the halakhic debates over *piyyut* focus almost exclusively on the legitimacy of these two types of poetic inserts.[26]

---

prayer, and even for vernacular *piyyut* in Avignon in the sixteenth century. See חירם פרי (פלאום), "התפלה והפיוט בלשון־לעז בימי־הביניים," תרביץ 24 (1955) 426–440.

19. See chap. 1, Principle B.4.
20. See chap. 1, Principle A.8.
21. See chap. 1, Principle A.9.
22. See chap. 1, Principle C.1.
23. See chap. 1, Principle C.3.
24. See chap. 1, Principles C.5 and 6.
25. See chap. 1, Principle B.7.
26. Although poetic versions of the *birkat hamazon* did circulate and created their own halakhic issues, we know much less about them because they were much less public. We will not consider them here. Similarly, poetic versions of individual blessings for special scriptural readings (after the *megillah* on Purim, the Ten Commandments on Shavuot, the completion of the Torah on Simḥat Torah, etc.) or parts of the Passover *haggadah* caused

To what extent was the debate over reciting *piyyut* in the synagogue service framed by the principles of liturgical law–and to what extent by rabbinic efforts to ensure *kavvanah* and counteract the tendency of invariant rituals to lose meaning? As we shall see, the sources to which Jews looked for inspiration and meaning changed over time; their need to integrate those sources with received liturgical traditions was a major factor influencing attitudes and halakhic stances toward *piyyut*.

## *Geonic Attitudes Toward* Piyyut

As a Palestinian Jewish creation, *piyyut* almost automatically became a bone of contention in the early Babylonian geonic struggles for hegemony over the Palestinian world.[27] In their struggles to establish the predominance of their own customs, early Geonim introduced many of the halakhic arguments that would echo against *piyyut* over the next millennium and more. For these rabbis, the authority of an invariant liturgy that could be legislated to other communities was an important and public political tool. Meaning came into the prayers, not through textual innovation, but through the intentionality the worshiper devoted to a narrowly defined, halakhically correct liturgy. Only as these geonic political concerns for halakhic hegemony became less compelling–and as the people outside of the academies, in spite of geonic objection, brought *piyyut* into the Babylonian synagogue itself–did the Geonim moderate their halakhic stance.

The earliest extant geonic responses to *piyyut* come from the school of the mid-eighth-century Rav Yehudai Gaon. The Babylonian rabbinic attitude of this period to the recitation of *piyyut* is preserved in two sources. One, *Sefer Halakhot Gedolot*, had vast influence and is widely cited by the Rishonim. The other, the letter written by Pirkoi ben Baboi addressed to the Jews of Kairouan, circa 800, was discovered in the Cairo Geniza. Our only clue as to the impact of this communication is that the number of fragments demonstrates the existence of multiple copies of this document–in a city that was neither its destination nor its place of origin. Its arguments against the recitation of *piyyut* were

eyebrows to be raised at certain periods, but never became longterm issues. After the expulsion from Spain and the removal of *piyyut* from the central parts of the service rite to before *barekhu*, some Sefardi authorities began to question too whether *piyyut* could legitimately interrupt *pesukei dezimra*. See below, p. 175.

27. Several important studies exist on the geonic rulings about *piyyut*. See especially Lawrence A. Hoffman, *The Canonization of the Synagogue Service* (Notre Dame, London: University of Notre Dame Press, 1979; rpt. 1986), 66-71; and Louis Ginzberg, *Ginzei Schechter*, II:504-573, especially 508-527: "יחס חכמי ארץ ישראל ויחס הגאונים אל הפיוט".

not cited directly by later authorities known to us, but its most important individual points continued to be rehashed. Its impact in Kairouan was not great, for Palestinian influences were still strong there several centuries later in the period of Sherira and Hai Gaon.[28]

We read in *Sefer Halakhot Gedolot*:[29]

> אמ׳ רב יהודה לעולם אל ישאל אדם צרכיו לא בשלש ראשונות ולא בשלש אחרונות אלא באמצעיות דאמר ר׳ חנינא בשלש ראשונות דומה לעבד שהסדיר שבח לפני רבו באמצעיות דומה לעבד שמבקש פרס מרבו באחרונות דומה לעבד שנטל פרס מרבו ונפטר והלך לו. ומהכה לא שבקינן רבנן למימר (מעומד) [מעמד] דאפילו זכרנו לחיים במגן לא אמרינן וכל שכן זכור רחמיך וכבוש כעסך במודים לא אמרינן אבל ובספר חיים אמרינן בשים שלום סליקו להו שמונה עשרה והוה ליה כתחנונים.
>
> Rav Yehudah said: One should never petition for one's own needs in the first or last three blessings [of the *amidah*], but only in the intermediate blessings [on weekdays], for R. Ḥanina said, "In the first three blessings, one is like a servant arranging the praise of his master. In the intermediate blessings, one is like a servant who requests a reward from his master. In the final three blessings, one is like a servant who received a reward from his master and took his leave."[30] Based on this, the rabbis did not allow the recitation of *piyyut*, for they do not even [allow the] recitation of the [the High Holy Day insert] *zokhreinu leḥayyim* in the *avot*, and they [objected] even more so to the recitation of *zekhor raḥamekha ukhevosh ka-askha* in *modim*; but they do recite *uvesefer ḥayyim* in *sim shalom*, because the *amidah* is completed and this is like a supplicatory prayer.

*Halakhot Gedolot* understands *B. Berakhot* 34a to have established a principle that petitionary prayer belongs only in the intermediate blessings of the weekday *amidah*. Therefore, this geonic text prohibits *piyyut* (*ma'amad*)[31] along with all but the last of the High Holy Day insertions, for *piyyut* should not be intermingled with the praise and thanksgiving of the beginning and concluding groups of blessings.[32] If these short inserts are halakhically problematic, then

---

28. See the discussion of the dating and identification of this letter, above, chap. 2, p. 51.

29. Ed. Azriel Hildesheimer, II: 33.

30. *B. Berakhot* 34a.

31. Hildesheimer here corrects all the received versions of this passage, which uniformly read מעומד, on the basis of citations of it that understand the word to refer to *piyyut*.

32. The final High Holy Day insert, *uvesefer ḥayyim*, is permitted because, coming at the very end of the *amidah*, it is like the beginning of the private supplicatory prayer. This is a very weak distinction, as this insert, to the best of my knowledge, always precedes the eulogy of the blessing, meaning that the *amidah* is not yet over. For some reason, the school of Geonim objecting to these insertions compromised with popular custom in this case.

how much more so is *piyyut*! Although *Halakhot Gedolot* was an influential text, especially in Ashkenaz,[33] we find that this particular passage had fairly limited impact. Rabbenu Tam, the great defender of *piyyut*, explicitly and harshly criticized those relying on this ruling.[34] Major manuscript traditions of *Halakhot Gedolot* fail to include it at all, perhaps simply because it contradicted the scribe's active practice.[35] Finally, this particular attack on the halakhic underpinnings of *piyyut* was itself, as we shall see shortly, undermined by later Geonim.

If we accept Pirkoi ben Baboi's[36] claim that he says nothing that he has not received from his teacher (a student of Rabbi Yehudai[37]), his lengthy arguments provide a much fuller witness to the venom spilled by that Gaon against those who recite *piyyut*. Those arguments may be summarized as follows:

1. Anyone who alters a talmudically ordained blessing fails to fulfill his prayer obligations. To add to the text is blasphemous and causes one to be uprooted from the world to come, because no one should even claim to relate all the praises of God. Any deletion from the text, even of only a single letter, makes one worthy of receiving a death sentence.[38]
2. Even worse than simple additions are additions with inappropriate content, especially petitions in the first and last three benedictions of the *amidah*.[39]
3. Even worse is reference in public, or even by an individual, to מעשה מרכבה, to mystical knowledge about the divine chariot or throne.[40]

---

33. See: ישראל תא־שמע, "קליטתם של ספרי הרי"ף, הר"ח, ו"הלכות גדולות" בצרפת ובאשכנז במאות הי"א–י"ב," קרית ספר 55 (תש"ם), 197–201.

34. *Maḥzor Vitry*, 364; *Shibbolei Haleket*, ed. Mirsky, 215.

35. Hildesheimer says (in his n.32 to this text) that he has added this passage here from the Warsaw edition because of its importance; he suggests that the scribes of the Milan and Berlin manuscripts deliberately omitted it because this section contradicted the liturgical tradition of their own communities. However, Neil Danzig dates the beginnings of these two manuscript traditions to the eighth (ninth?) century, which may make Hildesheimer's addition of this passage questionable. See Danzig's: מבוא לספר הלכות פסוקות עם תשלום הלכות פסוקות (ניו־יורק וירושלים: בית המדרש לרבנים באמריקה, תשנ"ג), 186–191. *Sefer Hapardes*, 230, ascribed to Rashi, cites our passage without any reference to *piyyut* at all. The situation is similar in *Or Zarua* 20, 12a-b and the *Tur*, OH 112.

36. Louis Ginzberg, *Ginzei Schechter* II: 504-573, 638-639 and ב.מ. לוין, "משרידי הגניזה," תרביץ ב (תרצ"א), 383–410.

37. *Ginzei Schechter*, 571.

38. These sentiments derive more and less directly from *B. Megillah* 18a and *B. Shabbat* 118b. Pirkoi ben Baboi has expanded the applications of the talmudic dicta.

39. *B. Berakhot* 34a; *Avodah Zarah* 8a.

40. *M. Ḥagigah* 2:1 and its discussion in the *gemara* (13a ff.) establish the esoteric nature of this subject. Ginzberg, 546, suggested that the reference here may be to a Kalirian piyyut. However, we now know that vast genres of *piyyut* elaborated specifically on mystical themes and that the mystics themselves produced poetry and prayer texts which influenced the

4. Even worse is any interruption of the statutory liturgy to insert *piyyut.*
5. One cannot claim that such interruptions are prohibited for the individual but allowed for the *sheliaḥ tzibbur.* The prayer of the *sheliaḥ tzibbur* is more important because it fulfills the obligations of many, not just of an individual.
6. The sages established prayers so precisely that they dictated exactly how and when to perform many minutiae like bowing,[41] waving the lulav,[42] and the posture for *shema,*[43] and in the last they established that anyone who does not follow the school of Hillel should be sentenced to death. If they were so exacting, then anyone who deviates by the tiniest hair from their words should be sentenced to death.[44]
7. God pays attention to everyone's prayers, except to those who add extra praises.[45]
8. Rav Yehudai derived from this: Any blessing not in the Talmud may not be recited, and one is forbidden to add a single letter. We can extrapolate from the few preserved talmudic arguments over wording (המלך הקדוש/מלך הקדוש and אהבה רבה/אהבת עולם),[46] that the sages struggled to establish exact texts for all the prayers, which we must respect.[47]
9. The Palestinian custom of reciting *piyyut* on the Sabbath comes from a period when persecutors would not allow them to pray normally. Now that the Christian decrees no longer hold, and Palestinian Jews are under Islamic rule, they are forbidden to recite anything other than the proper texts established by the sages in the right places in the right order.
10. No insertions of petitionary nature are allowed in the first and last three blessings for the Sabbath or the High Holy Days.[48]

Although we have no evidence that Pirkoi ben Baboi's letter had any influence, almost all of his arguments echo in later diatribes against–and in defenses

---

statutory liturgy. See, for instance, Fleischer's discussion of the אופן in his היוצרות בהתהוותם והתפתחותם, 252 ואילך; and מאיר בר־אילן, סתרי תפילה והיכלות, (רמת גן: אוניברסיטת בר־אילן, 1987).

41. *B. Berakhot* 34a.

42. *B. Sukkah* 37b.

43. *B. Berakhot* 11a.

44. *B. Bava Kama* 50a and *B. Yevamot* 121b, in midrashic contexts totally unrelated to our issue, indicate: שהקדוש ברוך הוא מדקדק עם סביביו כחוט השערה (that the Holy One, blessed be He, deals strictly with those round about Him even to a hair's breadth). Pirkoi ben Baboi's turning this into a death threat and applying it to liturgical issues has no preserved precedent.

45. This is an oblique reference to *B. Berakhot* 33b and *B. Megillah* 18a and 25a.

46. *B. Berakhot* 11b-12b.

47. See the preceding chapter for a detailed history of this legal principle.

48. Compare the argument of *Halakhot Gedolot,* above, p. 118.

of–the payyetanic endeavor. We may assume then that it genuinely reflects the content and tenor of the early geonic dispute with the proponents of *piyyut*, and that although it is the only such document we know of, it was not entirely unique.

Pirkoi ben Baboi makes extensive reference to the Babylonian Talmud, but in most cases, he extrapolates from or exaggerates the amoraic arguments. Clearly, his primary point develops the tannaitic principle that one may not change the established form of a benediction.[49] As discussed in Chapter One, the Babylonian Amoraim disapproved of any deviation from the decreed prayer formulae. In constrast, the Palestinians, while insisting on the established structure of the prayers, allowed more variation in specific wording. This geonic issue, then, at least in part, is a continuation of a long-standing debate between the two halakhic schools and liturgical traditions. If we assume that Yehudai Gaon and his students had a relatively fixed wording for their prayers, we can also understand their reading of the talmudic passages from which Pirkoi ben Baboi draws his arguments. He cites *B. Megillah* 18a, which, after describing the organization and establishment of the statutory *amidah* at Yavneh, reads: מכאן ואילך אסור לספר בשבחו של הקב"ה (from this point on, it is forbidden to speak praises of the Holy One, blessed be He). The Talmud continues with the warning attributed to Rabbi Yoḥanan: המספר בשבחו של הקב"ה יותר מדאי נעקר מן העולם (One who speaks too much in praise of the Holy One, blessed be He, will be uprooted from the world). If the amoraic warning against adding additional praises refers to the incidents recorded in *B. Berakhot* 33b and *B. Megillah* 25a, where prayer leaders were rebuked for expanding the biblical list of divine attributes in the *avot*, then it might naturally extend also to the recitation of *piyyut*. If, however, the Talmud in *B. Megillah* 18a, having listed the structure of the *amidah*, was merely warning against deviating from this structure by adding new paragraphs to it, the geonic reading does not reflect its original intention. The *gemara* specifically interdicts changes to the specific wording of the blessing only in a very few instances, the most notable being the opening praises of the *avot*.[50] Given that variant texts existed for the most basic prayers of the statutory liturgy, and that modern historians can demonstrate development in these texts even in Babylonia;[51] and that the Babylonian statutory prayers, perhaps already by the period of Yehudai Gaon and Pirkoi ben Baboi included much, even entire bless-

49. Chap. 1, Principle B.7. *Tosefta Berakhot* 4:5; *B. Berakhot* 40b; *P. Berakhot* 6:2, 10b.

50. *B. Berakhot* 33b; *B. Megillah* 25a.

51. See, for instance, among the various articles by Naphtali Wieder: "לחקר נוסח העמידה במנהג בבל הקדמון," סיני עח (תשל"ו), צו–קכב, רעט–רפד; "לחקר מנהג בבל הקדמון," תרביץ לז (תשכ"ח), 264–240 ,157–135.

ings,[52] that was not specifically prescribed in amoraic sources, Pirkoi ben Baboi's absolutist claims ring hollow. Even his sources could and would be interpreted differently.[53] Pirkoi ben Baboi interprets the halakhah narrowly and applies his theoretical rulings selectively. Obviously, factors other than halakhah itself were determinative.

Pirkoi ben Baboi's objections to the content of various insertions into the statutory prayers are potentially more serious; as we saw in *Halakhot Gedolot*, the tendency to add petitionary language to texts of praise and thanksgiving raised the ire of liturgical purists of this period. The talmudic principle is clear: it is impolite to petition God, except in the intermediate blessings of the weekday *amidah*.[54] Here in his fifth point, Pirkoi ben Baboi responds negatively to the counterargument itself recorded only in later geonic materials, that the restriction on the location of the petitions applies only to individual needs. The *sheliaḥ tzibbur* and even individuals, however, may add petitions anywhere for the communal good. In rejecting this provision, Pirkoi ben Baboi supports the logical reading of talmudic halakhah over and against those trying to justify minhag.

But Pirkoi ben Baboi also makes quite free use of talmudic materials, bending them to his own polemics. For instance, in his sixth point, he refers to God's precision in His demands, taking his proof from a stock line used in some talmudic midrashic discussions that have no integral connection to these liturgical issues at all. Pirkoi ben Baboi's tone, his piling on of details only vaguely relevant, and his constant threats of dire consequences, all lend to his halakhic arguments a sense of desperation and polemic, rather than the absolute authority he sought.

In his one non-halakhic argument, in his ninth point, Pirkoi ben Baboi, in the name of Yehudai Gaon, invokes a persecution theory for the origins of *piyyut*. His was probably not the only geonic document to voice this theory; *Sefer HaItim* cites it in the name of רבוותא, *rabbevata*, the rabbinic masters between the Savoraim and the Geonim."[55] Jews have, throughout history, resorted to such

52. We cannot date such blessings as ברוך שאמר and ברוך ה' לעולם/יראו עינינו, which have likely geonic origins. It is possible that they became current later than the period of Yehudai Gaon and his school.

53. See *Maḥzor Vitry*, 370, #331, which specifically labels *piyyut* as "praise of God" and argues for its inclusion in the blessings.

54. Chap. 1, Principle C.6.

55. *Sefer HaItim*, 252; Elbogen, *Jewish Prayer*, 222 (Heb. 213), understands the term to mean "early masters." I follow Robert Brody, *The Geonim of Babylonia and the Shaping of Medieval Jewish Culture* (New Haven: Yale University Press, 1998), 174. See too the description in the twelfth-century polemic, "Ifhâm al-Jahûd" by the apostate Samau'al b. Jahjâ

pseudo-historical claims to explain the development of customs that, from a halakhic and logical perspective, ought not to exist. Although *piyyut* flowered during the period of the early Christian persecution of Jews, it almost certainly did not originate then; it was much too complex an institution to have provided a universal and immediate response to "evil decrees." In addition, the appeal of *piyyut* was likely never limited to those areas directly affected by the Byzantine persecutions.[56] But the mythical connection of historical persecutions with the origins of the payyetanic institution helped the Babylonian opponents of *piyyut* justify its development in a community officially subject to rabbinic law. There is no indication that Palestinian Jews had a similar explanation for the origins of their custom. Thus they most likely shrugged off Yehudai Gaon's argument as mere polemic. And even if they did accept his explanation of the origins of *piyyut*, the arguments that Babylonian talmudic halakhah should now prevail in Palestine were of no impact, for they replied to Yehudai Gaon according to their tradition, מנהג מבטל הלכה (minhag nullifies halakhah).[57]

The only other extant geonic traditions that explicitly forbid the recitation of *piyyut* are quite problematic, as their content is inconsistent with other known opinions of their attributed authors. They derive from a commentary on the *Sheiltot* written by Rabbi Yoḥanan d'Ochrida in Bulgaria and published by J.N. Epstein, who surmises that the author is quoting *Sefer HaItim* or some other early Spanish work.[58] But even if this text is corrupt, it had some currency in Spain and later in the Balkans, and is thus of interest to us here. The first citation, questionably attributed to Rav Naḥshon, states that, in the academy and in any

al-Magribî, first published by Martin Schreiner, *MGWJ* 42 (1898): 220, in German; and in Elbogen, *Jewish Prayer*, 223 (Heb., 213-214). It is significant that *piyyut* seems to be one of the few cases where it is argued that a liturgical practice supposedly developed in response to persecution should be dropped once the persecution is over. The other exception is the inclusion of *shema* in the *kedushah*. On these matters, see Jacob Mann, "Changes in the Divine Service of the Synagogue due to Religious Persecutions," *HUCA* 4 (1927): 241-311.

56. Fleischer, ...שירת הקודש, 51-53. See, too, the editor's comment in Elbogen, *Jewish Prayer*, 223-224 (Heb., 214-215).

57. *Ginzei Schechter* II: 559-560. For a discussion of the status of minhag in Palestine, see: ישראל מ. תא־שמע, "הלכה מנהג ומסורת ביהדות אשכנז במאות הי"א - י"ב," בתוך מנהג אשכנז הקדמון - חקר ועיון (ירושלים: מאגנס, תשנ"ב; מסידרא ג (תשמ"ז), 85–161), 61–74, especially his discussion of the stance of Yehudai Gaon as expressed by Pirkoi ben Baboi, p. 71.

58. J.N. Epstein, "Sur les 'Chapitres' de Ben Baboi," *REJ* 75 (1922): 184, from Ms. Berlin Or. oct. 333, 124a-b. The texts are reprinted in *Otzar Hageonim*, *Berakhot*, *Teshuvot*, p. 70, #179. See also the comments of Simcha Emanuel, ...תשובות הגאונים החדשות, #166, p. 242, n. 22, who cites a manuscript that presents these three comments as more integrally connected one to another.

place where there are rabbis, no *piyyut* is recited, no *ḥazzan* is admitted who knows *piyyut*, and any synagogue that allows its recitation attests to the fact that its congregants are not scholars.[59] Questions of attribution and dating aside, it is quite clear that this diatribe attacks a world, most likely within the confines of Babylonia, in which *piyyut* had currency among the common people. Opposition arose from the elite scholastic culture of the academies.

The second citation, attributed to Rav Amram, is an objection to any changes in the talmudically ordained prayers, and a call for the removal of any *ḥazzan* who deviates from the official form of the blessings. However, only in the context of this *Sheiltot* commentary do these words seem necessarily to apply to *piyyut*. If read in the context of other discussions in *Seder Rav Amram Gaon*, the passage can be understood as an objection, not to *piyyut* per se, but to special forms of the benedictions for the Sabbath and holidays that were not the custom of the academy[60] or to grosser deviations from the proper outline of the prayers.

The final comment in this collection is attributed to Rav Tzemaḥ (b. Shlomo), the great judge of the gate, the vice-principle of the exilarch-run academy in the second half of the ninth century.[61] But again, like the tradition ascribed to Amram, this citation does not specifically mention *piyyut* and only calls for the excommunication and removal of any *sheliaḥ tzibbur* who adds to established prayers and expands the texts. Indeed, Louis Ginzberg tries to claim that Tzemaḥ is not referring to the recitation of *piyyut*;[62] but unlike Amram who speaks only of changing the forms, Tzemaḥ refers to additions and expansions to the text. This can have little reference to anything but *piyyut*. However, since this is the extent of his comment, we can learn little more from it.[63]

---

59. Ginzberg (*Ginzei Schechter*, II:510) strongly doubts the attribution to Naḥshon, as does Hoffman (*Canonization*..., 70), primarily on the grounds that a Suran Gaon, following directly after two very influential Geonim who allowed *piyyut*, would be unlikely to contradict his predecessors so blatantly. Ginzberg's attempts to emend the text need not concern us here.

60. *Seder Rav Amram Gaon*, ed. Goldschmidt, 61-62, 82. While these special forms of benedictions are at their heart payyetanic, these are *piyyutim* which have entered the realm of fixed liturgy. Although this category of concern is not unimportant, it is somewhat tangential to our question here. Note that Natronai, Amram's contemporary, voices a similar objection to the Kairouan community's expanded version of the *kedushat hayom* for the kiddush beginning the seder, on the grounds that the text should be identical for all holidays. *Otzar Hageonim*, *Pesaḥim*, *Teshuvot*, p. 90, #221.

61. Brody, *The Geonim*..., 41, 49, 60.

62. *Ginzei Schechter*, II:510.

63. His terminology does not allude to *M. Berakhot* 1:4 and its complex definitions of long and short benedictions, an argument that first appears only in eleventh-century Ashkenaz.

Thus the letter of Pirkoi ben Baboi remains the only known extensive geonic document to devote much energy to criticizing the legitimacy of *piyyut*; indeed, later Geonim, for the most part, moderated their opposition to the institution. They were less consumed with quests for political control over the Palestinian rabbinate[64] and, perhaps more significantly, were coming to accept *piyyut*, within limits, as a recognized part of Babylonian ritual. We can assume that *piyyut* did not arrive in Babylonia under the aegis of the great academies, whose scholars had the intellectual ability and piety to generate the *kavvanah* that kept their statutory prayers meaningful. More likely, as can be inferred from the geonic responsa cited above, common people were attracted to the aesthetics of *piyyut* and found that this poetry and its musical settings elevated their worship experience. We know that distinct congregations of Babylonians existed from relatively early times in Palestine. Some scholars speculate that the dean of all classical *payyetanim*, Elazar b"R. Kalir, belonged to such a group.[65] Those who traveled back to Babylonia no doubt shared their embellished Babylonian rite. Merchants trading between the two centers also served as conduits for cultural exchange. It was simpler for the theoreticians of the academy to compromise with this popular culture than to continue to crusade against it, especially when there were no longer political reasons for doing so.

Ezra Fleischer points to yet another element of this dynamic: the simple differential in the time required for the longer Babylonian annual cycle of Torah readings versus the shorter Palestinian "triennial" cycle. The Babylonians did not fail to appreciate the aesthetic qualities of *piyyut*; but they did not want to detract from the liturgical centrality of their Torah reading. Therefore, as is evident from the following responsum, they were more open to the inclusion of *piyyut* on festivals and fast days when their Torah readings were shorter.[66]

Consequently, we find most geonic texts either trying to justify the institution and place some limits on it, or else merely assuming its existence. Talmudic law could not be jettisoned, but loopholes could be found. Thus:

---

64. See Hoffman's *Canonization*..., 8-9, 60-171.

65. Ezra Fleischer, ...היוצרות, 94; and "לוח מועדי השנה בפיוט לר' אלעזר בירבי קיליר," תרביץ נב (תשמ"ג), 223–272. See, however, Fleischer's more recent discussion in his article, "קריאה חד־שנתית ותלת־שנתית בתורה בבית הכנסת הקדום," תרביץ סא (תשנ"ב), 40, where he speculates that some Palestinians always used the annual Torah cycle, and that Kalir belonged to such a tradition. If so, his having written for the annual Torah cycle does not prove participation in a community of Babylonians.

66. עזרא פליישר, תפילה ומנהגי תפילה ארץ־ישראליים בתקופת הגניזה (ירושלים: מאגנס, תשמ"ח), 294, הע' 5.

> לרבינו נטרונאי גאון זצ"ל האומרים פיוטים באבות וגבורות ובכל תפלות ובכל רגל ורגל מעניינו ומרבין בו דברי אגדה ובט"ב ובפורים. אם אומרים בכל ברכה וברכה מעין אותה ברכה ובר"ה וביוה"כ דברי ריצוי וסליחות ובט"ב דברי חורבן הבית הרשות בידו. ועקר שאומרין בכל ברכה וברכה מעין פתיחתה ומעין חתימתה. [ובאמצע אומרים דברי אגדה ודברי שבח של הקב"ה שפיר דמי] אבל בקבוץ גליות ובהקבץ בתולות וכל כיוצא בהן וכל הדומה להן אסור לאומרו, ואם אמר מלמדין אותו שלא יאמר כך.
>
> [A responsum] of Rabbenu Natronai Gaon, of blessed memory. Those who recite *piyyutim* in the *avot* and *gevurot* and in all the prayers, on each festival on the topic of the festival, and on the Ninth of Av and Purim, incorporating much aggadic material: if, in every benediction, they incorporate [*piyyut*] *me-ein haberakhah* (which expresses the essence of the blessing), and on Rosh Hashanah and Yom Kippur, they incorporate poetry asking for atonement and begging forgiveness (*seliḥot*), and on the Ninth of Av, poetry about the destruction of the Temple, they are allowed to do so. But the essential element is that, in each and every blessing, they use [transitional] language related to the statutory opening phrase and concluding benediction. In the middle, it is best that it discusses topics from the aggadah or praise of God. But one is forbidden to recite *bekibbutz galiyot* and *behikkavetz betulot* or anything similar to them or of their ilk, and if someone does recite them, we teach him not to do so.[67]

A short century after Yehudai Gaon's vehement renunciation of those who recite *piyyut*, the leading Suran Gaon, Natronai, explicitly permitted the practice, but with two restrictions: the content had to be appropriate to the blessing or the occasion; and, more essentially, one had to include the themes of the beginning and ending of the standard blessing. He adds a further note, prohibiting two specific *piyyutim* and any others like them. Unfortunately, without a certain identification of these particular texts, we cannot know the basis of his objection to them.[68]

Most of the arguments expressed by Pirkoi ben Baboi find no explicit counterargument here, for Natronai's assumptions in approaching the issue are com-

---

67. *Otzar Hageonim*, *Berakhot*, *Teshuvot*, p. 70, #178. Compare the similar responsum, apparently attributed to R. Sar Shalom, the immediate predecessor of Natronai, and not R. Yitzḥak bar Yaakov Gaon, as found in the collection חמדה גנוזה, #145, in the two recent publications of Ms. Guenzburg 566: תשובות הגאונים..., מהדורת אלעזר הורביץ, עמ' 224, חלק ב, סימן פ"א; תשובות הגאונים החדשות..., מהדורת שמחה עמנואל, עמ' 241, סי' קסו (See too the editors' notes to this responsum).

68. For a summary of the attempts to identify these texts, see Hoffman, *Canonization*, 209, n. 12. The version of this responsum found in *Shibbolei Haleket*, ed. Mirsky, 211, does not include this last prohibition.

pletely different. Most significantly, we know from the work of Natronai's contemporary, Rav Amram Gaon, that the recitation of *piyyut* at least on Yom Kippur was a fully accepted and expected part of the liturgy. However, the academy itself did not add extensively to the statutory texts, and Amram is consistently careful to indicate that payyetanic additions are fully optional.[69] For these Geonim, then, *piyyut* was no longer a cultural manifestation of a foreign group they were attempting to dominate. Without the motivation of a *Kulturkampf* and with the inroads made by this minhag into the popular custom of Babylonia itself, the rabbinic efforts turned to finding ways to make it halakhically acceptable.[70]

As Lawrence Hoffman has pointed out, Natronai's primary method was to understand the talmudic concept, *me-ein haberakhah* (the essence of the blessing), as broadly as possible.[71] This term and variations on it appear twice in the *gemara* in discussions of the *amidah*. The first is in *M. Berakhot* 4:3 and the *gemara* on it,[72] where the discussion is of the *me-ein shemoneh esreh*, the abbreviated *amidah*, to be recited by the person whose prayer is not fluent enough to enable him to pray the entire text properly. It is clear from the amoraic discussion that *me-ein* here refers to some sort of condensation of the text, which maintains its mandatory themes. The other discussion, in *B. Avodah Zarah* 8a, records various opinions on where individuals should include their private petitions in the *amidah*. Here, the *gemara* records an opinion of Rav, that if one adds one's petitions at the end of each individual blessing, מעין כל ברכה וברכה (on the topic of each individual blessing), one's obligations for prayer are still met. Here *me-ein* refers to an expansion on the blessing, but one that is thematically appropriate to the blessing.[73] Based on these talmudic precedents, Natronai restricts acceptable *piyyut* to those that are thematically appropriate. He expands

69. *Seder Rav Amram Gaon*, ed. Goldschmidt, 166-169. Amram does explicitly allow the recitation of *kerovot* in all Yom Kippur services, but he restricts the *seder ha-avodah* to *musaf*. The *Manhig* (ed. Raphael, I:369) cites Amram as permitting payyetanic insertions into *keriat shema* where they are customary.

70. It is significant that the arguments against *piyyut* never include anti-Karaite elements. Although the earliest post-Anan Karaite prayerbooks of which we are aware contain large quantities of *piyyut*, many of the early Karaite-like groups must have followed more closely rulings like that of Anan ben David, who insisted on only biblical language for prayer. Otherwise we might well have found the Geonim insisting that the Rabbanites distance themselves from this practice of the heretics. See Harkavy's ...ספר המצות לענן, 158.

71. *Canonization...*, 69-70.

72. *B. Berakhot* 29a.

73. The ברכה אחת מעין שלוש (one blessing summarizing three), referring to the shortened *birkat hamazon*, recited after eating less than a proper meal, is liturgically analogous to the מעין י"ח (the abbreviation of the weekday eighteen benediction *amidah*).

his definition, however, to include themes appropriate to the occasion and not merely to the individual blessing, as long as the *piyyut* incorporates some transition out of and back into the statutory text.

This is not a direct refutation of the arguments used by Pirkoi ben Baboi in the name of Yehudai. Hoffman correctly points out that these predecessors of Natronai had taken a very narrow interpretation of *B. Avodah Zarah*, restricting its permission to add petitions on the subject of the blessing only to those two instances specified in the next *memra*–namely, to the petitions for health and sustenance.[74] However, Hoffman places too much value on this point, suggesting that it was a prime argument by Yehudai's school against *piyyut* in general. Actually, it was quite overshadowed by Pirkoi ben Baboi's much more extensive argument that prayer texts are fixed and any change in them has dire consequences for the worshiper. In essence, Natronai changed the grounds of the debate; once *piyyut* was an acceptable addition to a blessing's text, issues of excessive praise, adding or deleting words, and creating an interruption (הפסקה) in the liturgy were no longer of any importance. Only the specific content remained to be regulated. We have no evidence that *piyyut* was ever again fully prohibited in Babylonia.

This is not to imply that all Geonim were enthusiastic about the inclusion of *piyyut*, or even that Geonim personally involved in creating liturgical poetry ever dropped all restrictions. Saadia, himself a prolific *payyetan* (his corpus includes *piyyut* written for recitation in the blessings of the statutory liturgy), specifically forbade certain works of others because of their improper content, improper language, and numerous errors.[75] A responsum ascribed to Sherira Gaon insists that sages pray with the community even if the communal service, prolonged by *piyyutim*, takes time away from their more important study of Torah. Clearly, some sages did not value *piyyut*![76]

Yehudai's argument, which appears in *Halakhot Gedolot* as well as in Pirkoi ben Baboi, that *piyyut*, like the High Holy Day inserts into the *amidah*, runs afoul of the talmudic prohibition against adding petitions in sections reserved for praise and thanksgiving, does receive extensive attention by later Geonim. We do not concern ourselves here with the issue of whether the standard holiday inserts[77]

---

74. This comment appears only in the fragment of Pirkoi ben Baboi published by Lewin, "משרידי הגניזה", 399.

75. *Siddur Rav Saadia Gaon*, 225; מנחם זולאי, האסכולה הפייטנית של רב סעדיה גאון (ירושלים: מכון שוקן למחקר היהדות, תשכ"ד), 78 ואילך, 142 ואילך.

76. תשובות הגאונים, מהדורת הורביץ, עמ' 239, חלק ב סי' צט.

77. Which included, in this period, inserts also for the Sabbath and festivals. See Pirkoi ben Baboi's objection, *Ginzei Schechter*, II:552; *Seder Rav Amram Gaon*, ed. Goldschmidt, 63,

were or were not acceptable, but rather with the underlying philosophical debate. As *Halakhot Gedolot* already recognized when it conflated the issues, if one form of insert of questionable content could be permitted, the argument permitting it must extend to other inserts, including *piyyut*. A close reading of the talmudic texts used by the early Geonim to prohibit these inserts revealed a loophole to those looking to allow *piyyut*:[78] the *gemara* phrases both versions of its limitation on the placement of petitionary inserts in the grammatical singular. *B. Berakhot* 34a reads: לעולם אל ישאל אדם צרכיו לא בשלש ראשונות ולא בשלש אחרונות (one should never request one's needs in the first and last three benedictions); the parallel passage in *B. Avodah Zarah* 8a reads similarly, שואל אדם (one requests). Because of this construction, the Geonim chose to interpret the restriction on petitions to refer only to the private requests of the individual and not to petitions made by or for the community. According to this reading, worshipers may legitimately insert petitions for communal needs at any point in the *amidah*, without concern that they violate the talmudically prescribed etiquette that dictates that the opening and closing blessings consist solely of praise and thanksgiving. As is made more explicit in the writings of the Rishonim and may already be implied in Pirkoi ben Baboi, the extension of this permission from petitions for communal needs to petitions and prayers recited by the *sheliaḥ tzibbur* for the community and on the community's behalf in the form of *piyyut* is quite simple.

The geonic traditions, then, created precedents for arguments both for and against the inclusion of *piyyut* in the blessings of the statutory liturgy. Those Geonim most dedicated to spreading the influence of the Babylonian Talmud and their academies' interpretations of it violently opposed *piyyut*, both as an obvious and accessible part of a popular culture they were trying to control, and as an institution that blatantly contradicted the halakhic norms they were at-

---

163; *Siddur Rav Saadia Gaon*, 21; נפתלי וידר, "לחקר מנהג בבל הקדמון," תרביץ לז (תשכ"ח), 144–147; and Lawrence Ahrin Hoffman, *Liturgical Responses Suppressed by the Geonim in their Attempt to Fix the Liturgy*, Ph.D diss., Hebrew Union College – Jewish Institute of Religion, Cincinnati, 1973, 121-122. The question of the poetic versions of the blessings for *shema* and *kiddush*, while not an issue of petition and praise, is also related.

78. Although our earliest preserved responsum on this topic is attributed to Paltoi Gaon, a slightly earlier Pumbeditan contemporary of the Suran Natronai, he is just reporting on pre-existent rulings. It is possible but not probable that these rulings were already known to Pirkoi ben Baboi, who responded to them obliquely. The fullest presentation of this approach is attributed to Tzemaḥ, and variants on it are attributed to Kohen Tzedek, Amram, and Hai. The texts are collected in *Otzar Hageonim, Berakhot, Teshuvot*, pp. 81-82, #221-225, and by Hoffman, *Liturgical Responses…*, 122-126. See too Wieder's discussion in his "לחקר מנהג בבל הקדמון", 144-147, where he posits a Babylonian origin for these inserts.

tempting to impose. However, once *piyyut* penetrated into the popular culture of Jews of undisputed Babylonian loyalties, other Geonim sought ways to justify the minhag, either from a sense that this poetry truly added to the beauty and meaningfulness of the liturgy, or because they recognized that popular favor would undercut any assertion of halakhic authority. Cultural realities, and not any theoretical halakhic stance, ultimately determined the geonic rulings.

### Piyyut *in the Medieval Synagogue*

Before examining later rabbinic positions and rulings regarding the inclusion of *piyyut* in the synagogue service, it is instructive to consider extant evidence for actual synagogue practice and the attitudes of the common folk to liturgical poetry. Few details are available; thus no full picture emerges for most times and places in the areas under discussion here. Nonetheless, the aggregate is of some significance, especially as similar situations often prevailed in widely scattered communities. By the end of the first millennium of the Common Era, *piyyut* of one style or another was a universal element of Jewish liturgy, with the exception of a few places where local authority had ruled otherwise.

The most extensive description of *piyyut* in a medieval synagogue service is the early thirteenth-century satirical account by Yehudah Alḥarizi in Chapter 24 of his *Taḥkemoni*, in which this Spanish cultural elitist describes his experiences one Sabbath while visiting a synagogue in the prosperous Babylonian city of Ashur.[79]

There, he found a congregation that was wealthy but totally unlearned. They took great pride, however, in the scholarliness of others, especially their reknowned *ḥazzan*, who, in addition to being supposedly generally well-learned, had a great voice and a broad knowledge of "treasured *piyyutim*." However, as Alḥarizi describes with great wit, this *ḥazzan* was, in fact, a total ignoramus who made myriads of errors even in the statutory liturgy. His *piyyutim*, which he began after the completion of the *zemirot*, lasted so long that by the time he returned to complete the statutory prayers, the entire congregation had either stretched out on the floor and fallen asleep or left the synagogue and gone home for the same purpose. Only four "asses" even tried to "bray" along with the

79. יהודה אלחריזי, תחכמוני, בעריכת י. טופורובסקי (תל אביב: מחברות לספרות, תשי"ב), 223–230. Victor Emanuel Reichert, *The Tahkemoni of Judah Al-Harizi* (Jerusalem: Raphael Haim Cohen's Ltd. Publishers, 1973), II: 110, identifies Ashur as Mosul, a city 220 miles northwest of Baghdad. Benjamin of Tudela reported finding a quite prosperous community of 7,000 Jews there in 1165.

*ḥazzan*, until even they could not continue. Alḥarizi finds the *piyyutim* themselves to be totally without literary merit.[80]

We cannot be certain of the nature of the *piyyut* recited in Ashur. Since Alḥarizi gives no indication that this was a special Sabbath, we can infer that this congregation weekly incorporated liturgical poetry into their Sabbath morning prayers, a custom that characterized the east much more than Europe. Their *piyyut* could well have been standard eastern-style poetry inserted into the statutory liturgy of every blessing from the *yotzer* through the *kedushah* of the morning *amidah*. But it is also possible that all the insertions came before the *barekhu*, which, as we shall see later, became a compromise between those who wanted to maintain the recitation of *piyyut* and those who felt it interrupted the flow of the statutory prayers.[81] Given the constant comparisons that one of the congregants makes between the local custom and that of the rest of the Jewish world, and his references to *kerovah* as one of the varieties of *piyyut*, most likely this congregation inserted *piyyut* into the blessings of their statutory liturgy.

Obviously, while the congregation officially valued *piyyut*, its members did not pay attention to it or try to understand it. After his description of the service itself, Alḥarizi records a debate about it between two congregants. The person speaking critically of *piyyut* points out the problematic nature of a system that encourages people to leave without even hearing the statutory liturgy, and that presents them with a service that not a single individual understands, let alone knows well enough to correct the errors made by their *ḥazzan*. The advocate of the current system counters that adding liturgical poetry has value precisely because it is the universal custom, from which one should not deviate. Certainly, he says, there must be others around the world who also fail to understand this poetry, yet their congregations do not change their customs! In addition, songs of praise like *piyyut* are the closest extant replacement for the levitical song of the Temple, and God cherishes them as much as sacrifices; as such, they have as much value as the statutory prayers.

Alḥarizi provides a glimpse of a situation where, operating outside the realm of direct rabbinic influence, some Jews had come to consider *piyyut* the highest available form of worship–and it was irrelevant whether or not they understood

---

80. Alḥarizi's judgment of the Babylonian poetry's merits reflects a vast difference in cultural esthetics, and cannot be used to assess the Babylonian poetry itself. In Gates Three and Eighteen, he discusses more directly the merits of Spanish poetry and denigrates that which he has heard during his travels to much of the rest of the Jewish world.

81. We find the earliest hint of such a system in an objection raised to the removal of the Rosh Hashanah *tekiata* from the appropriate blessings in *Maḥzor Vitry*, 370. See too: תשובות הרמב"ם, II: 363-366, #207. It only becomes common after the ruling of the *Tur* in the fourteenth century and especially after the expulsion from Spain. See below, p. 163f., 175f.

it. They made a token appearance in synagogue for an hour or so and were satisfied to know that their great *ḥazzan* was performing the necessary prayers. Totally reliant on authority (however misguided), they had no *kavvanah* at all in the traditional sense. Essentially, they had recreated for themselves a priestly system with their *ḥazzan* as the ritual intermediary, singing songs in conscious imitation of the levites.

Every one of the issues raised in Alḥaziri's account echoes in other sources from other periods and places in the Jewish world. In its inception in Palestine, *piyyut* was a constant source of creativity and intellectual challenge to the community; once it was entrenched in the liturgy, it often lost its meaningfulness. Maimonides claimed that the improper content, meters, and melodies added by *piyyut* turned prayer into a source of amusement, causing a loss of *kavvanah*, which in turn led people to think that since these prayers were not obligatory, they could act indecorously and chatter during the service.[82] Similarly, the *Tur*'s concluding argument against *piyyut* was that it should be abolished because it caused people to interrupt their prayers with inconsequential chatter.[83] The Rivash had the same complaint,[84] as did the Maharil, who objected to youths' studying instead of paying attention to the *piyyut*. He suggested that everyone study the Rosh Hashanah *piyyutim* ahead of time so they could pray with understanding and *kavvanah* and not be tempted to withdraw their attention from the *sheliaḥ tzibbur*.[85]

Rabbis objected to *piyyut* not only because of the loss of decorum but also because these additions simply were not comprehended by the congregation. This was one of Abraham Ibn Ezra's main objections to *piyyut*,[86] and similar objections may have spurred the French and German Jews, and especially the *Ḥasidei Ashkenaz*, to remedy the situation by writing *piyyut* commentaries.[87] Where people did not understand *piyyut*, they had only the authority of their ancestors who had originally included it in their ritual cycle to ensure its appro-

---

82. תשובות הרמב"ם, II: 467, #254.

83. *Tur*, OH 68.

84. שאלות ותשובות בר ששת, סי' עה, דף יד.

85. ספר מהרי"ל..., מהדורת שפיצר, הלכות תפלה, תלז; הלכות ראש השנה, רעא–רעב.

86. Commentary to Kohelet 5:1. Shmuel de Medina relies heavily on Ibn Ezra's argument in his: שו"ת מהרשד"ם, או"ח לה.

87. א.א. אורבך, ספר ערוגת הבושם, חלק ד' (ירושלים: מקיצי נרדמים, תשכ"ג), 6. See also Abraham Grossman's discussion in his חכמי צרפת הראשונים (ירושלים: מאגנס, תשנ"ה), פרק תשיעי, "פרשנות הפיוט". Grossman attributes the flourishing of this genre more to the general interest in writing commentary, combined with the high estimation given to *piyyut* in general in this period.

priateness. Situations could exist where, as the Radbaz colorfully described it:

> ...בזמננו זה חברו פיוטים ועניינים אסור לשומעם, כל שכן לפסוק בהם בתוך התפלה, ואין החזנים מבחינים בין שיר משורר לחמור נוער, וערבו דברי הטפשים הסכלים בתוך דברי אלהים חיים.
>
> ...in these times, they have composed *piyyutim* and matters to which it is forbidden to listen, let alone to interrupt prayer for them. The *ḥazzanim* do not distinguish between a song being sung and an ass braying,[88] and they have mixed words of foolish idiots in with the words of the living God.[89]

Constantly in the literature, we find claims for the reliability of the institution based on the status of the poet himself.[90] Although this is a major modus operandi of the entire Jewish halakhic system, it became problematic in this situation, where Jews had lost the ability to evaluate the poetry themselves. This practice was mentioned often, then, in the criticism leveled against *piyyut.*[91]

In spite of these issues and objections, people often ignored or even actively opposed attempts to eliminate *piyyut.* An Ashkenazi community that had been instructed to cease inserting it into their statutory liturgy on holidays appealed to Rabbenu Gershom, who supported their resistance to these changes.[92] Maimonides corresponded with a student, Saadia ben Berakhot Hamelammed, whose Alexandrian congregation was resisting Maimonides' ruling that would have eliminated the recitation of beloved *piyyutim* within the *amidah.* This congregation could not bring itself to omit the poetry of Yom Kippur or the *azharot* on Shavuot, and would not even accept the compromise of moving the recitation of all poetry to after the *amidah,* where it would be halakhically nonproblematic.[93] In another case, Maimonides ruled that the poetic forms of the Sabbath blessings might be preserved with minimal modification, because to impose the

---

88. Compare *Taḥkemoni,* 226.

89. ספר שו"ת הרדב"ז מכתב יד, חלק שמיני, סי' יג, עמ' י–יא.

90. Most famously, Kalir, whom Rabbenu Tam, in his widely cited lengthy responsum defending the payyetanic endeavor, identified as a Tanna and hence as an undisputable authority.(*Maḥzor Vitry,* 362-364; *Shibbolei Haleket,* ed. Mirsky, 213-218.) See my "Kalir Was A Tanna: Rabbenu Tam's Invocation of Antiquity in Defense of the Ashkenazi Payyetanic Tradition" *HUCA* (1996): 95-106.

91. See, for instance, Abraham Ibn Ezra's commentary to Kohelet 5:1; תשובות הרמב"ם, ב: 467–468, סי' רנד; ספר המצות ל...רבינו משה בן מיימון, הקדמה, עמ' ב דף ג; שו"ת מהרשד"ם, או"ח לה. See too the criticism by the Ḥasidei Ashkenaz of those who rely overmuch on the authority of the authors and include inappropriate content in their prayers, as recorded by Urbach, *Arugat Habosem* IV: 95.

92. תשובות רבנו גרשום מאור הגולה, מהדורת אידלברג, סי' א, 55–57.

93. תשובות הרמב"ם, II: 485-486, # 259.

halakhically mandated changes would create immense dissension within the community–and many worse transgressions were accepted by Jews in any congregation.[94] S.D. Goitein has suggested that the Maimonidean compromise might have been the result of an undatable letter found in the genizah, in which Jews, possibly from a provincial town, complained about their communal leaders' abolition of various insertions from their liturgy and asked the addressee to procure permission from the sultan for them to hold services in accordance with their ancestral customs.[95] To say the least, such interference by secular authorities, while not unheard of, would not have been well received by the rabbis whose halakhic authority was being undermined!

We also know from a letter dated from 1214 preserved in the Cairo genizah that, in spite of the active opposition to *piyyut* of Maimonides and his son, Abraham, there were groups of *ḥazzanim* in Egypt–among the community of Palestinian origins–who strove to collect new *piyyutim*, sending as far as France to locate texts. The same letter indicates that some of these *ḥazzanim* competed so fiercely, not to compose, but to collect these compositions, that they refused to share their knowledge with others.[96] The richness and variety of the genizah poetic collections, which largely date from this period, themselves attest to the vibrancy of the Egyptian payyetanic traditions.

Knowing that their changes would be resisted, later Sefardi rabbis sometimes chose not to impose their rulings on their communities or the communities of their correspondents even though they found *piyyut* objectionable. The *Tur*[97] records a responsum of R. Meir Halevi Abulafia, who, after detailing his halakhic objections to *piyyut*, notes that he did not force its elimination. He says he came to the synagogue anyway to participate in the *kedushah* and *kaddish*, and simply recited the statutory liturgy silently to himself. He adds:

> אך מה שהוגד לכם שיש בידי למחות לא הוגד לכם האמת על כן אמרתי הנח להם לישראל מוטב שיהו שוגגין ואל יהו מזידין וזה היא סיבת שתיקתי.
>
> But when you were told that I have the power to protest [effectively], you were not told the truth. Therefore, I said, "Let Israel be. It is preferable that they err from ignorance than that they willfully transgress."[98] This is the reason for my silence.

---

94. תשובות הרמב"ם, II: 329-330, # 181.

95. S. D. Goitein, *A Mediterranean Society*, Vol. II: The Community (Berkeley: University of California Press, 1971), 160, citing TS 8 J21 f. 12.

96. שלמה דוב גויטיין, סדרי חינוך בימי הגאונים ובית הרמב"ם: מקורות חדשים מן הגניזה (ירושלים: מכון בן צבי, האוניברסיטה העברית, תשכ"ב), 98–101.

97. OH 68. See the detailed discussion of this passage below, p. 161f.

98. *B. Shabbat* 148b; *B. Beitzah* 30a; *B. Bava Batra* 60b.

The Rivash reports that his teacher, Rabbenu Nissim, similarly followed a strict ruling for himself–refraining from reciting *piyyut*–but did not rebuke his congregation. Following that precedent, the Rivash stopped scolding his poorly educated congregation in Algiers when they did not heed his reprimands about talking during the statutory liturgy.[99] His younger colleague in Algiers, the Rashbatz, records:

> ואעפ"כ הרבה חכמים ז"ל הוקשה להן ענין הפיוטין אלא שאין בידן למחות לפי שנהגו בהן בכל המקומות ישראל ובכל מקום בעלי נפש ימעטו.
>
> And even so, many sages of blessed memory had difficulty with the matter of the *piyyutim*, but they were not able to protest [effectively] because it was such a universal Jewish custom, and there were so few conscientious people in any one place.[100]

Without a doubt, one of the elements that contributed greatly to the popular appeal of *piyyut* was its musical setting. The Babylonian apostate Samau'al b. Yaḥya al Magribi differentiates between the statutory liturgy recited solely by the *sheliaḥ tzibbur* without music and the *ḥizana* or *piyyut* sung with much congregational participation.[101] As we saw above, Maimonides attests that *piyyut* was performed more musically than the statutory prayers were when he lists melody among the aspects of *piyyut* that detract from the decorum of the service.[102] In contrast, the *Ḥasidei Ashkenaz* insisted on the invariance of the words of the liturgy, threatening death to anyone who exchanged one *piyyut* for another,[103] and the Maharil extended this invariance to include even the melodies of the service.[104] There is no doubt that music is an integral part of much human ritual experience; but as a nonverbal component, it can lessen the direct communicative value, the meaningfulness, of the words themselves and increase their illocutionary force.[105] In any case, the association of music with *piyyut* cannot be ignored when we try to understand the appeal of this generally obscure poetry to Jews around the world.[106]

---

99. שאלות ותשובות בר ששת, סי' עה דף יד:. For a discussion of the situation in Algiers, see Isadore Epstein, *The Responsa of Rabbi Simon b. Ẓemaḥ Duran as a Source of the History of the Jews in North Africa* (New York: Ktav, 1968; rpt. of 1930 ed.), 57, 73.

100. פירוש הרשב"ץ על ברכות, 47.

101. Elbogen, *Jewish Prayer*..., 222-223 (Heb. 213-214); Martin Schreiner, "Samau'al b. Jaḥjâ al-Magribî und seine Schrift "Ifḥâm al-Jahûd," *MGWJ* 42 (1898): 220.

102. תשובות הרמב"ם, II:468, # 254.

103. ספר חסידים שחיבר רבינו יהודה החסיד, מהדורת מרגליות, עמ' תב, סי' תרז.

104. ספר מהרי"ל, מהדורת שפיצר, הלכות שחרית דיום כפור, עמ' שלט.

105. See Bloch, "Symbols, Song, Dance...," 67, 69-71.

106. See יהודה רצהבי, "מעמד הפיוט בתפילה," בתוך מגנזי שירת הקדם (פיוט וחקרי פיוט) (ירושלים: משגב

Thus the vast majority of clues to the attitudes of ordinary Jews to *piyyut* come necessarily from sources critical of the endeavor. The evidence is admittedly spotty, but what emerges is a picture of a custom well entrenched at the popular level, not necessarily because it added cognitive content to the prayer services, but because it was part of the received liturgical experience, especially as it marked as different and significant the services for the various holidays and special Sabbaths. A large part of its appeal was its musical setting, and another was simply the sense that this was Torah study. Even if people did not understand *piyyut*, they knew it represented a "great tradition" of learning, which they valued even if they themselves were less educated.[107]

## *The Ashkenazi Defense of* Piyyut

Our earliest records of a learned Jewish presence in Italy, the Rhineland, and northern France indicate that *piyyut* was an embedded element of Ashkenazi minhag and that major rabbinic figures were themselves *payyetanim.* Among the most famous were R. Shimon ben Yitzḥak, R. Yosef Tov Elem, and members of the Kalonymos family. Their involvement helped maintain the inviolable status of the institution. We have no evidence of any Ashkenazi rabbi during the period of the Rishonim ruling that all *piyyut* should be excluded from the statutory liturgy.

It was, however, challenged at an early period–although probably only by outsiders questioning the halakhic validity of Ashkenazi custom. In contact with the Babylonian Geonim, northern European rabbis increasingly looked to the Babylonian Talmud as a primary source of literary halakhic authority.[108] As they began to incorporate Babylonian schools of thought into their own, they struggled to understand the legitimacy of their inherited customs, including their traditions of *piyyut.* Thus, although minhag and halakhah were never in real conflict over its inclusion in the Ashkenazi synagogue service, rabbis from

---

ירושלים – המכון לחקר מורשת יהדות ספרד והמזרח, 1991), 250. Especially noteworthy is his citation of Immanuel of Rome's description of the impact of his singing on his congregation. Amnon Shiloah, *Jewish Musical Traditions* (Detroit: Wayne State University Press, 1992), 113, 122-129; and Eric Werner, *A Voice Still Heard...: The Sacred Songs of the Ashkenazi Jews* (University Park: The Pennsylvania State University Press, 1976), 89ff., describe the musical aspects of *piyyut* primarily in the post-1492 period.

107. The concept of the "great tradition," which is esteemed even if not understood by the majority of the society, was developed by Robert Redfield, *Peasant Society and Culture* (1956; rpt. Chicago: University of Chicago Press, 1971).

108. See, for instance: אברהם גרוסמן, חכמי אשכנז הראשונים (ירושלים: מאגנס, תשמ"ט), 290–291, 424 ואילך.

this world had occasion to contribute to its halakhic defense and affect the subsequent history of the halakhic debates about *piyyut*.

As mentioned above, Rabbenu Gershom overruled an anonymous *ḥaver's* attempt to eliminate *piyyut* from the rite of some town.[109] He based his reasoning largely on geonic precedents and on the recognized authority of the most common *payyetanim*.[110] As Rabbenu Tam recorded, two of Rabbenu Gershom's French contemporaries, R. Yosi (Yosef) Tov Elem and R. Eliahu Hazaken of Le Mans, both of whom were themselves *payyetanim* with connections to the Babylonian Geonim, discussed the permissibility of inserting the poetry into the blessings.[111] Their questioning of *piyyut*, according to Abraham Grossman, only arose because their general adherence to Babylonian traditions created a conflict with the uniform acceptance of *piyyut* in France at that time. Although we have no record of their discussions, their final decision not only preserved the integrity of the Italian-German and French traditions but even elevated them.[112] They permitted *piyyut*, acknowledging that it was the finest way to fulfill the mitzvah of prayer and to direct the worshiper's thoughts to heaven. In other words, they understood it to significantly enhance *kavvanah*.

Our earliest preserved detailed defenses of *piyyut* are by Rabbenu Gershom's probable student and Rashi's teacher, the eleventh-century R. Yitzḥak Halevi,[113]

109. תשובות רגמ"ה, סי' א, עמ' 55–57. See above, p. 133. We have no means of identifying the source of the ruling this community is contesting. Eidelberg, in his commentary on this responsum, suggests that the challenge may be geonic, but none of the sources he refers to can be dated quite this late, and it would be strange for a Gaon to be referred to as a *ḥaver*, as in this responsum. However, as we have absolutely no evidence for such a strict ruling against insertions into the blessing ever coming from within the Franco-German schools of rabbis, it is quite likely that it originated with a travelling Babylonian or Babylonian-influenced sage or with some no longer extant correspondence with the Babylonian academies.

110. Rabbenu Gershom merely claims that Yannai and Kalir were מן החכמים הראשונים (among the early sages) and differentiates them only marginally from the contemporary Kalonimides, about each of whom he says, שחכם גדול היה (that he was a great sage)(p. 56). For him, this degree of antiquity establishes authority.

111. *Maḥzor Vitry*, 364; *Shibbolei Haleket*, ed. Mirsky, 216. For biographical information on these rabbis, see Grossman, חכמי צרפת הראשונים, 46ff., 84ff.

112. Grossman, חכמי צרפת הראשונים, 80-81, 91-92.

113. In: ספר הפרדס לרש"י ז"ל, מהדורת עהרענרייך, הלכות ראש השנה, עמ' רכג–רל. The responsum is identified in the text only as תשובת הלוי השיב ר'. Grossman, חכמי אשכנז הראשונים, 267, lists among the names by which others referred to R. Yitzḥak Halevi, Rashi's most common term, רבינו הלוי. Solomon Buber, in his introduction to the works of Rashi (*Sefer HaOrah*, 15, 101) explicitly identifies this responsum. Although more recent scholars have questioned this identification, Ta-Shma is inclined to support it. See his מנהג אשכנז הקדמון, 90–91, הע' 131. Certainly in content and methodology it predates R. Tam's discussions.

and, approximately a century later, by Rashi's grandson, Rabbenu Tam.[114] R. Yitzḥak Halevi's responsum was eclipsed by that of Rabbenu Tam, which became the primary authority in support of *piyyut*, cited in all serious subsequent discussions of the issue. However, R. Yitzḥak Halevi's responsum is significant as the first major source to document what were to become key foci of the European halakhic arguments about *piyyut*, as well as a (small) window to the historical reality of eleventh-century Worms.

The question posed to R. Yitzḥak Halevi no longer exists, but his response indicates that he was asked to justify his community's custom of inserting the High Holy Day additions and *piyyut* into the first three blessings of the *amidah*. This concern, as we have seen, goes back at least to the time of Yehudai Gaon. R. Yitzḥak Halevi's initial answer, like Rabbenu Gershom's, recapitulates the later geonic differentiation between the petitions of the individual, which were restricted, and the petitions of the congregation, which were not; but he adds a citation to similar effect from the Palestinian Talmud,[115] which he interprets to establish that, *ab initio*, the purpose of the entire repetition of the *amidah* is petitionary. He also points out that the talmudically ordained inserts, *yaaleh veyavo* on Rosh Ḥodesh and *al hanissim* on Ḥanukkah and Purim, are also petitionary additions to the last three blessings.[116] He asserts that the *sheliaḥ tzibbur* repeats the first and final three blessings only to maintain the standard form of the prayer.

The bulk of his responsum, however, treats a different halakhic issue. Although it is unlikely that he initiated the question, R. Yitzḥak Halevi's discussion is the oldest preserved application of the rather obtuse mishnaic concept of long and short blessings to the issue of the halakhic validity of *piyyut*. *Mishnah Berakhot* 1:4, referring to the blessings surrounding the *shema*, reads:

---

114. The fullest extant printed texts of Rabbenu Tam's responsum are in *Maḥzor Vitry*, 362-365 and *Shibbolei Haleket*, ed. Mirsky, 213-218. Although these two texts vary somewhat in the arrangement of the arguments, their content is fairly consistent. The version in *Shibbolei Haleket* contains fewer textual difficulties, but without a more critical edition of *Maḥzor Vitry* or manuscripts of the original responsum, we cannot judge the extent to which this is due to editing by the later source or some intermediate scribe. The problem is only compounded by the fact that the responsum cannot possibly have been included in R. Simḥah of Vitry's original text, as R. Tam was only a very young child when R. Simḥah died.

115. *P. Berakhot* 4:4, 8b.

116. *Sefer Hapardes*, 225. As R. Yitzḥak knew, Hai Gaon had indeed criticized the petitonary line in *al hanissim*, כשם שעשית עמהם נס פלא ונסים כן עשה עמנו נסים וגבורות והושיענו (just as You performed wonders and miracles for them, so too perform miracles and mighty deeds for us and save us) (*Otzar Hageonim*, *Berakhot*, *Perushim*, p. 48, #140). See *Sefer Hapardes*, 230.

בשחר מברך שתים לפניה ואחת לאחריה, ובערב שתים לפניה ושתים לאחריה; אחת ארוכה ואחת קצרה.

מקום שאמרו להאריך אינו רשאי לקצר, לקצר אינו רשאי להאריך, לחתום אינו רשאי שלא לחתום, שלא לחתום אינו רשאי לחתום.

In the morning, one recites two blessings before [*shema*] and one after it, while in the evening, one recites two before it and two after it, one short and one long.

Where they said to lengthen the blessing, one may not shorten it, and where they said to shorten it, one may not lengthen it. Where they said to recite a concluding benediction, one may not omit it; where they said not to recite a concluding benediction, one may not add one.

The Tosefta and the Palestinian Talmud already separate the Mishnah's discussion into two discrete units and understand the dictates about changing the length of the blessings as general comments applying to all sections of the liturgy, not just *keriat shema*.[117] Once read this way, rabbis could consider the second part of the Mishnah to be a principle of liturgical halakhah, forbidding any change in the length or structure of the blessings. Naturally, this presumes that the liturgy has an essentially fixed wording, and, most important for our issue here, the addition of any *piyyut* is prohibited. Because of the absolutism of the pronouncement and the difficulties later generations have had determining its precise application,[118] this "principle" became a major focus of the halakhic arguments of both the defenders and detractors of the payyetanic endeavor.

R. Yitzḥak Halevi argues strongly that there is enormous precedent for changing the lengths of blessings, and, in general, that there is nothing sacrosanct about the length or brevity of the service. He points to precedents where entire extra blessings were added (the *birkat haminim*, the additional six blessings on public fast days, and especially the third blessing after *shema* in the evening), and claims:

וכיון שרשאין על מניין של ברכות להוסיף אין צורך לומר שרשאין להאריך ביוצרות [ואופנים] וזולתות.

And once one is allowed to add to the number of blessings, there is no

117. *Tosefta Berakhot* 1:5-9, *P. Berakhot* 1:8, 3c. The Tosefta only makes the barest mention of the beginning of the Mishnah. Lieberman, תוספתא כפשוטה, I:5-7, cites Rabbenu Tam's comment that suggests that this is more a reference to the location in the Mishnah than an intrinsic part of the Tosefta's comment.

118. We need not concern ourselves here with the protracted and unresolvable debate as to whether "short" and "long" refer to the formal structure of the blessings or to their actual length. See the various medieval commentaries to *B. Berakhot* 11a-b, discussing these Mishnah and Tosefta passages.

> need to specify that one can lengthen the blessings with the payyetanic inserts into the blessings of *keriat shema*.[119]

The toseftan and talmudic listings of long and short blessings are not exclusive, and, in any case, the general prohibitions on changing length do not apply to the blessings of the *shema* and *amidah*. The only restriction on additions to prayers are those proscribed specifically as theologically inappropriate by the Talmud–namely, adding epithets to the description of God that begins the *avot*. Under certain circumstances, even an individual is allowed to deviate from the statutory texts. Contrary to the claims of the detractors of *piyyut*, the content of the addition, even if totally devoid of religious content, is of no halakhic import, as long as it is relevant to the blessing.[120]

R. Yitzḥak Halevi makes two additional arguments of import. Some detractor of *piyyut* must have claimed that it was a burden to the congregation because it prolonged the service–particularly on the Sabbath and holidays, when the statutory service had purposefully been shortened. To this, he responds that Moses commanded the Jews to study issues appropriate to the occasion, and, because diaspora Jews are not accustomed universally to preach sermons, sainted rabbis like R. Elazar b"R. Kalir and R. Shlomo Habavli and communities of the entire European diaspora[121] instituted *piyyutim* of appropriate content to fill the void. R. Yitzḥak Halevi also records the interpretation of his lesser known French contemporary, the *payyetan* R. Binyamin b"R. Shmuel of Coutances (Normandy),[122] that the Sabbath and festival services were shortened at a time when knowledge was widespread in Israel; now that it is not, sermons and *piyyutim* have become necessary modes of education. In desperate times, halakhic precedents (such as the shortening of the service) must be abrogated. Obviously, R. Yitzḥak Halevi and his contemporaries assumed that the content of *piyyut* would be understood not only by the elite, but by the entire congregation.[123] It was, then, not only a

---

119. p. 226. *Piyyut* for the *amidah* is implied earlier in this argument.

120. This caveat reflects the influence of the ruling of Natronai Gaon, discussed above, pp. 125-128.

121. p. 228. He specifies: גלות ירושלים אשר בספרד וגלות כנעני עד צרפת וגם בארץ רומי (the Jerusalemite exile which is in Spain and the Canaanite exile spread to France and also to Italy).

122. On the identification of this sage, see Grossman, חכמי צרפת הראשונים, 49. Grossman, 628, identifies the town as Constanz.

123. This assumption that people understand *piyyut* may also underlie the argument of others, rebutted by R. Yitzḥak Halevi, objecting to *piyyut* of secular content. Grossman (חכמי אשכנז הראשונים, 292) also notes, however, that R. Yitzḥak Halevi's students and successors cite his *piyyut* commentary. Engagement in this genre indicates an awareness of levels of *piyyut* that were not accessible without study.

source of *kavvanah* in prayer, but an effective means of integrating Torah study into the liturgy as a second potent form of worship.

In his conclusion, R. Yitzḥak Halevi moves away from his strictly halakhic approach and offers an argument typical of early Ashkenaz: he stresses the universality of the inclusion of *piyyut* and its importance as an ancestral custom. In this context, he includes other customs also under attack, such as the blessing over wine at a circumcision that falls on a fast day, the fixed poetic additions to the Sabbath *yotzer* blessing, and a petitionary line in *al hanissim.*[124] Those who criticize Ashkenazi minhag, he claims, do not understand that Torah has no validity unless it is inherited from a recognized authority. They are merely practicing self-aggrandizement, and their claims have no validity. For him, ancestral tradition is the ultimate authority, and it establishes that Ashkenazi Jews must recite *piyyut* and maintain all their other minhagim.

A century later Rabbenu Tam was similarly confronted by people criticizing *piyyut* both as a transgression of the talmudic prohibition against adding petitions to the first and last three blessings of the *amidah* and as an impermissible interruption to and elaboration of one's prayers.[125] His responsum, although presupposing and relying on many of the arguments of R. Yitzḥak Halevi, makes no direct reference to them. Although he offers important insights on the issue of communal petition and praise and the question of the length of the blessing texts, one senses that he included these matters only because they were part of the mandatory literary heritage of a discussion of the validity of *piyyut.* R. Tam's strongest claim, and the one on which he pins his entire argument, is the authority of the *payyetanim,* especially Kalir.[126]

Both Rabbenu Gershom and R. Yitzḥak Halevi had also invoked the credentials of the *payyetanim* as halakhic justification for reciting *piyyut.* However, R. Tam's argument transcends simple Ashkenazi reverence for ancestral custom and creates a halakhic bastion less easily refuted than the conventional talmudic and geonic arguments. He dates the entire payyetanic institution to early tannaitic times, to the time of the apostle Simon Peter, who was known to have composed a *seder avodah* for Yom Kippur.[127] More significantly, he suggests that Kalir could probably be identified as the Tanna R. Elazar b"R. Shimon, whose authority was unquestionable. R. Tam devotes a huge proportion of his respon-

124. p. 230.

125. *Maḥzor Vitry*'s version presents this as the actual question. It must be inferred in *Shibbolei Haleket,* which has reorganized the responsum somewhat to allow a smooth transition from the previous section.

126. See my more extended discussion of this aspect of R. Tam's responsum in my "Kalir Was A Tanna:..." 101ff.

127. On this curious attribution, see ibid., 101.

sum to establishing this identity, discussing the inspired nature of Kalir's work and validating Kalir's halakhic materials as consistent with the Palestinian Talmud.[128] Although he allows that Kalir may not have been R. Elazar b"R. Shimon, he asserts that his other evidence is, in any case, sufficient to prove Kalir's status as a Tanna.[129] It is noteworthy that R. Tam, unlike his Ashkenazi predecessors for whom we have evidence, makes no mention of the reliability and authority of *payyetanim* from more recent times; instead he argues only that the various great Ashkenazi and French rabbis themselves recited *piyyut*, endorsing it not only as permitted but even as the preferred way to worship God.

Why does R. Tam raise the Kalir argument, which is not without its weaknesses, with such force? After arguing that Kalir's work is consistent with the halakhic school reflected in the Palestinian Talmud, R. Tam also asserts that Kalir must have been a Tanna because no Amoraim, even in Palestine, differed so much from the traditions of the Babylonian Talmud. One senses here almost a degree of desperation and an attempt to defend, not only the institution of *piyyut*, but also the very reliance of the Franco-German school on Kalirian traditions. It is highly probable, although not fully demonstrable, that R. Tam was responding to Abraham Ibn Ezra's vehement attack on non-Spanish *piyyut*, especially the *piyyut* of Kalir.[130] R. Tam and Ibn Ezra corresponded with each other about poetics and may even have met as Ibn Ezra traveled and taught in France. R. Tam's insistence that Kalir was a Tanna, and hence a halakhic authority, was quite possibly an attempt disguised as an halakhic argument to bolster Ashkenazi minhag in the face of a new literary aesthetic. This may account for the conclusion of his responsum; after all the halakhic arguments and

---

128. This reverence for Kalir was, of course, not new, and was characteristic of the early schools of France and Germany. These rabbis studied Kalir's works minutely and attempted to emulate him. See for instance: אברהם גרוסמן, "על דרכו של הקליר בעשיית פשרה בדברי אגדה," נספח ב' לפרק ב של מנהגי ישראל של דניאל שפרבר, כרך ב (ירושלים: מוסד הרב קוק, 1991), עב-עה. They understood at least some of his poetry to be the result of a mystical ascent to heaven. See Moshe Idel, *Kabbalah: New Perspectives* (New Haven: Yale University Press, 1988), 12. As a consequence of Kalir's elevation to the status of a halakhic authority, interpretations of rabbinic materials embedded in his *piyyutim* became a legitimate source for understanding the intent of the Talmud. The *Tosafot* cite Kalir numerous times to elucidate otherwise obscure passages. See the many examples collected by R. Elazar Fleckeles in his תשובה מאהבה, Part I, #1; and see also R. Yosef Zekhariah Stern in his ספר זכר יהוסף, OH 19:3, p. 34c-35a. Neither of these later responsa confine themselves to Kalir's *piyyut*. The *Tosafot* make similar use of their more contemporary European *piyyutim*. On Rashi's citations of Kalir, see: מנחם זהרי, דברי משה הדרשן ופיוטי אלעזר הקלירי בפירושי רש"י (ירושלים: כרמל, תשנ"ו).

129. Some Spanish sources, citing R. Tam, speak of Kalir as R. Elazar b. Arakh, an even earlier tannaitic authority. See below, p. 161, n. 204.

130. See below, p. 105f., and see my "Kalir was a Tanna," p.102f.

a lengthy discourse on the issue of long and short blessings, R. Tam simply asserts: מנהג הלכה היא (minhag is halakhah).[131]

One of R. Tam's other halakhic arguments is also a significant contribution to the development of the discussion of *piyyut* and liturgical halakhah. R. Yitzḥak Halevi's discussion of long and short blessings, while extensive, never really resolved the question of how to understand the Mishnah's prescription of "one short, one long" for the blessings following the *shema* in the evening. Rashi understood this to refer specifically to the two blessings, *emet ve-emunah* and *hashkiveinu*, the first being long and the second short.[132] R. Tam finds this problematic, asking whether any technical element really differentiates these two blessings. He suggests, instead, that the language, אחת...אחת (one...one), is best understood to mean, בין...בין, (whether ... or). In other words, the Mishnah, instead of specifying lengths, has left the entire matter open. He goes on to explain that the only blessings that have predetermined lengths are those specifically listed in the Tosefta. Therefore this supposed "principle" does not apply at all to the issue of the legality of the payyetanic endeavor; it only forbids the inclusion of *piyyut* in the very few instances where the Tosefta has dictated that the blessing must be short.[133]

Rabbenu Tam's responsum, along with the geonic traditions, became the authoritative statement of those seeking a halakhic defense of *piyyut*. Almost every Ashkenazi or Ashkenazi influenced rabbi treating the issue cites or paraphrases it.[134] Within pre-modern Ashkenaz itself, no one else advances significant new halakhic arguments to defend their ancestral custom.[135] However, to some these

131. This appears only in *Maḥzor Vitry*. *Shibbolei Haleket* includes a much lengthier discussion of the Tosefta and ends rather abruptly without returning to the general issue of *piyyut*. Note the similarity between this and the response of the Palestinian Jews to Yehudai Gaon, as well as the thematic parallelism with the conclusion of R. Yitzḥak Halevi's responsum.

132. Rashi's specifying these blessings appears only as an alternative text in our editions of the Talmud, but it appears in the Rashi as printed with the *Rif*, and in many citations of Rashi by the Tosafists and others.

133. However, in his *Sefer Hayashar* (חלק השאלות והתשובות, סי' סג אות יב עמ' 146.), R. Tam modifies this reading and gives a different interpretation of the continuation of the Mishnah. He claims that in a place where the prayer has been fixed as short, one may substitute a long text only to meet some passing need. Such a change may not be permanent, or it would appear to the uneducated that there are two sources of Torah, and they would begin to mock it and rabbinic authority. He does not elaborate enough to differentiate between a standardized cycle of poetic inserts and objectionable fixed additions to the liturgy.

134. See, for example: תוספות רבנו יהודה שירליאון, קכד ואילך; פירושי רבנו אליהו מלונדריש ופסקיו, מח–מט; ספר אור זרוע, סי' יט, כ, עמ' יב; הגהות אשרי על הרא"ש, ברכות א:יב; הגהות מיימוניות, הלכות תפלה ו:ג.

135. The fifteenth-century Jacob Landau, in his *Sefer HaAgur*, (הלכות ברכות, עמ' לה, סי' קיז)

halakhic arguments were not entirely satisfactory. The human-derived halakhic basis for reciting *piyyut* was still sufficiently disputed for R. Yaakov of Marvège, a Tosafist of the late twelfth and early thirteenth centuries, to seek and receive mystical authorization from Heaven for the custom.[136] The language of the permission received does not conform to that of known halakhic debates; it states simply that humans should sing praises to God in any way they can. Some later rabbis accepted his visions as halakhic rulings.[137]

The only documentation of official rabbinic disapproval of *piyyut* from this period in the Ashkenazi realm indicates no discomfort with the halakhic validity of the general payyetanic endeavor, but rather a sense among the *Ḥasidei Ashkenaz* that congregations needed to be more careful about which *piyyutim* they recited. *Sefer Ḥasidim* calls for the elimination of a particular genre of *piyyut*, the *zulat*, because it was interfering with the proper sixfold recitation of *emet* in *emet veyatziv*.[138] It objected to any *piyyut* beginning with God's name lest one profane it by casually referring to the poem by its opening word(s).[139] It also called for Jews to be very careful to recite only the works of righteous *payyetanim*, for the character of the poet is embedded in the *piyyut* and redounds to the credit or discredit of the worshiper.[140] In general, however, these pietists not only approved of the inclusion of *piyyut*, but also insisted on the inviolability of the ancestral traditions dictating where and when each precise poem was to be recited. One who substitutes some alternative *kerovetz* for the conventional one by Kalir transgresses the commandments against encroachment on the bound-

---

merely recognizes the weighty Spanish opposition to *piyyut*, and then records a much longer list of geonic, Ashkenazi, and Sefardi authorities who do support the custom.

136. שאלות ותשובות מן השמים, סי' נח, עמ' כא.

137. See, for instance, תשובות הרדב"ז, חלק ג', סי' תקלב.

138. ספר חסידים שחיבר רבינו יהודה החסיד, מהדורת ראובן מרגליות, סי' רנח, עמ' רכב. Compare the similar statement, here referring specifically to the High Holy Day services, in R. Elazar of Worm's *Rokeaḥ*, 88-89. Margulies suggests that this *piyyut* was interrupting the continuity of the recitation of the statutory prayers. Fleischer (שירת הקודש העברית..., 426) indicates that *piyyut* continued to replace the statutory liturgy for the *shema* blessings for a while in Italy, and the *zulat* continued to do so in Ashkenaz. While he does not document his sources here, our text is probably the origin of this assumption. Margulies' suggestion makes less sense, for R. Yehudah Haḥasid's objection is to missing two of the six recitations. The text continues with a discussion of the cosmic problems created by missing other parts of the introductory section of the prayer if they are replaced by *piyyut* on Rosh Hashanah and Yom Kippur.

139. ed. Margulies, p. 555, # 1092.

140. ספר חסידים על פי נוסח כתב יד אשר בפארמא, מהדורת יהודה הכהן וויסטינעצקי, מהדורה שניה (פראנקפורט: מ.א. וואהרמאנן, תרפ"ד; מברלין: מקיצי נרדמים, 1891), עמ' 133–134, סי' תע.

aries (of customary law) established by one's ancestors.[141] Proof of this is that one person who replaced a Kalirian *piyyut* and another one who similarly replaced a *kerovetz* by R. Meshullam both died within thirty days of their transgressions.[142] As mentioned above, by the time of the Maharil, this sanctity ascribed to the *piyyutim* had been explicitly extended to the specific melodies with which the poetry was recited in any single community.[143]

A single but much later voice of full opposition, cited heavily by later Sefardi authorities, is that of the fifteenth-century R. Moshe Mintz, who took quite seriously the *Tur*'s concerns, to be discussed below, about interrupting the blessings of *keriat shema*. R. Mintz recorded that he did not separate himself from the congregation while they recite *piyyutim*, but essentially placed the *piyyut* before the blessings, reciting for himself the blessing's statutory beginning only after the congregation completed the poetry. He recited the *piyyut* himself only to avoid setting a negative or easily misinterpreted example for his congregation.[144]

Before turning to the Sefardi world, where the situation was much different, account must be taken briefly of those locales where the attitude towards *piyyut* was similar to that of Ashkenaz. I am aware of no discussions of the issue from the Byzantine and early Ottoman worlds, but we do know that the various Greek, Romaniote, and Middle Eastern rites included rich collections of *piyyut*. The same could be said for the indigenous traditions of North Africa,[145] although I have located no significant defense of their customs preserved in the literature.

It is clear that the Provençal rabbis also held no significant halakhic objection to *piyyut* and that it was an integral part of their liturgy. R. Zeraḥya Halevi, in his *Hamaor Hakaton*, objects to the specific content of the Yom Kippur *seder avodah*, but only because he disagrees with the payyetanic interpretations of the relevant Mishnah.[146] We may infer from this that although he considered the

141. *Sefer Ḥasidim*, ed. Margulies, p. 140, # 114. R. Yehudah derives the commandment from Prov. 22:28 and Dt. 19:14.

142. *Ibid.*, p. 402, #607. See, too the concern evidenced in the fifteenth-century *Leket Yosher* (pp. 17, 18, 21) about proper procedures to follow when the *ḥazzan* has mistakenly omitted the proper *piyyut*.

143. *Sefer Maharil*, 339. See p. 135, above.

144. שאלות ותשובות רבינו משה מינץ, מהדורת יונתן שרגא דומב, (ירושלים: מפעל תורת חכמי אשכנז, מכון ירושלים, תשנ"א), חלק ב', סימן פז.

145. R. Yitzḥak Alfasi approved of *piyyut* as long as the poem included a proper transition back to the subject of the blessing. See: ספר שלאות ותשובות ר' יוסף הלוי אבן מיגאש, מהדורת שמחה חסידה, עמ' עח–עט, סי' פז.

146. To the Rif, *Yoma* 1a.

meaning of the *piyyut* important, he did not find the poetry itself, as a category, problematic. The *Tur* and R. Shlomo ibn Adret explicitly cite R. Avraham ben David of Posquieres' approval of *piyyut* on the basis of an extension of the Ashkenazi argument about the length of the blessings. The Ravad apparently argued that the internal length of the blessings was of no halakhic import.[147] R. Avraham ben Natan Hayarḥi, in his *Sefer Hamanhig*, although not hesitating to voice his disapproval of inappropriate customs, recognizes the universality of the inclusion of *piyyut* on the basis of its being communal petition,[148] and cites several precedents from R. Amram Gaon justifying its recitation.[149] The Meiri similarly dismisses the problem of the length of the blessings, and merely stipulates that, ideally, inserts should be *me-ein haberakhah*, as the dictates of length refer to the ideational content of the blessings. According to him, the geonic and Spanish objection that *piyyut* alters the rabbinically ordained blessing format errs in its assumption that the prohibition against changing the form of the blessing refers to the internal wording of the blessing. Rather, it only defines the formal structure of the blessings beginning and ending the paragraph.[150] Thus, the Provençal rabbis, while defending their own customs, were not major players in the ongoing halakhic debates.

The primary literary defense of *piyyut*, then, came from the Ashkenazi rabbis. In their world, as in the world of most Jews, *piyyut* was an integral part of the liturgical experience and an embedded element of minhag. Why, then, do we find here, more than anywhere else, such an impassioned, innovative, and almost desperate defense of the custom? One reason was certainly the traditional Ashkenazi reverence for minhag. When non-Ashkenazim, probably oriented to the Babylonian geonic or Spanish schools, attacked Ashkenazi recitation of *piyyut* as inimical to talmudic halakhah, the response was to find halakhic ways to justify the custom. Thus, the Ashkenazim introduced two important new arguments, neither of which were fully irrefutable: they limited the mishnaic ruling about the length of the blessings to apply only to a very few specific cases; and they established *piyyut* as a minhag with origins in tannaitic antiquity.

However, behind these halakhic arguments lay the basic assumption of the

---

147. The Ravad's original discussion is lost. *Tur* OH 68; חידושי הרשב"א על הש"ס, לברכות יא., עמ' מג. See the similar arguments in "ספר ההשלמה לרבנו משולם ב"ר משה ב"ר יהודה מברדיש," עמ' רו–רז. The *Sefer Hahashelamah* makes reference to an argument of some that the only blessing among the statutory prayers to which one may not add *piyyut* is *hashkiveinu* because its special status as an elongated *geulah* means that it should not be too long.

148. ed. Raphael, 93-94.

149. pp. 349-350, 356, 419-420.

150. בית הבחירה על מסכת ברכות..., 23–24. *Orḥot Ḥayyim*, Hilkhot Tefillah, pp. 16b-17a, # 57, summarizes various pro-*piyyut* arguments but adds nothing new.

Ashkenazi schools that *piyyut* was essentially meaningful and hence appropriate and acceptable as prayer. We saw explicitly in the responsum of R. Yitzḥak Halevi the assumption that people did understand it; and in the writings of the Maharil and the very composition of *piyyut* commentaries, the view that if people did not, they had an obligation to learn to do so. Because *piyyut* carried so many levels of meaning–on a semantic level, on a mystic level,[151] and simply as a part of tradition, the halakhic justifications for continuing the custom in Ashkenaz were secondary.

### *The Debates in Muslim Spain*

Unlike most of the rest of the world of the Rishonim, where the custom of reciting *piyyut* found little or no opposition from halakhic theorists, Spain early became a center of controversy over the legitimacy of these additions to the statutory prayers. *Piyyut* was no less an integral part of the liturgy of the early Spanish Rishonim than it was in northern Europe, but whereas the Ashkenazim had adopted a corpus of poetry highly dependent on the classical *piyyut* of Kalir and his colleagues, the Sefardim, as part of the Arab world, had more direct contact with the ongoing eastern community of *payyetanim* and inherited their later, less refined traditions.[152] Some famous Spanish *payyetanim* like Yosef ibn Avitur continued to write eastern style poetry, but several factors soon led to a revolution, both in the nature of the poetry Spanish Jews composed, and in their theoretical halakhic attitudes to it.[153] Once traditional styles of *piyyut* were questioned and overthrown, the specific poems recited were no longer identified with ancestral custom. This crack in the armor of tradition allowed theoreticians to question the entire endeavor.

In spite of the traditions of geonic objections to *piyyut* (to which we should

151. Abraham Grossman, "הרקע לצמיחת פרשנות הפיוט בגרמניה ובצרפת במאה הי"א," בתוך ספר היובל לשלמה סימונסון: קובץ מחקרים לתולדות היהודים בימי הביניים ובתקופה הרנסנס (תל אביב: אוניברסיטת תל אביב, תשנ"ג), נה–עב, documents that *piyyut* commentary was early a regular activity of the Ashkenazi and Provençal academies, along with their better known activities of Talmud and Bible commentary. This commentary contributed to the use of *piyyut* as a source for understanding halakhic issues. Later *piyyut* commentaries from Ashkenaz, like the *Arugat Habosem*, are infused with the mystical knowledge of the *Ḥasidei Ashkenaz* and indicate that the mystical meanings inherent in or attributed to the poetic parts of the liturgy were highly esteemed.

152. Fleischer, ...שירת־הקודש העברית, 336.

153. For a detailed discussion of the eastern heritage of the Spanish poets and the revolution in its form and content, see: אהרן מירסקי, "שירת ספרד – תכניה וסוגיה," הפיוט: התפתחותו בארץ־ישראל ובגולה (ירושלים: מאגנס, תש"ן), 617–652.

add Rabbenu Ḥananel of Kairouan's rebuke to those changing the rabbinically established text of the first three blessings of the *amidah*[154]), halakhic factors played at best a secondary role in changing the Spanish Jews' attitude to their heritage of liturgical poetry. The most significant influence was Arabic culture. In Spain, the elite of Jewish society were well integrated into the life of the court and the Spanish intelligentsia. Inevitably, they accepted the norms of Hispano-Arabic culture and applied them to Jewish life wherever possible. Jews began to write Hebrew secular poetry incoporating Arabic forms and meters; beginning with Dunash ibn Labrat in the mid-tenth century and coming into full flower a century later with Shlomo ibn Gabirol, these new modes permeated the world of liturgical poetry too.[155] Similarly, Muslim study of the Koran and its grammar encouraged Jews to study the Bible and its language intensively. As the Muslims venerated koranic Arabic, the Jews came to venerate biblical

---

154. פירושי רבינו חננאל בר חושיאל לתלמוד, עא; *Otzar Hageonim, Berakhot, Nispaḥim*, p. 42, #144. Many citations of R. Ḥananel include only the first part of his statement, which accepts the legitimacy of communal petitions in the *amidah*. Out of context, this incomplete citation then becomes part of many rabbinic arguments *in favor* of the recitation of *piyyut*, especially as it becomes conflated by the Tosafists and those citing them with the more positive traditions of R. Hai Gaon and even Rabbenu Tam. See, for instance, the responsum of Rabbenu Tam in both *Maḥzor Vitry*, 362-365, and *Shibbolei Haleket* (Mirsky), 213-218; *Tosafot Berakhot* 34a, ד"ה אל ישאל אדם צרכיו לא בג' ראשונות ולא בג' אחרונות; *Mordechai* to *Berakhot* 5:104; *Rosh* to *Berakhot* 5:21; תוספות רבנו יהודה שירליאון על מסכת ברכות, חלק ראשון, קלא; רבנו פרץ ב"ר אליהו מקורביל, תוספות רבנו פרץ למסכת ברכות, מהדורת משה הרשלר (ירושלים: מכון שלם – צפונות קדמונים, תשד"ם), לד.; אבודרהם השלם, רסא–רסב; ר' ירוחם, ספר תולדות אדם וחוה, נתיב ג' חלק ג', דף כה עמ' א; שו"ת הרדב"ז, , עמ' 78, סי' תתקסז. Many of these are citing R. Tam. But the second half of R. Ḥananel's dictum does appear in a significant number of sources in one version or another. It says:

> ושמעי' מינה דאסור לכל מאן דמשני או מוסיף או גורע בג' ברכות ראשונות מן המטבע שטבעו חכמים בברכות ואלו חזנים שמניחים מטבע ברכות ואומרים קדושות (קרובות, קרוב"ץ) לאו שפיר עבדי...
>
> We derive from this that everyone is forbidden to change, add, or delete from the rabbinically established form of the first three blessings, and those *ḥazzanim* who abandon the established form of the blessings and recite *piyyut* are not acting appropriately.

The *Or Zarua*, 19d, #104 cites R. Ḥananel fully, but adds that R. Ḥananel would approve of "our" (13th century Viennese) *piyyutim* because they are really communal petitions. R. Eliezer b"R. Yoel Halevi (ספר ראבי"ה, כרך א', עמ' 71–72, סי' צב.) flatly disagrees with R. Ḥananel. For more direct citations, see *Shibbolei Haleket*, ed. Mirsky, 209, #28, which opens its collection of discussions with this one; *Hagahot Maimoniot* to *Hilkhot Tefillah* 6:3; and the *Beit Yosef*'s citation of *Hagahot Maimoniot*, OH 112 (he also cites others who fit into our previous category).

155. As Menaḥem Zulai has pointed out, these same factors influenced the poetry of Saadia Gaon in the east. Saadia's innovations may have influenced the Spanish Jews, but had relatively little influence in his own home. האסכולה הפייטנית של רב סעדיה גאון, יט.

Hebrew and to consider it the only worthy form, especially for liturgical creations. The study of philosophy increased the Jews' appreciation of meaningful prayer language and led them to reject incomprehensible poetic creations. The content of their prayers had to be philosophically accurate; instead of the language and ideas of rabbinic literature, the concepts of the rationalists permeated Sefardi *piyyut*.[156] As Naphtali Wieder has demonstrated, the strict decorum of Muslim prayer also impressed Jews[157] and may have motivated many to decry its absence in a Jewish service that was too long and understood by too few. All of these factors combined to allow criticism of the existing synagogue practice, the generation of some significant changes, and the weakening of the universal acceptance of the custom of inserting *piyyut* into the prayers. Since old *piyyut* was no longer a source of *kavvanah*, most of it was jettisoned.

Many of the earliest criticisms of *piyyut* in the literature of the Sefardi intelligentsia, rather than finding fault with the halakhic basis of liturgical poetry, instead objected to it on aesthetic or philosophical grounds. On the one hand, some scholars questioned whether the new forms, derived ultimately from Arabic secular poetry, were even an appropriate use of the language of divine revelation, let alone appropriate language for prayer. The grammarian Shlomo Ibn Parḥon and his teacher, the famous poet and intellectual Yehudah Halevi, were highly critical of the application of Arabic poetics, particularly metrical rules, to Hebrew verse, because it led to distortions of the holy tongue and grammatical abominations. Interestingly, Halevi, in his *Kuzari*, criticizes the application of meter to Hebrew verse and praises the traditional rhymed *piyyut*; we know, however, that he himself wrote liturgical poetry of immense beauty and impact in the new styles. Ibn Parḥon, on the other hand, could not justify any mode of poetry unknown in biblical times, extended his criticism to all forms of liturgical poetry, and reports that Halevi repented before his death for ever having written *piyyut*.[158]

---

156. אהרן מירסקי, "יצירתם של יהודי ספרד בפיוט ובשירה," בתוך מורשת ספרד, בעריכת חיים ביינארט (ירושלים: מאגנס, תשנ"ב), 140–142.

157. השפעות אסלאמיות על הפולחן היהודי (אוקספורד: ספרית־מזרח ומערב, תש"ז). Although Wieder is documenting a later period, that of the Maimonides clan in Egypt, there is no reason to suppose that Jews in Spain were immune to these same concerns about the perceptions of their neighbors.

158. Judah Hallevi, *Book of Kuzari*, trans. Hartwig Hirschfeld (New York: Pardes Publishing House, 1946), II:72-78. ר' שלמה ב"ר אברהם ן' פרחון (ממלכות ארגון), מחברת הערוך, ed. Salomo Gottlieb Stern (Pressburg, 1844; rpt. Jerusalem, 1970), 4d-5b, 74c (תעב). Ibn Parḥon's broadening of the argument may well reflect his reaction to the use of *piyyut* in Italy, where he settled after fleeing the religious persecutions instigated by the Almohad dynasty in Muslim Spain in 1149.

The most famous critic of *piyyut* from this period is, of course, Ibn Parḥon's other teacher, Abraham Ibn Ezra. His attack was highly influential, widely cited, and like the commentary of R. Ḥananel,[159] widely misquoted and used for other than its original purposes. Unlike Ibn Parḥon, Ibn Ezra did not oppose all *piyyut* per se. Although he found poetry written in biblical Hebrew acceptable according to the new Spanish aesthetics, he vehemently opposed Kalirian style *piyyut*, which he probably first encountered after fleeing to Italy to escape the Almohad persecutions in Spain.[160] We know from his *diwan* that Ibn Ezra himself wrote metered liturgical poetry, some of which was unquestionably designed to be incorporated into the blessings of the statutory liturgy.[161] But to him, improper *piyyut* could disrupt the halakhic validity of the entire prayer in which it was embedded. To be proper, it had to fit certain criteria: worshipers had to be able to understand their prayers and could not simply rely on the authority of those who composed them;[162] the prayer texts had to be in grammatical, purely biblical Hebrew; and they had to have proper non-aggadic, philosophically acceptable content appropriate for the serious task of divine worship. The *piyyut* of Kalir and his followers did not meet any of these criteria, and Ibn Ezra claimed that it would be better to omit classical *piyyut* entirely rather than include such poetry in one's worship.[163]

---

159. See note 154 above.

160. J. Yahalom, "The Poetics of Spanish Piyyut in Light of Abraham Ibn Ezra's Critique of its Pre-Spanish Precedents," in *Abraham Ibn Ezra and His Age, Proceedings of the International Symposium, Madrid 1989*, ed. Fernando Díaz Esteban (Madrid: Asosiacíon Espanola de Orientalistas, 1990), 387f.

161. שירי הקודש של אברהם אבן עזרא, מהדורת ישראל לוין, (ירושלים: האקדמיה הלאומית הישראלית למדעים, תש"ם). Note particularly the poems designated for inclusion in the *shema* blessings. Leopold Zunz, *Die Ritus des synagogalen Gottesdienstes geschichtlich entwickelt*, 2nd ed. (Berlin, 1919), 113, records that the Catalonian rite included Ibn Ezra's *zulat* and full *kerovot* for Yom Kippur *shaḥarit* and *minḥah* services.

162. Ibn Ezra singles out Kalir as the recognized model for Italian-Ashkenazi style *piyyut*. There is no evidence that he is responding to the added authority given to Kalir by R. Tam's identification of him with the Tanna, R. Elazar b"R. Shimon. As we saw above, R. Tam's predecessors relied on the authority of other *payyetanim* too without their having any such antiquity.

163. Ibn Ezra's commentary to Kohelet 5:1. See also the specific attacks in his grammatical treatises on the linguistic atrocities in the non-Spanish styles of *piyyut*, which he admits came from ignorance of the rules and search for novelty rather than deliberate attempts to pervert the language: שפה ברורה, מהדורת גבריאל הירש ליפמאן (פירת, 1839), יד; ספר שפת יתר, מהדורת גבריאל הירש ליפמאן (פרנקפורט אם מיין, 1843), עמ' כא:–כב., סי' עד. Compare the criticism of the descendant of another Spanish refugee from persecutions, David Kimḥi of Narbonne, who considered it a great sin to make grammatical errors such as those found in classical *piyyut*; repeating these errors liturgically brings the sins upon the shoulders of the worshiper as well.

Contemporary with this aesthetic revolution, some Spanish halakhists began to question the legitimacy of any insertion of poetry into the established blessings of the statutory liturgy. The chief exemplar of this criticism in Spain itself was R. Yehudah ben Barzilai of Barcelona, of whose work, *Sefer Haltim*, only a small section survives. Fortunately, this section includes a summary of his lost full scale attack on *piyyut*,[164] in which R. Yehudah argues adamantly that it is inappropriate to add the poetry of any individual, learned or not, to the texts of the blessings. Echoing the argument of Yehudai Gaon, *Sefer Haltim* claims that *piyyut* was a legitimate endeavor only in the period of its inception, when persecutions allowed the teaching of Torah in no other way. Without those persecutions, it has no place. Further, it maintains, *piyyut* often praises God to the point of blasphemy and includes content inappropriate to the blessings or petitionary material that should be reserved for weekdays.

Yehudah ben Barzilai concludes with a unique version of a responsum of Hai Gaon. Other forms of this responsum record that, in spite of there being no explicit talmudic precedent, and in spite of the disapproval of some, it was the custom of the yeshiva to recite the insertions into the *amidah* for the High Holy Days.[165] Other citations conflate Hai Gaon's opinion with that of Rabbenu Ḥananel and sometimes also that of Rabbenu Tam so that the *kerovetz* is among

---

(ספר השרשים, דויד בן יוסף קמחי הספרדי, ed. Jo. H.R. Biesenthal, F. Lebrecht, עתר.) See too Shmuel Ibn Tibbon's insistence on proper grammar and his elevation of biblical poetics, cited by A.M. Habermann, תולדות הפיוט והשירה (רמת גן: מסדה, 1970), א:74.

Three hundred years later, in the waning years of Jewish life in Christian Spain, Yosef Albo, in his *Sefer HaIkarim*, II: 711-712, cites Ibn Ezra to exactly this purpose. *Piyyut* itself is not bad, but in order that it not be burdensome and be esthetically pleasing, the poetry chosen must be brief and have meters that fit its music. To be acceptable prayer, it must also have suitable content and be recited with humility.

See too the comment of Zunz, *Ritus*, 163-4: "Abenesra, der Maamad-Dichter, tadelt–gleich Dunasch, der Saadia, und Chajudsch, der Menachem angegriffen–nur die Uncorrectheit, Dunkelheit, und Ueberladung, nicht den Piut überhaupt."

164. מהדורת יעקב שור, 251–252. Although R. Yehudah ben Barzilai resided in Christian Spain, which at this period generally had closer ties to Provence, he himself was closer to the Andalusian rabbinic traditions of Moslem Spain. See *Halakhot Gedolot*, ed. Hildesheimer, I:18, n. 15*; and ישראל מ. תא־שמע, רבי זרחיה הלוי בעל המאור ובני חוגו: לתולדות הספרות הרבנית בפרובאנס (ירושלים: מוסד הרב קוק, תשנ"ג), 68 ואילך. It is likely, given the evidence of later periods, that the Barcelonan synagogue had not fully participated in the revolution in payyetanic styles characteristic of Muslim Spain. This contrast may be a source of some of R. Yehudah's ire.

165. See: ספר שערי תשובה, מהדורת ירוחם פישל בן צבי הירש הלוי, סי' קנא. References to this responsum without inference that it applies to the question of *piyyut* appear also in *Maḥzor Vitry*, 365-366 (described only as a geonic responsum) and *Abudarham Hashalem*, 261-262.

the forms of customary petitionary insertions allowed as an expression of communal needs.[166] In contrast, *Sefer HaItim* specifically records that Hai Gaon's yeshiva chose to *omit* the High Holy Day insertions, in spite of their being the custom of most of Israel and justified as an expression of communal needs. The passage concludes with the editorial addition:

> שאר פיוטין כולהון דאינון דברי הבאי ודברי בורות אשר לא שערום אבותינו לא כש"כ שמצוה עלינו למנוע שלא להזכירן
>
> The rest of the *piyyutim* are entirely nonsensical and foolish matters beyond that which our ancestors could even have imagined. Therefore, it is incumbent upon us to desist from making any mention of them.

Although it is dangerous to draw conclusions from what is admittedly only a summary of a better developed argument, we can tentatively suggest that although he attempted to couch his argument in halakhic terms, Yehudah ben Barzilai was fundamentally uncomfortable with the nature of the poetry itself. His strongest arguments are against the inappropriate content of the poems and the poor credentials of the *payyetanim*, especially in comparison with the known antiquity and authority of the Prophets and men of the Great Assembly who established the statutory prayer texts. How could one possibly insert such foolishness into the elevated forms of the statutory liturgy? Although he refers to the legal principle forbidding alteration of the rabbinically ordained form of prayers–and to several of the arguments found in Pirkoi ben Baboi about persecutions, misplaced petitions, and excessive praise–he avoids the more serious halakhic points. Perhaps the lost section of the text better explained Yehudah ben Barzilai's unusual reading of Hai Gaon, which allowed him to extend the Gaon's logic to prohiting *piyyut*. In any case, it is abundantly clear that the author of *Sefer HaItim* vehemently opposed all *piyyut* and attempted to muster halakhic arguments that would uproot this errant custom. There is, however, no indication that his rulings affected actual practice.

Maimonides was the first truly influential authority to object to *piyyut* on halakhic grounds without merely rehashing geonic materials. However, we know of no single extensive Maimonidean treatise devoted to the topic. Maimonides never explicitly refers to *piyyut* in his *Mishneh Torah*, but his discussions of the sanctity of the prayer texts established by Ezra and his court and the consequent

166. *Tosafot Berakhot* 34a, ד"ה אל ישאל אדם צרכיו לא בשלש ראשונות ולא בשלש אחרונות; *Mordechai Berakhot* 5:104; *Hagahot Maimoniot* to *Mishneh Torah, Hilkhot Tefillah* 6:3; all of these are Ashkenazim. See note 154 above on the question of whether or not Rabbenu Ḥananel himself approved of *piyyut*.

inadmissability of any addition or subtraction from them imply that one who includes *piyyut* in the statutory liturgy is in error.[167] Several preserved responsa contain outright condemnations of the custom as forbidden and errant because the poems constitute interruptions in and deviations from the texts of the statutory prayers established in antiquity by Ezra and his court.[168] The content of *piyyut* can also be objectionable because it adds petitions that are inappropriate to the Sabbath and holiday liturgies, praises that are philosophically unjustifiable, or misinformation that reflects the poets' lack of learning.[169] While the preceding issues are all at least implicit in geonic arguments, Maimonides, as noted above,[170] also objects to the addition of meter, melody, and content foreign to Jewish traditions because these change prayer from a serious endeavor to a source of amusement; the result is a loss of *kavvanah* and a consequent lack of decorum because people sense that the prayers are no longer obligatory.[171]

Maimonides, of course, as a teenager, was among those Spanish Jews who fled the 1149 Almohad persecutions. Although firmly rooted in Spanish halakhic culture, he spent most of his adult life in Egypt, where the community included not only Jews who had accepted the authority of the Babylonian geonic traditions, but also a second group who had always looked first to Palestine as their cultural and halakhic home. We know from the evidence found in the genizah of their synagogue that this latter group had a rich tradition of *piyyut*; nothing suggests that Egypt's "Babylonian" community was different in this respect. The thriving Karaite community also filled their liturgy with *piyyut*, often poems of mourning for Jerusalem.[172]

---

167. See *Hilkhot Berakhot* 1:5 and *Hilkhot Keriat Shema* 1:7. *Hilkhot Tefillah* 6:2-3 establishes that the only permitted additions to the *amidah* are petitions properly situated in the weekday intermediate blessings.

168. תשובות הרמב"ם, II: 328-329, #180; 363-366, #207; 465-468, #254. For a detailed discussion of all the Maimonidean sources, see יעקב בלידשטיין, התפילה במשנתו ההלכתית של הרמב"ם (ירושלים: מוסד ביאליק ואוניברסיטת בן גוריון בנגב, תשנ"ד), פרק שישי. Yosef Tobi errs in his claim that the issue of interruption to the statutory texts appears first only in the late thirteenth century, as the technical terminology definitely appears in Maimonides' responsa (and even in the less influential Pirkoi ben Baboi), both in the questions posed to him and in his answers, indicating that the issue was not new. See his "יחסו של רב סעדיה גאון לפיוט," בתוך כנסת עזרא: ספרות וחיים בבית הכנסת, אסופת מאמרים מוגשת לעזרא פליישר, בעריכת שולמית אליצור, משה דוד הר, אביגדור שנאן, גרשון שקד (ירושלים: יד יצחק בן־צבי ומכון בן־צבי לחקר קהילות ישראל במזרח, 1994), 235, הע' 2; and his "השירה העברית בארצות־המזרח לאחר הגירוש," פעמים 26 (תשמ"ו): 37, הע' 22.

169. תשובות הרמב"ם, II: 465-468, #254; 487-489, #260; ספר המצות ל...רבינו משה בן מיימון, הקדמה, עמ' ב, דף ג; מורה נבוכים א:נט.

170. p. 132.

171. תשובות הרמב"ם, II: 465-468, # 254.

172. See תשובות הרמב"ם, II: 366-370, #208. Research into early Karaite liturgies is still in

Although the eastern Mediterranean communities knew and incorporated some of the new Spanish *piyyut*, no aesthetic revolution there ever resulted in the rejection of the old types of poetry. Yehuda Alḥarizi, in the thirteenth century, was appalled at the low levels of poetry common in the eastern communities.[173] We have no evidence that Maimonides attempted to impose the Spanish rite on his new community. Indeed, the siddur with which Maimonides concludes the liturgical section of his *Mishneh Torah* probably records the rite common in Fustat, which certainly differs greatly from the Spanish rite that we know from later periods.[174] However, this siddur contains absolutely no *piyyut*, not even for the *seder avodah* of Yom Kippur, and we know from his responsa that Maimonides actively discouraged the inclusion of liturgical poetry in Egyptian services.[175]

How can we account for Maimonides' attitude toward *piyyut*? Although the poetry indigenous to the Egyptian rite almost certainly did not meet the new elevated standards of Maimonides' Spanish heritage,[176] Maimonides never criticized it from the standpoint of a grammarian or biblical purist, but rather as a philosopher and halakhic expert who quickly became a recognized rabbinic leader of the community and was in a position to apply halakhic theory and influence local customs. As a highly regarded foreigner, he could scrutinize local customs and eliminate those that seemed errant to him. The halakhic grounds for criticizing *piyyut* had been laid by the Geonim and some of his Spanish predecessors. Because of his personal greatness and peculiar historical circum-

---

its infancy, but, as the majority of materials come from the Cairo genizah, we can assume that these texts had some use in the Egyptian Karaite community. See: חגי בן־שמאי, "היצירה הפייטנית וסדרי הקינות של אבלי ציון הקראים המסגרת והתכנים," בתוך כנסת עזרא: ספרות וחיים בבית הכנסת, אסופת מאמרים מוגשת לעזרא פליישר, בעריכת שולמית אליצור, משה דוד הר, אביגדור שנאן, גרשון שקד (ירושלים: יד יצחק בן־צבי ומכון בן־צבי לחקר קהילות ישראל במזרח, 1994), 191–234.

173. *Taḥkemoni*, Gates 3, 18, 24.

174. See: דניאל גולדשמידט, "סדר התפלה של הרמב"ם ע"פ כ"י אוקספורד," בתוך מחקרי תפילה ופיוט (ירושלים: מאגנס, תש"ם; מידיעות המכון לחקר השירה העברית בירושלים ז (תשי"ח), 183–213), 190. See, too, Stefan C. Reif, *Judaism and Hebrew Prayer: New Perspectives on Jewish Liturgical History* (Cambridge: University Press, 1993), 192f. There are no preserved manuscripts of twelfth-century Sefardi prayerbooks, and only a very few from the thirteenth century.

175. תשובות הרמב"ם, II:363-366, #207; 485-486, #259; 487-489, #260.

176. A standard subject in the education of a Jew in Maimonides' time was the tools necessary for the proper composition of Hebrew poetry. Nine poems, both secular and liturgical, can be clearly attributed to Maimonides. (See those listed in Davidson, אוצר השירה והפיוט.) Schirmann describes him as a competent but uninspired poet and suggests that Maimonides' rationalism prevented him from fully appreciating the artistic and non-practical aspects of poetry. ח. שירמן, "הרמב"ם והשירה העברית," אזנים ג, סידרא ב (תרצ"ה), 433–436; Salo W. Baron, *SRHJ*, VII: 105.

stances, Maimonides was one of the first detractors of the institution capable of influencing popular custom.

Whether or not he did so beyond his personal place of prayer in Egypt is difficult to determine. We have one responsum that records the difficulties encountered by his student, R. Saadia ben Berakhot Hamelammed, in executing a change that would have eliminated some highly cherished *piyyutim.*[177] Other evidence, discussed above, indicates that Egyptian congregations cherished *piyyut* and actively resisted its removal.[178] At times, Maimonides was forced to suggest compromise positions that maintained the poetry but simply moved it out of the context of the statutory blessings to halakhically neutral positions.[179] However, we do know that the Yemenite rite, which adhered extremely closely to that taught them by Maimonides, inserted no *piyyut* into the statutory blessings, and Maimonides' son Abraham seems to claim that this error (of *piyyut*?) has already been eliminated in Egypt.[180] We can also infer, from the Radbaz's

---

177. Possibly in Alexandria. תשובות הרמב"ם, II: 485-486, #259. It is likely that other students and colleagues of Maimonides imposed the same changes elsewhere. Since he makes no mention of problems at home, we may assume that Maimonides' personal prestige quashed any significant opposition in Fustat.

At issue here was Maimonides' elimination of the repetition of the *amidah*, requiring the prayer leader to recite his private prayers aloud and the congregants either to pray along with him if they were able or to respond *amen* appropriately. This resulted, almost incidentally, in the elimination of the *kerovot.* As Naphtali Wieder points out, Maimonides' motivation in allowing this unprecedented change was the loss of decorum when congregants failed to listen to the repetition of the *amidah.* Their talking, studying, turning away from their orientation to Jerusalem, and even leaving the synagogue meant that the formal prayers became *berakhot levatalah*, blessings in vain. Maimonides' sensitivity to this ancient problem was heightened by comparisons with the decorum of the mosque. See Wieder's discussion in his השפעות אסלאמיות על הפולחן היהודי, פרק ג', "ביטול תפלת לחש של י"ח," 26–30.

178. See p. 132f.

179. תשובות הרמב"ם, II:363-366, #207. Here, Maimonides suggests that if the commoners in the congregation are unable to give up *piyyutim* formerly inserted into the blessings of *shema*, the poetry can be recited before beginning the blessings, where it will no longer be an interruption. II:485-486, #259 records an attempt at a similar compromise that would move the *piyyutim* of the *amidah* to after the completion of the recitation of the entire statutory text. These two compromises allowed the mandatory juxtaposition of *shema* and *amidah* to remain undisturbed and allowed the preservation of *kerovot* even when the repetition of the *amidah* was dropped. Although direct influence cannot be demonstrated, especially as later halakhic sources do not refer to this precedent, these compromises were later used among the Sefardim. See below.

180. תשובות רבנו אברהם בן הרמב"ם, 132, סי' פז. The responsum, which is somewhat ambiguous, makes reference to a longer exposition elsewhere. I have been unable to locate any such passage in Nissim Dana's recent edition of his ספר המספיק לעובדי השם. See too S.D. Goitein, *A Mediterranean Society*, II:553, n. 20, and Salo Baron, *SRHJ* VII:103.

1539 reinstitution of the repetition of the *amidah*, that those Jews affected–in Egypt, Palestine, and Syria–had eliminated *kerovot* from any halakhically questionable role in this part of their services as a result of Maimonides' influence.[181] However, the total lack of any citation of Maimonides' objections to *piyyut* in the discussions of the Spanish Rishonim would indicate that his stance had little or no influence on the course of events in the west.[182]

### *The Debates in Christian Spain*

In the wake of Muslim persecutions and forced conversions, some Jews, like the Maimon family, had fled Spain altogether. Many others traveled north to Christian Spain, where new centers of Torah study were developing, especially in Barcelona, Toledo, and Gerona. There, constant comparisons with Arabic high culture and religious decorum were of lesser or no importance. More significantly, war zones no longer lay between these Spanish Jews and the French and German centers of rabbinic culture where *piyyut* was unquestioningly accepted. In addition, the persecutions and expulsions of the Jews from the various principalities of France and Germany eventually brought leading rabbis like the Rosh and his family to Spain. At the same time, however, the halakhic tradition of utter opposition to *piyyut* renewed by *Sefer HaItim* and made explicit by Maimonides was very much a part of continuing Spanish Torah traditions.[183] Thus, for the remainder of the Jewish sojourn in Spain, some halakhists actively opposed *piyyut*, others resigned themselves to popular custom but registered their personal discomfort with it, and still others accepted the authority of Rabbenu Tam and justified its inclusion.

To some extent, these variations were geographic. Until the very end of this

---

Tobi, "יחסו של רב סעדיה גאון לפיוט", 235, n. 3, claims that the Yemenites never inserted *piyyut* into their statutory prayers. However, the earliest preserved dated manuscripts of Yemenite prayerbooks come only from the fifteenth century, long after Maimonides' influence was felt.

181. שו"ת הרדב"ז, ד: סי' צד; Wieder, השפעות אסלאמיות..., 29.

182. Tobi, "השירה העברית...", 31, suggests exactly the opposite, but presents no evidence for Maimonides' influence other than the disappearance of *piyyut* from the Castilian rite (see below). It is strange that a strong halakhic influence would not be cited in the sources. A more likely factor is the cultural shift, which Tobi also discusses, that led to a devaluation of the actual collection of poetry in the rites.

183. Some Spanish siddurim indicate that not all communities add לאל אשר שבת..., the Shabbat insert into the Yotzer blessing to which the *Sefer HaItim* objected so vociferously. See, for example, Ms. Saragossa, Cathedral Library 1, dated to the 13-14th century; and Ms. Jewish Theological Seminary, Microfilm #4365, pp. 71a-b, dated to the 14-15th century, of probable Castilian origin.

period, Spain was not a single country but a collection of kingdoms, each with its own independent government and its own policies towards the Jews. The Jewish communities within each kingdom functioned fairly independently as self-governing bodies, responsible not only for the payment of taxes to the appropriate government, but also for their own internal administration according to Jewish civil, criminal, and religious law. However, there were distinct differences among the various kingdoms. While the Castilian congregations often operated as a single federation, communities in Aragon, Navarre, and Catalonia more frequently maintained strict autonomy.[184]

The Sefardi Jews themselves, not having been subject to constant expulsions like their northern European neighbors, tended to remain in the same area for generations.[185] This stability contributed to the consolidation of various local minhagim, which were sanctioned by their great antiquity, dating back to the origins of the Spanish Jewish community and to geonic precedents–and which we can assume included specific liturgical traditions, marked particularly by the selection of *piyyutim.*[186] The Castilian community, too, with its more centralized authority structure, seems gradually to have unified its liturgical customs. In contrast to the Jews in the other Spanish kingdoms, however, evidence suggests that Castilian Jews had eliminated almost all insertion of *piyyut* into the blessings of their statutory liturgy by the time of the community's destruction in 1492. In Castile, then–and only there–halakhah triumphed in the end.

These local minhagim notwithstanding, Spanish rabbinic culture operated fairly independently of political boundaries. Rabbis and students moved relatively easily from one area to another to study or take up new positions.[187] Rabbis from one kingdom were frequently called upon to help adjudicate disputes arising elsewhere on internal Jewish matters.[188] With Spain's rejoining the rest of Christian Europe, the Franco-German, Provençal, and Spanish halakhic

184. Yitzhak Baer, *A History of the Jews in Christian Spain* (Philadelphia: The Jewish Publication Society, 1961; rpt. 1971), I:212-216, 315.

185. Baer, *A History of the Jews in Christian Spain*, I:196.

186. Actual prayerbook evidence from Spain is scanty and insufficiently studied to allow precise description of the various rites.

187. Discussions of the halakhic output of the Spanish rabbis distinguish between the schools of individual rabbis to whom all of Spain gravitated, not between Castilian and Aragonese or Catalonian schools. See for instance: אברהם גרוסמן, "יצירתם ההלכתית של חכמי ספרד," בתוך מורשת ספרד, בעריכת חיים ביינארט (ירושלים: מאגנס, תשנ"ב), 150–173.

188. For example, R. Shlomo ben Adret of Barcelona probably consulted R. Asher ben Yeḥiel in Toledo before responding to a Provençal call for a ban on the study of philosophy by young adults. (Baer, I: 297-301, who also cites other examples. See, for instance, 289ff.)

schools began to influence each other even more. Naḥmanides was the first to implement Tosafist methodologies in the Spanish schools, and this process of merging the two halakhic traditions accelerated when other leading rabbis and Tosafists like the Rosh and his family, driven out of Germany, made their homes in Spain. Thus, while the actual liturgical rites of the various kingdoms seem ultimately to have differentiated themselves in their use or elimination of *piyyut*, no such statement can be made about the attitudes to *piyyut* of the rabbis active in the various locales. While those objecting to it most strenuously tended to be Castilian, not all were, and not all Castilian rabbis participated in the objection.

At the beginning of this period, we have no evidence that the earlier Spanish objections to *piyyut* had had any effect on popular custom. Although Maimonides' *Mishneh Torah* and *Guide for the Perplexed* quickly achieved widespread fame and became sources, respectively, of great authority and controversy, neither of these texts contain the outright condemnation and ruling to eliminate *piyyut* found in his responsa. Thus the Spanish communities did not participate in the Maimonidean reforms of the liturgy, perhaps because their recently adopted styles of poetry obviated some of the problems still found in the east, perhaps because they no longer had reason to compare themselves to the decorous mosque, or perhaps simply because Maimonides did not direct his responsa to them, allowing them to sidestep the issue.[189] Indeed, the new halakhic influences coming from the north–from areas in which the recitation of *piyyut* was firmly entrenched and supported by rabbinic culture–led the majority of rabbis of Christian Spain to find ways to support the existing minhag.

This northern influence is reflected in the new terms of the halakhic debates. Instead of questions of aesthetics, biblical language, aggadic content, and comprehensibility, the issues raised were now more similar to those found in the Tosafist schools. This change can be attributed, at least in part, to the rise of a new leadership of rabbis steeped in Talmud and kabbalah and to the decline in power of the more assimilated, philosophically oriented courtier class for whom the former issues were concerns.[190] Also, new Sefardi works had largely replaced the *piyyut* that had generated these issues.

The actual halakhic arguments of this period, however, display little novelty.

---

189. The Rashba does acknowledge and agree with Maimonides' stance, but goes on to argue for the perpetuation of this minhag based on the authority of Kalir. ספר שאלות ותשובות שחבר רבנו שלמה בן אדרת, I:469.

190. Bernard Septimus, "Piety and Power in Thirteenth-Century Catalonia" in *Studies in Medieval Jewish History and Literature*, ed., Isadore Twersky (Cambridge, MA and London: Harvard University Press, 1979), 205.

The supporters of the payyetanic endeavor continued to refine the Ashkenazi justification for changing the length of the blessings.[191] The Ra'ah[192] offers without attribution a version of R. Tam's argument in *Sefer Hayashar*[193] that temporary additions do not fall into the category of changing the length of the rabbinically established benedictions or improper petitions and hence are not forbidden. He and his colleague in Barcelona, the Rashba,[194] perhaps influenced by the teachings of the great German refugee, the Rosh,[195] are the earliest known Spanish rabbis specifically to employ R. Tam's argument for the tannaitic authority of Kalir. The Ra'ah integrates into his discussion of the length of the blessings an explicit acknowledgment and refutation of the two major geonic and Spanish arguments against *piyyut*: the legal principles respectively governing the placement of petitions and establishing the immutability of the rabbinically established texts of the blessings. The Rashba's extended discussion of R. Tam's interpretation of "one short, one long" is of interest largely because it shows the manipulations necessary to support the status quo–especially in light of the serious opposition, voiced by leading sages like his teacher, Naḥmanides, to *piyyut*'s lengthening of the blessings.[196] Basically, the Rashba, as he acknowledges in a responsum, realizes that not all *piyyut* can be fully justified on halakhic grounds, especially in light of Maimonides' opposition; but in this case, he claims, actual minhag should determine the halakhah.[197] One senses from his writings that, like the Ashkenazi rabbis, the Rashba per-

---

191. חידושי הרשב"א על הש"ס לרבינו שלמה בן אברהם בן אדרת, ברכות יא. לז–מג. In the previous generation, Rabbenu Yonah Gerondi, who had studied in France and Provence, made extensive use, without refutation, of R. Tam's arguments about the length of the blessings. He himself allowed changes in the prayers if expressed as communal petitions, at the end of the blessings of the *amidah*. However, in our texts, he never expressly allowed or prohibited *piyyut*, although his arguments make the latter unlikely. See his commentary on the Rif, *Berakhot* 5a, ד"ה מתני' בשחר מברך שתים לפניה וכו' אחת ארוכה ואחת קצרה וכו'; and 22a, ד"ה אע"ף שאמרו שואל אדם צרכיו בשומע תפלה.

192. פירוש הרא"ה על הלכות הרי"ף, מסכת ברכות, יד.

193. 63:12, p. 146. See above, p. 143, n. 133.

194. ספר שאלות ותשובות שחבר רבנו שלמה בן אדרת, I:469.

195. The Rosh calls on the authority of Kalir in his commentary to *Berakhot* 5:21 and in his *Tosafot* to *Berakhot* 34a, ed. Edwin, p. 63. Without dating each of these texts exactly, it is impossible to assign literary influence, but these rabbis were contemporaries and knew each other.

196. כל חידושי הרמב"ן לרבינו משה ב"ר נחמן, חלק ראשון, חידושי ברכות לדף מט ע"א, ג. Although neither the Ra'ah nor the Rashba explicitly cite Naḥmanides, they could not easily ignore their teacher either.

197. ספר שאלות ותשובות שחבר רבנו שלמה בן אדרת, I:469. We will return to this responsum below.

sonally felt no need to change existent custom, and his arguments arose only to defend the minhag from halakhic critique and to integrate it into halakhic theory.

In the next generation, the Ritva largely summarizes and reworks the discussions of his teachers, the Ra'ah and the Rashba.[198] In his *Hilkhot Berakhot*, he redirects and strengthens the emphasis of the Ra'ah's allowance of temporary additions, stressing that such *piyyut* is acceptable specifically because the rabbis never established an exact wording or length for any of the blessings.[199] The Ritva also makes an argument that is of some historical interest in his commentary to *Avodah Zarah* 8a. Apparently, the permission to elongate blessings caused some to justify following the old Palestinian text when including *piyyut* in the *avot*. Although we today know that this was a legitimate text in that rite, to medieval Jews it seemed like an abbreviated version of the prayer. The Ritva declares this "abbreviation" to be erroneous; the permission to change the length of the prayers works only in one direction.[200]

R. Shmuel b"R. Meshullam Gerondi, in his *Sefer Ohel Moed*,[201] also relies primarily on the arguments of R. Tam. He cites the Ra'ah's ruling that occasional inclusion of *piyyutim* is permitted, and concludes by stating that whether or not one considers *piyyut* permitted, no one claims that its inclusion prevents fulfillment of one's liturgical obligations. His contemporary codifier, R. Yeruḥam, makes no reference to *piyyut* in the *shema* blessings, but does defend its nature as communal petition in the *amidah*.[202]

One innovative argument, however, appears in this period–in the *Tzror Haḥayyim*, written by one of the Rashba's younger students, R. Ḥayyim b"R. Shmuel ben David of Tudela. Many had criticized *piyyut* as an improper interruption to the recitation of the statutory prayers. Rather than simply asserting its permissibility and sidestepping this problem, R. Ḥayyim sought to prove that, at least in the blessings of *keriat shema*, such interruptions create no obstacle to proper prayer. As he pointed out, the Mishnah itself assumes that these blessings will be interrupted and gives guidelines as to how and where these inter-

---

198. חידושי הריטב"א לרבינו יום טוב ב"ר אברהם אלאשבילי, מסכת ברכות, מז–נא.

199. הריטב"א: סדר ברכות הנהנין [הלכות ברכות], מהדורת מרדכי ליב קצנלנבוגן, עמ' ק, ו:יד. Note that the Ritva specifically speaks of *piyyut* as being within the blessing. Katzenellenbogen's commentary on this passage is completely confused. His misreading of the first line, נוסח שום ברכה מדבריהם הוא, to mean "the texts of *all* the blessings are their (the rabbis') words" makes the rest of the paragraph totally incomprehensible and necessitates his involved and difficult unraveling of the passage to fit its initial "premise." It is really quite simple when one understands it to mean that the rabbis did *not* dictate the texts of a single blessing.

200. חידושי הריטב"א על מסכת עבודה זרה (ירושלים: עם עולם, תשכ"ז), עמ' ז.

201. מהדורת אברהם יצחק גאגין, דרך רביעי, נתיב ג, עמ' לו:–לז.

202. ספר תולדות אדם וחוה, נתיב ג' חלק ג' דף כה עמ' א.

ruptions may occur.[203] To buttress his argument, he highlights the fact that the Tanna Kalir himself wrote *piyyut* for the evening *shema* blessings.[204]

The *Tzror Haḥayyim*'s reliance on this mishnaic ruling seems to be unique. However, responsa of Maimonides and the Rashba preserve evidence that some communities did insert *piyyut* between, instead of into, the blessings of *shema*. The language of the question posed to Maimonides indicates that this was most likely an attempt, derived from an interpretation of this mishnah, to lessen the degree of interruption created by the poetry. While Maimonides, characteristically, responded harshly that this custom is "totally erroneous and there is no way to permit it," the Rashba, curiously, answers that adding *piyyut* was the custom in his country too, not only for life cycle events, but also on festivals.[205] No other evidence suggests that it was the Barcelonan or Catalonian custom of this period to include insertions between the blessings. It is possible that the Rashba here merely intended to affirm the general custom of including *piyyut* within this section of the liturgy. But R. Ḥayyim's contemporaries, the Baal Haturim and Abudarham, as we shall see, argue specifically against its inclusion in the *shema* blessings. Most likely, R. Ḥayyim's innovative use of the mishnaic permission to interrupt these blessings arose in response to these influential sages.

Just as the supporters of *piyyut* mostly rehashed old arguments, so too did those opposing the custom.[206] R. Meir Halevi Abulafia, the Ramah, it is re-

---

203. *M. Berakhot* 2:1-2.

204. מהדורת שמואל חגי ירושלמי, עמ' ו'. Note that, like the Rashba (ספר שאלות ותשובות שחבר רבנו שלמה בן אדרת, I:469) and R. Shmuel b"R. Meshullam Gerondi, he identifies Kalir as R. Elazar ben Arakh, a first-century Tanna. R.Tam had found a second-century identification sufficiently authoritative and better buttressed by the actual tannaitic traditions about R. Elazar b"R. Shimon. See my "Kalir Was A Tanna...," 106 n.32, and the discussion of this identification in R. Elazar Fleckeles' תשובה מאהבה, I:1.

205. תשובות הרמב"ם, II:328-329, #180; שו"ת הרשב"א, I, #469. Since we have no evidence of anyone having dictated this compromise, we must also entertain the possibility that some communities developed this system when they began reciting the statutory liturgy instead of replacing it with *piyyut*. Rather than merge the two, as was done in most of the Jewish world, they simply moved the *piyyut* to after the eulogy of the blessing. For a somewhat analogous displacement of *piyyut*, compare the history of the poetic forms of the blessings like אשר הניא following the *megillah* on Purim and אשר בגלל אבות following the completion of the Torah on Simḥat Torah. (See: יהודה רצהבי, מגנזי שירת הקדם (משגב ירושלים, המכון לחקר מורשת יהדות ספרד והמזרח, תשנ"א), 291–293; אברהם יערי, תולדות חג שמחת־תורה: השתלשלות מנהגיו בתפוצות ישראל לדורותיהן (ירושלים: מוסד הרב קוק, תשכ"ד; תשמ"ט), 166–179.)

206. Chronologically, Yehuda Alḥarizi's criticisms of *piyyut* in his *Taḥkemoni*, discussed above, p. 130f., belong here. However, his is more a criticism of the payyetanic traditions outside of Spain that have not conformed to Spanish norms. He clearly had no theoretical objection to the insertion of *piyyut* into the blessings and was bothered primarily by the

corded, regarded *piyyut* inserted into the blessings of *shema* as an interruption, as an improper elongation of the blessing, and as a transgression of the principle forbidding change to the rabbinically established form of the benedictions. Of these, the second is noteworthy as the earliest recorded argument about the length of the blessings by an *opponent* of *piyyut*. It is unlikely, however, that the early Ashkenazim would have responded to this criticism without its ever having been raised! The Ramah also voices what becomes a constant refrain among those Spanish rabbis who opposed *piyyut* on halakhic grounds: he feels that he has no power to impose his halakhic concerns and effect a change in the actual minhag of the synagogue. Were he to impose a ruling, it would be purposefully ignored, and instead of being merely errant, the community would then sin deliberately, a much more serious offense.[207]

It is difficult to know if the Ramah actually limited his objections to *piyyut* in the blessings of the *shema*. No one cites a parallel objection to its insertion in the *amidah* in his name. His largely lost, massive Talmud commentary, from which this tradition likely derives, was a summation of the conclusions of the old Spanish talmudic school. The growing influence of Tosafist traditions and methods caused the Ramah's work to be little studied, and hence little cited. The Rosh, however, who had to learn the Spanish traditions to function in his new home, did study the Ramah and considered him the decisive local authority. He required his sons and students to do likewise–which accounts for the influence of the Ramah on Yaakov ben Asher's *Arba'ah Turim*.[208]

However, a century later, when R. Yaakov ben Asher wrote this code, the *Tur*, he did deliberately differentiate between the blessings in the *shema* and those in the *amidah* when determining the halakhic status of *piyyut*. Unlike his known predecessors on either side of the debate, who all seem to have treated insertions into these two rubrics of the statutory liturgy as a single issue,[209] the

---

recitation of *piyyut* by ignorant people who could not comprehend their prayers. *Piyyut* that had ceased to have semantic meaning as a source of *kavvanah* was, to him, inappropriate.

207. Cited by the *Tur*, OH 68; *Abudarham Hashalem*, 71.

208. Unlike the leading rabbis of the intervening generations, who had been primarily Catalonians, the Ramah spent most of his life in Toledo, the leading city of Castile, where the Rosh and his family ultimately settled. This geographical factor may also have been important in the Rosh's turning to the Ramah. See Israel Ta-Shma, "Abulafia, Meir," *Encyclopedia Judaica*, II: 189-193.

209. Many of our sources, because they are commenting on a specific talmudic passage or otherwise discussing a specific part of the liturgy, make reference to only one sort of *piyyut* or another, allowing us to draw no conclusions. But it is noteworthy how many of the extended discussions, particularly those based on R. Tam's responsum, clearly consider the two cases equivalent. The confusion of terminology in our sources referring to types of *piyyut* also suggests this lack of distinction. Although "*kerovetz*" technically refers to the formal

*Tur* rules separately on each, allowing *piyyut* as a legitimate form of communal petition in the *amidah*,[210] but suggesting that it would be more appropriate not to interrupt the blessings of *shema*.[211] On the question of the *amidah*, he seems simply to advocate maintenance of the status quo, based on authority going back to the Geonim, specifically to *Halakhot Gedolot*.[212] He does not even acknowledge here that opposition ever existed to this sort of *piyyut*.

In contrast, in his discussion of the *shema* blessings, the *Tur* calls for a radical change. After opening with the blunt statement that the interruptions caused here by *piyyut* should be eliminated, he cites as authoritative the arguments of the Ramah and Maimonides,[213] followed by the acknowledgment: אמנם נוהגין בכל המקומות לומר בהם קרובץ (in truth, it is customary everywhere to incorporate *piyyut* into the [blessings]).[214] A factor, he suggests, in the disregard of the halakhic stance of these great rabbis has been the authority of the *payyetanim* and of halakhic giants like the Ravad and R. Tam. However, the *Tur* rejects R. Tam's interpretation of the tannaitic rules about long and short blessings, opining that R. Tam created this forced interpretation for the sake of upholding the minhag (of *piyyut*). He notes briefly that this was also his father's opinion of R. Tam's responsum.[215] Whatever the validity of the halakhic arguments about changing the length of the blessings, he concludes with the suggestion: ומ"מ טוב ויפה הדבר לבטלה למי שאפשר כי היא סיבה להפסיק בשיחה בטלה בדברי הבאי (and in any case, it is best for whomever is able to, to abolish [*piyyut*], for it is an excuse to interrupt [prayer] with vain chatter about nonsense). *Piyyut* creates a breakdown of decorum and

series of *piyyutim* inserted into the *amidah*, it appears also referring to the *piyyutim* for the *shema* blessings in the *Tur*. "*Yotzer*" (or "*yotzerot*"), especially in Ashkenaz, at times refers to all the *piyyut* of the morning service, not just that of the *shema* blessings.

210. OH 112.

211. OH 68.

212. He seems to know only the first half of *Halakhot Gedolot*'s statement, and not its ruling against *piyyut*. See above, pp. 118f.

213. This is a paraphrase of *Hilkhot Keriat Shema* 1:7, and not of Maimonides' much stronger statement rejecting additions to the *amidah* in *Hilkhot Tefillah* 6:3. He does not refer to any Maimonidean responsa.

214. Although in the *Tur* these words read like part of the citation from Maimonides, they do not appear in our texts of the Rambam; more likely, they are the *Tur*'s recognition that previous halakhic opposition to *piyyut* inserted into the *shema* blessings had been to no avail in the face of universal custom.

215. No literary source of the Rosh supports this. The תוספות הרא"ש to *Berakhot* 11b, although not discussing *piyyut*, does cite R. Tam's responsum without criticism. The *Beit Yosef* suggests that the *Tur* received an oral tradition from his father. All other published comments of the Rosh about *piyyut* are on the question of communal petitions in the *amidah* (which he accepts).

leads to halakhically problematic interruptions in the prayers. Whoever has the power to do something about it ought to.[216]

Why did the *Tur* (or maybe the Ramah) distinguish between these two types of *piyyut*? There are several possible explanations. On a purely theoretical halakhic level, while arguments specifically supporting its inclusion in the *shema* blessings can be traced only to early Ashkenaz, the arguments for including it in the *amidah* are geonic, and hence of much greater authority, especially in Spain. However, as we have seen, the geonic support was by no means unanimous, and there was a strong tradition of Spanish opposition to its insertion into the *amidah* as well. Rather than being purely halakhic in nature, this curious differentiation may have arisen in deference to the reality of the synagogue. The Ramah's stance takes into account the communal nature of the recitation of the *shema* blessings. Although the individual fulfilled his own obligations with a private recitation of the *amidah*, he was expected to participate with the *sheliaḥ tzibbur* in *keriat shema*. When the *sheliaḥ tzibbur* interrupted his prayers with *piyyut*, this interruption was imposed upon the congregation, causing each individual also to transgress.[217] In the *amidah*, though, only the ignorant person who could not meet his own obligations was so tightly bound to the communal service. The rest of the congregation needed only to respond to the *kedushah* and the priestly benediction and recite the *modim derabbanan* to complete their obligations, making interruptions less of an issue.[218]

Very tentatively, we might suggest another possibility. The Ramah was also a kabbalist, and the increasing influence of kabbalah during this period, particularly in Castile, may also have influenced his thinking. Although I have found no references to discussions of *piyyut* in pre-Lurianic mystical texts, some of this group may well have objected to these poetic interruptions. The kabbalists insisted on proper recitation of the statutory prayers,[219] an attitude that arose at

216. *Tur* OH 68.

217. See, however, the discussion above, p. 160f., of the ruling of R. Ḥayyim of Tudela in his *Tzror Haḥayyim*, where he bases his ruling on an opposite interpretation of the Mishnah.

218. Maimonides could not have made this distinction. Once he had abolished the two-fold recitation of the *amidah* (תשובות הרמב"ם II:474-475, #256; 484, #258), all parts of the service required equal degrees of communal participation.

219. See the discussion of zoharic and kabbalistic conceptions of prayer in Isaiah Tishby, *The Wisdom of the Zohar: An Anthology of Texts*, trans. David Goldstein (Oxford: Oxford University Press, The Littman Library, 1989), III: 941-1016, especially 962ff. The Zohar itself does not discuss *piyyut* directly. See, too, the objection of Naḥmanides in his novella to *Berakhot* 49a, which although not couched in kabbalistic terms, evidences serious opposition to all poetic insertions into the blessings. His version of *Midrash Kohelet* 7:5, which interprets "song of fools" to refer to "the *ḥazzanim* who add to the fixed prayers," is not the standard version that refers to the *meturgemanim* (the ritual translators of Scripture), a much more

least partially in reaction to an extreme rationalist philosophy then current particularly among the courtier classes in Spain and Provence. These rationalists, influenced by Averroes, had taken the teachings of Baḥya ibn Pakuda and Maimonides to their extreme logical conclusion and asserted that conventional verbal and especially petitionary prayer were not only unnecessary but even sinful, as they suggested that God actually needed physically to hear prayers. The real sage required only contemplative prayer for proper worship, and participated in verbal prayer only for the sake of the foolish masses.[220] In addition to insisting on traditional verbal prayer, the kabbalists asserted the value of verbal petition of God for spiritual needs, specifically in the first three blessings of the *amidah*.[221] The proximity of this argument to the traditional justification for including *piyyut* in the opening blessings of the *amidah* may have made formal opposition to this poetry much more difficult.

The Rosh and his son are certainly known to have been among the major conveyors of German mysticism to Spain. Thus it is highly likely that R. Yaakov ben Asher knew of the Spanish mystical thought that had flowered in the thirteenth century. We still have to ask, however, how the *Tur*, grounded in the academies of the Ashkenazi Tosafists, came to oppose *piyyut*. In part, his reasons were probably analogous to those of Maimonides. Both men fled from persecution and, after much turmoil, found themselves living in a new culture with a new set of customs. The constant truth in their lives was not the active expression of their religion, but its theory, halakhah. Although the *Tur* would not have had Maimonides' reasons to be critical of the aesthetics of *piyyut* in his new home, Spanish liturgical poetry was essentially foreign to him. With no emo-

---

likely midrashic text. The kabbalists of this period maintained a strict separation between their esoteric and halakhic writings, making it extremely difficult to evaluate the influence of their mystical leanings on the halakhic process. This will be discussed in greater detail in Chapter Four. Additional and serious challenges to this explanation are that not only R. Yonah of Gerona, but also the Rashba and other students of Naḥmanides, all of known mystical leanings, argued *for* the legitimacy of the recitation of *piyyut*. Even more significant, there is no trace of references back to earlier mystical arguments against *piyyut* in the well-known Lurianic discussions.

220. For discussions of this notion, see Tishby, III:942f., and the sources he cites: גרשום שלום, ראשית הקבלה (1150-1250) (ירושלים: שוקן, תשי"ח), 135; מרדכי מרטארה, "ספר שער השמים לר' יעקב בר' ששת...," אוצר נחמד ג (תר"ך), 163–165. For a study of Maimonides' philosophical approach to prayer, which clearly intimates the sources of these European heresies, see Marvin Fox, *Interpreting Maimonides: Studies in Methodology, Metaphysics, and Moral Philosophy* (Chicago: University of Chicago Press, 1990), Ch. 11, "Prayer and the Religious Life."

221. Tishby, III:968, citing R. Azriel of Gerona, published by Scholem, "שרידים חדשים מכתבי ר' עזריאל מגירונה," ספר זכרון לאשר גולאק ולשמואל קליין (ירושלים: המכון למדעי־היהדות של האוניברסיטה העברית, תשי"ב), 213–214.

tional ties to it, he could more readily subject it to theoretical requirements.[222] Objections to *piyyut*, as we know, could be easily found among the rabbinic traditions of the Spanish school that the *Tur* had carefully studied as part of his assimilation into the halakhic culture of his new home.[223]

Because he himself did not hold a rabbinic post, the *Tur* only suggested to others that they attempt to abolish *piyyut* from the blessings of *shema*. Without the actions of others, then, his stance might have remained a contribution to the theoretical halakhah but with no impact on actual minhag. In his discussion of the Yom Kippur liturgy, however, we learn that these rulings were not merely the *ex cathedra* pronouncements of an academician concerned only with halakhic theory. He indicates with approval that the contemporary minhag in Toledo for this most solemn of days not only included no *piyyut* for the blessings of *keriat shema* but also moved all *piyyut* from the *amidah*, including the *seliḥot*, to after the repetition of this prayer.[224] If, on Yom Kippur–the day on which challenges to its customs are least likely to be allowed–this community inserted no *piyyut* into its statutory prayers, presumably in response to halakhic concerns, we can assume that this was most likely the case for the rest of their *maḥzor* also. The *Tur*'s primary rulings about *piyyut*, then, were not directed solely to the community in which he lived, but to the rest of the Jewish world. Not only did the Baal Haturim accept the ruling of the Ramah, which apparently had affected the local rite in Toledo, but he also rejected his Ashkenazi heritage to the point of ruling that the example set in Toledo should be followed universally.

In the course of the fourteenth and fifteenth centuries, the *Tur* became the primary halakhic authority of the Castilian communities, and its liturgy reflects his influence.[225] Outside of Castile, though, the Catalonian communities followed

---

222. Alfred Freimann, "Die Ascheriden (1267-1391)," *JJLG* 13 (1920): 160, remarks, "In seiner deutschen Heimat machte er sich mit dem synagogalen Ritus des Landes vertraut." Ta-Shma discusses the degree to which the Rosh and his family purposefully held themselves aloof from Sefardi ways. See his: "רבנו אשר ובנו ר' יעקב בעל הטורים: בין אשכנז לספרד," פעמים 46–47 (תשנ"א), 75–91.

223. Freimann, 163.

224. OH 620. The exception, noted in OH 621, is the *seder avodah* and two introductory poems, אוחילה לאל and עלינו, in the Yom Kippur *musaf* service. In his discussion of the Rosh Hashanah liturgy, OH 584, he only mentions, without further discussion, that it is customary in some places to recite *piyyut*.

225. For a discussion of the growing authority of the *Tur* in this period, see Freimann, "Die Ascheriden," 150, 191, 221-222. On the incident, c. 1340, when the Toledo community tried to make the *Mishneh Torah* its official halakhic code over the objections of its rabbi, Yehudah ben Asher, see: זכרון יהודה הוא ספר שאלות ותשובות לרבינו יהודה בן הרא"ש ז"ל, מהדורת יהודה ראזענבערג, סי' נד, עמ' ט.

authorities from the schools of Naḥmanides and the Rashba, and the Jews of Aragon and Valencia ruled according to Maimonides' *Mishneh Torah*.[226] Therefore, it is not surprising that the non-Castilian Spanish rites preserved *piyyut*. Not only did their lack of central political authority prevent any imposition of change from above, but their halakhic codes either supported *piyyut* or did not explicitly rule against it. The first printing of the prayerbooks of the Catalonian rite in Saloniki in 1527 maintained all *piyyut*, while that of the Aragonese rite in 1529 shows the impact of the *Tur* in its elimination of *piyyut* only from the blessings of the *shema*.[227]

The evidence from these prayerbooks is consistent with the literature generated by rabbis hailing from the non-Castilian areas of Spain in these last two centuries before the final expulsion. We saw above[228] that R. Ḥayyim of Tudela tried actively to buttress the arguments *for* interrupting the *shema* blessings with *piyyut*. The Rivash records that his teacher in Barcelona, Rabbenu Nissim, like the Ramah, personally *refrained* from such interruptions, but felt it futile to try to impose his stance on the rest of the community.[229] R. Shimon bar Tzemaḥ Duran, a native of Majorca who like his elder colleague, the Rivash, fled to Algiers in the wake of the 1391 persecutions in Spain, comments on *Berakhot* 11a:

> ...ושיטת הרשב"א ז"ל היא יותר נכונה להעמיד המנהג. ואעפ"כ הרבה חכמים ז"ל הוקשה להן ענין הפיוטין אלא שאין בידן למחות לפי שנהגו בהן בכל מקומות ישראל ובכל מקום בעלי נפש ימעטו.
>
> ...and the method of the Rashba, of blessed memory, is that it is best to uphold the custom. Even so, many sages had difficulty with the issue of *piyyut*, but they did not have the power to protest [effectively], because it was such a universal custom among the Jews, and there were so few men of principle.[230]

While far from wholeheartedly endorsing *piyyut*, he concludes that the minhag of including it should be upheld, especially since even those who object find

---

226. שמעון בר צמח, ספר התשב"ץ, כרך ג', שו"ת שכו. See too, for a summary of the halakhic authority structure of Spain, H.J. Zimmels, ***Ashkenazim and Sefardim: Their Relations, Differences, and Problems as Reflected in the Rabbinical Responsa*** (London: Marla Publications, 1976), 47. In Ashkenaz, this specific ruling of the *Tur* was explicitly rejected. See above, p. 143, n. 135.

227. דניאל גולדשמידט, "מחזורים כמנהג קהילות יוון," בתוך מחקרי תפילה ופיוט (ירושלים: מאגנס, תש"ם), 288–272.

228. p. 160f.

229. שאלות ותשובות בר ששת, סי' עה, עמ' יד:.

230. פירוש הרשב"ץ על ברכות, 47.

themselves unable to alter it. However, in order to eliminate concerns about improper elongation of the blessings, the topic of the *piyyut* must follow the topic of the blessing.[231]

The *Tur*'s ruling had only minimal effect on the rites of the eastern Spanish kingdoms, but the situation was quite different in Castile. David Abudarham's mid-fourteenth century commentary on the prayerbook, considered the authoritative work on Spanish liturgy, basically reproduces the arguments of the *Tur* and confirms that *piyyut* had already been largely marginalized in the rite of his community.[232] His siddur itself includes essentially no *piyyut* inserted into the blessings of the statutory prayers. In his discussion of Yom Kippur prayers, Abudarham cites, like the *Tur*, R. Amram Gaon's dictum that, while any community had full discretion in deciding the amount of *piyyut* to be said, his custom was to minimize the inclusions.[233]

Unlike the *Tur*, though, Abudarham makes no specific reference here to the customs of Toledo and their model for the actual elimination of *piyyut*. His limited discussion of poetry seems to derive primarily from his decision to write a commentary on a more universally accepted liturgy in order to stem the tide of ignorant and improper recitation of prayers.[234] To be sure, variations in local rites made inclusion of specific *piyyut* impossible in a book intended for broad use. Yet, one might have expected more reference in the context of this discussion as to where *piyyut* should be recited, if at all. In his siddur, Abudarham, like the *Tur*, specifically provides only for the recitation of the *seder avodah* in Yom Kippur *musaf* and its introductory *piyyut*, אוחילה לאל. Although he considers the latter to be part of the fixed liturgy on Yom Kippur, he does not mean that

231. p. 50. This hearkens back to the responsum of Natronai Gaon (above, p. 125f.) and his insistence that *piyyut* was acceptable as long as it was *me-ein haberakhah*. Among the Spanish rabbis, only R. Aharon Halevi had raised this issue even in passing (פירוש הרא"ה על הלכות הרי"ף מסכת ברכות, יד). Elsewhere, it appears explicitly in the Meiri (בית הבחירה על מסכת ברכות, 23) and in the responsum of Rabbenu Gershom (#1, p. 55), who considers a transition back to the subject of the blessing at the end of the *piyyut* satisfactory. The definition of this concept, as we have seen, varied from R. Gershom's requirement of a proper final transition to a full restriction of the topic of the *piyyut* itself. Although the former is consistent with the internal rules of payyetanic prosody, the latter was rarely enforced.

232. *Abudarham Hashalem*, 71. Abudarham combines the *Tur*'s two discussions and strengthens the arguments slightly by omitting the *Tur*'s acknowledgment that the Ravad saw no reason to be concerned about the length of the *shema* blessings. He also adds R. Tam's discussion about the credentials of Kalir.

233. *Abudarham Hashalem*, 287; *Seder Rav Amram Gaon*, ed. Goldschmidt, 166, # 125.

234. See his introduction, p. 6.

the individual should necessarily recite it on Rosh Hashanah too.[235] He refers to the *seliḥot*, but assumes that, with a single exception in Musaf, אדיר ונאור,[236] they will be recited after the conclusion of the repetition of the *amidah*.[237]

The mere existence of Abudarham's separate commentary on the *piyyutim* of Yom Kippur, *Sefer Tashlum Abudarham*, proves that *piyyut* was still an important part of the Yom Kippur liturgy, at least in his own community. The order of the *piyyutim* in this work confirms the picture gleaned from the comments of the *Tur* and from Abudarham's siddur,[238] for it includes no *piyyut* at all for the blessings of *keriat shema*, and, with the exception of the elaborated *kedushah* for all repetitions of the *amidah* and the *seder avodah* and its introductory *piyyutim*, the remaining poetry of this rite has been deferred until the conclusion of the *amidah*.[239]

The *Tashlum Abudarham* probably represents the customs of the Jews of Toledo, but not of Seville, Abudarham's home city. Two additional halakhic sources from Christian Spain confirm this elimination of *piyyut* from the Toledan rite. The outline of the Yom Kippur liturgy in the *Menorat Hamaor* of the Toledan rabbi, Yisrael Alnakava, specifies that one recites the *pizmonim* and *piyyutim* from the *maḥzor* after the conclusion of the repetition of the *amidah* at each service. It lists only the elaborated *kedushah* and the poetry connected with the *seder avodah* for insertion into the *musaf amidah* and makes no mention of *piyyut* at all in its discussion of the Rosh Hashanah liturgy.[240]

Our other source is even more significant, in that it indicates that Seville was not yet following the lead of Toledo in this matter. In his halakhic manual, *Tzedah Laderekh*, written specifically for the edification of the assimilated Sevillian courtier, Don Samuel Abravanel, Menaḥem ben Aharon ben Zeraḥ records approvingly that on Yom Kippur in Toledo (but, we can infer, not in

235. 271.

236. Davidson, 1095א.

237. He comments on some *seliḥot*: 285, 287, 288, 289, 291. The last is the only extensive discussion. Here he states that most of the *seliḥot* are too simple to need explanation. One wonders whether they are really so much simpler than the statutory liturgy to which he devotes the bulk of the work! However, his *Sefer Tashlum Abudarham* includes comment on close to one hundred *seliḥot*-type *piyyutim*, although they do not receive that specific title there.

238. Unless we assume that the comments about the Toledo rite are glosses into the *Tur*, and that some later copyist has reorganized the *Tashlum Abudarham* to correspond to some later version of the *maḥzor*. This seems unlikely.

239. This can be inferred from the appearance of the *piyyutim* for the first two blessings of the *amidah* (and all the rest of the poetry for that particular service) after those for the *kedushah* (and the *seder avodah* in *musaf*).

240. מהדורת הלל גרשום המכונה הימן ענעלאו, חלק ב, עמ' 398–400.

Seville) the custom was for the *sheliaḥ tzibbur* to recite all the *piyyut*, in order, after the conclusion of the *tefillah*.[241]

This elimination of *piyyut* from all statutory blessings in the Castilian rite had begun, as we saw above, at least by the early fourteenth century in Toledo.[242] We can only speculate as to the reasons. Perhaps the old Spanish *piyyut* had ceased to have meaning for these Jews, and it was simply time for a liturgical revival. Much of the corpus of Spanish *piyyut*, written in Muslim Spain, was permeated with philosophical speculation rather than rabbinic literature, which had a more timeless validity and which had become a more central part of the Sefardi curriculum with the introduction of Tosafist methods and ideologies.[243] In addition, pious Castilians were increasingly drawn to the practice of kabbalah, which very much opposed the secularism associated with the philosophical schools dominated by the courtier classes, but at the same time created new sources of *kavvanah* in mystical meditations on the texts of the statutory liturgy itself. Traditional *piyyut*, then, may well have become extraneous as well as objectionable in its content.[244] If this was the case, there was no need to differentiate–as the Ramah and the Tur had done–between *piyyut* composed for the *shema* and the *amidah*.

Why, then, was at least some of the *piyyut* simply moved to neutral locations before and after the statutory prayers? If it was objectionable, should it not have been fully discarded? One must bear in mind that kabbalah was at this period still a fairly esoteric doctrine, and its practice was certainly not universal. In addition, if the Castilian rabbis were able to impose essentially universal changes on the liturgy, their revisions had to recognize the needs both of the less educated (but pious) masses and of the elite, more assimilated courtier fam-

---

241. מאמר רביעי, כלל חמישי, פרק שביעי, עמ' קטז.

242. We can assume that, if the Baal Haturim had himself witnessed the change, he would have phrased his comment to reflect this.

243. For a discussion of the use of philosophical ideas in Spanish *piyyut*, see: אהרן מירסקי, "שירת ספרד – תכניה וסוגיה," 652–654.

244. Hints of this appear in the early fourteenth-century sermons of R. Yehoshua ibn Shuaib. (דרשות על התורה לר' יהושע אבן שועיב, דרשה לפרשת שמיני, דף מה עמ' ב.) After a discussion of the requirement of *kavvanah* in prayer–that has clear kabbalistic overtones–he distinguishes between two types of *piyyut*. One, the pure older style, written by sages like Kalir, who knew how properly to approach God, is appropriate. The other, metered poetry, concerns itself with its formal beauty, but in reality is only dross and ought not to be recited because it was not written with the *kavvanah* needed for proper prayer. This argument foreshadows that of Yitzḥak Luria, the Ari, in the sixteenth century. See below, p. 174f. The similarity may be incidental, though, as the northern Spanish rites had maintained the occasional Kalirian and Kalirian-style *piyyut*, creating the possibility of a reaction like Ibn Shuaib's; the Ari's native rite was that of Ashkenaz.

ilies (that had not become conversos). A total elimination of *piyyut* would have risked creating the situation rabbis throughout the centuries had tried to avoid: disregarding rabbinic ruling, people would become deliberate sinners instead of unwitting followers of errant customs. The compromise of moving *piyyut* out of the statutory liturgy–but maintaining it as a neutral part of the service–solved halakhic problems while allowing the preservation of the liturgy that popular associations deemed a necessary part of the observance of a particular day.[245]

The elimination of *piyyut* may also have been accelerated by historical events. The horrible persecutions of the final century and a half of Jewish life in Spain likely had two effects on Castilian liturgy. First, the destruction of the communities of Castile's leading cities, Seville, Toledo, and Burgos[246] inevitably led remaining Jews to band together, often in locations far from former homes. Under such conditions, a congregation would need to determine its ritual practice. Given the halakhic tendency to discourage interruptions to the statutory prayers, communities forced to choose between various cycles of poetic additions might well have simply jettisoned all such *piyyut* in order to create a neutral service.

Another probable effect of the disasters on the liturgy was the tendency to favor halakhah over minhag. After seeing their less committed neighbors and relatives convert to Christianity, the remaining Jews may have stressed their own piety and allegiance to Jewish law. The increase of messianic fervor in this period also encouraged the tendency to scrutinize actual practice and make sure it conformed to halakhic standards.

These conditions were no less true for the Jews of Catalonia and Aragon than those of Castile; yet only the Castilian rite eliminated *piyyut*.[247] At least two factors may account for this difference. First, the accepted halakhic code of the Castilian Jews, the *Tur*, was more strongly opposed to *piyyut* than were the codes accepted in the other kingdoms. The accepted code of Aragon and Valencia was the *Mishneh Torah*, in which Maimonides only hints of his opposition to *piyyut*. Secondly, the internal government of the Jewish community of Castile was much more centralized, making imposition of a universal ritual possible. The various synods of Castilian rabbis did make decrees on matters affecting

245. For examples of such a compromise, albeit in the sixteenth century, see the responsum of the Radbaz VIII:13 and almost all Sefardi rite *maḥzorim* of the post-expulsion world.

246. Baer, II:117.

247. In the fifteenth century in Barcelona, R. Yosef ben Ḥaviva, in his *Nimukei Yosef*, continues to promulgate arguments in favor of the inclusion of *piyyut* in all parts of the statutory liturgy. See his comment to *Berakhot*, 22-23. See also the discussion of the various specific rites in the following section.

the synagogue,[248] and while we have no direct evidence that they actually did so, one synod could well have established that all liturgy follow Abudarham, who, as we saw, ruled against *piyyut* in the *shema* blessings and inserted only *piyyut* for the *kedushah* itself and the *seder avodah* in the *amidah*, and then only on Yom Kippur.

Although, as we shall see, other Spanish rites persisted into modern times, in most of the Sefardi diaspora, not only did the Castilian rite come to represent the tradition of most Spanish Jews, but it became the liturgical tradition of many of the communities to which they fled. Constituting the vast majority of the Sefardim exiled in 1492, the Castilians represented an intellectual and, quickly, an economic elite in most of their new homes. Through sheer numerical superiority and through the tenacity with which they held on to and imposed the traditions of their homeland, they eventually absorbed the native populations of most communities of the eastern and southern Mediterranean.[249] Former Marrano families, adopting the Castilian–or Spanish and Portuguese–rite, formed vibrant communities in north-western Europe. For a substantial segment of world Jewry until today, then, *piyyut*, while still a living part of the liturgical experience, became a genre of prayer relegated to the sidelines, outside of the blessings of the statutory liturgy.

## Piyyut *in the Sefardi Diaspora*

To consider only the continuation of the "pure" Castilian rite, however, is to oversimplify the history of the recitation of *piyyut* in the Sefardi diaspora. A closer look reveals that actual practices were quite varied and affected by a number of factors: the strength of local custom; the influence of Lurianic kabbalah; the place of origin in Spain of the dominant exile community; and perhaps also the presence of former Marranos in the community. A study of

---

248. See Louis Finkelstein, *Jewish Self-Government in the Middle Ages* (New York: Phillip Feldheim, Inc., 1964), chap.13, especially p. 355; M. Kayserling, "Das Castilianische Gemeinde-Status," *Jahrbuch für die Geschichte der Juden und des Judenthums* 4 (1869): 263-334, especially 281.

249. On this phenomenon, see the articles of Joseph Hacker: "גאון ודיכאון – קטבים בהווייתם הרוחנית והחברתית של יוצאי ספרד ופורטוגאל באמפירה העות׳מאנית," בתוך תרבות וחברה בתולדות ישראל בימי־הביניים (ספר זכרון לחיים הלל בן ששון), בעריכת ראובן בונפיל, מנחם בן ששון, ויוסף הקר (ירושלים: מרכז זלמן שזר, תשמ"ט), 570–578; "יוצאי ספרד באמפירה העות׳מנית במאה הט"ז – קהלה וחברה," בתוך מורשת ספרד, בעריכת חיים ביינארט (ירושלים: מאגנס, תשנ"ב), 465–466. For an impassioned criticism of those non-Sefardim who wanted to revert to their ancestral customs, after having agreed to switch to the Sefardi rite in Turkish lands, see the responsum praising the superiority of the Sefardi rite of R. Shmuel de Medina, שאלות ותשובות מהרשד"ם, OH 35.

the prayerbooks of the period and of the halakhic discussions that attempted to shape them enables us to reconstruct this history.

As we have noted, the dominant diaspora Sefardi halakhic tradition uniformly disapproved of most *piyyut*. Yosef Karo, in his *Beit Yosef* to the *Tur*'s discussion of *piyyut* in the *shema* blessings,[250] comments that the inclusion of these *piyyutim* is no longer the custom, and that the *Tur*'s suggestion that they be eliminated is clear. In his discussion of *piyyut* in the *amidah*, Karo, after citing numerous authorities who supported the custom, notes R. Ḥananel's objection, and concludes: וכבר נתבאר בסימן ס"ח שהמנהג הנכון שלא לומר קרובץ (It has already been explained in paragraph 68 that the proper custom is not to recite *piyyut*).[251] At least in the dominant Castilian rite of Karo's world, *piyyut* had fully disappeared from the *shema* blessings, and it was, in spite of the lack of any formal ruling before Karo, largely gone from the *amidah* too, in accordance with Toledano custom.[252] Karo himself no longer differentiated these two categories. However, his contemporary, R. David ben Shlomo ibn Abi Zimra (Radbaz), more nuanced in his discussions, essentially continued the prohibition of *piyyut* for Sefardi (Castilian) Jews while allowing other customs to persist in his Egyptian community. Drawing on the authority of the great *payyetanim* of Ashkenaz and Sefarad, the Radbaz did not find *piyyut* in theory to be an inappropriate interruption in the statutory prayers. He did, however, claim that most later poetry does constitute an interruption and, because most cannot discern between *piyyut* of appropriate and inappropriate content, ruled that it all is best avoided unless the local custom specifies specific ancient poems. Thus, the Castilian rite, which no longer had a tradition of *piyyut*, could not begin to include any beyond their elaborate *kedushah piyyutim*, preserved by Abudarham.[253]

Others were less tolerant than the Radbaz about allowing communities to maintain their own minhagim. Shmuel de Medina (Maharashdam) advocated that all take on the Sefardi rite as the superior formulation of prayer; the only substantial difference between rites, he claimed, was the corpus of *piyyut*, which

250. OH 68.

251. OH 112.

252. R. Meir ibn Gabbai's sixteenth-century mystical prayerbook commentary, *Sefer Tolaat Yaakov*, makes no mention of *piyyut* at all, with the exception of אוחילה לאל introducing the *malkhiyot* in the Rosh Hashanah *musaf* service. As indicated above, this *piyyut* seems to have become statutory liturgy in the Castilian rite.

253. *Shut Haradbaz* III:967 [532]; VIII: 13. The Radbaz did not permit the Sefardi immigrants to Egypt to establish formal supremacy in synagogue affairs over the local communities, with the exception of reversing Maimonides' elimination of the silent *amidah* (IV:94). Thus, he had to design his rulings for Castilian Jews in such a way that they would not impact the rites of others.

was best omitted anyway because it was incomprehensible, and incomprehensible prayer could never fulfill anyone's obligations. In reality, the Maharashdam and others like him were dealing not only with the question of *piyyut* but with a more general problem. If individuals were required to maintain their ancestral customs, how could a mixture of immigrants from various areas of Spain, local Jews who were perceived as less sophisticated, and occasionally Ashkenazim too, form a new community? In large cities like Salonika, separate congregations developed, but in most areas this was impossible. The domination of the Castilian rite, advocated by the Maharashdam, eventually became the reality.[254]

Another factor that significantly shaped approaches to *piyyut* was the impact of Lurianic kabbalah. No earlier kabbalistic comments about *piyyut* were cited by later authorities in mystical or non-mystical contexts, but R. Ḥayyim Vital's *Shaar Hakavvanot*[255] records specific traditions of R. Yitzḥak Luria, the Ari, that were considered exemplary for later generations. Luria, of course, was himself of Ashkenazi extraction, although most of his immediate and most influential followers were Sefardim. According to Vital, the Ari recited no poetry by later poets like Ibn Gabirol; because these men did not know the ways of kabbalah, their poetry was certain to be full of errors. However, because Tannaim such as R. Akiva, R. Elazar ben Arakh, and R. Neḥuniah ben Hakanah established their poetry according to true wisdom, the Ari ruled that their *piyyutim*, plus all of Kalir's found in the Ashkenazi *maḥzor*, may be recited, even in the middle of a blessing. At the same time, though, the Ari understood that individual Jews were obliged to pray according to their ancestral minhag in order for their prayers properly to ascend to heaven. Thus, his traditions affected discussions not only about *piyyut*, but also about the legitimacy of any change to a community's established prayers.

Followers of the Ari, both in the Ashkenazi and Sefardi worlds, struggled to understand these traditions and to apply them. The Italian R. Yosef Yedidiah Carmi claimed that the Ari ruled this way because he actually understood the difficult and often obscure Kalirian poetry. His acceptance of it thus verified its conformity to the teachings of kabbalah. Carmi also hints that the Ari had a special mystical connection with R. Elazar b"R. Shimon.[256] Although other ref-

254. *Shut Maharashdam* OH 35. An interesting discussion of this responsum occurs in R. Yoshiyahu Pinto's *Shut Nivḥar Mikesef* OH 1, which confronts the communal anarchy resulting from immigrants wanting to continue their own ancestral customs. Based on the Maharashdam, he rules that although Ashkenazim may continue to pray according to the Ashkenazi rite, all others must follow the dominant Sefardi (Castilian) tradition.

255. 50c bottom – d.

256. ספר כנף רננים (ויניציאה, 1626), ח. It would seem from Carmi's comments that he fol-

erences to the Ari and mystical traditions appear in intervening generations, the most important and influential sage to continue this discussion was R. Ḥayyim Yosef David Azulai (Ḥida). Referring to Carmi's discussion, he reports that the Ari revealed that Kalir was the בן ניצוץ של נשמתו של ר' אלעזר ברבי שמעון (the offspring of a spark of the soul of R. Elazar b"R. Shimon).[257] In this, he essentially uses the Ari to buttress R. Tam's identification of Kalir with the Tanna.[258]

More influential, though, was the Ḥida's application of other aspects of the traditions of the Ari. A leading Sefardi rabbi and mystic, the Ḥida managed to gain attention for and adherence to many changes less successfully suggested by both predecessors and contemporaries. The Ari had objected strenuously to the corpus of Sefardi *piyyutim* and contributed to their removal from the statutory prayers of *keriat shema* and the *amidah*. However, many of the *piyyutim* for *keriat shema* had simply been moved to before these blessings, occasionally before *nishmat*, and more often following it, before and after *kaddish* and *barekhu*. In addition, *piyyut* composed for *nishmat*, to introduce it and as insertions into it, had not come under serious question in earlier Sefardi discussions of *piyyut*. But now the Ḥida and his colleagues were asking: as *nishmat* is mentioned in the Zohar, and the Zohar predates the Mishnah, how can it be interrupted?[259] Rabbi Yehudah Halevi and his colleagues obviously did not know the mystical meanings of the prayers –that heavenly secrets and divine names are contained in the precise numbers of letters and words. If they had, they would not have dared to compose *piyyut* to be inserted in the liturgy, since there should be no insertions into the prayerbook from *barukh sheamar* until the completion of the repetition of the *amidah*.[260] The Ḥida similarly objected to the remnants of *piyyut*

---

lowed an Italian or Ashkenazi rite, rather than counting himself among the Sefardim. His other comments show a general openness to flexibility in the payyetanic corpus.

257. *Sefer Maḥazik Berakhah* 112. Carmi's statement is actually quite different, referring to a relationship between the Ari and Kalir, not Kalir and the Tanna.

258. This work of the Ḥida was published in 1777, approximately half a century before the various identifications of Kalir as a medieval poet by Zunz, Luzzatto, and Rapoport (noted in Elbogen, *Jewish Liturgy*, p. 439, n. 19).

259. Although *nishmat* appears in the Babylonian Talmud as a version of the *birkat hashir* to follow *hallel* in the seder (*B. Pesaḥim* 118a), it never appears there in the context of *pesukei d'zimra*. The prayer was definitely known in this context by the time of the Geonim. It appears in all the manuscripts of Amram used by Goldschmidt, 69-70, in Saadia, p. 119-120, and in multiple genizah texts, several of which are cited by Fleischer, ...תפילה ומנהגי תפילה, as listed in his index of prayers, p. 339. The Zohar today is generally understood by historians to be the work, probably of R. Moshe de Leon, in the late-thirteenth century, pseudepigraphically presented as the work of R. Shimon bar Yoḥai, an early second-century Tanna.

260. *Shut Tov Ayin* 18, #35. Compare also #40 and his *Sefer Birkei Yosef* OH 68:2. Ironically, the question posed here concerns the *mi khamokha* of Halevi for Shabbat Zakhor,

that had generally not yet been removed from the *amidah*–i.e., the poetic elaborations for the liturgical shifts to the seasonal mentions of dew or rain on Pesaḥ and Sukkot respectively. Curiously, his comments on the extended *kedushot* on Yom Kippur are somewhat contradictory, recognizing that they are problematic but accepting that perhaps minhag must prevail. He makes no direct comment about the extended Yom Kippur *vidui* common in the Sefardi rites or on the insertion of the *seder avodah*.[261]

The reiteration of these arguments over several centuries suggests, of course, that there was no immediate conformity to this halakhic guidance in the rites of the various communities of the Sefardi diaspora. Indeed, one cannot generalize about the impact of any halakhic decisions on these diverse communities.

---

originally composed for insertion into the third blessing of *keriat shema*, but understood by the Ḥida and his contemporaries to have been composed for insertion into *nishmat*, the place to which it was moved in most Sefardi rites when insertions in the blessings of *keriat shema* came under question. This is not an unique case of a community completely forgetting that their poetry had ever been recited in a different station. This particular *piyyut* is one of the few almost universally preserved, even today, in one location or another, in the Sefardi rites.

The objection to *piyyut* inserted between *yishtabaḥ* and the *yotzer* appears already in Yisrael Yaakov Algazi's *Sefer Shalmei Tzibbur*, Ḥelek Ḥalvei Hashelamim 23. Following the Ari, Algazi makes an exception for *piyyut* of Kalir and other Tannaim. Similarly, David de Raphael Meldola, in his *Sefer Divrei David* 24 documents a recent change in his Amsterdam community, following the custom common in Israel, the western lands, Turkey and Italy, to remove this *mi khamokha* from *nishmat* to after the repetition of the *amidah*. He reports that earlier sages had objected to interruptions in this prayer. While acknowledging the difficulty of changing an established minhag, he calls on the Jews of Pisa to extend this stricture and to remove *piyyut* from this section of the liturgy on Rosh Hashanah and Yom Kippur too. Curiously, though, he extends Kalir's credentials to Halevi, Gabirol, and Najara, perhaps in an attempt to continue the elevated status granted to them by the Radbaz in his responsum, III:532, or in response to the *Shut Vayikra Avraham* 122c, who claimed that anyone who eliminated Halevi's *piyyut* would have to settle personally with Halevi. Note that the Ḥida does not defend the Spanish *payyetanim* at all.

261. See his *Shut Tov Ayin* 18 #40; and *Sefer Birkei Yosef* OH 112. This objection too was not original with the Ḥida. See Shmuel Aboab's *Sefer Devar Shmuel* 149, which approves of the removal in Israel and a few Italian congregations of the *piyyut* for *tal* and *geshem* to before *musaf*. However, he suggests that such a change would not work in most communities. See also R. Yosef ben Imanuel Ergas' *Sefer Divrei Yosef* 5, which points to the difficulties of forcing the community to change its custom based on kabbalistic rather than talmudic rulings, especially when the Ari considered any extra words to constitute an interruption, and the general community considered words of praise on the topic of the blessing or day to be acceptable. But, he insists, individual sages can change the customs of their communities, and he points to examples where communities have removed the dew, rain, and fast-day poetry from the repetition of their *amidah* and Halevi's *mi khamokha* from *nishmat*.

From northwestern Europe to east Asia, different social realities determined the extent of *piyyut's* persistence in the various "Sefardi" liturgical traditions. However, the general trend–which eventually became essentially universal and which continues even today[262]–was to eliminate it. The extent of that trend can be adequately illustrated by looking at a few specific schools of minhagim.

As discussed above, to the extent that it can be reconstructed, it seems that in Spain itself, only in the Castilian rite, and perhaps there initially only in Toledo, was *piyyut* fully removed from the statutory blessings before the expulsion. The *Tashlum Abudarham*, commenting on the *piyyut* of the Toledan Yom Kippur liturgy, indicates that the rite includes no *piyyut* for *nishmat* or *keriat shema*. Its placement of the extended *kedushah* before the *kedushta* itself indicates that only the former was inserted; the rest of the *piyyut* was deferred until after the repetition of the *amidah*. Thus this pattern goes beyond the dictates of the *Tur* and represents either conformity to a lost halakhic protocol or a popular loss of interest in *piyyut*.

It is almost impossible to know which of the post-expulsion rites are authentic heirs of the Castilian traditions. If those printed in Italy, Amsterdam, and Constantinople for the general use of Sefardi Jews represent the Castilian rite, we do perceive a consistent ritual, one developed at least in part to provide a new, halakhically legitimate rite for the former Marranos who turned to the Sefardi rabbis of these centers for guidance as they learned to conform to Jewish tradition.

In the early editions of these prayerbooks, no *piyyut* is inserted into the statutory prayers of *keriat shema* and the *amidah*. The *kedushta*, where it has been preserved, is deferred until after the repetition of the *amidah*, either before or after the *sheliaḥ tzibbur* has recited kaddish. The *ofan* typically precedes the kaddish before *barekhu*,[263] the *guf hayotzer* sometimes follows *barekhu*, and the rest of the *yotzer piyyutim*, where preserved, precede the *kedushta* after the repetition of the *amidah*. *Piyyut* for *nishmat* may be inserted into the prayer or precede it. On Yom Kippur, the extended poetic *kedushah* and *vidui* are inserted into the repetition, as is the *seder avodah*. On the appropriate festivals, the seasonal announcements of the shifts to mentions of dew and rain are also inserted into the *musaf* repetition.[264]

---

262. According to Shulamit Elizur, in a private conversation.

263. This is a curious transposition of themes of sanctification–moving a *piyyut* tightly bound to the verses of the *kedushah deyotzer* and tying it instead with the kaddish.

264. See, for example, the *maḥzorim* printed in Ferrara, 155-; Venice 1572; 1600; Amsterdam 1642, 1716; Salonika 1526. For the insertion of the dew and rain *piyyut*, see for

Interestingly, this situation shifts slightly, particularly into the eighteenth century, when new urgency suffused rabbinic calls for the elimination of kabbalistically inacceptable *piyyut*; the *kedushta*, first deferred to the end of the repetition, disappears entirely.[265] Essentially at the same time, these prayerbooks begin to reflect concern about the insertion of *piyyut* into *nishmat*, either moving it to before *barukh sheamar* or adding multiple notes at *nishmat* indicating that this *piyyut* should be said earlier or deferred to after the repetition.[266]

While the Castilian rite is perhaps the most important and widespread, it is not necessarily the most interesting or dramatic exemplar of these changes over the centuries. The halakhic opinions summarized above influenced the other Spanish rites as well, even of those communities whose primary halakhic decisors in Spain had supported the recitation of *piyyut*.

As documented by Daniel Goldschmidt, even those Spanish rites in Salonika that maintained their autonomy eventually removed some *piyyut* from their statutory prayers. The Catalonian community maintained the original placement of their poetry in 1527 when their rite was first printed, but the next printing, in 1863, eliminated insertions into *keriat shema* while continuing to insert the *kedushta*.[267] The Aragon rite printed in 1527[268] seems already to have moved the *piyyut* for *keriat shema* to before *barekhu*, but because the printer did not reproduce the statutory texts, it is difficult to be certain whether the *zulat* included was said before *barekhu* or inserted into its original location. The *kedushta* was inserted into the statutory texts. The 1804 edition transposes this *zulat* with the *ofan* preceding kaddish, indicating that there was a question about its previous location. Thus, neither of these communities in Salonika removed *piyyut*

---

example the *siddurim* and festival *maḥzorim* printed in Venice, 1656; Amsterdam, 1659, 1726, 1825/6; Florence 1736.

265. See, for example, the *maḥzorim* printed in Leghorn, 1797, 1821 and the Constantinople rite texts in the following note.

266. The Constantinople rite *maḥzor* printed in Venice, 1796 continues to list the *piyyutim* before and after *nishmat*, but includes multiple instructions that these are best deferred to after the repetition. It also suggests that one should not change local minhag. Clearly, this is an ambivalent nod to prevalent halakhic opinion, which persists in the editions printed in Leghorn in 1858 and 1888 (?1894) and Jerusalem, 1908. In contrast, the *maḥzor* printed in Salonika in 1792 directly cites the Ḥida and prints all the *piyyut* before *barukh sheamar*. This inclusion persists in the edition printed in Salonika in 1876 and reprinted in Tel Aviv in 1963. Here, though, the *piyyut* for Yom Kippur is not merely moved to before *barukh sheamar*, but even to before the Psalms preceding it.

267. מחקרי תפילה ופיוט, 272-279. The 1927 edition continues this format.

268. Goldschmidt, מחקרי תפילה ופיוט, 279-288, dates this edition to 1529–which does not correspond to the dating of the JTS copy (Microfilm #4849) that he does not cite.

from the repetition of the *amidah*, but both eventually followed the *Tur*'s strict ruling about interrupting the blessings of *shema*.

These communities were fairly unique in withstanding pressures to change their minhag. The rites of two other communities are closely related to the Catalonian rites because of geographical propinquity–the Jews in the Provençal Papal states and those of North Africa–but they proceeded quite differently.

Representing the only French communities not expelled in 1305, the rites of the Papal states are the sole remaining examples of the authentic Provençal traditions. They are quite well documented because they relied on locally produced manuscripts into the eighteenth century rather than infrequent mass printings. In the fifteenth-century manuscripts of these rites, *piyyut* is inserted into all of the statutory prayers, as in the Catalonian rites.[269] By the seventeenth-century, though, all *piyyut* on High Holy Days had been removed from the statutory prayers; although the *piyyut* for *nishmat* remained in place, parts of the *yotzrot* remained inserted between the end of *nishmat* and the beginning of the *yotzer* blessing itself, and the rest appeared with the *kedushta* after the repetition of the *amidah*.[270] However, for festivals and especially for the four special Sabbaths before Purim and Passover, the transition to the new placement of *piyyut* was less smooth. Although these communities did not maintain the full gamut of possible *piyyut* for any one of these days, it is quite clear that they persisted in inserting the *yotzrot* on Shabbat Zakhor and on the festivals long after these had been abandoned on Rosh Hashanah and Yom Kippur.[271]

However, by the eighteenth century, even this inconsistency had disappeared; by mid-century even the insertions for rain and dew had been moved, as had Halevi's *mi khamokha* for Shabbat Zakhor.[272] Unlike in the traditions

---

269. See the manuscripts of the community of Avignon, Jewish Theological Seminary Microfilms 4844, 4511, and perhaps 4783 and 4287 (The rites of these two manuscripts are not so precisely identifiable).

270. See, for example, from Avignon in the eighteenth century, JTS 4476, 4235; also the 1765/6 edition, printed in Amsterdam (Hebrew Union College). From Carpentras in the seventeenth century, JTS 4746, 4470, 4535, 8145; from the eighteenth century JTS 4490, and the editions printed in Amsterdam in 1739-1740. From Cavaillon in these same centuries, JTS 4842, 4839, 4840, 4493. From Lisle, similarly, JTS 4394, 4669, 4474, 4835, 4206, 4197.

271. See the seventeenth-century manuscript of the Carpentras rite, JTS 4471. Note that they had no *kedushta* for these days.

272. Avignon rite: JTS 4829 (1701/2), 1767 edition. Carpentras rite: JTS 4504 (1720, maintains insertions for dew and rain only), 1759 Amsterdam edition of festival *maḥzor* maintains no insertions, 1761 Amsterdam edition of Sabbath siddur instructs that the Halevi *mi khamokha* is best recited after the repetition.

discussed above, we do not find in these texts extensive citations of halakhic authorities justifying changes, perhaps because most of these texts are manuscripts, written for the use of an individual, rather than printed editions whose multiple copies would reach the hands of many. The only comment, about the moving of Halevi's *mi khamokha* for Shabbat Zakhor, does indeed appear in the first printed edition of the siddur.[273] However, it is quite obvious that these rites were adjusted to conform to the prevailing rulings of the Sefardi rabbis of the post-expulsion world. It would be fascinating to investigate the archives of these communities and perhaps find recorded evidence of the dynamics accompanying these shifts.

When we travel south to North Africa, especially to Algeria, we find other rites that show strong Catalonian influence, consonant with the economic ties between the communities in the thirteenth and fourteenth centuries and the influx of Catalonian refugees to Algeria from the 1391 persecutions in Spain. Relatively few refugees sought a safe haven in Algeria in the aftermath of 1492, and the only other major influx of Jews into the community was of former Marrano families, coming via Italy, in the seventeenth and eighteenth centuries.[274]

Consequently, the Algerian prayerbooks through most of the eighteenth century fully insert *piyyut* of all types into their statutory prayers.[275] However, contemporaneous again with the rulings of the Ḥida and his colleagues, a shift occurs. A note added to the front of the Jewish Theological Seminary's copy of a 1759 *maḥzor*–likely by E.N. Adler, from whose collection this volume comes–indicates that there were two rites in Algiers since 1782, that of the פשטנים (simple people, non-mystics), who had only two synagogues and who read *piyyut* in their prayers, and that of the kabbalists, who read the *piyyut* after the *amidah*.[276] The first written evidence of the kabbalistic change appears in a 1772 prayerbook for special Sabbaths and festivals, where Halevi's *mi khamokha* for Shabbat Zakhor is deferred until after the repetition of the *amidah* and isolated *yotzer piyyutim* appear before *barekhu*.[277] From 1800 on, with the exception

273. Amsterdam, 1761, p. 48.

274. See Leopold Zunz, *Die Ritus des synagogalen Gottesdienstes geschichtlich entwickelt*, 2nd ed. (Berlin: Louis Lamm, 1919), 46ff.; and "Algeria," *Encyclopedia Judaica* 2:612-4.

275. See JTS 4717 (15th c.), 4604 (16-17th c.), 4801 (17-18th c.), 4489 (17-18th c., Constantine rite), 4664 (18th c.), 4556 (18th c., Tlemcen rite), 4726 (1759), 4556 (1769, Oran rite), 4523 (1772), 4540 (18th c.), 4830 (18th c.). The last three are for festivals and special Sabbaths and are more inconsistent in their inclusion of all genres of *piyyut*. However, none obviously defer or displace any poetry.

276. JTS 4726, ENA 2305. Adler seems to have provided two dates, the first of which, also in the eighteenth century, is illegible.

277. ספר חכמת מסכן והוא ספר קרובץ, מנהג ארג'יל, Leghorn, 1772. It is not obvious whether or

of the rite of Oran, essentially every prayerbook conforms to the Sefardi halakhic norm, where, if *piyyut* is printed with *nishmat*, notes accompany it suggesting that it be deferred until after the repetition.[278]

A similar if more complex process seems to have taken place in Corfu, where the community was continually struggling to maintain its own rite while using the prayerbooks printed for the Sefardi community at large. The seventeenth-century texts for the High Holy Days indicate a community in transition. The *piyyut* for *keriat shema* appears before *barekhu*, but with the notation that some insert it in its original locations, and notes in those locations refer the worshiper back to that *piyyut*. In addition, at the point of the *ofan* and the *mi khamokha*, additional *piyyut* is recited in conjunction with the statutory liturgy. On the other hand, this *mahzor* includes no *kedushta* for any service, and does not even insert the *seder avodah* into the Yom Kippur *musaf* repetition.[279] A similar text from a century later moved the inserted *ofan* to before *barekhu* and included a *kedushta* only for Yom Kippur.[280] A similar conformity with Sefardi halakhic norms may be observed with the poetry for festivals and special Sabbaths, with, perhaps, a tendency to be careful about use of *piyyut* on festivals evident earlier than on Sabbaths.[281]

---

not this text calls for the insertion or deferral of the *kedushta* in the services for which it is provided. Compare JTS 4523, a manuscript from the same year, which does indicate insertion of the *kedushta*.

278. See JTS 4505, of obvious kabbalistic leanings, where all *piyyut* is printed after the repetition, or, on Yom Kippur, also before *barukh sheamar*. The מחזור לראש השנה כמנהג ק"ק ואראן תלמסאן ומעסכר ואגפיה (Vienna, 1888) and the second volume for Yom Kippur include no *piyyut* for the *amidah*, but do indicate that Oran inserts poetry into *nishmat*, *keriat shema*, and does recite a *kedushta* (although it is not necessarily inserted into the prayers). Most prayerbooks, however, merely suggest moving the *piyyut* out of *nishmat*, if that. See, for example, those printed in Leghorn in 1852, in Susa in 1925 (Constantine rite), in Casablanca in ?1940. Although the evidence available in the libraries I have consulted is less extensive, a similar process can be posited for the Moroccan, Tunisian, and Libyan communities.

279. JTS 4559, c. 1650. The removal of the *seder avodah* apparently derives from a concern that the *sheliah tzibbur* would move his feet, and hence prematurely signify the end of his prayer, while prostrating himself in response to the High Priest's rituals recounted in this poem. Compare also the 17th c. manuscripts JTS 4768 and 4582.

280. JTS 4641, (1741/2). This text, in its instructions to the congregations, also reflects directly dialogue with the Sefardi prayerbooks. Compare also JTS 4583 (17-19th c.) which explicitly lists the *zulat* among the displaced *yotzer piyyut*. See too JTS 4636, 4637, 4171, 4173, 4338.

281. JTS 4507 (16th. c.) demonstrates inconsistencies in whether it inserts parts of the *yotzer piyyut* or removes it to before *barekhu*. JTS 4769 (17th c.) seems to insert less *piyyut* on festivals. JTS 4585 (18-19th c.) clearly inserts Halevi's *mi khamokha* in the blessing on

There can be no question, then, that halakhic concerns about interruptions to the statutory prayers–a category eventually expanded to include *pesukei d'zimra*–eventually uprooted minhag in every Sefardi rite, including those that clearly differentiated themselves from the Castilian traditions. The reasons halakhah took precedence over minhag largely lie in changing conceptions about the source of meaningful liturgy. As is clear from the traditions of the Ari, especially as they were re-presented by the Ḥida and his colleagues, the meaning of a prayer was now determined on kabbalistic grounds. The fixed liturgies were effective because of mystical powers hidden in their precise number and order of words. *Piyyut* composed without consciousnes of these kabbalistic meanings could render a prayer useless in affecting the heavenly realms. According to these sages, only the *piyyut* of Kalir and his colleagues could be trusted. However, Kalir's compositions were not part of the rites of those conducting this discussion, and the Ari also taught that to pray in other than one's own rite rendered one's prayer equally ineffective. Hence, Sefardi-style *piyyut*, the only kind included in most of these rites, could not interrupt these statutory prayers. It was sidelined and increasingly dropped as meaningless.[282]

### *The Late Ashkenazi Discussions*

These arguments did not fail to affect the Ashkenazi communities as well. The modern shifts away from Ashkenazi recitation of *piyyut*, however, came less from its halakhic or kabbalistic insuitability than from a sense that the poetry had indeed lost its meaning. The dominant Ashkenazi halakhic tradition had

---

Shabbat Zakhor, and may insert other *piyyut* on the other special Sabbaths. JTS 4821 (18-19th c.) and 4692 (1797) still add instructions for the transition to the statutory liturgy at the conclusion of the *zulat* and *mi khamokha* for some services, but by the nineteenth century, this inconsistency ceases to appear. (JTS 4579 (1817)). In contrast, the Corfu Jews seem to have been much more careful about insertions into the *amidah*, in direct contradiction to the Spanish halakhic concerns. By the eighteenth century, the elaborate announcements of the rain or dew liturgy were to be recited before *musaf* (JTS 4581, 4816, 4555).

282. Many of the later prayerbooks that list *piyyut* after the repetition drop the designations for the original locations of the *piyyut*. From one printing to the next, individual *piyyutim* in this listing were dropped as the communities shortened their liturgies. Centralized printing of Sefardi prayerbooks also hastened this change. However, individual communities may well have added their own traditions of *piyyut* to the now impoverished prayerbook. Indeed, the library liturgy collections which I have consulted contain extensive *diwans*, especially from North African communities. Unfortunately, these collections only rarely indicate when or where a particular poem was to be recited; their organization by author or melody or alphabet makes reconstruction of the rite from the text itself impossible.

always supported the preservation of minhag, including necessarily the recitation of *piyyut.* Increasingly, though, important sages voiced ambivalence about the issue. The Rema, Moshe Isserles, while generally supporting *piyyut,* acknowledged that if one skips it, no harm is done. However, separating oneself from the community and studying silently while the congregation is reciting it might well lead one to talk and create a more serious interruption in the prayers. Therefore, one *must* recite *piyyut.*[283]

The *Magen Avraham* considered the Ari's precedent supportive of Ashkenazi minhag, but continued with citations of various precedents for avoiding its recitation.[284] Similarly, Yair Ḥayyim Bachrach upheld Ashkenazi minhag. He suggested that Kalirian *piyyut* was not problematic because it was in the repetition of the *amidah,* which was no longer needed to fulfill the obligations of the unlearned, so there need be no concerns about interrupting it. However, he did suggest that individuals try to find ways to avoid interrupting the *yotzer* with *piyyut,* while fulfilling their obligation to recite the poetry.[285]

Issues of meaning enter more directly into the comment of R. Yehudah Leib b"R. Shimon of Frankfurt in his *Yad Yehudah.* He agrees with Ibn Ezra that *kavvanah* is impossible without understanding the prayers, but limits that requirement to individual prayers, and not to those recited by the *sheliaḥ tzibbur,* as long as the *sheliaḥ tzibbur* himself understands the prayers. The *Yad Yehudah* represents a radically different and historically more accurate understanding of the function of the repetition of the prayers than that voiced by Bachrach. Both allow *piyyut* to interrupt the repetition of the *amidah,* but for different reasons.[286]

By the late eighteenth and nineteenth centuries the Ashkenazi debates had become more heated. While R. Elazar Fleckeles vigorously defended all Ashkenazi traditions of *piyyut,* especially those of Kalir,[287] the Vilna Gaon eliminated all inserted *piyyut* except that of the High Holy Days and the announcements of the mentioning of rain and dew on the festivals. He did preserve the *piyyut* for festivals and the four special Sabbaths, but only if deferred to after *hallel* or the repetition respectively. Unfortunately, these traditions do not preserve his reasons for advocating these changes.[288]

Indeed, evidence in this period points to a general loss of Ashkenazi interest in reciting *piyyut*–even though sages like R. Abraham Lowenstamm argue that

283. OH 68:1, 112:2.

284. OH 68:1.

285. *Shut Ḥavat Yair* 235, 238.

286. מנחם עזריה מפאנו, ספר עשרה מאמרות עם פירוש יד יהודה מהור"ר יהודה ליב ב"ר שמעון... (למבורג, 1858; ד"ח ?1973), מאמר אם כל חי, חלק א' סימן לא

287. *Teshuvah Meahavah* I:1; I:90.

288. *Sefer Maaseh Rav,* 127, 163, 205; *Sefer Shaarei Raḥamim* 91.

if the Ari recited it, so should we. Not only can one rely on the greatness of the ancient poets, Lowenstamm maintains, but now that Heidenheim has made the poetry accessible through translation and commentary–and the entire congregation has prayerbooks that provide the texts–there is no reason to reject what sages like the Rema considered a mitzvah.[289] In other words, Lowenstamm's response to those wanting to reform the liturgy was not so different from those in early Ashkenaz who required study of *piyyut* before its liturgical recitation.

Responses to the issue were also tied up in the religious politics of the period. In 1892 R. Yosef Zekhariah Stern, although acknowledging the validity of various arguments for eliminating *piyyut*, insisted on maintaining the minhag, not simply for its own sake, but because its abolition would open the doors to reforming pressures on the rest of the liturgy.[290] Thus sages who might have otherwise jettisoned the custom felt that such a move was dangerous in a world where traditional practice was being increasingly challenged.[291]

On the other hand, respected sages like R. Tzvi Hirsch Chajes pointed to the unpopularity of *piyyut* as a reason for changing the custom–arguing that the *Tur* and Karo were able to rule so strongly against it precisely because it was unpopular in their immediate worlds (as opposed to Isserles, who, because it was widespread, did not want to abolish it). Although, in the past, support of *piyyut* had persisted despite serious halakhic arguments against it, Chajes considered it appropriate now to abolish this errant custom since most Polish and Russian Jews no longer followed it, proving that it no longer met the needs of the time. However, he advocated letting it evolve and die naturally, rather than assertively legislating against it and confusing a community that could not distinguish between important and unimportant matters.[292]

The result of these various voices was the gradual loss of *piyyut* from traditional Ashkenazi rites, except for on the High Holy Days. A few communities maintained rich traditions of *piyyut* until the Holocaust, and even fewer reinsti-

---

289. *Sefer Tzror Haḥayyim, Shut Biyeshishim Ḥokhmah.* See also Yitzḥak Isaac, *Sefer Binyan Olam* #6, for additional evidence of the general communal loss of interest in reciting *piyyut.*

290. *Sefer Zekher Yehosef* OH 19:3-4.

291. See Jakob J. Petuchowski, *Prayerbook Reform in Europe: The Liturgy of European Liberal and Reform Judaism* (New York: The World Union for Progressive Judaism, 1968), 30, 117, 122, 125, 147, 155-6, 160-1, 165.

292. *Darkhei Horaah,* Ch. 6, Ofan 3. A fascinating document of a phase of this opposition to *piyyut,* which also summarizes the arguments raised against *piyyut* up to his own day, is the monograph of the chief Rabbi of Denmark, Dr. A. A. Wolff, עתרת שלום ואמת, *Die Stimmen der ältesten glaubwürdigsten Rabbinen über die Pijutim* (Leipzig, 1857).

tuted these traditions after the war.[293] Never sidelined in Ashkenaz for halakhic reasons, *piyyut* simply lost its meaning. The result was its virtual elimination in the Reform rites, the maintenance of selected High Holy Day *piyyut* in the Conservative, and a custom closely conforming to that of the Vilna Gaon in most Orthodox synagogues.

* * *

*Piyyut* originated as an expression of *kavvanah*, a characteristic that early rabbinic traditions established as necessary for prayer to be meaningful and effective. The Palestinian *ḥazzanim*, by infusing prayer with ever-renewing content, provided their congregations with a source of this *kavvanah*. However, the resultant poetry was culture-specific, and although Jews in Palestine persisted in reciting their corpus of *piyyut* and Jews in other communities imported and imitated it, some Jews no longer understood it or valued the heavily aggadic content it conveyed. Others found meaning only in interpretation of the statutory prayers themselves. Nevertheless, *piyyut* persisted–out of habit, because it was an established part of the minhag, because of the aesthetic qualities it added to the service, and because of the value placed on it by a rabbinic elite who interpreted it and wrote new compositions.

This persistence brought the recitation of *piyyut* to various points of crisis during its long history. The Geonim and various Sefardi sages, both Rishonim and Aḥaronim, hurled halakhic arguments against it, criticizing its interruption of the statutory prayers and its introduction of inappropriate, sometime incomprehensible, content into the liturgy. Supporters of *piyyut* countered with arguments that tried to create a halakhic basis to support the existing custom as a legitimate addition to the statutory prayers with sanction from antiquity. Both sides were ultimately arguing about the impact of *piyyut* on the acceptability of the community's prayer.

Ultimately, though, through the ages it was not the pure halakhic arguments that determined a community's ritual course, but the general cultural milieu of its worshipers. If the corpus of *piyyut* in the liturgy had meaning and associations for them, if it was not perceived as burdensome and aesthetically offensive, then it was likely to persist in spite of objections by halakhic authorities. Recognizing this reality, some sages struggled to find ways to understand and legitimate the

293. See, for example, the documentation of such a community founded in Cincinnati in 1939, in Benny Kraut's *German-Jewish Orthodoxy in an Immigrant Synagogue: Cincinnati's New Hope Congregation and the Ambiguities of Ethnic Religion* (New York: Markus Wiener Publishing, 1988), especially Appendix C: The New Hope *Minhagim*.

custom, establishing the precedents that later broadened into full-scale authorizations for recitation.[294] Others, quietly broadcasting their concerns about *piyyut* and avoiding its recitation themselves, refrained from ruling directly against the minhag of a specific community.

Thus cultural shifts were the real catalyst to changes in the custom. Jews in Muslim Spain ceased to value the aesthetics of eastern-style *piyyut*; they replaced it with new poetry that not only employed different linguistic and aesthetic norms, but also replaced midrashic allusions with more philosophically acceptable content. Maimonides, as an immigrant to Egypt, was ready and, because of his personal stature, able to abolish much of the local practice. Jews in parts of Christian Spain apparently lost their regard for their corpus of *piyyut* by the fourteenth century and were already eliminating it or reciting it outside of the statutory prayers. The Baal Haturim was able to capitalize on this lack of interest in Toledo to create a strong halakhic precedent accepted without apparent opposition in Castile. The dislocations of Jews during the Spanish persecutions and expulsions spread this process further; Jews looking to create a new, uniform rite in a new place could easily eliminate *piyyut*.

The most significant cultural change to affect its recitation in the later Sefardi world was the popularization of kabbalah. The mystical concerns for the purity and inner meaning of the statutory liturgy, combined with the direct criticism of Sefardi *piyyut* by the Ari–especially as those concerns and that criticism were reiterated over the next two centuries–led to the sidelining and elimination of *piyyut* even in those rites that had most carefully preserved it. Were these arguments halakhic? At some level, yes, but their implementation depended on a totally new attitude to prayer on the part of the populace. Average Jews now felt themselves encouraged to participate in the grand task of repairing the world and preparing for the coming of the Messiah by meticulous observance of halakhah–and that halakhah, in the Sefardi realm of influence, happened to frown on the insertion of *piyyut* into the statutory prayers. In addition, the standardization of prayerbooks brought about by printing and the turning of new Jewish communities of former Marranos to rabbinic authorities for direction in the development of the minhag of their new communities also militated against *piyyut*.

The advent of modernity in the Jewish communities of Europe had a revolutionary effect analogous in many ways to the exposure of Sefardi Jews to Arab culture hundreds of years earlier. The received corpus of *piyyut* simply ceased to have meaning for many Jews who, comparing the liturgical life of their Chris-

294. For instance, Natronai Gaon's permission to recite *piyyut* had much more impact than his little heeded requirement that the *piyyut* be *me-ein haberakhah*.

tian neighbors with their own, found the incomprehensible poetry and lack of decorum that often accompanied its recitation particularly irksome. The studies of the Wissenschaft historians made it clear that Kalir was by no means a Tanna; arguments supporting the authority of his poetry above all others had to be jettisoned. The renaissance of modern Hebrew poetry must also have affected the attitudes of some.

As a result, most but not all of the most strictly orthodox communities simply ceased to recite much of their *piyyut*, restricting it to days of highest significance in the liturgical calendar. By the late twentieth century, very few prayerbooks even include *piyyut* for the four special Sabbaths (and even fewer congregations recite them); *piyyut* for the statutory prayers of the festivals, except for the announcements of rain and dew, is printed in the back of *maḥzorim* if at all, and only orthodox congregations maintain a full array for the High Holy Days. Again, it is not halakhic arguments that determined the change. Ashkenazim did not remove their *piyyut* to halakhically neutral sites while continuing to recite it, but rather removed it totally from the communal liturgy. No longer a source of *kavvanah*, it distracted people from serious prayer.

Thus, in all sectors of the Jewish world, a liturgical revolution took place. But only when the minhag was ready for change could the halakhah effectively play an active role.

# 4

# Individual Recitation of the *Kedushah*: The Impact of Mysticism on Minhag and Halakhah

The theophanies of Isaiah and Ezekiel presented to the world tantalizing glimpses of the workings of the heavenly realms. Subsequent generations understood these visions to represent an ongoing reality, one that mystic adepts might themselves perceive. Even simple people, under proper circumstances, might regularly participate in the angelic praise of God by ritual recitation of the words these prophets heard. This liturgy, consisting of various elaborations on Isaiah 6:3 and Ezekiel 3:12, became known as the *kedushah* (sanctification), or, in the parallel Church tradition, the *trisagion* or *sanctus*. Because its words originated on high, they could undoubtedly be acceptable praise of God, with a powerful efficacy that might even exceed that of any other human utterance. Hence, they were very attractive to devout worshipers, who at the same time recognized that their misuse carried with them a possibility of transgression of holy realms and an element of danger far more serious that any caused by extraneous blessings or improper prayer language. The words of the *kedushah*, then, could not be treated cavalierly.

As it moves through the medieval period, the halakhic debate over the proper setting for the recitation of the various *kedushah* prayers is an excellent forum for our analysis of the forces shaping liturgical law. As we shall see, the rabbinic sources treating this liturgy leave many vague precedents of unclear application. Already in antiquity, it is evident that forces encouraging its inclusion lay outside the realm of exoteric rabbinic Judaism. As such, decisions vis-à-vis its status provide a ready opportunity to study the impact of esoteric mystical traditions on the halakhah of the synagogue, a dynamic we have been able to trace only in very late periods in previous chapters. But as with issues we have already discussed, struggles over the *kedushah* also involved popular custom and the almost constant unwillingness of the people to conform to rabbinic strictures.

Only the popularization of mystic traditions in the sixteenth century, combined with the halakhic genius of Joseph Karo, allowed for a lasting compromise between the mystically influenced and the popular definitions of acceptable prayer.

To understand this compromise, we need first to determine how the *kedushah* fit into categories of communal prayer and why. What were the textual traditions on which later generations could base their rulings? What role did mysticism play during late antiquity and what precedents did it create? And specificially, what were the attitudes of mystics and the official rabbinic community to this liturgy?

One of the primary early categories of liturgical law as it applied to the *kedushah* was the rabbinic tradition that certain liturgical rituals could be effectively and appropriately performed only in a communal setting, defined as a quorum of ten adult males. Surviving texts leave no clues as to the origins of this concept of minyan; the midrashic assertion that God's presence is found in the synagogue only when ten men gather there is early, but clearly was developed to justify an existing institution.[1] The rabbis integrated this concept into their requirements for proper performance of their recently formalized, non-sacrificial mode of worship and, on a more practical level, used it to inculcate a system of public prayer that would make the new form of worship accessible to the common people. According to this conception, only in the setting of a minyan would those corporate rituals that presuppose a public communal setting or a congregational response be acceptable to God; and only in such a gathering could a *sheliaḥ tzibbur* propose to fulfill the obligations of others, most importantly of the unlearned, for recitation of crucial parts of the liturgy.

*Mishnah Megillah* 4:3 specifically restricts certain rituals to this communal setting, saying:

> אין פורסין את שמע ואין עוברין לפני התבה ואין נושאין את כפיהם ואין קורין בתורה ואין מפטירין בנביא ואין עושין מעמד ומושב ואין אומרין ברכת אבלים ותנחומי אבלים וברכת חתנים ואין מזמנין בשם פחות מעשרה.
>
> With less than a quorum of ten [men], one may not lead the communal recitation of *shema*, lead the congregation in reciting the *amidah*, recite the priestly benediction, ritually read the Torah or prophetic portions, perform rituals blessing and consoling the bereaved, recite the wedding ben-

1. See *Avot* 3:6; *Mekhilta* Yitro 11 (Horowitz-Rabin, p. 243); *B. Berakhot* 6a. It is also by no means certain that the minyan always consisted of ten men in the Palestinian tradition. See *Masekhet Soferim* 10:6, Higger ed., which indicates that there the minimum number was six or seven.

edictions, or recite the form of the invitation to the grace after meals that invokes God's name.

The Mishnah provides no explanation for the inclusion or exclusion of the specific rituals in this list. Whether it merely records tannaitic custom, or whether it ascribes particular significance to the communal recitation of these rituals cannot be determined with any certainty. But early in the amoraic period, the rabbis extrapolated from this list a concept that could be applied to other liturgical issues and that resolved the antiquity of this Mishnah. By citing a complex midrash ascribed to rabbis of the third century that establishes that the proper and acceptable sanctification of God can occur only in a gathering of ten men, the *gemara* transforms the simple tannaitic specification of the community required for particular rituals into an overarching principle of liturgical law applicable to any setting in which worshipers seek an enhanced degree of holiness.[2]

This new principle, כל דבר שבקדושה לא יהא פחות מעשרה (nothing involving sanctity [or alternatively, the sanctification of God], no *davar shebikedushah*, may be recited in the presence of less than ten men), received essentially no further definition, either in the *gemara* or in later rabbinic writings. *B. Megillah* 23b explicitly applies it to the Mishnah's list of rituals requiring a minyan, but does not discuss the possibility that it might apply beyond this list. *P. Megillah* 4:4, 75a-b does suggest that the ceremony sanctifying the new month should require a minyan too, but it does not introduce the concept of the *davar shebikedushah*. Only the discussion in *B. Berakhot* 21b expands the list, very narrowly, to include the *kedushah*, here specifically in the context of the *amidah*. By and large, then,

---

2. *B. Berakhot* 21b; *B. Megillah* 23b. Compare also *P. Megillah* 4:4, 75b, which applies the midrash establishing the reason for the quorum of ten to our Mishnah, but without reference to the idea of sanctification that appears in the Babylonian versions. Although the rabbis mentioned in all these versions were mostly leaders of the Palestinian community, it is noteworthy that only the Babylonian literary traditions employed the more elevated and abstract concept of sanctification. Further study may determine whether this differentiation is of historical significance.

Max Kadushin, in his *Worship and Ethics: A Study in Rabbinic Judaism* (Northwestern University Press, 1964), chap. 6, endeavors to determine the significance of this communal requirement for worship. He specifically discusses what others would term the *performative* aspects of the minyan, claiming that the corporate act of worship creates the setting in which people can achieve a consciousness of God's holiness; it concretizes the idea of *kedushat hashem* (the sanctification of God). However, his discussion of how this applies to the *kedushah* itself is not helpful because it is highly influenced by then-dominant methodologies of liturgical studies and the thinking of his day vis-à-vis the origins of the *kedushah*.

the legal statement that the Amoraim leave for posterity leaves the matter open to dispute by later generations of rabbis.[3]

The most logical extension of the Mishnah's list is to the *kedushah* itself, as occurs in *B. Berakhot* 21b. Although the linguistic connection might seem obvious (what could be more a *davar shebikedushah* than the *kedushah* itself?) and might similarly include the kaddish, it could not be extended to the early home ritual of sanctification, the kiddush. More significantly, by analogy to the list of rituals in the Mishnah, the concept of the *davar shebikedushah* extended easily to prayers of obvious communal nature, especially those incorporating a congregational response. Hence, kaddish and the *barekhu* preceding *keriat shema*[4] easily met the criteria and logically, so should the *kedushah* in all its forms, since its very structure implies a congregational response and its primary content, the angelic praise of God, could not be more elevated. However, in this case, it was not to be so simple.

As we know it today, the *kedushah* appears in three distinct places in the liturgy: in the *yotzer*, the first blessing preceding *shema* in the morning; in every repetition of the *amidah*; and as a relatively distinct liturgical unit known as the *kedushah desidra*, originally recited after the study of Scripture in the *bet midrash*, the study hall, and eventually incorporated into the synagogue service, primarily, but not exclusively, as a concluding prayer.[5] Of these three, none was necessarily viewed by the definition of the Mishnah as a communal prayer. The public repetition of the *amidah* required a minyan, whether or not the *kedushah* was recited,[6] and the possibility exists that some individuals recited this *kedushah* without a minyan. The *kedushah desidra* was not an integral part of the ritual Torah and Haftarah readings listed by our Mishnah; it merely followed them.

3. When one follows the usage of the term *davar shebikedushah* through the responsa literature to the present day, one notices a growing trend in more recent centuries to apply this term not only to words, but also to objects.

4. The *barekhu*, for which we have no indisputable evidence until geonic times in this context, was already part of two rituals included in the mishnaic definition of the *davar shebikedushah*: Torah reading, and the tannaitic *zimmun* when the leader could exclude himself and maintain the minimum number. Later redefinitions of *perisat shema* assume *barekhu* to be essential to the ritual.

5. For a summary of theories on the origin of this prayer, see Ismar Elbogen, *Jewish Liturgy: A Comprehensive History*, trans. Raymond P. Scheindlin (Philadelphia, New York, Jerusalem: The Jewish Publication Society, The Jewish Theological Seminary of America, 1993), 404, n. 23 (Heb. ed., 403).

6. In the repetition of the weekday *amidah* in the Palestinian rite, there was no *kedushah*. See below, p. 196.

Finally, the *kedushah deyotzer*[7] may or may not be a critical part of the liturgy to which later generations applied the label of the mishnaic ritual requiring a minyan, פורס על\את שמע, *pores al/et shema*.[8]

In the redacted literature of the rabbinic period, even the existence of these three separate forms of the *kedushah* is not clearly demonstrable. Indeed, one of the few texts that even explicitly mentions it is *B. Berakhot* 21b, which discusses the appropriate procedure for one who arrives so late in the synagogue that the congregation is already reciting the *amidah*. Two third-century Amoraim differ as to the extent of permitted overlap between the individual's private *amidah* and the public repetition of the *sheliaḥ tzibbur*. Rav Huna gives the latecomer until *modim* to finish his private prayer,[9] but Rabbi Yehoshua ben Levi gives him only until the *kedushah*. The anonymous talmudic editor explains that the issue underlying this dispute is that Rabbi Yehoshua ben Levi does not allow private recitation of the *kedushah* under any circumstances, while Rav Huna does allow it (at least when the individual is physically in the presence of a minyan). The *gemara* then records the tradition of Rav Adda bar Ahavah, also of the third century, who derives midrashically that the individual may never recite the *kedushah* without participating in a minyan because it is a *davar shebikedushah*.

The tradition of Rabbi Yehoshua ben Levi, at least, documents that by the third century something called the *kedushah* was an established part of the repetition of the *amidah*.[10] The entire passage, though, indicates that its status as a

7. Also sometimes, especially in later literature, called the *kedushah deyeshivah* (the "sitting" *kedushah*), in contrast to the *kedushah de-amidah* (the "standing" *kedushah*).

8. The Amoraim already do not understand the tannaitic referent of this technical term. By the time of the Geonim, it has acquired new meaning, and this becomes an important factor in our discussion. See below.

9. The second to last blessing of the 18 (19), at which point the congregation is expected to say the *modim derabbanan*, a prayer paralleling the reader's.

10. Louis Ginzberg, who takes the stance that the *kedushah* in the *amidah* is Babylonian and hence later than the *kedushah deyotzer*, asserts that the references to the *kedushah* in this *sugya* do not necessarily indicate that the third-century synagogue knew of the *kedushah* as a separate paragraph. Rather, they may have been discussing some reference to Isaiah 6:3 interwoven into the standard wording of the third benediction of the *amidah*, a wording that was appropriate for recitation by the individual. See his *Geonica* (New York: The Jewish Theological Seminary of America, 1909), I: 131-2. More recent research into the nature of early Jewish mysticism, to be discussed below, indicates that the *kedushah* as a liturgical unit was known very early, making it highly unlikely that third-century rabbis did not know the term as explicitly referring to participation in or description of the angelic liturgy. Questions of the historical reliability of rabbinic texts, of course, apply here too, but the very irregularity of the situation described in this passage vis-à-vis later practices heightens the chances that this a a reliable transmission.

prayer restricted to public recitation was not yet firmly established. In the most conservative reading, we can assert that since Rav Huna still allowed the individual to recite it while in the physical presence of a minyan, it is not out of the question that he might have allowed it in a private setting as well. The appearance here of a third tradition, that of Rav Adda bar Ahavah, may well reflect the hand of a later redactor. He was not necessarily referring to this specific debate at all. Indeed, later authorities often chose to consider his tradition as a free-standing assertion of broad application. As it stands, this passage demonstrates only the inclusion of the *kedushah* in the *amidah* and its developing status in the third century as an independent *davar shebikedushah* requiring the presence of a minyan.[11]

The existence of the *kedushah desidra*–or at least of some prayer by this name–in the talmudic period is also attested. The anonymous talmudic editor in *B. Sotah* 49a, commenting on a tannaitic tradition bewailing the world's problems since the destruction of the Temple, asserts that in the absence of the Temple, the world is now sustained by the *kedushah desidra* and by the congregational response to the kaddish. However, an anonymous passage cannot help us trace the origins of a custom; we cannot even be sure it refers to a specifically liturgical setting. As a matter of fact, the juxtaposition of these two prayers, both of which Heinemann has identified as being of *bet midrash* origin,[12] justifies the assumption that the *gemara* is really stating that it is the formal (most likely communal) study of Torah (and not the synagogue's liturgical reading of Scripture), customarily followed by these prayers, that really sustains the world. Thus, although we know the *kedushah desidra* existed in talmudic times, we cannot necessarily locate it in the context of rabbinic prayer or its requirements of minyan.

When we turn to the *kedushah deyotzer*, we find no definitive evidence that it was even an element of talmudic liturgy. Two sufficiently vague sources have sparked speculation. *Tosefta Berakhot* 1:9 reads:

ר' יהודה היה אומר עם המברך קק"ק וגו' וברוך וגו'. כל אילו היה קורא ר' יהודה עם המברך.

Rabbi Yehudah used to say "Holy, holy, holy..." and "Blessed"[13] with the

11. One midrashic text clearly describes an aspect of the recitation of the *kedushah* in the *amidah*, but it comes from a late enough composition that it is not helpful in this context. See the printed *Tanḥuma*, *Tzav* 13. Other midrashic passages combine the verses that form the core of the *kedushah*, but do not place them in a human liturgical context.

12. *Prayer in the Talmud: Forms and Patterns*, trans. Richard S. Sarason (Berlin, New York: Walter de Gruyter, 1977), 262, 266-267.

13. Isaiah 6:3, Ezekiel 3:12.

prayer leader. Rabbi Yehudah recited all of these (responses) with the prayer leader.

This source records the public recitation of some sort of *kedushah* in Palestine in the mid- to late second century, but does not specify when or how this occurred. Louis Ginzberg claimed that it must be the *kedushah deyotzer*, as the technical term מברך (prayer leader, one who blesses) indicates a setting in the blessings for the *shema*.[14] More recently, Ithamar Gruenwald has suggested that קורא (recite) in the summary sentence should also be understood as a technical term for the *shema* blessings.[15] This verb, though, may only refer here to the *kedushah* verses themselves and not their actual liturgical context. As Heinemann has indicated, these words were not always applied consistently to specific parts of the liturgy, and we may not be justified in reading the language of this period as true technical terminology. For instance, *Mishnah Rosh Hashanah* 4:9 uses the verb ברך (bless) in a context that clearly indicates the *amidah*.[16] Another problem is that our *Tosefta* text only mentions two verses, like our received *kedushah deyotzer* and unlike the other *kedushot*, which commonly include more. However, as Meir Bar-Ilan has demonstrated, the earliest forms of the *kedushah* show flexibility in their texts–in their number, order, and selection of verses. Several sources also include verses beginning with *barukh*, "blessed," that do not derive from Ezekiel, so again we must be cautious in our assumptions about the referent of the *Tosefta*.[17] It is impossible, then, to claim absolute identification of the referent of this *baraita*.

The second source presents similar problems, allowing us to glean even less. *P. Berakhot* 5:4, 9c records an incident in the mid-fourth century when one Betitai, who was leading the congregational prayers, went silent in the middle of the אופנייה (*ofanaya*), a term usually referring to the part of the *kedushah* describing the animated wheels of the heavenly chariot as seen by Ezekiel. Not knowing the proper procedures for continuing the service, the worshipers consulted Rabbi Abun, who responded that the one who takes Betitai's place before the ark (שעובר) should begin at the place where Betitai had stopped. When questioned further, because he was contradicting the principle that the substitute should begin from the beginning of the blessing in which the error occurred,

---

14. *Geonica*, I:129.

15. איתמר גרינולד, "שירת המלאכים, ה'קדושה' ובעיית חיבורה של ספרות ההיכלות," פרקים בתולדות ירושלים בימי בית שני, ספר זכרון לאברהם שליט, בעריכת אהרן אופנהיימר, אוריאל רפפורט, מנחם שטרן (ירושלים: יד יצחק בן צבי, תשמ"א), 478. See too, Lieberman, תוספתא כפשוטה, I:11, who assumes this reading.

16. *Prayer*..., 230-231.

17. מאיר בר־אילן, "קווי יסוד להתהוותה של הקדושה וגיבושה," דעת 25 (תש"ן): 5–20. He refers to, among other sources, I Enoch 39:14, 61:12; IV Enoch 39:1-2, 48B:2 (Charlesworth ed.).

Rabbi Abun answered that, because the congregation had already recited the *kedushah*, it should be considered as if they were at the beginning of a blessing. In other words, the sacrality of Isaiah 6:3, the core of the *kedushah*, is so great that it should not be repeated, even if the *sheliaḥ tzibbur* has erred before completing the entire blessing.

Once again, it is not entirely clear which *kedushah* was being recited in this congregation. The mention of the *ofanaya* leads some to claim that it must have been the *kedushah deyotzer*, for in known rites, it is the only one that explicitly refers to this particular group of heavenly creatures.[18] On the other hand, the technical term עובר refers only to the *sheliaḥ tzibbur*, who stands before the Torah ark to lead the repetition of the *amidah*. In addition, one might argue that the entire discussion in this source of whether or not the substitute leader needs to return to the beginning of the blessing applies primarily to the repetition of the *amidah*.[19] Only in this repetition of the *amidah* is the leader fully fulfilling the congregation's obligation to pray, and hence the rabbis stress the requirement that his prayer be correct. Our sources contain no similar discussion about the *shema* benedictions, probably because early precedents established that they could be omitted if absolutely necessary.[20] Most likely, the *ofanaya* referred to here was a recognized section of the Palestinian *kedushah* of the *amidah* of the time, perhaps even a standard poetic section, one that has not been preserved.[21]

---

18. See, for instance, the *P'nei Moshe* on this passage.

19. *B. Berakhot* 29a-30a, 34b; *P. Berakhot* 5:2-3, 9a-c; and *P. Taanit* 1:1, 63d, all establish the protocol an individual or the *sheliaḥ tzibbur* must follow to repeat the prayers properly after erring in the blessings of the *amidah*.

20. Indeed, *B. Berakhot* 13b cites the precedent of Rabbi Yehudah Hanasi, who fulfilled his obligation to recite *shema* by reciting just its first line so as not to interrupt his teaching. Later rabbinic authorities did not consider the blessings dispensable, but did recognize their lesser status, reflected in the mishnaic permission to interrupt this section of the liturgy but not the *amidah*. While we have multiple traditions preserved in talmudic sources about prayer leaders erring and being removed in the *amidah*, discussions of error in the blessings surrounding *shema* are never couched in the context of communal prayer.

21. Reuven Kimelman has asked the intriguing question (in a private conversation) whether *T. Megillah* 3(4):28 might also possibly contain a hint of some connection between *pores al shema* and angelic themes. Is the anonymous retort: הרבה דרשו במרכבה ולא ראו אותה מעולם (Many have expounded on the "chariot" who have never seen it) more than a simple response to Rabbi Yehudah's comment (compare *M. Megillah* 4:6): כל שלא ראה מאורות מימיו לא יפרוס על שמע (Anyone who has never seen the heavenly luminaries may not lead the public recitation of *shema*)? Is the emphasis of the *Mishnah* simply a question of whether one needs relevant experience to participate in ritual, or does the *Tosefta*'s answer imply some connection between mystical learning and one's ability to lead the *yotzer* benediction, with its references to the heavenly luminaries and its angelic liturgy? The apparent assumption of this *Tosefta* that the *yotzer* benediction, with its themes of light, is an integral part of *perisat shema*

No other passages in the talmudic corpus refer to liturgical recitation of the *kedushah.*[22] The only other pre-geonic rabbinic source to yield information about the synagogue's use of the prayer is the corpus of Palestinian liturgical poetry (*piyyut*) preserved in the Cairo genizah.[23] As Ezra Fleischer has demonstrated,[24] the early payyetanic compositions closely followed the structure of the liturgy. When the *kedushah* was not to be recited in a particular service, there was no reference to it in the preserved *piyyut*; conversely, beginning perhaps as early as the late amoraic period, when the *kedushah* was to be recited, it became a focal point of the *piyyut.* This literature establishes that, in the Palestinian rite, the *kedushah*, whether in the *amidah* or the *yotzer*, was never recited on weekdays, but only on Sabbaths and festivals, and in the case of the *amidah*, also on Rosh Ḥodesh, Ḥol Hamoed, Hoshanah Rabba, and Ḥanukah. In addition, in the case of the *kedushah deyotzer*, the genizah evidence suggests that its recitation was not universal, even on Sabbaths and holidays, and that it was never recited privately by individuals.[25] However, there do exist early examples of *piyyut* for the morning *shema* benedictions that clearly include *ofanim*, i.e., the angelic liturgy of the *kedushah deyotzer.* The style of the earliest of these poems is similar to that of Yose ben Yose, dating them tentatively to the end of the amoraic period. That these older texts were preserved at all is evidence for the persistence of this custom among at least some Jews of the Palestinian rite.[26] Fleischer claims, therefore, contrary to earlier scholarly conception, that when Pirkoi ben Baboi fulminated against the Palestinian customs regarding the recitation of the *kedu-*

---

is itself important. Note too that this is likely the same Rabbi Yehudah who recited the *kedushah* in the passage cited above.

22. *B. Ḥullin* 91b describes the angelic liturgy, but makes no reference to a human counterpart. This is particularly curious, because the passage does compare human and angelic praise of God, asserting the superiority of Israel. Compare also *Pirkei d'Rabbi Eliezer*, chap. 4, end.

23. As we shall see shortly, mystic texts from this period are an important source of information about the *kedushah*, but they do not teach us about regular public recitation of this liturgy.

24. "לתפוצתן של קדושות העמידה והיוצר במנהגות התפילה של בני ארץ ישראל," תרביץ 38 (תשכ"ט), 284–255.

25. The omission of the *kedushah deyotzer* from the pure prayer texts of the Palestinian rite found in the genizah has confused many scholars and led them to claim that the Palestinian rite did not include it at all. However, Fleischer, "לתפוצתן...", 257, n. 8, points out that some of these texts were weekday liturgies that never included the *kedushah* in Palestine; we might add that others may have been the texts that individuals were to recite outside of the communal context. The replacement of the standard prayer texts by *piyyut* on days when the *kedushah deyotzer* was recited may also account for the omission of this *kedushah* from the preserved statutory prayer texts.

26. Fleischer, "לתפוצתן...", 266-272, 276, 282.

*shah*,[27] he was not attempting to introduce the *kedushah* into the rite of the Palestinians–whose traditions confined recitation to days of greater sanctity, when more people would have come to the synagogue to pray. The Babylonians sought to impose only its daily recitation.[28]

Given this additional material, we can establish without serious doubt that the *kedushah* was recited, at least in some circles, in the *yotzer* and in the *amidah* by at least the later years of the amoraic period. The genizah evidence also suggests that at least the Palestinian Jews considered this liturgy sacred, elevated, and inappropriate for recitation by the individual. This being the case, the reticence of the rabbinic texts is surprising. Two explanations are possible: either there were no major issues surrounding the *kedushah* and no reason to discuss its timing, setting, placement in the service, or requirements of posture, *kavvanah*, or community;[29] or, as angelic liturgy, it was understood to belong to the domain of esoteric mysticism, which the rabbis preferred to keep totally separate, if possible, from the traditions of exoteric learning.[30] The second explanation is more consistent with our understanding of general rabbinic tendencies. Indeed, although the understanding of Jewish mystical prayer is still in its infancy, the assertion that the origins of the *kedushah* lies in mystic circles is well accepted by modern scholars.

Late Second Temple period apocalyptic traditions, texts from Qumran, as well as the surviving *heikhalot* mystic traditions themselves evidence a preoccupation with angelic liturgies and with the participation of human beings in these praises of God. An integral part of many of these liturgies is, of course, the words heard by Isaiah and Ezekiel in their theophanies, the verses that became the standard responses of the synagogue's *kedushah*.[31] Such a preoccupation is particularly

---

27. *Ginzei Schechter*, II: 555-556.

28. Fleischer, "לתפוצתן...", 255-257. Note, though, that Fleischer has also published a text for Shabbat that does not contain a *kedushah*. See his היוצרות בהתהוותם והתפתחותם (ירושלים: מאגנס, תשמ"ד), 355–353.

29. This is indeed the argument of Eric Werner, "The Doxology in Synagogue and Church, A Liturgico-Musical Study," *HUCA* 19 (1945-46): 298.

30. *Mishnah Ḥagigah* 2:1 restricts the settings in which mystic lore may be discussed, and the various comments on this Mishnah make clear that this knowledge was considered esoteric; the power and danger involved in the mystic experience and gnosis for the unqualified person made it essential that it be kept separate from the general traditions of halakhic learning. Therefore, all discussions that touch on mystic traditions in the talmudic corpus are truncated and allusive. See, for instance, on this subject, Ithamar Gruenwald, *Apocalyptic and Merkavah Mysticism* (Leiden/Köln: E.J. Brill, 1980), chap. 3, "The Attitude Towards the Merkavah Speculation in the Literature of the Tannaim and Amoraim."

31. For a summary of the various *kedushah* traditions, see: מאיר בר אילן, "קווי יסוד...", 20–5.

marked in *Heikhalot Rabbati*, which in certain sections uses the *trisagion* as a constant refrain, almost as a marker for the conclusion of the section, not dissimilar to the synagogue's eventual use of the kaddish.[32] However, the dating of the various literary traditions of the *yordei merkavah* is a matter of considerable dispute; consequently, we can only tentatively treat them as evidence for the liturgical usage of the *kedushah* during late antiquity.[33]

The biblical verses that constitute the core of the *kedushah* were early considered the central components of the angels' daily praise of God, and this angelic liturgy played a key role in the religious experience of the apocalyptics and mystics; but the forms of the *kedushah* that became standard in the synagogue liturgy never appear in the *heikhalot* literature.[34] Modern scholars can only speculate as to how this religious experience functioned and how it entered the public synagogue.

Indeed, the complexities involved in deriving historical data from texts compiled and recompiled over as much as a millennium preclude consensus about such critical issues as the degree of early rabbinic involvement in mystical speculation, the interface between this speculation and the populace at large, and even the nature and purpose of the mystic gnosis and experience. The synagogue service did eventually fully integrate, however, not only the *kedushah* in multiple forms, but also several other prayers identifiably originating in the world of *heikhalot* mysticism.[35] Although any briefly developed model exploring this phenomenon would necessarily be overly simplistic,[36] several crucial points may be made.

---

For a more detailed discussion of angelic liturgies at Qumran, see Carol Newsom, *Songs of the Sabbath Sacrifice: A Critical Edition* (Atlanta: Scholars Press, 1985), 20-21, 59-72; and Bilhah Nitzan, *Qumran Prayer and Religious Poetry*, trans. Jonathan Chipman (Leiden: EJ Brill, 1994), especially chap. 8, "Mystical Poetry" and the appendix, "The Qedusa (Trishagion)." See also Gruenwald, *Apocalyptic...*, 39-41.

32. See, for instance, Peter Schäfer, *Synopse zur Hekhalot Literatur* (Tübingen: J.C.B. Mohr (Paul Siebeck), 1981), §94-106. On p. XI, he designates this group as the *kedushah* songs.

33. It is now generally agreed that the phenomenon of ascent/descent to view the divine chariot was probably an active form of mystic experience by the second century C.E. However, many of the texts have reached us in much later recensions, and we have to assume that the liturgical passages included are among those most likely to have been "updated" by copyists. On the problems of dating these texts, see Peter Schäfer, *The Hidden and Manifest God: Some Major Themes in Early Jewish Mysticism*, trans. Aubrey Pomerance (Albany: State University of New York Press, 1992), 5-8, and the literature he lists there.

34. איתמר גרינולד, "פיוטי יניי וספרות יורדי מרכבה," תרביץ לו (תשכ"ז), 272.

35. See Meir Bar-Ilan's discussion of many of these in his: סתרי תפילה והיכלות (רמת גן: אוניברסיטת בר־אילן, תשמ"ז).

36. See, as an example, Philip Alexander's "Prayer in the Heikhalot Literature," in *Prière,*

Like rabbinic prayer, these mystical traditions responded to the fundamental crisis of post-Temple Judaism: how to gain access to God. God's place, *hamakom*, "God-the-Place," has now fully removed to the heavenly realms. The search for nearness to God and, even more, the search for access to divinely derived power and information permeates this literature. Effective use of language, prayer and adjuration is a significant tool in achieving all of these. And whatever the dynamics between these mystics, the rabbis, and the synagogue, it is evident that some of the mystic prayers were known, not considered esoteric, and deemed appropriate for public use. One need not be a mystic to want to join in the angelic liturgy and to demonstrate how, in the absence of the Temple, God's "Place" is still accessible to human praise.[37]

A glimmer of this dynamic may lie behind the difficult passage from the *Tosefta Berakhot* 1:9 discussed above.[38] Gruenwald posits that if this Rabbi Yehudah who answered the *kedushah* with the prayer leader was the same Rabbi Yehudah of *Mishnah Megillah* 4:10–who allowed a prophetic reading from the visions of Ezekiel–he was probably sympathetic to the introduction of mystical studies into the communal prayer setting.[39] Here we may have an example of a mystic and rabbi who participated in the angelic liturgy in a non-mystical public liturgical context and actively encouraged discussion of mystical topics among the non-initiates–in seeming contradiction to the esotericism of these traditions, so strongly suggested by their obvious exclusion from the "mainstream" of rabbinic literature. However, such exclusion is curiously not supported by the mystical texts themselves. Gruenwald and Halperin, using different considerations and different methodologies, both point out that substantial strata of these texts actively encourage the mystics to reveal at least certain elements of their visions to all of Israel.[40] I would suggest that there was a tension in the Jewish

---

*mystique et judaïsme*, Roland Goetschel, ed. (Presses Universitaires de France, 1987), 43-64. While intriguing in its possibilities, Alexander's reconstruction is based on a single ascent narrative in *Heikhalot Rabbati* and fails to take into account the many other models in the literature.

37. See David J. Halperin, *Faces of the Chariot: Early Jewish Responses to Ezekiel's Vision* (Tübingen: JCB Mohr [Paul Siebeck], 1988), especially chap. 9.

38. See p. 193f.

39. "שירת המלאכים...", 478.

40. Gruenwald, *Apocalyptic*..., 156-157, generalizes from the situation in *Heikhalot Rabbati* to all of the *merkavah* literature, contrasting this to the apocalyptic strict emphasis on secrecy. See, too, in this context, his article, "פיוטי יניי וספרות יורדי המרכבה," תרביץ לו (תשכ"ז), 257–277, which demonstrates this sixth-century *payyetan*'s knowledge of *heikhalot* traditions and his willingness to embed them in his public poetry. Halperin, *Faces*..., 288, 316, 372, 374f., 386, 439f., understands the entire phenomenon of chariot mysticism to have deep roots in synagogue ritual and to have a strong popular emphasis.

world between those who suppressed discussion of mystic concerns in the exoteric talmudic traditions–non-mystics wanting to limit the spread of mysticism or mystics concerned by the dangers of its abuse–and mystics wanting to include others in their gnosis. As we shall see, a similar tension shaped the tradition of liturgical recitation of the *kedushah* in the medieval world.

For much of the last century, scholars have debated the question: Which of the liturgical forms of the *kedushah* developed first? Greater understanding of the role of mysticism in Jewish life in the rabbinic world–plus the movement away from the philologically based assumption that the *kedushah* evolved from only one source–make this question obsolete. As Meir Bar-Ilan has demonstrated, participation in or active awareness of the angelic liturgy was a powerful and compelling experience, one that developed concurrently among many different strands of Judaism during the late Second Temple period. Increasingly, the combinations of biblical verses that rabbinic Judaism came to see as the core of the *kedushah* crystallized into recognizable units. Different groups eventually incorporated these independent *kedushah* rituals into different aspects of the synagogue liturgy, resulting in, among other things, different traditions of the occasions on which to recite a particular *kedushah.* And rather than discarding *kedushah* texts when the parts of the liturgy coalesced into a single service, the rabbis retained them all, on the model of our principle of liturgical law that variant customs can be combined to create a universal norm.[41] In addition, different rites maintained different forms of the *kedushah* within the now universal stations for it. Hence, it is historically fallacious to claim priority of one form of the synagogue *kedushah* over another.[42]

The picture developed so far, then, is of a basic uniformity of halakhic status for all three accepted forms of the *kedushah* in the synagogue liturgy. All developed ultimately from the preoccupation of the early rabbinic mystics and their predecessors with human participation in the angelic liturgy. Because of mystic concerns about the power or knowledge embedded in these prayers, all seemingly required a communal setting for their recitation; all were tolerated but largely ignored by the official establishments of rabbinic law. A major limitation of this reconstruction, though, is that it lacks a date. Does it represent the reality in the third century, when we find our first reference to the *kedushah* as a *davar shebikedushah,* or does it apply only to an undefined earlier period? The evidence from the payyetanic corpus suggests that, at least by the late amoraic period, the Palestinian rite differentiated between the *kedushot* of the *amidah* and the

41. See chap. 1, Principle C.7.
42. מאיר בר־אילן, "קווי יסוד...", 17–19.

*yotzer*, at least in their frequency of recitation. But this may have been more a product of their independent development (as is the Babylonian daily recitation of both *kedushot*) than a reflection of any real differentiation in their halakhic statuses.

What *kedushah* traditions, then, did medieval Jews inherit? Almost certainly, it was known and widely recited in the three basic forms in which we know it today. The halakhic parameters for its recitation, however, were vague. Its association with heavenly realms and traditions of mystical schools lent its recitation an extra aura of sanctity. The medieval halakhic mind, struggling with the implications of that aura, had to decide exactly how to integrate these mystically based prayers into the rabbinic liturgical system. It is to that process that we now turn.

### *Geonic Views of the Issue*

Geonic rulings uniformly and consistently attempted to restrict recitation of the angelic liturgy to the ritually constrained and less ecstatic public setting of the minyan. Rabbinic tradition teaches that God's indwelling presence, the *Shekhinah*, can be found in the presence of ten Jews praying together.[43] Therefore, recitation of the *kedushah*, the direct liturgical reaction to God's presence, is appropriate only in a communal context. Continuing rabbinic pronouncements, however, demonstrate not only that private recitation continued to be an issue, but that earlier rulings did little to change the actual and otherwise undocumented customs of the local synagogues.

#### Masekhet Soferim

One of the most important sources for the history of the *kedushah*, the first to differentiate halakhically between its various settings, is the statement found in *Masekhet Soferim*:[44]

> וקטן שאינו פורס את שמע אינו יכול לומר קדוש ביוצר ביחיד, אבל בציבור עונה עמהם. וגדול שהוא פורס את שמע, יכול לומר קדוש, לפי שהוא כסודר, אבל קדוש של עמידה, כיון שצריך לומר נעריצך ונקדישך, אינו מן הדין לומרו פחות מעשרה.
>
> A minor, who is not qualified to lead the public recitation of *shema*, may not recite the *kedushah* in the *yotzer* when he is alone, but in a congregation, he may respond with the others. An adult, who is qualified to lead the

43. *B. Berakhot* 6a.
44. 16:9, ed. Higger.

> public recitation of *shema*, may recite the *kedushah* (as an individual) because he is like one reciting verses; but it is not proper for him to recite the *kedushah* of the *amidah* with less than a minyan, because he needs to say "Let us extol and sanctify You."

The community whose rite this text represents[45] knew the *kedushah* as firmly established in two settings, both with some understood tie to mystic origins. In the *amidah*, its recitation was absolutely forbidden without a minyan, a prohibition derived here from the introductory words of the liturgy itself: "Let *us* extol and sanctify..." Behind this interpretation, though, must have been a sense that human participation in the angelic liturgy was inappropriate or impossible outside the communal setting. The Talmud, after all, establishes that individuals must always consider themselves part of a community and pray in the plural.[46]

In contrast, this text proscribes individual recitation of the *kedushah deyotzer* (which merely describes the angelic liturgy and does not suggest human participation in it) only for the minor outside of the communal setting. Does an attempt to shield the uninitiated or unqualified from mystic praxis lie behind this distinction? The child is, of course, not qualified to lead the public recitation of the *shema* because he is not yet obligated to pray and thus may not fulfill the obligations of others in this or any other public prayer. In this case, the text suggests that the minor also lacks the discernment to recite and even more so to lead the *kedushah deyotzer* with proper intent. Unprepared and unqualified to deal with the sanctity involved in the angelic liturgy, he may not even voice the verses, except as an adjunct to the adult community.[47] An individual adult, on the other hand, could be trusted to understand that, apart from the minyan, his *kedushah deyotzer* must merely be a descriptive recitation of the biblical verses recording the angels' prayers. Unlike the child, an adult could be trusted to meet

---

45. The precise dating and provenance of *Masekhet Soferim* are unclear, with serious suggestions ranging from the sixth to the twelfth centuries and from Babylonia to Italy. See Higger's introduction; Harry Freedman, "Soferim," *Encyclopedia Judaica*, XV:81; M.B. Lerner, "The External Tractates," in *The Literature of the Sages*, part I, ed. Shmuel Safrai (Van Gorcum, Assen/Maastricht; Philadelphia: Fortress Press, 1987), 397-400; and Debra Reed Blank's dissertation (Jewish Theological Seminary, 1998). There is no reason to believe that this passage necessarily represents the Palestinian rather than the Babylonian practice. In fact, its assumption that the introductory line of the *kedushah* of the *amidah* is fixed and meaningful would argue against Palestinian roots. Palestinian *piyyut* routinely replaces this introduction.

46. *B. Berakhot* 29b-30a. See chap. 1, Principle A.2.

47. A ruling requiring children to refrain from participating as congregants in the adult liturgy would be impractical and pedagogically difficult.

the prerequisites of purity and knowledge that would shield him from danger if he were to use the angelic liturgy as a platform for more extensive speculation about the heavenly realms. Thus we learn from *Masekhet Soferim* not only that these two *kedushot* were established parts of the liturgy of an early medieval community, but, more importantly, that there was also a halakhic distinction made between them, based both on their wordings and on a perceived difference in their mystical impacts.

Before *Masekhet Soferim*, except for the interpretation of Rav Huna's statement in *B. Berakhot* 21b, we have no indication that individuals ever sought to recite the liturgical *kedushah* outside of a communal context.[48] (Indeed, our only unequivocal evidence for the existence of the *kedushah deyotzer* comes from the *piyyut* written for the public recitation of the *shema* blessings.) Because the *kedushah* never appeared in the obligatory private *amidah*, only in its public repetition, the prohibition against the individual's active participation in the angelic liturgy in the *amidah* was easily accepted. Worshipers would also naturally shy away from involvement in this numinous experience in an unauthorized setting. But as the *kedushah deyotzer* and the *kedushah desidra* came to be worded, they did not technically signify any human participation in the acts of sanctification of God; they merely included a description of the angelic liturgies–similar to one an individual might encounter elsewhere during a reading of the appropriate biblical passages or even through study of certain rabbinic traditions. In addition, in both of these settings, the participants in the minyan always recited the same prayer as the *sheliaḥ tzibbur*; the *yotzer* was among the mandatory prayers for every individual. Thus it was difficult to convince the masses to omit this *kedushah* when they prayed without a minyan, especially in communities such as those in Babylonia, which recited it daily.[49] The evidence of *Masekhet Soferim*, then, suggests that individuals did recite the *kedushah deyotzer* when praying alone, and that the rabbinic authority represented in this text only tried to limit this minhag for those least able to distinguish between a description of and actual participation in the angelic liturgy.

48. One might indeed question whether the reiteration of the *kedushah* verses in the *Heikhalot* literature reflects just such a custom.

49. It must have been even more difficult to teach only children to recite a different text! One might justifiably wonder about the practicality of establishing a different requirement for children. As we shall see, very few of the Rishonim who cite *Masekhet Soferim* include this element.

### *The Babylonian Geonic Precedents*

We have no evidence that a single geonic authority ever fully approved of the recitation of the *kedushah deyotzer* and *kedushah desidra* without a minyan, but the existence of multiple geonic rulings against such practices teaches us that at least some communities must have allowed it. This strict geonic attitude is consistent with our sense that all forms of the *kedushah* originated in mystic circles and carried with them, when they entered the public synagogue liturgy, assumptions of their elevated, sacred, and necessarily communal nature. Because the various *kedushot* have, by this period, acquired well defined and separate identities, we will deal here with them individually.

Only two sources rule directly against private recitation of the *kedushah deyotzer*, one attributed to the late ninth-century Rav Naḥshon Gaon, and the other to the early tenth-century gaon, Saadia. The responsum attributed to Naḥshon is a gloss preserved in the Vatican manuscript of *Halakhot Gedolot* in its logical position, and at the end of *Hilkhot Tzitzit* in Hildesheimer's primary text.[50] The Vatican manuscript's version is the earliest extant source explicitly to apply the mishnaic requirement of a minyan for *perisat shema* to a prohibition of the individual's recitation of the *kedushah* in the *yotzer* blessing.[51] In this responsum, Naḥshon is asked how one should pray the morning service when

50. ed. Azriel Hildesheimer, I:470-471, n. to line 41; and 507, where he notes that it is missing in Ms. Vatican 142. Clearly, the scribe of that manuscript moved it to its logical location. The two versions are not identical.

51. This connection is ambiguous in *Masekhet Soferim*, above, where it is possible to read the text as simply applying the qualifications of one ritual to the other. There is no doubt among scholars today that the original meaning of the tannaitic technical term *pores al/et shema* had been totally forgotten even by the Amoraim and certainly by all later generations. The term referred originally to a communal responsive recitation of the biblical verses of the *shema* itself. See Reuven Kimelman, "The Shema' and its Rhetoric: The Case for the Shema' Being More than Creation, Revelation, and Redemption," *Journal of Jewish Thought and Philosophy* 2 (1992), Appendix I: 154-155, and the sources he cites there. The Amoraim no longer knew this ritual and never required a minyan for any form of recitation of *shema* itself. However, with the development of the liturgy, prayers came to surround *shema* that did require a minyan, such as kaddish, *barekhu*, and, according to some, the *kedushah deyotzer*. Later authorities understood this liturgical complex to be the referent of the Mishnah, either as it appears during the regular morning service (in which case this term refers to the act of being the *sheliaḥ tzibbur* for all of the *shema* and its blessings), or in a special repetition of these prayers–especially *barekhu* and less frequently the *kedushah*–for the sake of those who came late. Such an arrangement is found today in Sefardi rites at the end of the service. (See Rashi and Tosafot to *B. Megillah* 23b for examples of the latter understanding.) See: עזרא פליישר, "לליבון ענין ה'פורס על שמע'," תרביץ 41 (תשל"ב), 133–144.

alone. The preserved fragment addresses only the *yotzer* benediction; it provides a text of the benediction that omits the *kedushah* and ends, saying:

> **ולמה ידלג קדושה וברוך שאי אפשר ליחיד לומ' קדושה[52] וברוך והיינו דתנן אין פורסין על שמע פחות מעשרה.**
>
> Why should he skip *kedushah* (Isaiah 6:3) and *barukh* (Ezekiel 3:12)? Because an individual may not recite *kedushah*[52] and *barukh*, for it is taught in the Mishnah: one does not *pores al shema* with less than ten [men present].

Naḥshon operates on the assumption that the mishnaically defined public ritual, *pores al shema*, includes the *kedushah deyotzer.* He does not provide any further reasoning, but the editorial introduction to the reponsum hints at mystical concerns, labeling the verses of the angelic liturgy *ma'aseh merkavah*, the rabbinic term for the restricted mystical lore about the divine chariot of Ezekiel's vision. Unfortunately, because this introduction seems to be a gloss on a gloss, we know nothing of the provenance of these explicit mystical concerns.

The responsum attributed by some to Saadia Gaon[53] is very similar to Naḥshon's, with one major addition. Saadia also forbids the individual to *pores al shema*, which involves saying the *kedushah*, but explains that it is forbidden to say a *davar shebikedushah* with less than a minyan. Although that concept is implied in Naḥshon's reference to *Mishnah Megillah* 4:3, Saadia's responsum is the earliest preserved source specifically to include the *kedushah deyotzer* in the Talmud's category of elite rituals.

Both of these responsa, in addition to their halakhic pronouncements, also dictate substitute texts for the individual to recite when omitting the *kedushah deyotzer.* These liturgical alternatives, indeed, are the content of most preserved geonic comments on this matter at all.(See Appendix, p. 255f.) Most striking about this group of responsa, aside from the uniform assumption that the individual should not recite the *kedushah deyotzer* privately, is the wide variation in substitute texts they suggest. The most radical omit completely everything from the slightest introductory reference to the angelic liturgy to most of the paragraph following it. At the other extreme are those that omit just the scriptural verses and any transitional text between them. Faulty transmission of the texts and confusion in attribution make it virtually impossible to establish which

---

52. The gloss at the end of *Hilkhot Tzitzit* ends here in Hildesheimer's text.

53. The comment attributed to Saadia Gaon appears only in the British Museum manuscript of the *Seder Rav Amram Gaon* (ed. Goldschmidt, 13), where, once again, it cannot be original. Goldschmidt also cites a similar ruling, which appears in Chaim M. Horowitz, תורתן של ראשונים, I:52, #21, there attributed only to the *Seder Rav Amram.* Goldschmidt questions the attribution to Saadia and suggests a number of alternatives. However, the position taken in the responsum is consistent with the liturgy of Saadia's *Siddur.*

Gaon proposed what text.[54] While some of this variation–especially when two versions are attributed to the same Gaon–may reflect traditions of later communities introduced by copyists, the lack of any unified approach and the multiplicity of responses on this issue indicate that the rabbinic leaders were not successful in defining and and implementing a halakhic alternative acceptable to their communities. In this case, popular minhag, especially on an issue with no public ramifications, resisted any change.[55]

In contrast, turning to the *kedushah desidra*, we find that a preserved responsum on this issue did indeed have vast impact. Rav Tzemaḥ Gaon of Pumbedita, when asked if the individual could recite this *kedushah*, responded:

> אם תלמיד חכם הוא יעסוק בשמעתא דגיד הנשה כגון ג׳ כתות של מאלכי השרת אומרי׳ שירה בכל יום, שיש בה דברי שבח קדושת הקב״ה, אם אינו תלמיד חכם יעסוק במקרא בפסוקים שיש בהם קדושה, כגון שרפים עומדים ממעל לו, ומה טעמו של חכם שאומר ומודה כך, כלומר תפלה זו וסדר זה נביאים הראשונים תקנוה וזקנים הקדמונים תקנוה לומרה בקהל, ויחיד לא יסיג גבול הקהל לפי שכל דבר שבקדושה אינו בפחות מעשרה, הילכך יאמר מקרא או תלמוד שפירשנו ונמצא אומר אותה ממילא. ויש חכמים שאומרים, כיון שהן מקראות אומרם, ומה בכך. הלכך נהגו יחיד האומר קדושא דסידרא קורא הפסוקין בטעמן כדרך התינוקות שקורין לפני רבן.
>
> If he is a scholar, he should study a talmudic discussion from *Ḥullin*, Chapter 7, like "Three groups of ministering angels recite the song daily,"[56] which includes praise of the sanctity of the Holy One, blessed be He. If he is not a scholar, he should study scriptural verses that include elements of sanctification, like "Seraphs stood in attendance on Him..."[57] What is the reason that the sage should agree with this? This is to say that the first Prophets established this prayer and this order of sanctification, and early elders established that it should be recited in a community; and the indi-

54. A. Buechler, "La Kedouscha du «Yocêr» chez les Gueonim," *REJ* 53 (1907): 220-230, tried valiantly to sort out the conflicting evidence of the preserved geonic responsa and to understand the history of the halakhic rulings for and against the recitation of the *kedushah deyotzer* by the individual. Like his contemporaries, he assumed all geonic differences of opinion to reflect differences between Palestinian and Babylonian traditions and, within Babylonia, between the Suran and Pumbeditan academies. We now know that these rites themselves were not so precisely delineated, and that many more regionalized customs existed. Buechler failed to take into account the influence of mysticism, both during the geonic period and later, and the ongoing impact of popular minhag. Thus, his analysis is seriously flawed.

55. An anonymous responsum is the only geonic source to accept this popular minhag. It apparently assumes that the individual may recite the *kedushah deyotzer*. See pp. 207-208.

56. 91b.

57. Isaiah 6:2f.

> vidual should not encroach upon the rights of the community, because no *davar shebikedushah* may be recited with less than ten [men present]. Therefore, he should recite the biblical verses or talmudic passage that we have laid out, and you will find that he has recited the *kedushah* anyhow. There are sages who say that because these are verses, he should just say them, and what is the issue? Therefore, it is customary that the individual who recites the *kedushah desidra* recites the verses with their melody like children who recite them for their teacher.[58]

Tzemaḥ begins from an ideological stance that the *kedushah desidra* is indeed a *davar shebikedushah* and that the individual must consequently find some alternative mode of recitation. In contrast to all of the geonic rulings about the *kedushah deyotzer*, though, he does not call for the elimination of the sensitive verses. Instead, recognizing their centrality, he suggests the recitation of alternative, non-liturgical texts that contain these words. Apparently, however, these texts would replace the entire *kedushah desidra*, a move possible only for a prayer lying outside the statutory liturgy. It would be impossible to apply such a method to the *kedushah deyotzer* and eliminate the mandatory *yotzer* benediction; even interrupting that prayer with non-liturgical texts would be problematic. But Tzemaḥ, having accepted the notion of substitution, found it possible to justify the existing popular custom that allowed this non-liturgical recitation of just the *kedushah* verses to occur within the context of the intact prayer. This apparent compromise with popular minhag becomes very important.

Two other preserved geonic sources continue this discussion. The *Siddur Rav Saadia Gaon*[59] reflects Tzemaḥ Gaon's theoretical stance, although not his practical compromise, for the *kedushah desidra* appears only in the section on communal prayer and not at all among the prayers for the individual. The other source, in an anonymous responsum, reacts to Tzemaḥ's compromise.

> וששאלתם, קידושא דסידרא יש ליחיד לאומרה או לא? כך ראינו שאעפ"י שפסוקין הן [ואינו] דומה לקדושה דקרית שמע ולא לקדושה דתפילה, כיון שקבעוהו בתפילה מדמי לה לקדושה של תפלה ואין לו רשות ליחיד לאמרו. אבל לאחר שגמר תפילתו ובודל מן התפילה, אם רצה לומר כקורא בנביאים הרשות בידו.
>
> You asked: May the individual recite the *kedushah desidra* or not? It seems

58. Cited in the *Seder Rav Amram Gaon*, ed. Goldschmidt, 41; *Otzar Hageonim*, *Berakhot*, *Teshuvot*, p. 53, #136, and by numerous Rishonim, some of whom Goldschmidt notes. Compare also the brief citation of Amram and R. Natan in ספר ארחות חיים, דין התחנות והמזמורים שאומרים אחר י"ח, סי' ד, דף כא עמ' ג–ד.

59. 39-40.

> appropriate to us, that even though these are verses, and they are [not] comparable to the *kedushah* of *keriat shema* and not to the *kedushah* of the *amidah*, once they established it in the liturgy, it became comparable to the *kedushah* of the *amidah*, and the individual does not have the right to recite it. But, once one has completed one's prayer and ceased to be engaged in worship, if one wishes to say [the verses] like one who is reading from Scripture, one may.[60]

While continuing to refine the ideological stance that the *kedushah desidra* is to be treated like the *kedushah* of the *amidah*, this responsum also accepts Tzemaḥ's compromise and attempts to strengthen the difficult-to-enforce distinction between recitation as liturgy and as biblical text.

Although the evidence is not sufficient to make an absolute assertion, there are reasons to believe the geonic insistence that all forms of the *kedushah* required a minyan was a product of their perception that even descriptions of the angelic liturgy had mystic import. We know that *merkavah*-style mysticism was practiced until the end of the geonic period,[61] and evidence points directly to the participation of the last influential Bablylonian Geonim, Sherira Gaon and his son, Hai Gaon, in mystic knowledge.[62] The editor of the *Halakhot Gedolot* manuscript viewed the *kedushah deyotzer* as *ma'aseh merkavah*, mystic lore, and explicitly prohibited its private recitation. However, Rav Tzemaḥ Gaon and reluctantly after him, the anonymous Gaon, found a way to justify the existing popular minhag of reciting the *kedushah desidra* privately. *Masekhet Soferim* made a similar compromise for the *kedushah deyotzer*. In both cases, halakhic theory did not change. Rather, the prayer changed status, and as a mere recitation of

60. תשובות הגאונים החדשות ועמן תשובות, פסקים ופירושים מאת חכמי פרובאנס הראשונים, מהדורת שמחה עמנואל (ירושלים: מכון אופק, ספריית פרידברג, תשנ"ה), סי' קלב, עמ' 178; תשובות הגאונים עם תשובות ופסקים מחכמי פרובינציה, מהדורת אלעזר הורביץ (ניו־יורק, תשנ"ה), חלק ב, סימן מה, עמ' 168; אוצר הגאונים, ברכות, תשובות סי' קלה, עמ' 53, מגילה, סי' קנא, עמ' 41. Hurwitz's edition omits the word אינו (not), creating a distinction between the *kedushot* of the *yotzer* and the *amidah*, which is characteristic of *Masekhet Soferim* but not of geonic thought. Emanuel may have added it based on comparison to the shortened version cited in *Otzar Hageonim*, which does not mention the *kedushah deyotzer* at all.

61. Joseph Dan, "The Religious Experience of the *Merkavah*," in *Jewish Spirituality from the Bible through the Middle Ages*, ed. Arthur Green (New York: Crossroad, 1989), 289.

62. *Otzar Hageonim*, *Ḥagigah*, pp. 11-12, #16; p. 14, #20. In the first responsum, these Geonim refuse to answer fully and openly the question posed to them by correspondents from Fez about the nature of the *gemara*'s restrictions on teaching mystic lore. Their language justifies an assumption that these Geonim knew what they were refusing to discuss. The second responsum contains one of the few extant descriptions of how these mystics would induce their experiences of ascent/descent. Both responsa suggest active mystic practice and gnosis in the geonic courts.

scriptural verses that just happened to describe the angelic liturgy, it no longer signified powerful active human participation in the awesome heavenly praise.

## *The Private* Kedushah *Among the Rishonim:* *The* Kedushah Desidra

In the Europe of the Rishonim, Tzemaḥ Gaon's compromise stance on the *kedushah desidra* not only established a nearly unanimous precedent for individual recitation of the *kedushah desidra*,[63] but influenced some to accept private recitation of the *kedushah deyotzer* as well. Among the Ashkenazim, from the texts of the Rashi school on, we find citations of, or allusions to, this responsum.[64] Many of the twelfth-century Provençal[65] and leading thirteenth- and fourteenth-century Spanish scholars[66] similarly used it as a precedent. All ruled that the individual may recite the *kedushah desidra* without a minyan; many stated explicitly that because these are only scriptural verses, there can be no real concern. Others emphasized that one must say them in the mode of a schoolhouse recitation, with proper melody, trope, and vocalization, specifically differentiating a private recitation from a communal liturgical

63. There is some evidence of opposition to this position. *Orḥot Ḥayyim*, *Din Kedushah Demeyushav* 1, p. 24, cites Rabbenu Yonah as reporting that those who opposed the individual's recitation of the *kedushah deyotzer* believed that the individual should skip the verses in the *kedushah desidra* as well. This line does not appear in the version of his comment printed with the Rif, *Berakhot*, 13b-14a.

64. See, for example *Siddur Rashi*, 36, #61 (this may be the referent of the *Beit Yosef* OH 59, to *Pardes*, where this citation does not appear); *Maḥzor Vitry*, 25-26, #46; תשובות ופסקים לר״י הזקן, רטז, סי׳ פד; סידור רבנו שלמה ב״ר שמשון מגרמייזא, עמ׳ קכב; ספר האגור השלם לרבנו יעקב ברוך בן מהר״ר יהודה לנדא, מב, סי׳ קעח.

65. אברהם ב״ר יצחק מנרבונא, ספר האשכול, מהדורת צבי בנימין אויערבך, כרך א, עמ׳ 33, סי׳ טו. This passage does not appear in Shalom Albeck's edition of the text, which is understood to be more authentic. (Saul Aaron Adler, "Abraham ben Isaac of Narbonne," *Encyclopedia Judaica*, II:147.) The Rashba cites the Ravad as allowing the verses to be recited in his manner. (*Shut Harashba* V:9.) Note, though, that a direct tradition of the Ravad does not make this allowance. (See: רבנו אברהם בן דוד תשובות ופסקים, מהדורת יוסף קאפח, רלב, סי׳ קצג.) See also *Manhig*, ed. Raphael, I:106. ארחות חיים, דין התחנות והמזמורים שאומרים אחר י״ח, סי׳ ד, ascribes this view to R. Natan, as confirmed by R. Amram; there can be little doubt that this is the same tradition, as found in a version of the *Seder Rav Amram Gaon*.

66. Although these rabbis, for the most part, do not refer explicitly to the responsum of Rav Tzemaḥ, they consistently permit the individual to recite the *kedushah desidra* as scriptural verses, chanted as they are in the biblical text. See: ספר שאלות ותשובות רבנו יוסף הלוי אבן מיגאש, קכה–קכו, סי׳ קלא; רבינו יונה על הרי״ף, ברכות יג.–:; שו״ת הרשב״א ה:ט; חידושי הריטב״א, ברכות, עמ׳ קכט; חידושי הריטב״א, מגילה, קעג; תוספות הרא״ש לרבינו אשר ב״ר יחיאל, מסכת ברכות, מב, לברכות כא:; טור, אורח חיים קלב; רבינו נסים על הרי״ף, מגילה יג:; נמוקי יוסף על מסכתות מגילה ופסחים, פ.

experience. The only other authority cited was an apparent extension of *Masekhet Soferim*'s ruling regarding the *kedushah deyotzer*. Scholars who viewed the latter as simply a description of the angelic liturgy and not a human liturgical participation in the sanctification of God often applied this conception to the *kedushah desidra* as well. However, rather than seeing it as a recitation of biblical verses, as in the geonic precedent, they spoke of it as simply a description of the angelic activities. This shift in reasoning had little practical impact except that it omitted any requirement that the individual recite the verses in their non-liturgical, scriptural mode.[67]

Only with the growing impact of the Zohar was there any substantial change in this status quo. Restricting the Aramaic translation of the *kedushah* verses to the individual and forbidding recitation of the Hebrew originals in a prayer setting without a minyan, the Zohar, II:132b, states baldly:

> כל קדושה דאיהו בלשון הקודש יחיד אסיר ליה למימר. תרגום לעולם ביחיד ולא בסגיאין יחיד איהו תקונא דיליה ודאי ולא סגיאין. וסימן לרזא דא שנים מקרא ואחד תרגום. שנים לישנא דסגיאין איהו דודאי קדושה דלשון הקודש אסיר איהי ביחיד. קדושת תרגום חסיר (צ"ל אסיר) איהו בסגיאין אלא ביחיד לעולם. אחד תרגום תנינן ולא תרין ולא יתיר...
>
> The individual is forbidden to recite any *kedushah* in Hebrew. The Aramaic translation is always (recited) by the individual and not by the congregation, for it was certainly instituted for the individual and not for the congregation. The indication of this secret is "Twice/two the Hebrew Scripture and once/one its translation."[68] "Twice/two" is plural, so the Hebrew *kedushah* is definitely forbidden to the individual. The Aramaic *kedushah* is forbidden to the public congregation, but the individual always (recites it). It is taught: "once/one its translation," not two and not more...[69]

---

67. See, for instance, *Sefer Ravyah*, ed. Aptowitzer, 5-6, #2, and 42, #66, which explicitly conflates the rulings about the two *kedushot*; the comment of Rabbenu Peretz to *Sefer Tashbetz* of R. Shimshon b"R. Tzaddok, #221, cited also in the note to Yitzhak Zeev Kahana's collection of R. Meir of Rothenburg's תשובות פסקים ומנהגים, #46; *Hagahot Maimoniot* to *Hilkhot Tefillah* 7:17 cites the Ravyah and indicates that this was also the ruling of his teacher, R. Meir of Rothenburg; Michael Higger, *Masekhet Soferim*, 295, n. 45, cites a similar comment from a manuscript of *Mordekhai* to *B. Berakhot* 21b. The Maharil continues this tradition (שו"ת מהרי"ל החדשות לרבינו יעקב מולין, טו, סי' י). See too the Meiri to *Berakhot* 21b; *Tur* OH 59 (but note that in 132 he invokes the geonic precedent).

68. *B. Berakhot* 8a, referring to obligations for study of the weekly Torah portion.

69. Compare II:129b: קדושה די בסופא איהי תרגום כמה דאוקימנא ודא אפילו יחיד יכול לומר לה אינון מלי דתרגום אבל מלין דלשון הקדש דקדושה לאו אינון אלא בעשרה. בגין דלשון הקדש שכינתא מתחברא בהדיה. ובכל קדושה דשכינתא אתיא לאו איהו אלא בעשרה דכתיב ונקדשתי בתוך בני ישראל וגו' בני ישראל אינון לשון הקדש ודאי ולא שאר עמין דאית לון לישן אחרא (The *kedushah* at the end is in Aramaic, as I have established, and here even the individual can recite these Aramaic words; but the words of the *kedushah* in the holy tongue

The text continues with more esoteric explanations, which need not concern us here. For our purposes, the critical point is that the Zohar, rereading a well-known talmudic tradition, limits the liturgical settings for the Hebrew verses of all three forms of the *kedushah* and its Aramaic translation included in the *kedushah desidra*.

There are some precedents for the Zohar's statement. It cites the *gemara*'s "Twice/two the Hebrew Scripture and once/one the translation," in which the numbers appear in their grammatically masculine forms even though their most likely referents, *pa'amim* (times) or *parshiot* (portions), are feminine. This leaves open the possibility that these numbers actually refer, not to the frequency with which one must study Torah, but to something else–most obviously the number of people involved. Indeed, Rabbi Eliezer ben Natan (Ravan), in his *Even Haezer*,[70] understands the *gemara* to refer to the minimum of two people, the reader and one more, who must stand at the Torah while it is read.

There is also some precedent for differentating between the Hebrew verses of the *kedushah* and their Aramaic translation. Although it gives no indication as to why, *Maḥzor Vitry*[71] specifies that the *sheliaḥ tzibbur* should say aloud the first three verses of the *kedushah desidra*, i.e., through Isaiah 6:3, and then recite the rest, i.e., beginning with the translation of this verse, silently along with the congregation. That this is, at least in some places, the actual custom, is attested in a ruling of R. Eliahu of London, who wonders about the reason for saying the translation silently when the *gemara* has established that the recitation of the *kedushah desidra* is one of the human actions sustaining the world.[72] He concludes: ואמת כי יש עיקר גדול וסוד כמוס ויסוד גדול בתרגום... (In truth, there is a great principle and a hidden secret and a great foundation in the Aramaic translation...). He does not indicate what this esoteric understanding might be, but does admit that people generally ignore it. Lying behind this may also be the concept, established in the Talmud, that the angels do not understand Aramaic.[73] Hence,

---

may be recited only by a quorum of ten, because the *Shekhinah* is intimately associated with the holy tongue. And any *kedushah* that invokes the *Shekhinah* may only (be recited) with a quorum of ten, as it is written, "I will be sanctified among the children of Israel, etc." "The children of Israel" certainly indicates the holy tongue, unlike the rest of the nations, who have another language).

70. p. 63b, #88, cited by R. Yom Tov Lipman Heller in his *Ma'adenei Yom Tov* and *Divrei Ḥamudot* to the Rosh, *Berakhot* 1:8.

71. p. 74.

72. פירושי רבנו אליהו מלונדריש ופסקיו, לד-לה, citing *B. Sotah* 49a. However, in the conclusion of his comment, R. Eliahu justifies the recitation of the *kedushah desidra* by the individual, based on geonic precedent.

73. *B. Sotah* 33a; *P. Sotah* 7:1, 21b.

an Aramaic recitation of the *kedushah* is as distant as one can be from imitation of or participation in the angelic liturgy while still using the ideational content of its language.

Naḥmanides, himself a kabbalist, takes an approach very similar to that which would appear in the Zohar and does not allow the individual to recite any *kedushah* privately. However, in the communally recited *kedushah desidra*, the Hebrew verses should be said aloud and the Aramaic translations silently כיון שאין בתרגום משום דבר שבקדושה ואינו צריך עשרה (since Aramaic does not fall into the category of a *davar shebikedushah* and does not require a minyan).[74] Unlike R. Eliahu of London, who posited great meaning behind the Aramaic verses, Naḥmanides insists that they carry no special sacrality at all. Although he does not here (or in any other text I have located) take the step of permitting the individual to recite the *kedushah desidra* privately as long as the Hebrew verses are omitted, this is a logical corollary to his statement. Indeed, the Zohar, which was first circulated not long after Naḥmanides' death, seems to make exactly this assumption. We must suppose that there was some tradition to this effect among the kabbalists of northern Spain in the thirteenth century.

The theoretical resolution of these conflicting rulings begins to appear as early as the Rashba, although there is no evidence at this point that it impacted popular custom broadly. In general, the Rashba includes all *kedushot* under the umbrella of *devarim shebikedushah* and restricts their recitation to the public setting.[75] He gives a rather hesitant nod to the precedent of the Geonim, as transmitted by the Ravad, for the individual to recite the scriptural verses as if at school. Then he rules that there are no restrictions on recitation of these verses in translation, and from this he derives that even the individual can silently recite the *kedushah* in Aramaic.[76]

However, there was no universal tradition among the Rashba's students as to his actual ruling in this matter. The Ritva cites, as the opinion of his teacher (which may mean either the Rashba or the Ra'ah), that the individual may recite the *kedushah desidra*, because he is only like one who reads from the Prophets and translates.[77] This comment implies that the individual may still recite the Hebrew verses. In contrast, R. Ḥayyim b"R. Shmuel ben David of Tudela, in

74. חידושי הרמב"ן על מסכת ברכות, בתוך ספר חידושי הראשונים הרמב"ן ורשב"א והריטב"א על מס' ברכות ושבת, א' עמ' ב–ג.

75. *Shut Harashba* I:7. Here, he concludes his responsum with the very strong statement: ואנחנו אין אומרין אותה כלל וכל דבר שכיוצא בו הנכון שבהן לנהוג בו במניעה דשב ואל תעשה שאני (We do not recite [any *kedushah*] at all or anything similar to it. The proper way to behave is with restraint, according to the principle: sit and do nothing [in matters such as these]).

76. *Shut Harashba* V:9.

77. חידושי הריטב"א, מגילה, קעג.

his *Tzror Hahayyim*,[78] specifically cites the Rashba as forbidding the recitation of any *kedushah* without a minyan, in spite of Maimonides'(!)[79] permission to the individual to recite the verses as Scripture.

Perhaps because of the strong halakhic leadership exerted by the Rosh and the Baal Haturim (whose rulings on this issue followed the dominant German trends and were not influenced by Spanish kabbalah), we find no further influence of the Zohar and the tradition behind it in this matter during the remainder of the Spanish period. Most likely it was simply impossible to change popular custom based on esoteric mystic lore to which people were not privy, especially when there were long-standing traditions justifying a minhag that continued to be supported by major rabbinic authorities. However, after the expulsion from Spain, with the broadening influence of kabbalah, we find rabbis again actively ruling according to the concerns generated by the Zohar. R. Meir ibn Gabbai in his kabbalistic commentary on the siddur, *Tolaat Yaakov*,[80] cites Rav Tzemaḥ Gaon(!) and the Maor Hakadosh,[81] that the individual may recite the *kedushah desidra* only in Aramaic, but not in Hebrew. Similarly, the Radbaz[82] rules strictly in these controversies, directing that the individual is under no circumstances permitted to recite any *kedushah*, unless it is in Aramaic. In support of this stance, he cites the responsum from heaven of R. Yaakov of Marvège,[83] which in our printed version makes no reference to the *kedushah desidra* or to Aramaic; he also cites the Rashba.

However, Joseph Karo, who was attempting to create a more universal code of Jewish law, does not quite take this strong a stance. He follows the Zohar to the extent that he does not permit the communal recitation of the Aramaic verses, ruling that these must always be recited silently. However, he continues

---

78. p. 5.

79. We have no evidence that Maimonides ever made this statement. Our only indication of Maimonides' stance regarding the *kedushah desidra* is his omission of it in his discussion of the prayers of the individual, as opposed to his inclusion of it in the congregational liturgy (*Hilkhot Tefillah* 7:17 and 9:5). Any number of other sources could be the true attribution of this statement, or this may be an extension of Maimonides' ruling about the *kedushah deyotzer* in his responsum.(תשובות הרמב"ם, II:581, #313; IV:24.) See below, p. 225f.

80. p. 20c.

81. Such a passage does not appear in our editions of the *Sefer Hamaor* of R. Zeraḥya Halevi. Roland Goetschel, *Meir Ibn Gabbay: Le Discours de la Kabbala Espagnole* (Leuven: Peeters, 1981), 33-36, seems also to have been unable to identify this reference, for in his list of Ibn Gabbai's sources, he includes all of those mentioned in the context of interest to us here, except this one.

82. שו"ת הרדב"ז, חלק רביעי, ב עמ' א–ב, סי' אלף סד.

83. שאלות ותשובות מן השמים לרבינו יעקב ממרויש, מבעלי התוספות (ירושלים, תשל"ב), כו, סי' פ. See below, p. 218.

to allow the individual to recite the original biblical verses with their trope in the schoolhouse mode.[84] We will explore Karo's stance in more detail below in connection with his ruling regarding the *kedushah deyotzer*. Briefly, it seems that, realistically, in the light of popular custom and established halakhic stances permitting it, he found himself unable to promulgate a strict ruling in accordance with his mystical leanings. Among Karo's supercommentators, all accept that the individual may recite the *kedushah desidra* privately. Most restrict the recitation of the Aramaic translations to the individual (meaning they are recited silently even in the congregational setting),[85] and many explicitly allow the individual to recite the Hebrew verses. Hence, in spite of a resurgence of mystic concern about the legitimacy of the individual's recitation of the *kedushah desidra*, popular minhag ultimately prevailed.

## *The Private* Kedushah *Among the Rishonim:* *The* Kedushah Deyotzer

As we have seen, until the advent of kabbalah, permission for the individual to recite the *kedushah desidra*, although with some reservations, was almost universal. Variation appeared more in the rationales created to allow this recitation than in the resultant rulings promulgated for the community. The rulings about the *kedushah deyotzer*, in contrast, present no obvious unanimity, even when analyzed according to geographical or chronological criteria. Only when we categorize the sources according to the mystic leanings of their authors can we begin to understand the history of this halakhic issue–and even then, some schools of thought are difficult to explain. But for the most part, rabbis of mystic bent were more seriously concerned about the latent powers inherent in this angelic liturgy and restricted its recitation to the public setting. Those who found mystic concerns less compelling tended to accept the authority of *Masekhet Soferim* and to permit the individual to recite the *kedushah deyotzer* privately. Outside the walls of the academy, however, we can still glimpse a world in which common people disregarded rabbinic opinion and recited the same prayers whether or not they were with a minyan.

Before analyzing the rabbinic halakhic stances, it is worthwhile to summarize

84. *Beit Yosef* OH 59.

85. Note, however, the discussion of the *Shaarei Teshuvah*, OH 132:1, which records that the Ari did say the Aramaic verses aloud. However, he modifies this precedent, saying that the concern that the congregation not recite the Aramaic verses together remains. A person may recite the verses aloud in the presence of others, but not with them.

the evidence available for the actual customs common in the various worlds of medieval Jewry. A note of caution is in order, though, for a rabbinic statement about the universality of a custom may not be historically accurate; it may represent what the rabbi wishes were universal custom, or the "universe" intended may refer to something far less than the entire Jewish world. Without corroborating evidence, which we generally do not have, we cannot know the difference.

In Ashkenaz itself, in the twelfth and thirteenth centuries, we find two rabbinic claims that individuals, instead of reciting the *kedushah* verses and the transitional liturgy between them, actually recited just the first words of the verses, *kadosh* and *barukh.* However the first source, by R. Ephraim of Bonn, records all sorts of other alternative halakhic rulings, indicating that this custom was not really so firmly established.[86] The second appears in R. Peretz of Corbeil's comments on R. Meir of Rothenburg's ruling that the custom of abbreviating the *yotzer* is unnecessary.[87] We cannot know whether the "universal custom" of saying just the first words, to which R. Peretz refers, is that of the French Jews, the German Jews, both, or just a mystically inclined elite. That this custom of abbreviating the *yotzer* was actually current somewhere in the middle of this time period is clear from the *Manhig*'s objection to it,[88] but the ruling of R. Meir of Rothenburg and his students ended this custom, at least eventually, if it was indeed ever popularly widespread.[89] In the fifteenth century, the *Agur*[90] and, in the sixteenth century, R. Moshe Isserles[91] record that the custom had spread for individuals to recite the entire *kedushah deyotzer* privately.

We have no similar traditions about the actual customs of Provence or Italy.[92] In Spain, both Rabbenu Yonah,[93] in the thirteenth century, and Abudarham,[94] in the fourteenth, record that all actual prayerbooks make no distinction be-

86. סידור רבנו שלמה מיוחס לרבנו שלמה ב"ר שמשון מגרמייזא וסידור חסידי אשכנז מבית מדרשם של ר"י החסיד ור"א מגרמייזא בעל הרוקח, פז–פח. Ephraim E. Urbach, *Arugat Habosem*, IV:65, identifies this as the commentary of R. Ephraim of Bonn.

87. שמשון ב"ר צדוק, ספר תשב"ץ...עם הגהות רבינו פרץ זצ"ל, סי' רכא.

88. ed. Raphael, 63.

89. See below, p. 223. One might suggest that it is possible that this custom, in Ashkenaz, evolved from the Palestinian tradition of never reciting the *kedushah* on weekdays. However, all evidence suggests that when the Palestinians omitted the *kedushah*, they also omitted all reference to it, above and beyond even the geonic compromise texts (except that of Saadia).

90. p. 33, #101-102.

91. *Darkhei Moshe* to the *Tur* OH 59; comment on the *Shulḥan Arukh*, OH 59:3.

92. The *Manhig*, while objecting to the customs of others, only indicates his own halakhic stance, which may or may not reflect a living reality.

93. To the Rif, *Berakhot* 13b.

94. *Abudarham Hashalem*, 74.

tween the text of the *yotzer* for the individual and that of the community, and contrast this situation to the text of the *amidah*.[95] Again, we cannot know the real applicability of this claim of universality, but prayerbook manuscript evidence supports it. The single exception I have located is a poorly preserved prayerbook, tentatively identified as of the Sefardi rite in North Africa in the fifteenth century, which does provide an alternative text for the individual.[96] Finally, Joseph Karo records reluctantly that it has become universal custom for the individual to recite the *kedushah deyotzer*.[97]

### *The* Kedushah Deyotzer *in Ashkenaz*

Restricting the *kedushah deyotzer* to the public realm, a significant number of Ashkenazi scholars recorded that the custom was for the individual simply to omit it when praying alone. Our evidence is spotty, but it seems clear that they based this opinion on two sources of authority: the geonic responsa and the mystic heritage. Reliance on geonic precedent appears in *Sefer Hapardes*,[98] which cites, without attribution and without further comment, the geonic responsum attributed to Saadia found in a manuscript of Amram forbidding private recitation of this *kedushah* because it is a *davar shebikedushah*.[99] However, we must note that none of the other texts of the Rashi school reflect such a position,[100] although none of the evidence to the contrary is unequivocal. In *Sefer Hapardes* itself, this paragraph comes in the midst of a series of geonic

95. These cases, of course, are not exactly analogous, as the *kedushah* appears only in the repetition of the *amidah*, which the individual never recites, even in the presence of a congregation, whereas the *yotzer* has no repetition.

96. Jewish Theological Seminary Microfilms, #4112, p. 16a.

97. *Beit Yosef*, OH 59.

98. Ehrenreich ed., 327; Warsaw ed. #61.

99. See above, p. 205 and n. 53, and the text labelled "Geonic, attribution unclear" in the appendix.

100. *Maḥzor Vitry*, 65, simply includes the *kedushah deyotzer* without any discussion of a differentiation to be made for the individual. This would be a strange point for such a comprehensive liturgical work to omit, were it of any importance. *Sefer HaOrah*, Buber ed., 11, #21, discussing another aspect of the *kedushah*, mentions that the *kedushah deyotzer* does not involve a human sanctification of God, a significant argument for those who do allow the individual to recite this *kedushah*. However, *Sefer HaOrah* does not directly address our issue. Finally, *Hagahot Maimoniot* to *Hilkhot Tefillah* 7:17 cites Rashi as supporting the recitation of the *kedushah deyotzer* by the individual, based on the authority of *Masekhet Soferim*. However, this is not independently supported in any of the literary traditions we have received.

responsa that are only loosely related to the subject of the preceding material, raising the possibility that it is not original or integral to the work.

Among the received traditions of the various Tosafists, the matter is clearer. Rabbi Yitzḥak of Dampierre explicitly rules according to a paraphrase of this same geonic responsum.[101] *Shibbolei Haleket* cites the Tosafist R. Elazar of Verona's support for a geonic style omission of the intervening liturgy and all but the first words of the *kedushah* verses themselves. It then cites another Tosafist, a Rabbi Barukh, who insists on maintaining the intervening liturgy so that it does not appear that the same groups of angels are saying both verses.[102]

While these sages appear to rely largely on geonic precedents, we cannot ignore possible mystical influences as well–especially in the cases of Rabbi Yitzḥak of Dampierre and his student, R. Elazar of Verona. Urbach documents R. Yitzḥak of Dampierre's interest in mysticism and his connections with R. Yehudah Haḥasid in Germany and possibly also with the early Provençal kabbalists through his student, R. Avraham b"R. Natan Hayarḥi, the author of the *Manhig*. R. Elazar of Verona was also in contact with R. Elazar of Worms and the circles of the Ḥasidei Ashkenaz in the Rhineland.[103] However, because these sages do not explain their reasoning, it is difficult to determine the extent of these mystical influences on their halakhic thought.

But even the overtly mystically-based Askenazi rulings against the individual's recitation of the *kedushah deyotzer* show little unity or dependence on one another. Rabbi Ephraim of Bonn,[104] although a bit ambivalent, refutes the position of those who would follow the position of *Masekhet Soferim*. His primary argument is that one must rule strictly on anything involving a *davar shebikedushah*. However, earlier he responds to the assertion of others that the *kedushah deyotzer* is permitted because it merely relates the angelic sanctification of God's name. He says: אבל אסור לספר בינתיים מרוב שמות שיוצאים ממנו (but it is

---

101. תשובות ופסקים לר"י הזקן, רמב–ג, סי' קלד. Note, however, that on p. 216, #84, he makes the opposite ruling regarding a *kedushah*. Given the language that he uses and his reference to a similar ruling in *Amram*, this second ruling most likely applies to the *kedushah desidra*. No exact determination can be made.

102. ed. Mirsky, 171, #1:13, cited also by the *Agur*, 33, #102. There are at least two contemporaneous sages by the name of Barukh among the Tosafists: R. Barukh ben Shmuel of Mainz, c. 1150–1221; and R. Barukh ben Yitzḥak of Worms, a student of R. Yitzḥak of Dampierre, c. 1170–c. 1240. The comment here uses the same language found in *Arugat Habosem* III:81 at the beginning of a citation from R. Elazar of Worms regarding the *kedushah deyotzer* (see below, p. 219f., for discussion of other aspects of this text). However, he uses the citation for a different purpose.

103. א. א. אורבך, בעלי התוספות, תולדותם, חיבוריהם, שיטתם, מהדורת חמישית מורחבת ומתוקנת (ירושלים: מוסד ביאליק, תשמ"ו), 237, 433 ואילך.

104. סידור חסידי אשכנז, פז–פח, and in Urbach, *Arugat Habosem*, IV:65.

forbidden to relate this in the meanwhile because of the large number of [holy] names that are thereby articulated). This statement, whose exact referent is unclear, has no parallel in the direct commentaries on the *kedushah deyotzer* in either the *Siddur Ḥasidei Ashkenaz* or in the siddur commentary of the Rokeaḥ.[105] It would seem to refer to a mystical result of the liturgical recitation of the *kedushah* verses, perhaps one derived from permutations of the words, gematria manipulations, or the mere utterance of God's name, all of which would occur regardless of the actual setting of the words. In his conclusion, R. Ephraim discusses the geonically endorsed or inspired substitute liturgies that the individual should recite instead.

Similar concerns appear in the responsum received from heaven by R. Yaakov of Marvège.[106] Faced with conflicting rulings on our issue, he sought enlightenment directly from God, who replied:

> למה תאמר יעקב וגלוי וידוע ונקדשתי בתוך בני ישראל כל קדושות אינם בפחות מעשרה. עשרה בטלנים עומדים לפני כל היום ובהם קדושתי עומד, ואין פותחים בקדושה בלתם, ושמי הנקרא בקדושה אינו ביחיד לעולם.
>
> "Why do you say, O Jacob"?[107] It is well known, "And I will be sanctified among the children of Israel,"[108] [means that] no *kedushah* may be recited with less than a quorum of ten. Ten otherwise idle men[109] stand before Me all day, and My sanctity depends on them. One may not begin the *kedushah* without them. My name, which is recited in the *kedushah*, is never recited by the individual.

Here we see the same two arguments: as a *davar shebikedushah*, the *kedushah deyotzer* may, on clear halakhic grounds, be recited only in the communal setting.[110] And on mystic grounds, the sanctification that God needs can only

---

105. However, some hint of R. Ephraim of Bonn's meaning may be found in their commentaries on the *kedushah* of the *amidah*. See: פירושי סידור התפלה לרקח: פירוש התפילה וסודותיה לכל ימות השנה לרבנו אלעזר ב"ר יהודה מגרמיזא, מהדורת משה הרשלר ויהודה אלתר הרשלר (ירושלים: מכון הרב הרשלר, תשנ"ב), כרך א, עמ' 325; סידור רבנו שלמה, סידור חסידי אשכנז, מהדורת משה הרשלר (ירושלים, תשל"ב), קז.

106. שו"ת מן השמים, כו, סי' פ.

107. Isaiah 40:27, referring here, of course, to R. Yaakov of Marvege.

108. Leviticus 22:32, the biblical basis of the midrashic derivation of the requirement of a minyan for the *davar shebikedushah*, used in *B. Berakhot* 21b and *B. Megillah* 23b.

109. A term derived from *Mishnah Megillah* 1:3's definition that what constitutes a large city is the presence of ten men sufficiently free of obligations that they are always available to constitute a minyan.

110. This identification of the *kedushah deyotzer* as a *davar shebikedushah* becomes a more central element of the halakhic argument, particularly in Spain. We should note here that the Italian *Shibbolei Haleket* (ed. Mirsky, 1:9, p. 157; 1:13, 171-172) and, after him, the *Tanya Rabati* (Warsaw, 1879, p. 15 #4) rule explicitly on this basis against the recitation of the

come from this community of ten, and that sanctification is tied somehow to the recitation of the Name in the *kedushah* itself, not to the entire verses. Reciting the divine Name in whichever setting is forbidden to the individual as, at the very least, an ineffective sanctification, but probably as a source of danger to the individual. It may even have a negative effect in heaven.[111]

Finally, we find in the *Arugat Habosem* of R. Avraham b"R. Azriel[112] a positive statement of clear mystic import about the value of the individual's reciting just the two introductory words of the *kedushah* verses.

> כלומ'[113] יש מלאכים שאומ' קדוש ואינם אומרים ברוך ויש מאלכים שאומ' ברוך ואינם אומ' קדוש. אבל קהילות ישראל הם אומרים קדוש וברוך. אברהם יצחק ויעקב בגימט' קדוש וברוך וזהו שאמ' בברא' רבא אומ' ריש לקיש האבות הן הן מרכבה שנ' ויעל אלהים מעל אברהם, ויעל מעליו אלהים, הנה ה' נצב עליו. פי' האבות הן הן המרכבה, כלומ' מרכבת שכינה עליהם ורמז לדבר ודמות פניהם פני אדם בגימ' המרכב"ה אבו"ת עול"ם יתר א', בע"א המרכבה אבות העולם כלומ' מרכבת שכינה על אבות, ה"ר אלע' ז"ל. ואחרי שהשכינה הן אבות, והאבות קדוש וברוך, ע"כ אומ' יחיד ביוצר אור קדוש וברוך במקו' קק"ק ה' צבאות וגו' ברוך כבוד ה' ממקומו. כי קדוש וברוך היא השכינה. ע"כ די בקדוש וברוך.
>
> That is to say, there are angels who say *kadosh* and do not say *barukh*, and there are angels who say *barukh* and do not say *kadosh*. But the congregations of Israel say (both) *kadosh* and *barukh*. In gematria, the combined

---

*kedushah deyotzer* by the individual. We have no evidence linking R. Tzidkiah b"R. Avraham Harofe with the mystical circles of Ashkenaz, Provence, or Spain. He invokes the precedents of the Geonim and the Tosafists, as well as his teacher's refutation of *Masekhet Soferim*. Given these literary precedents, his position may be based purely on theoretical, legal criteria and be unaffected by mystic concerns.

111. A more detailed study of the interpretations of the *kedushah* among the Ḥasidei Ashkenaz would enhance our understanding of these comments, but is beyond the scope of and not fully relevant to this study. Note should be made, though, of the following:

In his Tosafot to *B. Berakhot* 21b, Rabbi Yehudah Haḥasid explains the talmudic disagreement between Rav Huna and Rabbi Yehoshua ben Levi to refer to the terms of our medieval debate. (ספר ברכה משולשת על מסכת ברכות, יב:.) This comment gives no insight into R. Yehudah's practical halakhic stance on our issue.

Although the evidence of his position is not unambiguous (see below, p. 221f.), R. Elazar of Worms in his *Sefer Harokeah*, 249ff., #362, when he gives substitute texts for the individual to recite so as to allow him to say the various *devarim shebikedushah*, includes many texts with obvious links to the *merkavah* literature.

R. Eliahu of London, who makes reference to the secret meanings embedded in the translation of the *kedushah* verses in the *kedushah desidra*, also rules in passing against the recitation of the *kedushah deyotzer* by the individual, citing Maimonides' ruling in *Hilkhot Tefillah* 7:17. (פירושי רבנו אליהו מלונדריש ופסקיו, לד.).

112. III: 81-82. This discussion appears in his commentary on the *piyyut* לך אלים, an *ofan* (the *piyyut* intervening between the *kedushah* verses in the *yotzer*) for a Shabbat Rosh Ḥodesh.

113. To the line: לך קהילות בשבתות ובחדשים.

numerical values of the words "Abraham," "Isaac," and "Jacob" equal "*kadosh*" and "*barukh*" (638), which is what is meant in Genesis Rabbah[114] when Resh Lakish says: The patriarchs are the chariot, for it is said, "God went up from upon Abraham,"[115] "God went up from upon him (Jacob),"[116] and "Behold the Lord stood upon him (Jacob)."[117] This means that the patriachs are the chariot, that is to say, the chariot of the *Shekhinah* [rests] upon them. There is an intimation of this in that the numerical value of "The form of their faces was human"[118] (826) is in gematria only one less than "*hamerkavah* (the chariot), *avot* (patriarchs), *olam* (world)" (827). In another matter [we find], the chariot is the patriarchs of the world, i.e., the chariot of the *Shekhinah* [rests] on the patriarchs. [So according to] R. Elazar of blessed memory.[119] Since the *Shekhinah* is the patriarchs,[120] and the patriarchs are *kadosh* and *barukh*, the individual should recite in the *yotzer* [just the single words] *kadosh* and *barukh* instead of the full verses, because [the words] *kadosh* and *barukh* [represent] the *Shekhinah*. Therefore, [the words] *kadosh* and *barukh* are sufficient.

R. Avraham b"R. Azriel argues here against those who permit the individual to recite the *kedushah deyotzer* privately. The crux of his argument, however, is not based on his halakhic stance, which, he assumes, is established and accepted–as we have seen it was, at least among members of his immediate circle of early European mystics. Instead, he concentrates on establishing that even the individual's abbreviated *yotzer* text has mystic significance. Although individuals may no longer be able to participate in or describe fully the angelic praise of God, on reciting this abbreviated text with awareness of its hidden numerical significance, they invoke the *Shekhinah*, God's presence itself, or the divine chariot; at the very least they help to form the foundation on which the chariot rests. Therefore, R. Avraham argues, individuals should have no desire to recite the full *kedushah*, which is restricted to the communal setting.

Did R. Elazar of Worms himself take this route? There is no mention of anything related to the individual's recitation of the *kedushah deyotzer* in his

114. 47:6, 69:3, 82:6, ed. Theodor-Albeck, 475, 793, 983. Note the absence in this tradition of a verse referring to Isaac!

115. Genesis 17:22.

116. Genesis 35:13.

117. Genesis 28:13. In the biblical text, עליו refers to the ladder, not Jacob.

118. Ezekiel 1:5.

119. It is not clear how much of the preceding material is cited from R. Elazar of Worms. Urbach notes that material preceding "In another matter" has a parallel in R. Elazar's *Sodei Razaya*, pp. 120-121, but that text really uses the midrash and gematria for another purpose.

120. Note the logical leap here!

prayerbook commentary. We find in his *Sefer Harokeaḥ*,[121] in the manner of Rav Tzemaḥ Gaon's solution for the *kedushah desidra*, several alternative texts designed to enable individuals non-liturgically to recite the words of the various responses requiring a minyan, including the *kedushah deyotzer* verses. However, the nature of these substitutions indicates that they were not intended for insertion into the course of the individual's standard prayers, but rather for separate recitation. It is possible that the Ḥasidei Ashkenaz tried both to find higher meaning in the individual's abbreviated *yotzer* and to provide a mechanism to compensate for the omissions at the conclusion of the prayers.

Thus in addition to geonic precedents, considerations of the mystic import of the *kedushah* influenced the halakhic stance of the early northern European rabbis on this issue. But this approach was not universal. Another significant group of authorities, basing themselves on *Masekhet Soferim*, ruled that the individuals may indeed recite the *kedushah deyotzer* exactly as they would in a communal setting. Documented use of this argument in Ashkenazi circles dates to at least the twelfth century. The *Hagahot Maimoniot*[122] knows of a tradition that cites the argument in the name of Rashi. Similarly, Rabbenu Yonah ascribes it to "the French rabbis and a few Geonim."[123] I have located no such statement in the literary works of Rashi or his school. The earliest documentation to which we can assign a date is R. Ephraim of Bonn's *rejection* of the arguments of others who were relying on *Masekhet Soferim*. He himself did not object to this text as a halakhic source, but found other considerations more compelling.[124]

The earliest extensive, and, incidentally, influential discussion by a scholar who relied on the arguments of *Masekhet Soferim* is that of R. Eliezer b"R. Yoel Halevi, the Ravyah. In explicating the *baraita* in *B. Berakhot* 3a[125] that relates Rabbi Yose's experiences when he prayed in a ruined building in Jerusalem, the Ravyah records that there are those who, when they are not with a minyan, compensate by reciting this *baraita* because it includes the response to the kaddish, then *Mishnah Berakhot* 7:3 because it includes *barekhu*, and finally the *baraita* from *B. Ḥullin* 91b or Isaiah 6 because they include the *kedushah*. Such a custom corresponds to the initial compromise position in the responsum of Rav

121. 249-250, # 362. See further discussion of this passage below, p. 222.

122. *Hilkhot Tefillah* 7:17.

123. To the Rif, *Berakhot* 13a-b. Note, though, that he does not specifically use the characteristic language of, or cite, *Masekhet Soferim*.

124. *Siddur Ḥasidei Ashkenaz*, 87-88; also in Urbach's introductory essays to *Arugat Habosem*, IV:65. Indeed, this passage contains an additional reference to *Masekhet Soferim*, 10:6, which seems to accept it as a legitimate halakhic source.

125. *Sefer Ravyah*, ed. Aptowitzer, I:5-6, #2.

Tzemaḥ Gaon about the *kedushah desidra*, which also suggests substitution of talmudic texts. Here, though, the Ravyah indicates that the precedent of *Masekhet Soferim* establishes that only in the case of the *kedushah* of the *amidah* is the individual prohibited from reciting the *kedushah* without a minyan. He quite specifically excludes both the *kedushah deyotzer* and the *kedushah desidra* from categories requiring any such liturgical compromise.

In his comment to *B. Berakhot* 21b, the Ravyah expands upon this position, explicating the meaning of the passage in *Masekhet Soferim*. There, the text uses an unusual participle, claiming that the individual who recites the *kedushah deyotzer* is like a סודר. The Ravyah explains this term, saying:

> פי' מספר והולך היאך משבחים המלאכים והוי לי' כקורא פרשת בשנת מות המלך עוזיהו שיש בה קק"ק.
>
> This means that he simply relates how the angels are praising; and this is as if he were reading the sixth chapter of Isaiah, which includes the *trisagion*.[126]

Therefore, one does not need to create a substitute text for this *kedushah* because it is already functioning as that substitute text would. It does not constitute a praise or sanctification of God by human beings, but is merely a description of the angelic liturgy using biblical verses. As such, he continues, it is distinct from the *kedushah* of the *amidah*, which, as a *davar shebikedushah*, requires a quorum of ten. The concerns of the discussion of *B. Berakhot* 21b, then, do not apply to the *kedushah deyotzer* because it is not a *davar shebikedushah*.

It might seem that Rabbi Elazar of Worms, a younger colleague of the Ravyah, also allowed the individual to recite the *kedushah deyotzer* and considered *Masekhet Soferim* to be the determinative literary halakhic authority. In the discussion of the *yotzer* blessing in his *Sefer Harokeaḥ*,[127] he simply lists relevant halakhic sources on various issues. On the *kedushah*, he only cites *Masekhet Soferim* without any elaboration. However, later in the book, he gives alternative texts, like those described by the Ravyah, with which individuals may compensate for missing their communal synagogue recitation of the relevant prayers. In this extensive list, he includes substitute texts for *kadosh* and *barukh* alone, and for *barekhu*, kaddish (read *kadosh*) and *barukh*–that is, for the responses of the *kedushah deyotzer*.[128] Given that Rabbi Elazar was a leader of the Ḥasidei

126. I:41-42, #66.

127. p. 210, #320. The פירושי סידור התפילה לרוקח itself contains no discussion of any special protocol for the individual at this point.

128. pp. 249, 250, #362.

Ashkenaz and consequently deeply involved in mystic pursuits, this second source is more likely representative of his personal practice and halakhic stance.

The most influential Ashkenazi ruling regarding the matter was that of Rabbi Meir of Rothenburg (Maharam), who, as is clear from the various reports of his students, was heavily influenced by the Ravyah on this issue. The reports of his decisions and those of his students acknowledge the well-grounded halakhic stance that required the omission of these *kedushah* verses, but they rule decidedly according to *Masekhet Soferim*, using the language of the Ravyah's arguments.[129] Rabbi Meir's stance does determine the subsequent minhag of Ashkenaz, as is evident from the *Agur*,[130] the Maharil,[131] and, later, from the Ashkenazi supercommentators on Karo's works. It also becomes highly influential, as we shall see, in Spain, through the influence of the Rosh and the Baal Haturim.

How do we explain this permissive position? We have sufficient evidence from known Ashkenazi mystics to show that these schools did not take lightly the recitation of any *kedushah* by an individual. Although the Ravyah and the Maharam were not isolated from these circles (Ravyah studied with Rabbi Yehudah Haḥasid, author of the *Sefer Ḥasidim*, and among his pupils was R. Avraham ben Azriel, author of *Arugat Habosem*), Urbach asserts that Aptowitzer was essentially correct in claiming that the Ravyah was not actually part of the school of Rabbi Yehudah Haḥasid and R. Eliezer of Worms, to whom mysticism was a central concern.[132] While the Ravyah himself may have been peripherally involved in mystic pursuits, this seems not to be true for the Maharam. According to Urbach, there is no question that he accepted the teachings of the Ḥasidei Ashkenaz, following in all liturgical matters Rabbi Yehudah Haḥasid and the *Rokeaḥ*, including their numerological explanations for the prayers. He is also known to have relied on visions from dreams for halakhic guidance.[133] This influence notwithstanding, we know that in this case he does

129. רבי מאיר ב"ר ברוך (מהר"ם) מרוטנבורג, תשובות פסקים ומנהגים, חלק א: עמ' קלה, תשובה קמג; עמ' קמה, פסק מו (=ספר תשב"ץ, סי' רכא.); הגהות מיימוניות, הלכות תפלה ז:יז; כ"י מרדכי לברכות, פרק ג' רס"ה א', מודפס ע"י מיכאל היגגער, מסכת סופרים, 295, הע' 65.

130. p. 33, #101-102. Note, however, that Landau, in citing the *Tur*, OH 59, includes Maharam among those agreeing with Maimonides. Maharam does not appear in the *Tur*'s list of authorities on this issue. However, even though he reviews various opinions to the contrary, Landau does not suggest that the current custom, to say the *kedushah*, ought to be changed.

131. שו"ת מהריל החדשות לרבינו יעקב מולין, טו, סי' י. See also R. Isaac Tirnau's ספר המנהגים, מהדורת שלמה י. שפיצר (ירושלים: מפעל תורת חכמי אשכנז, תשל"ט), עמ' ט.

132. Urbach, *Baalei Hatosafot*, 387-388.

133. Urbach, *Baalei Hatosafot*, 547.

not follow the *Rokeaḥ*, but instead the less mystically inclined Ravyah and perhaps the leanings of the French rabbis with whom he had studied extensively.

Joseph Dan describes the thirteenth century as a period in which German Jews gradually lost interest in their esoteric theology, both because of internal problems–generated by the disintegration of their early centers and the state of social and economic crisis characteristic of the period–and because of the appeal of kabbalah, which was percolating northward.[134] We have no evidence for Maharam's involvement in kabbalah-style mysticism or in the writing of new mystic works. Instead, he seems to have devoted his energies to more practical halakhic matters and to the active guidance of his community. His reliance on the liturgical pronouncements of the Ḥasidei Ashkenaz may then reflect more tradition than personal involvement. If the "universal custom" of reciting an abbreviated *yotzer* described by R. Peretz and others reflects more a pietistic minhag than true popular custom, then we can understand the Maharam's ruling. In troubled times, and without a deep commitment to mystic practice himself, he may well have chosen to rule according to the popular custom, especially in a case where such a lenient ruling had the authority of Rashi,[135] the Ravyah, and *Masekhet Soferim.*[136]

### *The* Kedushah Deyotzer *in Provence and Spain*

While two very distinct and conflicting rulings were developing in northern Europe, the rabbinic authorities of southern France and Christian Spain were independently discussing the legitimacy of the individual's recitation of the *kedushah deyotzer.* As in Ashkenaz, many of the sages ruling on this issue were involved in mystical pursuits. However, in the south the extreme concern of the early kabbalists to preserve the secrecy of their doctrines limited the penetration of even hints of such reasoning into their halakhic works, requiring us often to guess the true motivation behind a ruling. Although the correlation is not perfect between kabbalistic leanings and decisions against private recitation, it is still statistically significant. With the spread of the Zohar in Spain and the contemporaneous arrival of the Maharam's traditions carried by the Rosh and the Baal Haturim, lines of demarcation became even clearer.

134. יוסף דן, תורת הסוד של חסידות אשכנז (ירושלים: מוסד ביאליק, תשכ"ח), 252.

135. If the *Hagahot Maimoniot* (*Hilkhot Tefillah* 7:17) cites Rashi on this issue, it is not unreasonable to assume that the Maharam was also aware of this tradition.

136. Referred to as "Yerushalmi" in a report of the Maharam's ruling in the responsum of an unidentified scholar, printed by Kahane from a manuscript source (תשובות פסקים ומנהגים, תשובה קמג, עמ' קלה).

Before we turn to these later *posekim*, we must introduce the influential but conflicting rulings of the Rambam, the only figure from the period of Muslim Spain whose treatment of our question survives. In his *Mishneh Torah*, Maimonides ruled explicitly that "the individual is to skip the *kedushah* in the *yotzer* because an individual never recites the *kedushah*."[137] He added no further explanation, but presumably considered the *kedushah* to be a *davar shebikedushah*, part of the Mishnah's *perisat shema*, which requires a quorum of ten men. However, in a responsum[138] known to later sages also from the independent testimony of his son Abraham,[139] Maimonides ruled that the individual should recite the same text as does the *sheliah tzibbur*. In this responsum, directed to Yosef ben Gabir of Baghdad, he acknowledges that most of the (Babylonian) Geonim disagreed with this position; he asserts, however, that most western "Geonim" agree with him because this *kedushah* is just a description of the angelic liturgy. Although Maimonides does not cite *Masekhet Soferim* by name, this is clearly the source, at least indirectly, of his ruling. As further support, he cites the work on liturgy of Ibn Gasos, the student of Rav Nissim Gaon.[140]

To what can we attribute this about-face? As we have seen in previous chapters, Maimonides was not one to accede to popular custom if it contradicted his sense of halakhah or propriety. But here, we can assume, he was made aware of a legitimate, halakhically valid case for existing minhag, supported by sages hailing from different parts of the Jewish world. In addition, Maimonides, as his philosophy developed, came to ascribe less and less real value to human verbal praise of God[141] and understood the prophetic visions of the angelic liturgies in such a way that active human participation in them could not really exist.[142] This about-face, however, created confusion for subsequent generations, espe-

137. *Hilkhot Tefillah* 7:17.

138. תשובות הרמב"ם, II:581, #313; IV:24.

139. ארחות חיים (ירושלים, 1955), דין קדושה דמיושב, א, עמ' 24; *Shut Harashba* I:7; *Beit Yosef* OH 59. Attested to directly in his ספר המספיק לעובדי השם, 199-200, where R. Abraham ben Moshe Hamaimon describes his father's own custom of reciting the *kedushah deyotzer* when alone.

140. There is some confusion as to the name of this scholar, some reading גאסום instead of Blau's גאסוס. Fragments of his work on liturgy have been found and published by Simḥah Assaf, "קטע מחבורו של אבן אלגסוס (או אלגסום) בעניני תפלה," קרית ספר כח (תשי"ב–תשי"ג), 101–109. Unfortunately, these fragments do not include his discussion of the *kedushah deyotzer*.

141. See Marvin Fox, *Interpreting Maimonides, Studies in Methodology, Metaphysics, and Moral Philosophy* (Chicago and London: University of Chicago Press, 1990), chap. 11, "Prayer and the Religious Life," especially 306-310, 316-321; and Ehud Benor, *Worship of the Heart: A Study in Maimonides' Philosophy of Religion* (Albany: SUNY, 1995), especially chap. 2, "Prayer as Worship."

142. Maimonides does not discuss the *kedushah* itself in his *Guide of the Perplexed*, but see his discussions of angels in II:6 and of Ezekiel's vision in the opening chapters of Part III.

cially for those communities that regarded the *Mishneh Torah* as their primary and authoritative code of Jewish law.

In Provence, the evidence suggests that most kabbalists prohibited the individual's recitation of the *kedushah deyotzer*. R. Avraham b"R. Yitzḥak Av Beit Din of Narbonne, the earliest Provençal rabbi known to have engaged in kabbalist speculations, explained in his *Sefer HaEshkol*[143] that the Mishnah prohibits *perisat shema* with less than a quorum of ten because it includes the *kedushah*, and every *davar shebikedushah* requires no less than this quorum. Although in his comments afterwards he recognizes that the human liturgy here is just mentioning the angelic praise, he indicates in an earlier discussion that the *kedushah* only appears in the *yotzer* because this is the time of day when the angels praise God in imitation of Israel.[144] Some active participatory element in the human recitation of the *kedushah deyotzer* thus apparently precludes its private recitation.

This supposition is supported by R. Azriel of Gerona's discussion of the issue, in which he identifies the specific effects the angelic liturgy has on the *sefirot*. Seth Brody explains:

> Sanctus, corresponding to God's compassion (here probably *Tiferet*) is recited by the Seraphic beings who embody its energy. In response, the wheels and holy beasts, who support and rotate before the Throne, ascend upwards in a mighty rush and acclaim the quality of Justice, most likely the Shekhinah, which gathers blessing from the realm of Holiness (*ḥokhmah*) and conveys it throughout the universe.

As Brody indicates, the very words of the *kedushah* carry "profound esoteric meaning." When spoken by angels, they allow the heavenly beings to participate in and attain renewal "from the same ceaseless outpouring of divine light which reconstitutes Creation. By reciting their song, humanity too celebrates a cosmic liturgy of praise of this process of constant rebirth."[145]

---

143. ed. Shalom and Hanokh Albeck, I:38.

144. p. 12: זכירין קדושה ביוצר אור, כי המלאכים כמו כן מקלסין ומקדשין כמו ישראל כדכ׳ ברן יחד כוכבי בקר אלו ישראל והדר ויריעו כל בני אלהים אלו המלאכים (We mention the *kedushah* in the *yotzer*, because that is when the angels praise and sanctify [God] like Israel, as it is written, "When the morning stars sang together"–these are Israel–and then "And all the divine beings shouted for joy" (Job 38:7)–these are the angels).

145. Seth Lance Brody, *Human Hands Dwell in Heavenly Heights: Worship and Mystical Experience in Thirteenth Century Kabbalah* (Ph.D. diss., University of Pennsylvania, 1991), 493, commenting on R. Azriel's *Commentary to the Morning Liturgy* (פירוש לתפילות, Ms. Oxford 1938/10, p. 217b). See also Brody, 491f. Unfortunately, the surviving manuscript material includes no commentary on the *kedushah* in the *amidah*, valuable to us for comparative pur-

In contrast, it seems that R. Avraham ben David of Posquieres (Ravad), in a comment not preserved among his own works, permitted the *kedushah deyotzer* (but not other *kedushot*[146]) to be recited privately since human beings are only describing what the *ofanim* are saying.[147] Little is known about this early kabbalist's mystical thought; thus we can neither verify the attribution of this tradition nor explain this apparent exception to other mystic halakhic rulings about the issue.[148] The *Manhig*, written by the Ravad's student, R. Avraham b"R. Natan Hayarḥi, objects even to the common Ashkenazi custom of preserving the first words of the *kedushah* verses and follows the geonic position espoused by another of his teachers, R. Yitzḥak of Dampierre, which requires their total omission. He argues against *Masekhet Soferim* and gives priority to the talmudic category of the *davar shebikedushah*.[149] Here, too, we know that the author of the *Manhig* was influenced not only by the early kabbalah of his native Provence, but also by the northern French traditions of R. Yitzḥak of Dampierre and by the Spanish mystics he met later in life.[150]

In northern Spain during this period of the late twelfth and early thirteenth centuries, we find a similar situation. R. Yehudah b"R. Yakar, a Provençal student of the leading kabbalist R. Yitzḥak Sagi Nahor, son of the Ravad, moved to Spain as a young man, where he wrote his kabbalistic liturgical commentary. His discussion of the *kedushah deyotzer* clearly depicts the human *kedushah* as paralleling the angelic liturgy, even though it is just a description of it. Much of

---

poses. There is all too little research devoted to the kabbalistic understandings of prayer. See also Elliot Wolfson, "Mystical and Theurgical Dimensions of Prayer in *Sefer Ha-Rimmon*," in *Approaches to Ancient Judaism in Medieval Times*, vol. III, ed. David R. Blumenthal (Atlanta: Scholars Press, 1988), 41-79; and his publication of this text, *The Book of the Pomegranate: Moses de Leon's Sefer Ha-Rimmon* (Atlanta: Scholar's Press, 1988). De Leon's commentary on the *kedushah deyotzer* on pp. Heb. 72-73 insists that the individual may not recite this prayer because the human recitation is bound to the actual angelic praise and acts with it.

146. See above, p. 209, n. 65, about the confusion over the Ravad's stance regarding the *kedushah desidra*.

147. The clearest citation of this tradition appears in חידושי הר"ן לרבינו נסים על מסכתות מגילה ומועד קטן, מא. This Rabbenu Nissim was a student of Naḥmanides, and is not identical to the Ran whose comments are published with the Rif. See too: נמוקי יוסף על מסכתות מגילה ופסחים, פ.; ר' שמעון בר צמח, ספר תשב"ץ, סי' סו (שאלה), עמ' יד:; ספר אורחות חיים, דין קדושה דמיושב, סי' א', עמ' 24

148. Gershom Scholem, *Kabbalah* (N.P.: The Jewish Publication Society of America, Quadrangle/The New York Times Book Co., 1974), 43; Joseph Dan, "Introduction," in *The Early Kabbalah*, ed. Joseph Dan (New York, Mahwah, Toronto: Paulist Press, 1986), 31.

149. ed. Raphael, I:63. See Raphael's introduction, 16f. for a list of R. Avraham b"R. Natan's teachers.

150. Raphael's introduction, 19, 29.

what he says echoes themes raised in the *Sefer HaEshkol*, but his conclusion is novel. He asserts that one can prove that the individual may not recite the *kedushah deyotzer*, because when one is *pores al shema*, i.e., when one repeats elements of the service for people who come late, one recites just the *yotzer* benediction because of its *kedushah*, and not the second benediction before *shema* or the *shema* itself–which the individual has been able to recite alone. This existing custom, which has, in the medieval world, assumed the name of the long-forgotten mishnaic ceremony, would not include the *yotzer* were individuals permitted to recite its *kedushah* on their own.[151] Curiously, R. Yehudah b"R. Yakar justifies his restrictive stance not by talmudic or geonic precedents, but by the very existence of the custom that had developed to compensate for the ritual benefits denied individuals because of the restrictions on their recitation of the *kedushah deyotzer*! We can assume, though, that without a modern sense of history, R. Yehudah b"R. Yakar simply assumed that his contemporary *perisat shema* was that of the Mishnah and that the ritual had always existed. In the preserved writings of R. Yehudah b"R. Yakar's student, Naḥmanides, we find only a remark in passing that the individual does not recite the *kedushah deyotzer* or any *kedushah* without a minyan.[152] However, R. Yehudah b"R. Yakar's ingenious and convoluted argument proving that the *kedushah deyotzer* requires a minyan from the inclusion of the *kedushah deyotzer* in the *perisat shema* for the latecomer reappears in elaborate development in the commentary of one of Naḥmanides' students, a R. Nissim.[153]

In contrast, Rabbi Yonah of Gerona, another influential rabbi of probable kabbalist leanings, permitted private recitation. Understood by Joseph Dan to have been among those Geronese kabbalists who heeded R. Yitzḥak Sagi Nahor's admonition to avoid writing kabbalist works so as to maintain the esoteric nature of their knowledge, R. Yonah included so few kabbalist allusions in his works that many, wrongly, do not consider him a kabbalist at all.[154] Be that as it may, in his discussion of the *kedushah deyotzer* recorded by his stu-

151. פירוש התפלות והברכות, חלק א',כה–כו.

152. See: חידושי הרמב"ן על מסכת ברכות, דף א', עמ' ב–ג.

153. To the Rif, *Megillah* 13b. Scholars cannot identify him precisely, but generally agree that he is not R. Nissim Gerondi, the author of most of the rest of this commentary.

154. *The Early Kabbalah*, 35. Dan claims that R. Yonah's works are totally lacking in such allusions. However, Moshe Idel, *Kabbalah, New Perspectives* (New Haven and London: Yale University Press, 1988), 297, n. 113 cites a passage from R. Yonah's *Shaarei HaAvodah* (Bnei-Brak, 1967), 58, that includes clear kabbalistic content. He also discusses epistles sent from R. Yitzḥak Sagi Nahor to R. Yonah on kabbalistic matters (p. 22). There can be no question, then, of R. Yonah's involvement in mystical speculation. For sources omitting this side of his life, see Ephraim Kupfer, "Jonah ben Abraham Gerondi," *Encyclopedia Juda-*

dents,[155] R. Yonah is specifically responding to and rebutting the kabbalists' concerns about private recitation of this sanctification.

He begins by acknowledging their major halakhic argument, that this *kedushah* is a *davar shebikedushah.*[156] He then presents the opposing view with a paraphrase of *Masekhet Soferim*, specifically excluding the *kedushah deyotzer* from the category of *davar shebikedushah.* He attributes that view to the French rabbis and a few "Geonim"–whose precise identity can be only a subject of speculation, since we have no direct literary evidence of such an approach from them. But R. Yonah studied in the Tosafist academy of Rabbis Moshe and Shmuel ben Shneur of Evreux and with the Provençal R. Shlomo b. Avraham of Montpellier. He thus must have had first-hand knowledge of their teachings and minhagim. At any rate, R. Yonah's students commented that his opinion tended to follow the *Masekhet Soferim* position, which he buttressed by establishing that the *gemara*'s ruling regarding "every *davar shebikedushah*" cannot refer to everything that has sanctity, for a most sanctified part of Jewish liturgy, the *shema* itself, does not require a minyan. The *gemara* refers only to the specified list of prayers to be said with a minyan, and the *shema* and *kedushah deyotzer* are not among them. He argues that actual minhag did not support any restriction on the individual's recitation of the *kedushah deyotzer.* Indeed, he observed that in actual prayerbooks, this *kedushah* appears in every text of the *yotzer* blessing written for the individual, something not true of the *kedushah* of the *amidah*, which all agree requires ten men.

However valiant his attempts to justify actual minhag, R. Yonah does not succeed in constructing a convincing argument against the standard kabbalist invocation of *davar shebikedushah.* He fails to consider the Mishnah's term *pores al shema*, which clearly is relevant to a discussion of the application of the rules

---

*ica*, X:179-181; *The Rishonim...*, ed. Hersh Goldwurm (Brooklyn: Mesorah Publications, Ltd., 1982), 87-88.

155. To the Rif, *Berakhot* 13a-b.

156. The citation of R. Yonah in *Orḥot Ḥayyim*, *Din Kedushuh Meyushav*, 24, #1, adds to this account of the positions of other authorities that if the individual does recite the *kedushah*, he is sentenced to death by fire. Therefore, the Men of the Great Assembly (!) established the abbreviated text that includes just the first word of each verse and omits the intervening liturgy. It is difficult to know for sure whether the *Orḥot Ḥayyim* knew a more extensive version of R. Yonah's comments, or whether he interpolated other materials at this point. The text does not identify the end of his citation from R. Yonah, but his inclusion of a citation from the Rashba, R. Yonah's student, as differing from R. Yonah, indicates that many of the additions may indeed be later interpolations not original to R. Yonah's discussion. Thus, we cannot assume that the material that the *Orḥot Ḥayyim* cites from the Ravad, Maimonides and his son, and the *Eshkol* were originally part of the tradition of R. Yonah.

of minyan to the *shema* and its blessings. And one wonders if he really would have removed *barekhu* and kaddish from the list of those prayers requiring a minyan–which would be the logical extension of his argument.

Although R. Yonah was widely cited, only Abudarham[157] includes his attempt to exclude the *kedushah deyotzer* from the *davar shebikedushah* category. R. Yonah's impact on the halakhic traditions of Spain and Provence thus seems to have been slight, perhaps because in the century after his death, the center of the debate over our issue did indeed move to Spain, and the authorities around which any discussion centered changed dramatically. On the one hand, Spanish kabbalah came into its own increasingly under the leadership of R. Yonah's colleague, Naḥmanides, who remained firmly in the tradition of opposition to recitation of the *kedushah* by the individual. The major literary summation of Spanish mystical thinking, the Zohar, as we have seen,[158] also limited recitation of Hebrew *kedushah* verses to the public setting. On the other hand, the arrival of the Rosh and the Baal Haturim, both of whom stood firmly, on this matter, in the camp of R. Meir of Rothenburg, brought with them a strong halakhic precedent to permit the private recitation. Many of those who cite R. Yonah do so primarily as an explication of the position stated rather briefly in the *Tur.*

Before turning fully to the Spanish schools, we must return briefly to the late traditions of Provence, where we find comments on our problem in the works both of the Meiri and in the *Sefer Orḥot Ḥayyim* of R. Aharon Hakohen of Lunel. We know that the Meiri opposed Naḥmanides' attempt to impose Spanish Catalonian customs on the Provençal community and that he was in contact with R. Yonah of Gerona, although it is not clear that he actually studied with him.[159] As far as I am aware, there is no evidence for the Meiri's involvement in mysticism; on the contrary, he supported and himself engaged in the study of philosophy and secular subjects. These pursuits correspond with his firmly granting permission, based on the precedents of *Masekhet Soferim* and Maimonides' responsum, to the individual to recite the *kedushah deyotzer.*[160]

In the case of R. Aharon Hakohen of Lunel,[161] there is even less information

157. *Abudarham Hashalem*, 74.

158. Above, p. 210.

159. Israel Ta-Shma, "Meiri, Menahem ben Solomon," *Encyclopedia Judaica*, XI: 1257-1259.

160. בית הבחירה על מסכת ברכות..., 76; בית הבחירה על מסכת מגילה..., 76.

161. ספר ארחות חיים (ירושלים, 1955), דין קדושה דמיושב, א, עמ' 24; ספר כל בו, ח, עמ' ג דף א. According to Shlomo Zalman Havlin, "Aaron ben Jacob Ha-Kohen of Lunel," *Encyclopedia Judaica*, II:13, the *Kol Bo* is most likely an earlier draft of the *Orḥot Ḥayyim*, rather than an abbreviation of it, as some have asserted.

about his involvement in mysticism or philosophy, except that he knew well the works of his contemporaries, including the Rashba (see below) and others who were indeed involved in mysticism. In his long encyclopedic work *Orḥot Ḥayyim* his views on our issue are somewhat ambiguous because of the number of contradictory interpolations he has added to his basic sources: Rabbenu Yonah; a discussion of Maimonides' contradictory decisions, resolved according to Abraham's report of his father's actual change of mind; and the *Eshkol*'s discussion of the omission of the third *kedushah* verse (*yimlokh*) in the *yotzer*,[162] combined with the tradition of *Masekhet Soferim*.[163] These same sources appear in his *Kol Bo*, where he clearly allows the individual to recite the *kedushah deyotzer*. We have to assume that his opinion remained unchanged in the later, larger *Orḥot Ḥayyim*, the last work of the Provençal school, written on Spanish territory after R. Aharon's expulsion with the rest of his compatriots from France in 1306.

The next generations of kabbalist Spanish rabbis, including students of R. Yonah, ruled fairly consistently to forbid the private recitation of the *kedushah deyotzer*. R. Shlomo ben Adret states unequivocally that it falls into the category of a *davar shebikedushah*, that Maimonides' *Mishneh Torah* carries halakhic authority over his responsa, and that, in any case, one may not rule according to *Masekhet Soferim* when it contradicts the *gemara*. Further, he objects even to the custom of those who find some substitute method of reciting the angelic liturgy as biblical verses, along the lines of the accepted geonic compromise for the *kedushah desidra*.[164] He summarizes his extreme conservatism on this matter, saying:

ואנחנו אין אומרין אותה כלל וכל דבר שכיוצא בו הנכון שבהן לנהוג בו במניעה דשב ואל תעשה שאני.

We do not say it at all, and in any similar matter, it is proper to act with

162. The *Eshkol* itself does not apply this discussion directly to the question of the individual's recitation of the *kedushah deyotzer*.

163. This may be an indirect citation of the work of his contemporary, about whom little is known, R. Natan b"R. Yehudah, in his work, *Sefer Hamaḥkim*, ed. Freimann, 9, whom Havlin, *EJ* II:13, indicates is cited without attribution in the *Orḥot Ḥayyim*. (See Freimann's introduction, xviii-xix.) According to Freimann, ix, R. Natan b"R. Yehudah was the student of R. Yitzḥak b"R. Todros, known for his kabbalist writings. In any case, these are the first medieval rabbis to emphasize *Masekhet Soferim*'s requirement that the individual have reached the age of thirteen before reciting this *kedushah* when alone.

164. *Shut Harashba* V:7. see above, p. 206.

> restraint, on the principle of "sit and do nothing"[165] (in matters of doubt like this).[166]

Students of the Rashba, and his students' students were loyal to his opinion. R. Yom Tov ibn Asevilli (Ritva) explicitly refutes the position of R. Yonah and presents instead a recapitulation of the arguments of R. Yehudah b"R. Yakar and the Ran, which claim that the discussion of *perisat shema* in *P. Megillah* 4:4, 75a precludes any recitation of the *kedushah deyotzer* by the individual.[167] R. Ḥayyim b"R. Shmuel ben David of Tudela, in his code *Tzror Haḥayyim*, follows the Rashba exclusively here.[168] Rabbenu Yeruḥam, a student of the Rashba's student, also invokes the authority of his unnamed teacher in this matter to refute arguments to the contrary, which, as we shall see, were becoming increasingly influential in the mid-fourteenth century.[169]

Before turning to these other arguments, though, it is important to recognize that these later kabbalists may well have already known the Zohar–and certainly knew some of the traditions from which Moshe de Leon drew. As we saw above in the discussion of the *kedushah desidra*, the Zohar[170] rules against the recitation of any Hebrew *kedushah* verses by the individual, based on its novel interpretation that the talmudic dictum, "Two/twice the [Hebrew] Scripture, one/once the [Aramaic] translation," refers to the size of the community in which such verses may be uttered. Because of the firm line of demarcation in Spain at this time between esoteric and exoteric lore, we cannot expect that sages, in their practical halakhic rulings, would make any overt reference to the Zohar. However, the Rashba and his students were kabbalists, and we may assume that their mystic inclinations did influence their halakhic stance in matters of dispute where the Zohar and kabbalah had something to say. Whether or not the label *davar shebikedushah* has any special significance in Spanish mystic traditions, it was a convenient halakhic category in which to cast their objections to the individual's recitation of the Hebrew *kedushah* verses.

---

165. *B. Berakhot* 20a; *B. Yevamot* 90a. Neither locus deals with matters relevant here.

166. *Shut Harashba*, I:7; compare also his novellae to *Berakhot* 21b and *Megillah* 23b, which discuss *pores al shema* as a separate ritual for latecomers that still requires a minyan because of its inclusion of the *kedushah*.

167. חידושי הריטב"א, ברכות, קכט–קל; מגילה, קעב–קעג. The Yerushalmi discussion establishes that there is no difference in the requirement of a minyan for *perisat shema* and *amidah*.

168. p. 5.

169. ספר תולדות אדם וחוה, נתיב ג', חלק ג.

170. II:132b-133a. In the text before and after what I have cited above, the Zohar also elaborates on the cosmic effects of the properly recited *kedushah*. If one were to recite the *kedushah* improperly, it is implied, these effects might go awry.

In 1306, R. Asher ben Yeḥiel (the Rosh) arrived in Spain with his family, including his son R. Yaakov, the Baal Haturim. The leading disciple and successor of R. Meir of Rothenburg, the Rosh, and his son after him, promulgated the rulings of his teacher and of the Tosafist schools in Spain. Therefore, at the same time that the Rashba and his students were ruling unequivocally against the private recitation of the *kedushah deyotzer*–ostensibly as a *davar shebikedushah*, but more probably because of mystical concerns–these world-renowned German sages were permitting it, arguing from *Masekhet Soferim* that it was merely a description of the angelic praise of God and involved no direct human act of sanctification.[171] We cannot fully explain why Rabbi Meir and his disciples, steeped in the lore of the Ḥasidei Ashkenaz,[172] allowed private recitation. Most likely their own traditions of halakhic authority, the existence in Spain of a significant tradition to permit it, and a minhag among the non-kabbalist majority not to differentiate between their prayers in private and in communal settings (as documented by Rabbenu Yonah), all contributed to the Asherides' halakhic decisions.

That these factors may indeed have been significant can be sensed in the non-mystical and influential liturgical commentary of R. David Abudarham, a student of the Baal Haturim, which was apparently written during his teacher's lifetime.[173] As we have seen in our discussions of *piyyut*, Abudarham does at times follow his teacher very closely. Here, though, rather than citing the brief comment of the *Tur*, he quotes instead the full comment of Rabbenu Yonah (as we have noted on p. 229). The final halakhic statement is no different, but he is able, in this way, to discuss more fully the various opinions current in his world and to refute directly the claim that the *kedushah deyotzer* is a *davar shebikedushah*.[174] In addition, he repeats Rabbenu Yonah's argument that no written prayer texts provide a separate text for the individual to recite in the

171. Rosh, *Berakhot* 3:18, *Megillah* 3:7; תוספות הרא"ש לרבינו אשר ב"ר יחיאל, מסכת ברכות, מב–מג. Note that the Rosh does not explicitly cite *Masekhet Soferim*, and that, while he does acknowledge other opinions, he neither discusses the reasoning behind them nor argues against them. Rather, he simply states his own opinion and why it makes sense. The *Tur*, OH 59, after acknowledging Maimonides' and Rav Natronai's rulings against the individual's recitation, cites his father, buttressing the Rosh's words with a direct, if abbreviated, citation from *Masekhet Soferim*.

172. See, for instance, the *Tur*'s numerological introductions to various prayers in OH.

173. *Abudarham Hashalem*, 73-74.

174. Abudarham clarifies somewhat the language of Rabbenu Yonah's argument on this matter, making a stronger case by distinguishing clearly between a technical *davar shebikedushah* as specified in the Mishnah, which must be recited in a minyan, and a דבר שיש בו קדושה (a matter that has intrinsic sanctity) like the *shema* (and the *kedushah deyotzer* and *kedushah desidra*) which may be recited by the individual.

*yotzer*. We have to assume that, if Abudarham repeats this statement without comment, he was accurately describing the prayerbooks common to the Jews of fourteenth-century Castile.[175]

In contrast, the traditions available to us from the growing Sefardi diaspora from the late fourteenth century and later all come from known mystics and, true to form, all object to the individual's recitation of the *kedushah deyotzer*. The existence of weighty halakhic opinions on both sides of the issue, combined with a popular minhag that contradicted the stricter ruling of the kabbalists, indicate that even after centuries of debate, this was still a very real question. People still turned to the leading rabbis of their generations for guidance, as can be seen in the continuing discussions in the responsa literature. Although it might be suggested that regional differences had developed in Spain between the Catalonian schools, which followed the more mystically oriented traditions of Naḥmanides and the Rashba, and the Castilian schools, which followed the authority of the Rosh and the *Tur*, the evidence is insufficient to support such a conclusion. Indeed, that among those forbidding the individual's recitation is Rabbenu Yeruḥam, who spent the latter half of his life in Toledo and who studied with the Rosh, as well as, more intensively, with R. Avraham ben Yishmael, himself a student of the Rashba, gives some indication that these halakhic traditions were not regional or reflections of regional realities.[176]

Two responsa from the fifteenth and sixteenth centuries directly confront our issue. The earlier is that of R. Shimon ben Tzemaḥ Duran, who identified himself as a kabbalist and cited the Zohar directly in his various writings.[177] His correspondents were confused by the contradictory traditions of Maimonides, as well as by some French traditions for which I have found no other evidence. The Rashbatz answers in the language of the Rashba, pointing out that later rabbis consider the *Mishneh Torah* to be the source of halakhic authority and hence they follow Maimonides' original position. Further, one may not over-

175. Although not drawing directly upon this tradition, R. Yosef Ḥaviva, in the early fifteenth century, also seems to accept the individual's recitation of the *kedushah deyotzer*, based on the authority of the Ravad and *Masekhet Soferim*. Although little is known about him, it would seem highly possible that he was not a kabbalist, for he was a student of the Ran along with the Rivash, both of whom were known to oppose kabbalah. He was also a student of R. Ḥasdai Crescas, the philosopher. See his נמוקי יוסף על מסכתות מגילה ופסחים, פ. For biographical data, see Yehoshua Horowitz, "Ḥabiba, Joseph," *Encyclopedia Judaica*, VII: 1026 and *The Rishonim...*, 109.

176. Scholars have yet to identify the precise provenance of the few existing Spanish prayerbook manuscripts, a necessary task before we can buttress this observation with actual liturgical customs.

177. H. J. Zimmels, "Duran, Simeon ben Ẓemaḥ," *Encyclopedia Judaica*, VI:304.

rule, on the basis of *Masekhet Soferim*, the Talmud's inclusion of *pores al shema* as a ritual requiring a minyan. Like the Rashba, he concludes: ובכיוצא בזה הממעט הרי זה משובח דשב ואל תעשה שאני (In matters like this, it is best to take the cautious position, on the principle of "sit and do nothing").[178] The Rashbatz's direct commentary on the issue in *Berakhot* makes much the same argument, but adds that the French rabbis, as a result of this halakhic stance, called either for the omission of the actual *kedushah* verses–substituting just their first words and enough transitional liturgy to indicate that the *ofanim* say the second verse–or for the full omission of any reference to the verses altogether.[179]

Similarly, in the sixteenth-century responsum of R. David ben Shlomo ibn Zimra,[180] the correspondent is also confused by the variety of opinions passed down. The Radbaz also rules according to the tradition of the Rashba, cited here by name, but he adds the authority of the mystical vision of R. Yaakov of Marvège. Particularly of interest to us is the correspondent's comment that it is the Sefardi custom for individuals to recite these verses. Since we know nothing about this correspondent, we cannot place him in any specific Spanish community. But it is curious that in spite of his statement about common custom and the Radbaz's ruling against it, the Radbaz makes no effort to enlighten his correspondent as to how to conduct private prayer without the *kedushah deyotzer*.

Unlike the Geonim, the Ashkenazi rabbis, and some of the Italian and Provençal sages who forbade individuals to recite the *kedushah deyotzer*, many of the Spanish rabbis did not bother with the necessary corollary to their halakhic stance–providing an alternative prayer text.[181] This omission severely limited the practicality of their rulings, especially given the wide range of alternatives available in the literature. The Ritva and Rabbenu Yeruḥam are the only two Sefardi sages whose explicit but differing directions have been pre-

---

178. ר' שמעון בר צמח, ספר תשב"ץ, חלק שלישי, סי' סו, עמ' יד:.

179. פירוש הרשב"ץ על ברכות, קכה–ו. See the appendix for the actual liturgical text. Note that this attribution to the French rabbis is directly contradicts Rabbenu Yonah's widely cited statement of the French position. Does the Rashbatz really mean the Provençal rabbis or Tosafists like the Ri Hazaken? These are also not the same French rabbis referred to by the Rashbatz's correspondent in his responsum, for those French rabbis permitted the individual to recite the *kedushah deyotzer*, based on an obscure argument based on the permission given (to the individual?) to recite the *piyyut* inserted into this prayer. The reference to this French responsum is too truncated to enable us to understand it fully.

180. שו"ת הרדב"ז, חלק ד', סי' אלף סד (י), ב, עמ' א–ב.

181. See, however, my discussion below of the responsa of the Rashba as they appear in the *Beit Yosef*, p. 238f.

served;[182] but later authorities cite the prayer texts of neither source. Thus it would seem that, unlike the German communities, who were presented with too many alternative texts, the Spanish communities were essentially given none. In both cases this made it nearly impossible for halakhic theory to impact significantly on popular custom.

This reality notwithstanding, the authority of the Zohar and its explicit ruling against recitation of the Hebrew *kedushah* outside the communal setting continued to weigh heavily on the halakhic authorities who engaged in kabbalah. Two sixteenth-century sources deal with this issue directly. The first, the *Tolaat Yaakov*, the commentary on the prayerbook of R. Meir ibn Gabbai,[183] provides insight into the type of thinking behind the various halakhically couched positions of the kabbalists on our issue. He discusses the mystic significance of the inclusion of the *kedushah* in the *yotzer*, saying:

> ...ולטעם זה נתקנה הקדושה ביוצר להורות כי סדר תפלתנו סודר כפי הסדר העליון וזו היא כוונת הנביאים מסדרי התפלות ואמר קדוש וברוך פי' קדוש למעלה וברוך למטה כי הוא הגן הצריך השקאה
>
> ...for this reason the *kedushah* was established in the *yotzer*: to teach that our prayers are organized according to the order above [in the divine realm]. This was the intention of the prophets who organized the prayers. One says *kadosh* and *barukh*; *kadosh* has impact above [in the higher *sefirot*? in the realm of the *sefirot*?], and *barukh* has impact below [on the lower *sefirot*? on earth?[184]] for this [lower region] is the garden that requires watering [by the flowing down of emanation from the upper realms].

Having established this understanding, Ibn Gabbai continues in a purely halakhic vein to reject arguments based on *Masekhet Soferim* and to rule according to the *Mishneh Torah* and the Zohar. He then explains that we present the *kedushah deyotzer* as a description of the angelic liturgy not because of any intrinsic difference between it and the *kedushah* of the *amidah*, but because, until we have ourselves recited the *amidah*, we cannot consider ourselves worthy of

182. חידושי הריטב"א על הש"ס, מגילה, קעב–ג; ספר תולדות אדם וחוה, נתיב השלישי, חלק השלישי. We must exclude such sources as the Rashbatz, who buttresses his own objections to the individual's recitation of the *kedushah deyotzer* by citing two *different* "French" traditions. We also have to assume that authorities who cite geonic and German sources for substitute texts, but rule against them, like the Rosh and the *Tur*, did not inspire anyone to recite these substitutions, which they deemed unnecessary.

183. 13b-c.

184. The second readings in these two translations/interpretations may be more accurate, for the Zohar II:133a speaks specifically of Israel's being sanctified through all the liturgical *kedushot*.

being counted among the angels. We phrase the *kedushah deyotzer* differently, then, only out of modesty.

The massive upheavals caused by the expulsion from Spain created a need for a more comprehensive, up-to-date, and universally accepted legal code. At the same time the emergence of kabbalah as a ubiquitous force in the Jewish world necessitated a resolution of tensions between the now crystallized positions of the mystic and non-mystic camps. It seems that the vast majority of the Jewish world did not follow the theoretical halakhic stance advocated by the mystics. But to the kabbalists, improperly performed prayer had drastic negative effects on the upper realms, and this situation was intolerable.[185] Our second source, the great codifier of Jewish law and active mystic, Joseph Karo, creatively solved this dilemma, and his solution quickly found universal acceptance. Indeed, after his *Beit Yosef* and *Shulḥan Arukh* were published, discussion of our issue essentially ceases.

What was Karo's solution? In the *Beit Yosef*,[186] he works out the problem at great length, first reviewing the various halakhic rulings on both sides of the issue, even though his primary authorities, his "pillars of halakhah," actually do agree.[187] He had no received ruling of the Rif, and the Rosh allows the individual to recite the *kedushah deyotzer*, as does Maimonides in his responsum and in his documented personal practice. Karo knows this responsum or the tradition of R. Abraham Maimon regarding his father's practice only second hand, but he never indicates, as others did, that one should continue to consider the *Mishneh Torah* authoritative in this matter. Therefore, based on the rulings of the Rosh and Maimonides, Karo could simply have declared the *kedushah deyotzer* permitted for the individual and have gone no further.[188]

His "pillars of halakhah," however, did not deal with the tradition of the kabbalists. Therefore, he summarizes the arguments of many of the Sefardi authorities discussed above,[189] with the addition of the Provençal *Manhig*, *Orḥot Ḥayyim*, and *Kol Bo*. His only source of Ashkenazi tradition, other than that

185. See Daniel C. Matt, "The Mystic and the Mizwot," in *Jewish Spirituality from the Bible through the Middle Ages*, ed. Arthur Green (New York: Crossroad, 1989), 386-388, for a discussion of this idea in terms of the entire system of mitzvah observance in the Zohar.

186. OH 59. His discussion in the *Kesef Mishneh* is less elaborate, but does not contradict what he says here.

187. For a concise summary and discussion of Karo's methodology for determining the halakhah, as outlined in his introduction to his *Beit Yosef*, see Menaḥem Elon, *Jewish Law...*, III:1316-1319.

188. This is the implication of R. Moshe Isserles' comment here in his *Darkei Moshe*.

189. Plus Yitzḥak Aboav, whose work is lost.

brought by the Asherides to Spain, is the *Agur*, his source for the Tosafist tradition preserved in *Shibbolei Haleket* debating substitute texts for the individual to recite. In this section, he does not refer to the rulings of Naḥmanides, the Rashba, or the Mordekhai, all of whom we have discussed above, and all of whom, according to his theoretical plan, should have constituted the next level of authority for determining the law.[190] While the traditions of Naḥmanides and the Mordekhai on our question are not part of larger discussions, are not widely cited, and may simply have been unknown to Karo, this is not the case with the ruling of the Rashba. Instead of following his pre-ordained methodology, Karo chose here to deviate–allowing him to cite the Rashba alone and at length, not as an independent authority from whom halakhah may be derived, but as a support for his own independent position in the matter.

Having acknowledged both sides of the halakhic dispute, Karo then acknowledges that the universal custom follows Rabbenu Yonah and the Rosh–that is, even children, contrary to the limitation of *Masekhet Soferim*, recite the *kedushah deyotzer* outside of the communal context. He contrasts that custom with the ruling of the Zohar, which he cites in full, that no Hebrew *kedushah* may be recited by an individual, and concludes:

> ואע"פ שהעולם נהגו לומר קדושת יוצר ביחיד נלע"ד שמאחר שאין דבר זה מפורש בתלמוד יש לנו לתפוס כדברי הזוהר.
>
> Even though it is a universal custom for individuals to recite the *kedushah deyotzer*, it appears, in my humble opinion, that since the matter is not explicitly decided in the Talmud, we should follow the words of the Zohar.[191]

As support, Karo finally cites the Rashba and his unequivocal ruling that the individual should not recite the words of the *kedushah* under any circumstances.[192] However, having made clear his theoretical stance, Karo then deals with reality. The Rashba, after asserting that the Talmud has absolute authority over *Masekhet Soferim* and before stating his final ruling in this responsum, had entertained the possibility of private recitation, saying:

---

190. Elon, *Jewish Law…*, 1317, citing Karo's introduction to his *Beit Yosef.* Karo does cite the Ran here, in a position that agrees with that printed in our editions of the Rif. However, as noted above, the attribution of this commentary on *Megillah* to the Ran is considered erroneous.

191. That this is characteristic of Karo's use of the Zohar in such cases has been demonstrated by Yaakov Katz, "יחסי הלכה וקבלה בדורות 'התגלות' הזוהר," הלכה וקבלה (ירושלים: מאגנס, תשמ"ו), 69–68.

192. *Shut Harashba* I:7.

ושמעתי משמן של גדולי החכמים שאותה קדושה שביוצר כיון שהוא מזכיר סדר קדושות שמלאכי השרת אומרים אם בא לאומרה כקורא במקרא בנעימה אומר.

I have heard in the name of influential sages that because the *kedushah deyotzer* mentions the sanctifications recited by the ministering angels, if one happens to recite [the verses] in the manner in which one reads Scripture with [its] cantillation, one may recite them.[193]

Although the Rashba ends up absolutely rejecting this possible mode of individual recitation, Karo omits the refutation and cites yet another responsum of the Rashba that uses the precedent of recitation of the *ofanim* and *kedushah* verses in their scriptural mode as a justification for private recitation of another *davar shebikedushah*, the "Thirteen Attributes of God." However, once again, the original responsum does not allow a private liturgical recitation of the "Thirteen Attributes," for they are like a *davar shebikedushah* and require a minyan. The permission to recite them "as one recites the *ofanim* and *kedushah* verses" seems more a nod to actual minhag than the Rashba's own ruling.[194] In any case, Karo is the first of all the sages to consider these particular statements of the Rashba significant.

Having "established" the Rashba's "support" for some alternative means by which the individual may recite the *kedushah* verses, Karo draws upon other

---

193. The responsum of the Rashba, as we have received it, adds another phrase: שאין זה אלא כיחיד שקורא פרשת סדר קדושת המלאכים בישעיה (for this is just like an individual who reads the chapter describing the sanctification of the angels in Isaiah).

194. *Shut Harashba* I:211. It is also not entirely clear that the Rashba here refers to the *kedushah deyotzer*. *Ofanim*, the name of a group of heavenly beings that recite the verse *barukh*, is the subject of the text recited between the *kedushah* verses. Many texts calling for the omission of the *kedushah* omit these words too–but not as an independent entity, with its own sanctity. I am not aware of anyone who specifically calls for the omission of these words. The referent of this term, then, is vague. "*Kedushah* verses," could apply, of course, to the *kedushah desidra*, where recitation of the verses in non-liturgical mode had found broad acceptance very early. It is possible that the Rashba simply used the term "*ofanim*" here as a label for the *kedushah deyotzer*.

A third responsum, *Shut Harashba* V:9, is also relevant to this issue. Here, the Rashba reaffirms his position that the individual is not to recite any *kedushah* without the presence of a minyan. But according to the long-standing (geonic) precedent, he does allow recitation of the verses of the *kedushah desidra* as long as they are recited with their cantillation, like one reading the Prophets in school. Then he adds: מ"מ נראה לי שאם בא לומר בין ביוצר בין בסדר קדושה בלשון תרגום אומר ואינו נמנע (In any case, it appears to me that if, whether in the *yotzer* or whether in the *kedushah desidra*, [the individual] recites the verses in Aramaic, he can do so without hesitation). This is yet another alternative; it is evident that in these responsa, the Rashba was searching without great success for an acceptable bridge between his halakhic stance and common practice.

authorities who have provided such alternatives. The *Hagahot Maimoniot*[195] had cited the custom of those who did not want to recite the various *devarim shebikedushah* as individuals and substituted the various talmudic passages in which the responses occur, allowing them to say the words in a non-liturgical context. What Karo omits here, because it would defeat his purposes, is the conclusion of the *Hagahot Maimoniot*'s comment, which states clearly that all this is unnecessary in light of *Masekhet Soferim*'s permission to the individual to recite the *kedushah deyotzer.* But Karo recognizes that the origins of this idea of a non-liturgical recitation of the words of the *kedushah* lie in Rav Tzemaḥ Gaon's responsum about the *kedushah desidra*, which he cites from the *Sefer Hapardes.*[196] Finally, Karo cites the *Terumat Hadeshen*, which directs the individual to recite the *kedushah deyotzer* and the *kedushah desidra* with melody and trope.[197] Indicating that this is a suitable way for the individual to avoid reciting a liturgical *kedushah*, he adds, as an afterthought, a reference to the alternative passages found in the *Rokeaḥ.*

To be sure, Karo's solution to his inherited conundrum had precedent. There is no question that some Jews must have been advocating an extension of the method of Rav Tzemaḥ Gaon's responsum to the *kedushah deyotzer* as early as the time of the Ravyah, whom the *Hagahot Maimoniot* cites without attribution. We know from the inclusion of alternative texts in the *Rokeaḥ* that in the world of early Ashkenaz there were those who sought to provide individuals with some means of articulating the words they could not recite liturgically. But no single text, unless we include the late and rather off-hand comment of the *Terumat Hadeshen*, actually advocated such a compromise in a halakhic discussion of our problem. Indeed, the later Ashkenazi traditions themselves deemed such attempts purposeless, as they accepted the authority of *Masekhet Soferim* in this matter where the Talmud made no clear statement.[198] In Spain, and

195. *Hilkhot Tefillah* 7:17. This tradition, like most of the traditions of the school of R. Meir of Rothenberg on our issue, can be traced back to the Ravyah (5-6, #2).

196. I have not been able to locate this in the *Sefer Hapardes* ascribed to Rashi; it does, however, appear in *Maḥzor Vitry*, 25-26, #46.

197. חלק ראשון: שאלות ותשובות, סי' ח. This responsum is curiously like the responsum Karo cites from the Rashba. Its primary question has to do, not with the *kedushah*, but with the recitation of God's "Thirteen Attributes." Isserlein rules that, although the individual may recite this passage, it is best if he does so with melody and trope as if reading in the Torah. As an afterthought, he adds that he saw written somewhere that this applies too to the *kedushah deyotzer* and the *kedushah desidra.* Was the composition that he saw a collection of the responsa of the Rashba? The evidence of the Maharil and the *Agur* (see above, p. 223) suggests that such senses of substitution were no longer considered necessary in Ashkenaz.

198. See R. Moshe Isserles' *Darkhei Moshe* on Karo's discussion here. Isserles also objects to Karo's attempt to rule according to the Zohar and against *Masekhet Soferim* when the estab-

among the Sefardi kabbalists, though, the problem persisted. The Rashba was clearly aware of attempts to extend the model of the *kedushah desidra* to the *kedushah deyotzer*, but he was very uncomfortable with it, and we have no evidence that any later Sefardi halakhic authorities, until Karo, cited his opinion as justification for such practice.

Karo's innovation, then, was in applying this little known, possibly non-rabbinic, solution to his inherited halakhic problem. By allowing the individual to recite the *kedushah* verses in their scriptural mode, rather than with their liturgical melodies, he successfully removed most mystical concerns about an unqualified liturgical recitation of, and participation in, the angelic liturgy. At the same time, he provided individuals with a way to continue reciting what they had been reciting all along, the biblical verses that record the angelic sanctification of God. The only adjustment required was a relatively minor one of melody; no longer would Jews be asked to recite one set of words in synagogue and another, less familiar and more awkward, at home.

* * *

To insure that Jews' worship of God would be received on high with utmost favor, one obvious course was to imitate and to try to participate in the liturgy of the angels and other higher beings described in prophetic visions. From early on, though, such a course was fraught with tension: although this liturgy could undoubtedly be effective, it was also a potentially dangerous transgression of realms. Consequently, its contemplation and development was probably confined to an elite group of mystics. The resulting rabbinic ambivalence about making this lore public was reflected in the extreme reticence of the tannaitic and amoraic literature to discuss mystical matters, including this element of the liturgy. Consequently, although we can document that the *kedushah* was recited in the early amoraic synagogue, the Talmud contains no details about its meaning or specific halakhic status. This vagueness, aggravated in the cases of the barely mentioned *kedushah deyotzer* and the *kedushah desidra*, left the door open for a variety of rulings based on different understandings of the talmudic texts, *Masekhet Soferim*, and the preserved responsa of the Geonim.

In the case of the *kedushah desidra*, most later authorities found the solution of Rav Tzemaḥ Gaon satisfactory: these verses could be recited in a non-liturgical mode, thus removing this *kedushah* from the category of a *davar shebikedushah*. However, for a variety of reasons, such a solution was not readily applied to the *kedushah deyotzer*. On the one hand, no explicit geonic tradition, widely known

---

lished custom, in itself a major consideration in Ashkenazi halakhic deliberations, already follows the latter.

or otherwise, advocated this compromise. On the other hand, the ruling of *Masekhet Soferim*, if accepted, made such a compromise unnecessary; and if not accepted as authoritative, it was difficult to defend.

To be sure, these two *kedushot* are not liturgically equivalent. The *kedushah desidra* is not part of the liturgical structures strictly regulated by halakhah. It is not included in the mishnaic list of rituals requiring a minyan.[199] In addition, some rabbinic traditions trace this ritual specifically to a time when the government forbade the Jewish recitation of the *kedushah* because it objected to their comparison of themselves to angels. Consequently, worshipers waited until the authorities had left the synagogue and recited the angelic liturgy at the end of the service. After the persecution ended, they maintained the liturgical change out of a sense of thankfulness, but restored the real *kedushah* to its original place.[200] Accepting such a tradition moves the later recitation of the *kedushah desidra* one notch further from a sense that it has intrinsic sanctity.[201]

In contrast, the *kedushah deyotzer* is embedded in the first blessing preceding the recitation of *shema* in the morning–a mandatory, halakhically significant part of the liturgy. The mishnaic inclusion of *pores al shema* in its list of rituals requiring a minyan raised the real possibility, especially because the original meaning of this term had been forgotten, that it should be understood to refer not only the *barekhu* but also to the *kedushah deyotzer*. If so, these rituals fall into the category *devarim shebikedushah*. So far as later rabbis were concerned, this *kedushah* had always been part of the (communal) *yotzer*. No pre-modern traditions assign it late origins; nor do rabbinic memories exist about its Palestinian inclusion only on Sabbaths and holidays. For all these reasons, rabbis could not simply extend the leniency applied to the *kedushah desidra* to the *kedushah deyotzer*.

There are several reasons for the persistence of this halakhic dispute, which continued for centuries with ever-developing new arguments. To begin with, rab-

---

199. See, however, attempts to invest this *kedushah* with additional sanctity by tying it to the kaddish that follows it, by Yisrael Isserlein in his *Terumat Hadeshen*, Part I, #15 (cited in the *Leket Yosher*, 29.) The kaddish itself is, of course, another example of the rabbinic extension of the idea of a *davar shebikedushah*.

200. See E.E. Urbach, *Arugat Habosem*, IV:65-66, for the Ashkenazi traditions on this matter. See too Jacob Mann, "Changes in the Divine Service of the Synagogue Due to Religious Persecutions," *HUCA* 4 (1927): 267-270. From the standpoint of "objective" history, this tradition is suspect.

201. Some sources do indeed try to emphasize the significance of the *kedushah desidra* based on the tradition of *B. Sotah* 49a that, in the absence of the Temple, its recitation helped insure the continued existence of the world. However, this function does not necessarily require a minyan.

binic concerns about the legitimacy of the individual's recitation of the *kedushah deyotzer* only rarely percolated down to popular practice. These halakhic objections remained an element of the elite culture of the rabbis–the "great tradition," as described by Robert Redfield–and did not affect the "little tradition."[202] Indeed, before the widespread availability of printed prayerbooks, the average Jew did not own a siddur; normal practice was to memorize the standard prayers and to rely on the *sheliaḥ tzibbur*'s repetition for the more infrequent holiday prayers.[203] Thus, the prayer first memorized for the *yotzer* would be the version for the communal prayer setting, which in almost every known rite except the Palestinian included the *kedushah*.[204] For the average Jew, this text would be the one that came fluently. Even if he had been taught an alternative one for those occasions when he could not attend the communal synagogue service, his presumably infrequent use of such a text, its lack of communal reinforcement, and its inherent awkwardness would make it easily forgotten. Prayerbooks, where available, largely ignored the question of private recitation. Hence, the various abbreviated texts of the *yotzer* could not have found widespread use. And by the time printed prayerbooks were becoming common, rulings permitting recitation of the *kedushah deyotzer* were also increasingly accepted.

Thus, although we have to assume that Jews sometimes did pray together without a minyan,[205] rulings advocating abbreviated texts probably were only followed within the scholarly community itself. Less educated Jews, even if once taught this ruling, were probably not able to apply it immediately and consistently in a private setting. Further, the mystics' deep concern about the impact

202. Redfield writes in his *Peasant Society and Culture* (Chicago: University of Chicago Press, 1956; rpt. 1971), 41-42: "In a civilization there is a great tradition of the reflective few, and there is a little tradition of the largely unreflective many. The great tradition is cultivated in schools or temples; the little tradition works itself out and keeps itself going in the lives of the unlettered in their village communities. The tradition of the philosopher, theologian, and literary man is a tradition consciously cultivated and handed down; that of the little people is for the most part taken for granted and not submitted to much scrutiny or considered refinement and improvement."

203. For evidence of actual opposition to the use of written prayerbooks, see L. Ginzberg, *Geonica*, I:120 and the references he makes there to the medieval literature. See also Stefan C. Reif, *Judaism and Hebrew Prayer* (Cambridge: Cambridge University Press, 1993), 184f.

204. There is no evidence of a parallel halakhic dispute among Palestinian rite Jews.

205. We have to assume that most synagogues were able to gather a minyan. There is evidence, though, that in Ashkenaz, some communities had difficulties. See, for instance, אברהם גרוסמן, חכמי אשכנז הראשונים (ירושלים: מאגנס, תשמ"א), 7, 135, 299–300, and the sources he lists there. Does such a problem also lie behind the relative leniency of some Ashkenazi authorities in allowing the recitation of the *kedushah deyotzer* without the presence of a quorum at all?

of improper recitation of the angelic liturgy was driven by understandings based on esoteric knowledge that could not be divulged to the uninitiated. Mystically oriented rabbis did not disclose their full reasons or even the determinative factors for restricting the recitation of the *kedushah deyotzer* to the communal setting. Had they been more explicit in warning the populace of the dire consequences of improper participation in the sanctification of God, their rulings might have had greater effect on the prayer life of the greater community.[206]

Various traditions tried to reconcile the harsh rabbinic position with the reality of popular minhag, but none received recognition or acceptance in their own day until, in the wake of the greatest upheaval since the destruction of the Temple, Joseph Karo, largely quoting out of context, collected these traditions and used them to justify popular custom. He did not invalidate the mystic concerns; in fact, as a member of the Safed community, he was among the first to make them fully public. This enabled him to advocate a compromise like that made centuries earlier for the *kedushah desidra*. Without taking the extreme position of *Masekhet Soferim* and legitimating the individual's recitation of the *kedushah deyotzer*, he created a non-liturgical mode in which the individual could recite the *kedushah* verses privately. By removing the individual's recitation from the realm of angelic liturgy and, hence, from the realm of mystic concerns, Karo enhanced the mystical impact of the communal recitation of the *kedushah deyotzer*. In reality, of course, his dictate that individuals be careful to recite the verses in schoolhouse rather than in synagogue mode could have little practical effect. But in the chaotic aftermath of the expulsion from Spain, the practice advocated all along by popular custom was now justified by mystically influenced halakhic opinion.

206. See Stefan Reif, *Judaism and Hebrew Prayer*, 203.

# 5
# Conclusions

Because Jews understand worship to be one of the key pillars supporting their covenantal relationship with God, they want to be certain that their prayer is acceptable, that it reaches God and has beneficial effects, and that it does not transgress divine commandments and cause offense or worse in Heaven. To these ends, rabbis have struggled to define the details of proper worship, encoding these details in halakhah.

After the destruction of the Temple, most aspects of Jewish life and law could basically continue adapting to new times and places. The biblically sanctioned official worship of God, however, came to an abrupt halt. The tannaitic leadership quickly stepped in to fill this void, formalizing the status of specific prayers as the halakhically mandated forms of covenant-maintaining worship for the new situation. The details of the new liturgy derived from various oral traditions and extant customs–and not from written Scripture, which provided ample examples of verbal prayers but no models for communal covenantal prayer in the absence of sacrifices. Thus rabbinic halakhah and liturgy evolved concomitantly as Jews sought ways to penetrate the "wall of iron" cutting them off from God.

Although tannaitic and amoraic halakhic texts defined many aspects of the new liturgical system, they left much to the discretion of individual and communal customs. In some cases this was a deliberate nod to popular practice and the preservation of flexibility. In others, it reflected more the inchoate state of rabbinic liturgical development and authority and the fact that, in matters of liturgy at least, the talmudic corpus was not ready to function as a comprehensive legal code. Only as the system developed did questions emerge that led to the further definition of the requirements for acceptable worship of God.

By the time of R. Yehudai Gaon in the eighth century, the leaders of the Babylonian geonic academies were transforming their Talmud, as interpreted through their academic traditions, into the authoritative statement of the Oral Law. When the Talmud ruled or even implied a ruling in a liturgical matter, it was understood to be the halakhah. When the Talmud was vague, the legal traditions and customs of the academy theoretically carried the same authority. The Babylonian geonic traditions treated the Talmud as a code whose liturgical rulings would shape the further development of Jewish liturgy.

As time went on, however, rabbinic liturgy had to confront the tension between the ideal world of theoretical halakhic pronouncements and the actual world of popular worship, each of which considered its own ways to constitute proper worship of God. Indeed, rabbinic attempts to reconcile halakhah with minhag became a major factor shaping the halakhah itself. Only during periods of extraordinary rabbinic influence did sages successfully uproot what they considered errant customs and obtain closer adherence to theoretical halakhic standards. More often, they found ways to legitimate minhag, even when they had significant doubts about its ultimate halakhic propriety. To maintain or establish effective leadership of their communities, they could not do otherwise. Thus in matters of liturgy, rabbinic sages almost never cast themselves as prophetic voices "crying out in the wilderness,"[1] making halakhic pronouncements they knew would be disregarded.[2] Instead, the dominant mode was one of compromise.

Such compromises began early. They fill talmudic literature and account for such rulings as the permission for vernacular prayer,[3] leniency regarding the precise times of prayer,[4] the institutionalization of the abbreviated *amidah*,[5] and permission to recite *hallel* on Rosh Ḥodesh.[6] In many other instances, actual rabbinic or popular custom was the sole source of the halakhic ruling, for it was the only existing precedent. However, in the post-talmudic world, authoritative literary sources on rabbinic prayer did exist and were increasingly utilized as yardsticks by which to evaluate customs. Rabbis still searched for compromises, but now they had to find new interpretations of either the halakhah or the custom itself to make the two conform. Their abilities to do so and the directions they took were shaped by their changing understandings of acceptable prayer.

---

1. Isaiah 40:3.

2. As in the case of the Sefardi rabbis who personally objected to *piyyut* but refrained from imposing a ruling on their congregations, reasoning that it was better for the congregation to err from ignorance than deliberately to transgress a halakhic pronouncement. See above, chap. 3.

3. *Mishnah Sotah* 7:1-2; *B. Sotah* 32b-33a; *P. Sotah* 7:1, 21b.

4. *B. Berakhot* 26a, 27a, allows that even though the ideal time for the morning *amidah* is at sunrise, it may be recited until the fourth hour or even noon.

5. *Mishnah Berakhot* 4:3; *B. Berakhot* 29a; *P. Berakhot* 4:3, 8a; *P. Taanit* 2:2, 65c.

6. *B. Taanit* 28b. See also the discussion of Mark Washofsky, "Minhag and Halakhah: Toward a Model of Shared Authority on Matters of Ritual," in *Rabbinic-Lay Relations in Jewish Law*, ed. Walter Jacob and Moshe Zemer (Tel Aviv and Pittsburgh: Rodef Shalom Press, 1993), 103-107.

In the geonic world, Natronai Gaon extended the understanding of the talmudic *me'ein haberakhah* to allow for the insertion of *piyyut* pertinent to the topic of the day. Other Geonim restricted the individual, but not the community as a whole, from inserting petitions into the first and last three blessings of the *amidah*, creating a loophole that would permit the insertion into these blessings not only of the customary High Holy Day additions, but of other communally recited *piyyut* as well. Beginning in Ashkenaz, many Rishonim made sure to develop an understanding of the mishnaic distinction between long and short blessings and to allow for the elongation of the blessing texts by the insertion of poetry. These new interpretations of existing halakhic concepts were informed by rabbinic and communal understandings that *piyyut* added meaning to the endeavor of prayer and provided a source of *kavvanah*.

In the case of the *birkat betulim*, rabbis troubled by its non-talmudic status and misuse of the liturgical blessing formula changed their understanding of the blessing itself, either interpreting it as a *berakhah* for the recognized mitzvah of a man's having intercourse with his new wife, or rereading the Rosh's vague attribution of geonic origins to allow the history of the blessing to extend back to talmudic times and the authority associated with that period. Ascriptions of antiquity also limited challenges to the status of prayers like *barukh sheamar* and the *birkat hapesukim* and were a dominant element in the Tosafists' defense of their payyetanic heritage.[7] Such attempts at compromise were attractive: they prevented destructive breaches between the rabbinic leadership and the community at large and eliminated the difficult process of changing popular custom.

However, compromise was not always possible or desirable. Under certain circumstances, rabbinic authorities–utterly convinced that it was absolutely wrong and even dangerous for the community to continue in its errant ways–attempted and succeeded in overthrowing minhag. To be effective, such changes required strong leadership by a scholar of recognized authority who

---

7. We can add to this list R. Hai Gaon's references to both the *birkat betulim* and the priest's blessing at the *pidyon haben* as legitimate traditions of the academy. In the geonic world, this too was a source of authority.

Another major series of examples of rabbinic compromise with popular custom is discussed by Jacob Katz in his article, "מעריב בזמנו ושלא בזמנו – דוגמא לזיקה בין מנהג, הלכה וחברה," בתוך הלכה וקבלה: מחקרים בתולדות דת ישראל על מדוריה וזיקתה החברתית (ירושלים: מאגנס, תשמ"ו), 200–175. In addition to his general discussion of the sages' attempts to deal with the popular custom of reciting the evening *amidah* before the appropriate time for the evening *shema*, see his discussion on pp. 176-7 of the shift from the talmudic definition of the evening *amidah* as *reshut* (optional), to its geonic designation as mitzvah (commanded), as a compromise with the popular understanding that it was *ḥovah* (obligatory), like the other services.

was personally willing to risk his relationship with the community whose custom he was threatening. Often this occurred when the minhag itself had become less valued by the community or, conversely, when shifts in religious ideology influenced by the teachings of philosophical or mystical schools enhanced the value of the theoretical halakhah in the thinking of the rabbi concerned.

Among the most famous and influential halakhic authorities of the medieval world were Maimonides, the Rosh and his sons, and Joseph Karo, all of whom, in the wake of persecutions, emigrated to countries where their wisdom and knowledge brought them recognition and leadership positions, but where the dominant minhag was quite different from that of their birthplaces. As members of small immigrant families, the Maimonideans and Asherides could not realistically hope to recreate their original ritual worlds in their new homes, except, perhaps, among a small circle of family and followers. At the same time, they were often hesitant to take on new customs, especially if they found them problematic. Unable to be fully invested in their original customs and unwilling to adapt fully to the *minhag hamakom*, they tended to devalue the halakhic weight of minhag as a category and enhance the status of the strict theoretical halakhah in their rulings. The esteem in which they and their works were held, which varied from community to community, determined the effectiveness of these rulings. By and large, however, their pronouncements were turning points in the history of the development of Jewish liturgy.

Among the instances of such rulings discussed here, we should note particularly Maimonides' vehement stands against the public *birkat betulim* and against the addition of *piyyut* into the statutory blessings, both customs that assumed different forms in Egypt than they had in his native Spain. Maimonides, however, did not address either issue directly in his *Mishneh Torah*. These rulings are preserved in his responsa and in the writings of his son, Abraham, and although they evidently affected practice in Egypt and, to a lesser extent, the eastern Mediterranean, they did not enter the halakhic mainstream of the dominant Sefardi and Ashkenazi schools. Maimonides' strict stance prohibiting non-talmudic benedictions and any unnecessary blessings for the performance of actions that were merely customary–positions that necessarily caused upheaval when applied to the actual practices of specific communities–did, however, eventually become more influential, especially in Sefardi communities after the expulsion from Spain.

In the case of the individual's recitation of the *kedushah*, Maimonides' stance also played a wider role. Initially he followed his general tendency to rule according to stringent theoretical principles and encoded his prohibition against the individual's recitation of the *kedushah deyotzer* in his *Mishneh Torah*. Later in life, when he was more integrated into the Egyptian world and its customs, his personal practice changed, and he promulgated the opposite ruling in a responsum. Thanks at least in part to his son, this responsum received notice in Europe. Later scholars did not dismiss Maimonides' authority, but they did struggle to determine which tradition carried real weight. Maimonides, then, represents the type of immigrant sage who applied theoretical halakhic principles to the customs of his new community and who had the force of personality–in this case aided by a lack of rabbinic competition–to implement his halakhic strictures, at least locally. The one apparent exception discussed here, the *kedushah deyotzer* responsum, is not a significant deviation from his general trend, as *Masekhet Soferim* presented a sufficiently strong legal precedent to justify the more lenient stance.

The Rosh and his sons were also refugees who did not hesitate to express strong objections to the customs of their new home. These followers of R. Meir of Rothenburg maintained their identities as Ashkenazi Jews, disdaining Spanish customs and halakhic traditions, even while serving as leaders of the Castilian community.[8] Thus it is not surprising that the Rosh invoked the theoretical halakhic principle forbidding non-talmudic benedictions and vehemently opposed the recitation of the priest's blessing at the *pidyon haben*, a custom unknown in Ashkenaz. The degree to which this was a reaction to an unfamiliar minhag, rather than a purely halakhic stance, is emphasized by comparing the *pidyon haben* ruling with his attempts to justify a more universally practiced ceremony, the equally non-talmudic *birkat betulim*.

Similarly, the Tur's ruling against the inclusion of *piyyut* in the blessings of *keriat shema* was more a reaction to Spanish custom than an abstract theoretical decision. It is highly unlikely that the Baal Haturim objected to the German *piyyut* traditions, which Ashkenazi Jews considered a venerated, ancient, and central part of their liturgical minhag, sanctified by antiquity. But the Spanish rites had eliminated all poems to which such antiquity could be ascribed, either because of their authorship or because of their adherence to the literary models of ancient authors. In their place, they substituted poetry that bore little formal or linguistic relationship to that known in Ashkenaz. While we know that the Rosh perpetuated the traditions about Kalir's authority, it was easy perhaps for him and certainly for his son to separate Spanish *piyyut* from this source of legitimation and apply other theoretical halakhic concerns to it. This stance was aided by strong Sefardi traditions of opposition to *piyyut* and by the fact that, by the time of their arrival, it had apparently already been moved from halakhically questionable positions in the rite of Toledo, the city of their resi-

8. See: ישראל מ' תא–שמע, "רבנו אשר ובנו ר' יעקב בעל הטורים: בין אשכנז לספרד," פעמים 46–47 (תשנ"א), 80, 86–90.

dence in Spain. The Tur's rulings against *piyyut* thus applied only to other Spanish communities.

Whereas Maimonides and the Asherides had been members of individual families who fled persecutions - parts of relatively small groups of refugees who settled in lands with established Jewish communities–Joseph Karo belonged to the vast wave of emigres from Spain who relatively quickly overwhelmed the pre-existing communities of the eastern Mediterranean. Thus, his concern was less with the legitimacy of local customs than with the re-establishment of Sefardi Jewry and its traditions on new ground. Nonetheless, the breakdown of the customs of individual Sefardi communities when Jews from different areas of Spain formed new homogeneous communities[9] created some of the same conditions for halakhic re-examination of customs.

Karo ruled adamantly in favor of Sefardi liturgical customs and against those of Ashkenaz.[10] He maintained the Castilians' elimination of all *piyyut* from *keriat shema* and from the *amidah* (the latter had resulted more from a change in custom than from direct halakhic rulings). This ruling ultimately affected not only the rites of refugees from Catalonia and other parts of Spain who had not accepted the ruling of the *Tur*, but also the Romaniote and other eastern Mediterranean rites that had maintained active payyetanic traditions[11]–even though Karo did not mention those rites specifically. Similarly, Karo invoked the prohibition of non-talmudic blessings only as it applied to specifically Ashkenazi traditions of *birkhot hashaḥar*, and not when it applied to non-talmudic blessings accepted by his own Sefardi community. Finally, although Karo wanted to follow those who prohibited the recitation of the *kedushah* by the individual, common custom, both of Sefarad and of Ashkenaz, dictated otherwise. Like the other refugee codifiers, he defended the customs of his homeland, invoking halakhic principles only when they furthered that defense. Unlike Maimonides and the

---

9. This did not happen to the same extent in large cities where the large Jewish population could easily subdivide into separate synagogue communities, each representing a different minhag.

10. The material discussed here does not support the claim of Israel Ta-Shma, that in accord with his desire to be recognized as the rabbinic authority for all Jews, in cases where the Talmud and Maimonides do not present clear rulings, Karo ruled according to the halakhic traditions of Ashkenaz. See his: "רבי יוסף קארו בין אשכנז לספרד – לחקר התפשטות ספר הזוהר," תרביץ נט (תש"ן), 158–153.

11. Steven B. Bowman, *The Jews of Byzantium 1204-1453* (University of Alabama Press, 1985), 129-130, remarks that the Romaniote efforts in composition of *piyyut* reached their peak in the years 1350-1550. Much of this material has been published by Leon Weinberger. See his *Jewish Hymnography: A Literary History* (London: The Littman Library of Jewish Civilization, 1998), chaps. 4-6.

Asherides, however, Karo still lived with the remnants of his community; for the most part, he was not confronted with a fully alien minhag. His results, therefore, were different.

Such a summary raises important and irreverent questions: If only ulterior motives and the circumstances of their lives drove these sages to uphold halakhic principles, how important was and is this halakhah? Is it simply a convenient tool, or does it have an independent authority? Is the definition of acceptable liturgy derived from a theoretical absolute against which actual practice must be measured, or is it dependent upon the emotional tie of the sage to a particular custom? While the anthropologist, standing outside the culture, would argue for the social, humanly grounded basis of the Jewish legal system, Jews through the ages have not considered it this way. The Oral Torah, the ultimate authority for liturgical acceptability, is a process, not an immutable, codified Law. The rabbis, heirs of the Oral Torah in its various recensions and codifications, have an ongoing mandate to interpret and apply it to their contemporary worlds. Changing circumstances and new intellectual currents open rabbinic eyes to new issues of halakhah and provide new opportunities for its application. Rabbis must not only understand it differently over time; they must preserve its authority by decreeing only what a community is able to accept. Over the centuries these considerations account for the lack of rulings by those sages who felt their hands were tied by popular minhag. They also account for vehement stances taken on our issues by this group of immigrant rabbis and for the renewed interest in strict readings of halakhah in the modern world in the light of the immense cultural shifts brought about by European emancipation and enlightenment, by the Holocaust, and by the founding of the State of Israel.

Liturgical halakhah thus was shaped not only by the historical circumstances of its great codifiers, but also by changes in the cultural status of minhagim. These changes altered the balance between the authority of the particular minhag and the authority of the relevant halakhah. In the case of the *birkat betulim*, Jewish practice reflected shifting influences from the environment in which the Jews were living. Where the surrounding Christian or Islamic society considered the establishment of the bride's virginity a crucial part of the wedding itself, popular Jewish custom incorporated a parallel ceremony of recognition that included this blessing. The exact form of the ceremony was limited only by efforts to preserve the modesty of the bride and, eventually, in later centuries, by halakhic concerns about the recitation of a non-talmudic blessing. Even after surrounding Christian cultures fairly universally moved away from the custom of the morning gift–preferring other financial arrangements to seal the marriage–Jews preserved their now hallowed custom, but in such a quiet, private manner that it eventually ceased to be of real concern because it had lost any vestige of meaning in the culture.

In the case of *piyyut*, the dramatic shift in the aesthetic norms applied to Hebrew poetry in Muslim Spain developed directly from the efforts of Jewish poets to participate, within their own culture and religious tradition, in the great literary and intellectual flowering of the period. No purely halakhic concerns led to the abandonment of the earlier traditions of oriental Hebrew poetry; rather, scholars like Abraham Ibn Ezra and his contemporaries objected to the innovative grammar and lexica and the infusion of midrashic and talmudic ideas characteristic of eastern *piyyut* as inappropriate for the serious task of prayer. Ibn Ezra's objections, although couched in halakhic language, really reflect the desire of a grammarian and philosopher to glorify Hebrew and the Bible as his fellow intellectuals had done with Arabic and the Koran. They were able to do so because, in his society, eastern-style *piyyut* had ceased to be meaningful; people did not understand it and questioned the values it represented.

However, this total revamping of the liturgical poetry of the Spanish synagogue ultimately backfired. With the Reconquista and the cessation of Arab influence, Spanish Jewish culture moved towards mysticism and away from philosophical rationalism. Persecutions upset local minhagim, and new halakhic influences produced a culture in which the rabbinic elite was troubled by, and the populace was little invested in, the incorporation of this newer corpus of *piyyut* into their statutory prayers. Many generations of Spanish rabbis had proclaimed their inability to make minhag conform with halakhic theory in this matter. Only a shift in the minhag or the value placed on it could have allowed this ultimate triumph of halakhah. Indeed, those *piyyutim* that the people did care about—those for Yom Kippur and particularly Halevi's *mi khamokha* for *Shabbat Zakhor*—survived, at least for a while.

Just as changing communal attitudes affected the invocation of theoretical halakhic norms, so too did changing currents of rabbinic thought. Some extra-halakhic intellectual influences, like the philosophers' and grammarians' attitude to eastern *piyyut* voiced by Abraham Ibn Ezra, discussed above, were common to a broader segment of society but affected rabbinic thought as well; others, like mysticism in its various forms, essentially remained the specialized knowledge and practice of the rabbinic elite.

The study of mystical prayer and the impact of mysticism on synagogue prayer deserves much more attention than it has received to this point. Indeed, prayer and mysticism have a natural affinity, in that both offer ways to communicate with God or affect the workings of the divine realm. It is not surprising, then, that mystics have much to say about prayer, and that mystical thought should have influenced both the development of Jewish liturgy and its halakhah. Those rabbis who practiced mystical pursuits could not easily ignore those values when making practical halakhic pronouncements, even if they hid the mystic lore itself behind the veil of esotericism. Our studies here have demonstrated that mystical concerns for the impact of prayer in the heavenly realms played a major role in the halakhic stance taken by individual rabbis–particularly in the case of individual recitation of the *kedushah.* We have also posited that the kabbalists' reinterpretation of the *birkat betulim* contributed to the persistence of this custom, especially since the ceremony itself had lost significant elements of its original meaning. And kabbalistic attitudes toward prayer quite possibly also influenced later Spanish opposition to all non-talmudic benedictions and to the inclusion of *piyyut* in the blessings of *keriat shema* and the *amidah.* This was certainly the case for the followers of the Ari. The fact that these *piyyutim* were, at least initially, simply moved to stations outside of the statutory liturgy and not eliminated entirely indicates that their location, not their content or even the loss of local customs, was a primary issue.[12]

In sum, most Jewish synagogue practices developed in accordance with the principles of liturgical halakhah, both because early halakhah was formulated to conform to actual practice, and because worship was a sufficiently serious endeavor that most Jews relatively early accepted rabbinic guidance. But talmudic halakhah was not comprehensive, and, as time went on, Jews living in varied environments were subjected to new influences and needed or wanted new liturgical outlets. Thus, customs considered by their practitioners to be efficacious prayer developed on the fringes of this halakhically defined liturgy, and some of these challenged aspects of the halakhah itself. For the most part, in matters of competing understandings of efficacious liturgy, we must conclude that מנהג מבטל הלכה, minhag indeed overrides theoretical halakhah. In most cases, successful elimination of doubtful customs occurred only when the customs themselves were no longer of major value to the communities. Halakhah could then be invoked to dispose of them.

---

12. Additional case studies would certainly reveal other areas where mysticism and other trends of Jewish piety and thought affected rabbinic halakhic pronouncements about liturgy. For example, the Ḥasidei Ashkenaz were greatly concerned about the precise wording of their prayers, and we have seen that this concern extended to certain halakhic matters also. Their impact on liturgical halakhah and their attitudes to the talmudic-geonic traditions deserves a study of its own. Similarly, studies of the effects of post-expulsion kabbalah, or, on the other hand, academic pilpul methodologies on liturgical halakhah are a desideratum. From yet another perspective, a study of the nineteenth- and twentieth-century Orthodox reactions to modernity would aid us in understanding the dynamics of the contemporary situation of Jewish liturgical law.

At the same time, we have explored three specific situations when theoretical halakhah and its definitions of effective worship of God gained dominance over halakhically questionable liturgical customs in the medieval world: (1) when immigrant halakhic authorities, the leading Torah scholars of their times, who were not invested in local customs, ruled in their law codes against the regnant minhag, without great concern for popular reaction to their rulings; (2) when shifts in popular culture, caused by influences from the surrounding society or simply by changing times, devalued the minhag itself and created an opening for the halakhic concerns to be effectively expressed; (3) and when shifts in the values of the academy influenced the seriousness with which various infractions of theoretical halakhah were viewed. As we have seen, even where theoretical halakhah seemed victorious over errant customs (except in cases where the minhag itself had ceased to matter to the community), popular needs usually dictated some degree of compromise. The conflict between halakhah and minhag often had to be resolved by redefining halakhah, or by creating a new understanding of the law or custom involved. Rarely was theoretical halakhah itself able to influence popular practice significantly.

# *Appendix*

## Alternative Texts for the Individual When Omitting the *Kedushah Deyotzer*

PALTOI GAON:

1. ויחיד מדלג מנעימה לנעימה כלל, מבשפה ברורה ובנעימה לאל ברוך נעימות.[1]

NATRONAI GAON:

1. בשפה ברורה בנעימה ובקדושה כולם כאחד לאל ברוך נעימות יתנו...[2]
2. בשפה ברורה ובנעימה, לאל ברוך נעימות יתנו...[3]
3. עונין באימה ואומרים ביראה קדוש וברוך...[4]

NAḤSHON GAON:

1. ...וכלום פותחין בקדושה ובטהרה ומברכין ומשבחין ומקדישין לאל שמו האל המלך הגדול הגבור והנורא קדוש הוא [ויתחיל ויאמר] ולו זמירות יאמרו ותשבחות ישמיעו...[5]
2. יאמ׳ יוצר אור על הסדר כמות שהיא עד שיגיע וכולם פותחין את פיהם בקדושה ובטהרה ומשבחים ומברכים ומקדישין לאל שמו האל הגדול הגבור והנורא ויתחיל ויאמר לו זמירות יאמרו ותשבחות ישמיעו ומסיים תפלתו...[6]
3. ונותנים רשות זה לזה להקדיש לעושה אורים גדולים כי לעולם חסדו כו׳[7]

---

1. From a responsum of R. Ephraim of Bonn, cited by E. E. Urbach, *Arugat Habosem* IV, 65; and in *Siddur Ḥasidei Ashkenaz*, 87-88.

2. *Otzar Hageonim*, *Berakhot*, *Teshuvot*, 52, #131; cited from *Shibbolei Haleket*, ed. Mirsky, 171, #13. See also *Tanya Rabbati*, 15.

3. *Manhig*, ed. Raphael, I:63. Cited by the *Beit Yosef* OH 59.

4. *Tur* OH 59. We can question the accuracy of this attribution, based on comparisons of other statements attributed to Natronai and the prevalence of this alternative text in Europe.

5. *Halakhot Gedolot*, ed. Hildesheimer, I:470-471, n. to line 41. The text appears in *Halakhot Gedolot* only in Ms. Vatican 142.

6. *Halakhot Gedolot*, ed. Hildesheimer, I: 507. This a scribal addition, clearly out of context, filling in empty space at the end of a section in a manuscript. Does the previous passage, found only in one manuscript, represent another scribe's decision to insert this material in its logical place? Note, however, that the two traditions vary slightly, a fact of possible significance, but also attributable to scribal changes in the liturgical texts.

7. *Shibbbolei Haleket*, ed. Mirsky, 171, #13; *Tanya Rabbati*, 15, #4 omits the last three words.

SAADIA GAON:

1. ... ואי אפשר לו נמי לפתוח בבורא קדושים שכיון שהתחיל אסור לגמור, אלא מברך כך. ברוך אתה ה' אמ"ה יוצר אור ובורא חשך עושה שלום ובורא את הכל. המאיר לארץ ולדרים עליה ברחמים. טובו מחדש בכל יום תמיד מעשה בראשית. כאמור לעושה אורים גדולים כי לעולם חסדו בא"י יוצר המאורות.[8]

2. ברוך אתה ה' אלהינו מלך העולם יוצר אור ובורא חושך עושה שלום ובורא את הכל המאיר לארץ ולדרין עליה ברחמים רבים וטובו מחדש בכל יום תמיד מעשה בראשית ב'א' ה' יוצר המאורות.[9]

GEONIC, ATTRIBUTION UNCLEAR:

בסדר רב עמרם: וששאלתם יחיד המתפלל בינו לבין עצמו בשחרית יכול לומר בורא קדושים עד יחד כולם עונין באימה ואומרין ביראה. או דילמא כיון דקדושה היא יחיד אינו (כצ"ל) אומרה כל עיקר. כך המנהג. יחיד המתפלל אם אמר עונין באימה ואומרין ביראה צריך לומר קק"ק אבל אין לו רשות לומר קדושה כולן כאחד עונין וכו' אלא אומר בורא קדושים וכשיגיע עד שפה ברורה ובנעימה מדלג ואומר לאל ברוך וכו'.[10]

ADDITIONAL ALTERNATIVES PRESENTED BY THE RISHONIM:

1. יחיד המתפלל לבינו לבין עצמו בשחרית אינו עונה בעצמו קק"ק וכו' אלא כך הוא אומר, כשמגיע לשפה ברורה ובנעימה קדושה כולם כאחד עונים ואומרים ביראה, ואינו אומר אלא שתי תיבות: קדוש וברוך, ומדלג ואומר לאל ברוך וכו'.[11]

---

8. *Otzar Hageonim, Berakhot, Teshuvot*, 52-53, #133; cited from the *Seder Rav Amram Gaon*. Goldschmidt, in his edition of *Seder Rav Amram Gaon*, 13, correctly indicates its status as a gloss. Note, however, that *Shibbolei Haleket*, Mirsky ed., 171, #13, cites this solely in the name of Amram, as does *Tanya Rabbati*, 15, #4, which has a corrupted text.

9. *Siddur Rav Saadia Gaon*, 13, morning service for the individual. Contrast this with his service for the community, 36-37, that, although still shorter than our customary texts, does contain the *kedushah*.

10. *Seder Rav Amram Gaon*, ed. Goldschmidt, 13-14, from Horowitz, תורתן של ראשונים, I:52, #21. This text does not appear in any manuscripts of the *Seder Rav Amram Gaon* used by Goldschmidt. Goldschmidt suggests that although it is possible that this text is original to Amram, it is also possible that it is really a version of a responsum of Natronai or Naḥshon Gaon known to the Rishonim. Note the slight difference between this responsum and the answer attributed to Saadia. This responsum merely says that once individuals introduce the *kedushah*, they must complete it, but Saadia absolutely forbids individuals to complete the prayer, leaving them literally stuck.

This responsum also appears without attribution in *Sefer Hapardes*, ed. Ehrenreich, 327; תשובות ופסקים לר"י הזקן, שיטת הקדמונים על מסכת עבודה זרה, חלק שלישי, רמב–ג, סי' קלד. In the latter source, it appears in conjunction with Saadia's responsum on "אור חדש," as it does in the material cited by Goldschmidt, indicating that the source may well be a version of Amram.

11. רבי מאיר ב"ר ברוך (מהר"ם) מרוטנבורג - תשובות פסקים ומנהגים, תשובה קלה, סי' קמג. This seems to be a citation of the position of others, for Maharam goes on to refute this. Rabbenu Peretz, in his commentary on Rabbenu Shimshon b"R. Tzaddok's collection of the Maharam's rulings, ספר תשב"ץ, #221, indicates that it is the general custom not to say the *kedushah deyotzer*, but instead to say: עונים ואומרים ביראה קדוש וברוך. *Hagahot Maimoniot* (*Hilkhot Tefillah*

2. האומרים עונים ביראה ואומרים קדוש וברוך לא יפה הן עושין, משום שאותו כת האומרת קדוש אינה אומרת ברוך...אלא הכי לימא: עונים ביראה ואומרים קדוש והאופנים וחיות הקודש כול׳ משבחים ואומרים ברוך. ואינו גומר הפסוקים ומתחיל לאל ברוך נעימות יתנו כול׳.[12]

3. ונותנים רשות זה לזה להקדיש לקדוש וברוך לאל ברוך נעימות יתנו וכו׳.[13]

4. בשפה ברורה ובנעימה קדושה כולם כאחד עונים באימה ואומרים ביראה קדושה והאופנים וכו׳ לעומתם משבחים [וכו׳] לאל ברוך נעימות יאמרו.[14]

5. עונין באימה ואומרים ביראה קדוש והאופנים אומרין ברוך.[15]

FROM A PRAYERBOOK MANUSCRIPT:

יחיד המתפלל כשיגיע כאן אין אומ׳ קדושה שכך אמרו כל דבר שבקדושה אין אומ׳ אותו בפחות מעשרה ויאמר כך ואומרים קדוש וברוך לאל ברוך נעימות ולמטה כתובה קדושה של יחיד שאומ׳ בכאן אם ירצה.[16]

---

7:17) lists this as the alternative for those wishing to skip the *kedushah deyotzer*, in spite of their being permitted to say it. This is the position advocated by the earlier Tosafist, R. Elazer of Verona, cited in *Shibbolei Haleket*, Mirsky, 171, I:13; and *Sefer HaAgur*, p. 33, #102. The *Manhig*, ed. Raphael, I:63, rules this custom improper. The *Orḥot Ḥayyim*, *Din Kedushah Meyushav*, 1, 11c, cites Rabbenu Yonah (in a comment not included in his commentary on this matter in *Berakhot*), that some are of the opinion that this alternative was established by the Men of the Great Assembly (the absolute authoritative source for all rabbinic liturgy in its sacred history). See too, the Rosh, *Berakhot* 3:18 and *Tosafot Harosh* to *Berakhot* 21b, who reports this opinion; the *Tur* OH 59, who attributes it to Natronai; Rabbenu Yeruḥam, ספר תולדות אדם וחוה, נתיב השלישי, חלק שלישי, who rules that this is the proper alternative; and the *Beit Yosef* on this passage in the *Tur*, who cites various of these authorities.

12. Attributed to a Tosafist, R. Barukh, whose exact identity is unclear. Cited by *Shibbolei Haleket*, ed. Mirsky, 171, I:13; *Agur*, 33, #102; *Beit Yosef* OH 59. This may be the alternative preferred by the Ritva in his commentary to *Megillah* 23b, but a scribal abbreviation prevents full identification. The Rashbatz (פירוש הרשב״ץ על ברכות, קכה–ו.) cites this as the preferred version of the French rabbis. Note, however, that all his predecessors referring to the French rabbis in this context, beginning with Rabbenu Yonah, have ascribed to them the opposite opinion!

13. This text appears only in *Sefer Tanya Rabati*, 15, #4, where it is presented as the custom of the author's teacher, R. Yehuda bar Binyamin Harofe. This was clearly an attempt to improve the literary level of the alternative text and to maintain the allusions to the prophetic verses while in effect using the words for new purposes.

14. חידושי הריטב״א על הש״ס, מגילה, קעב–ג.

15. פירוש הרשב״ץ על ברכות, קכה–ו. The Rashbatz presents this opinion as that of the French rabbis, an attribution for which we have no precedent.

16. Jewish Theological Seminary, Microfilm #4112, identified as possibly a fifteenth century Sefardi siddur from North Africa. The manuscript is in poor condition, and I was unable to find the full text for the individual referred to here.

# *Bibliography of Works Cited*

## A. Hebrew Primary Sources

(Alphabetized by title. Standard editions and the commentaries included in them are not listed. Responsa consulted through the Bar Ilan University Responsa Project CD-ROM also do not appear.)


ר׳ דוד אבודרהם. ספר אבודרהם השלם. ירושלים: אושא, תשכ״ג.

שמואל ב״ר משולם ירונדי. ספר אהל מועד. מהדורת אברהם יצחק גאגין. ירושלים, תרמ״ו; תשכ״ט.

אוצר הגאונים: תשובות גאוני בבל ופירושיהם על פי סדר התלמוד. בעריכת ב. מ. לוין. י״ב כרכים. ירושלים: הוצאת ח. וגשל, תדש״מ.

יצחק ב״ר משה מווינא. ספר אור זרוע. זיטאמיר, תרכ״ב; ד״ח 1959.

ספר ארחות חיים לר׳ אהרן הכהן מלוניל. מהדורת משה בן אליקים שלעזינגער. ירושלים: יהדות, תשמ״ו. דפוס ראשון, ברלין, תרנ״ט.

איילנבורג, יששכר בער. ספר באר שבע. ירושלים, תשכ״ט.

עמדן, יעקב. בירת מגדל עוז.... חלק א. בולוגנא, תק״ח.

בית הבחירה על מסכת ברכות לר׳ מנחם ב״ר שלמה לבית מאיר המכונה המאירי. מהדורת שמואל דיקמן. מהדורה שניה. ירושלים: מכון לתלמוד הישראלי השלם, תשכ״ה.

בית הבחירה על מסכת פסחים לר׳ מנחם ב״ר שלמה לבית מאיר המכונה המאירי. מהדורת יוסף הכהן קליין. ירושלים: מכון התלמוד הישראלי השלם, תשכ״ד.

אייזיק, יצחק. ספר בנין עולם. ווארשא, תרי״א.

אפשטיין, ברוך הלוי מפינסק. ברוך שאמר. תל אביב: הוצאת עם עולם, תשכ״ח.

ספר ברכה משולשת על מסכת ברכות. ווארשא, תרכ״ג. דפוס חדש, ירושלים, תשכ״ח.

אזולאי, חיים יוסף דוד (חיד״א). ספר ברכי יוסף. ווינא, 1859; ד״ח ירושלים, ?196.

אבואב, שמואל. ספר דבר שמואל. ויניציאה, תס״ב.

מילדולה, דוד ב״ר רפאל. ספר דברי דוד. אמשטרדם, 1753.

אירגאס, יוסף. ספר דברי יוסף. ליוורנו, 1742; דפוס חדש, ?1990.

חיות, צבי הירש. ספר דרכי ההוראה. בתוך כל ספרי המהרי״ץ חיות. ירושלים, תשי״ח.

דרשות על התורה לר׳ יהושע אבן שועיב .ירושלים: מקור, תשכ״ט. צילום מדפוס קראקא, של״ג.

ספר האגור השלם לרבינו יעקב ברוך בן יהודה לנדא. מהדורת משה הרשלר. ירושלים, תש״ך.

ספר האורה, כולל פסקי דינים והלכות מיוחס לרבינו שלמה בר׳ יצחק. מהדורת שלמה באבער. לבוב, תרע״ה. דפוס חדש, ירושלים, תשכ״ז.

ר׳ אברהם ב״ר יצחק אב״ד מנרבונא. ספר האשכול. כרך א׳. מהדורת שלום אלבק וחנוך אלבק. ירושלים: ראובן מס, 1945.

אברהם ב״ר יצחק מנרבונא. ספר האשכול. כרך א׳. מהדורת צבי בנימין אויערבך. האלברשטאדט, תרכ״ח. דפוס חדש, ?196.

״ספר ההשלמה לרבנו משולם ב״ר משה ב״ר יהודה מברדיש.״ בתוך גנזי ראשונים, ברכות. מהדורת משה הרשלר. ירושלים: מכון התלמוד הישראלי השלם, תשכ״ז.

ספר הישר לרבנו תם, חלק השאלות והתשובות. מהדורת שרגא ראזענטהאל, אפרים זלמן מרגליות. ברלין, תרנ״ח; ירושלים תשל״ב.

ספר הלכות גדולות. מהדורת עזריאל הילדסהיימר. כרך א. ירושלים: מקיצי נרדמים, 1971.

חאגיז, יעקב שמואל. ספר הלכות קטנות. ויניציאה, תס״ז; ניו־יורק, תשי״ח.

ספר המחכים לר' נתן ב"ר יהודה. מהדורת יעקב פריימאנן. ישראל, n.d. מהאשכול ו (תרס"ט), 94–162.

ספר המנהגים לרבינו אייזיק טירנא. מהדורת שלמה י' שפיצר. ירושלים: מפעל תורת חכמי אשכנז, תשל"ט.

ספר המנהיג לרבי אברהם ברבי נתן הירחי. מהדורת יצחק רפאל. ירושלים: מוסד הרב קוק, 1978.

ספר המנוחה, הוא פירוש רבינו מנוח מנרבונה על הרמב"ם. חלק א': הלכות קריאת שמע תפלה וברכות. מהדורת אלעזר הורביץ. ירושלים: מוסד הרב קוק, תש"ל.

ר' אברהם בן הרמב"ם. ספר המספיק לעובדי השם, הוא כתאב כפאיה אלעאבדין. מהדורת נסים דנה. רמת גן: אוניברסיטת בר אילן, 1989.

ספר המצות ל...רבנו משה בן מיימון. ווארשא, 1891.

אזולאי, חיים דוד בן יצחק (חיד"א). עין זוכר. בתוך ספר יעיר אזן. למברג, 1865.

יוסף אלבו. ספר העיקרים. ישראל: מחברת לספרות, תשכ"ד.

יהודה בר ברזילי אלברצלוני. ספר העתים. מהדורת יעקב שור. קראקא: מקיצי נרדמים, תרס"ג. דפוס חדש, ירושלים, תשמ"ד.

ספר הפרדס. וורשא, 1870. דפוס חדש, ישראל, 1959?.

ספר הפרדס לרש"י ז"ל. מהדורת חיים יהודה עהרענרייך. בודאפעשט, תרפ"ד.

משה בן מימון. הקדמה לפירוש המשנה. מהדורת מרדכי דב רבינוביץ. ירושלים: מוסד הרב קוק, תשכ"א.

ספר הרוקח הגדול חברו...רבינו אלעזר מגרמיזא. מהדורת ברוך שמעון שניאורסון. ירושלים, תשכ"ז.

הריטב"א: סדר ברכות הנהנין [הלכות ברכות]. מהדורת מרדכי ליב קצנלנבוגן. ירושלים: מוסד הרב קוק, תשמ"ג.

דויד בן יוסף קמחי הספרדי. ספר השרשים. Edited by Jo. H.R. Biesenthal, F. Lebrecht. Berlin, 1847. Reprinted, Jerusalem, 1967.

שמעון בר צמח. ספר התשב"ץ. לעמבערג, תרנ"א. דפוס חדש, תל אביב, n.d.

שטערן, יוסף זכריה. ספר זכר יהוסף, שאלות ותשובות. תרנ"ט–תרס"ב; דפוס חדש, ירושלים, תשכ"ח.

זכרון יהודה הוא ספר שאלות ותשובות לרבינו יהודה בן הרא"ש ז"ל. מהדורת יהודה ראזענבערג. ברלין, תר"ו. דפוס חדש, ירושלים, תשכ"ח.

זכרון לראשונים וגם לאחרונים. חלק ראשון: זכרון לראשונים. מחברת רביעית: זכרון כמה גאונים וביחוד רב שרירא ורב האיי בנו והרב ר' יצחק אלפאסי. מהדורת אברהם אליהו הרכבי. ברלין, תרמ"ז. דפוס חדש, ישראל, תשכ"ו.

חידושי הריטב"א לרבינו יום טוב ב"ר אברהם אלאשבילי, מסכת ברכות. מהדורת משה הרשלר. ירושלים: מוסד הרב קוק, תשמ"ה.

חידושי הריטב"א לרבינו יום טוב ב"ר אברהם אלאשבילי, מסכת מגילה. מהדורת יחיאל מיכל שטרן. ירושלים: מוסד הרב קוק, תשל"ו.

חידושי הריטב"א על מסכת עבודה זרה. ירושלים: עם עולם, תשכ"ז.

חידושי הרמב"ן על מסכת ברכות. בתוך ספר חידושי הראשונים המרב"ן ורשב"א והריטב"א על מס' ברכות ושבת. מהדורת רפאל בלום. ניו־יורק, תשל"ז.

חידושי הר"ן לרבינו נסים על מסכתות מגילה ומועד קטן. ירושלים: מכון הרי פישל לדרישת התלמוד ומשפט התורה, תשכ"ו.

חידושי הרשב"א על הש"ס לרבינו שלמה בן אברהם בן אדרת. ברכות. ירושלים: מכון אור, תש"מ.

חידושי רבינו שלמה בן אדרת על מסכת מגילה. מהדורת חיים דימיטרובסקי. ניוארק: פעלדהיים, תשט"ז.

ספר חמדה גנוזה. ירושלים, תרי"ח. דפוס חדש בתוך קובץ ספרי הגאונים תשובות ופסקים. חלק ראשון. בני ברק: מסורה, תשמ"ה.

ספר חסידים על פי נוסח כתב יד אשר בפארמא. מהדורת יהודה הכהן וויסטינעצקי. מהדורה שניה. פראנקפורט: מ.א. וואהרמאנן, תרפ"ד. מברלין: מקיצי נרדמים, 1891.

ספר חסידים שחיבר רבינו יהודה החסיד. מהדורת ראובן מרגליות. ירושלים: מוסד הרב קוק, תשי"ז.

ר' שלמה לוריא. ספר ים של שלמה. ניו יורק: ח'י'ל, תשי"ג.

ספר כל בו. לעמבערג, 1860. דפוס חדש, ניו יורק: Shulsinger Bros., 1946.

כל חידושי הרמב"ן לרבינו משה ב"ר נחמן. חלק ראשון. ירושלים: אור עולם, תרפ"ח. דפוס חדש, פ. פעלדהיים, תש"י.

בנבנישתי, חיים. ספר כנסת גדולה. ירושלים, תשכ"ה.

קרמי, יוסף ידידיה. ספר כנף רננים. ויניציאה, 1626.

אישתורי הפרחי. כפתור ופרח. מהדורת אברהם משה לונץ. ירושלים, תרנ"ט.

ליקוטי פרדס מרש"י ז"ל. ירושלים, תשכ"ד.

ספר לקט יושר לרבנו יוסף ב"ר משה. מהדורת יעקב פריימאנן. ברלין, תרס"ג. דפוס חדש, ניו יורק: מנורה, מכון למחקר ולהוצאת כתבי־יד וספרים עתיקים, תשי"ט.

ספר מהרי"ל: מנהגים של רבינו יעקב מולין. מהדורת שלמה י. שפיצר. ירושלים: מפעל תורת חכמי אשכנז, תשמ"ט.

ר' שלמה ב"ר אברהם ן' פרחון (ממלכות ארגון). מחברת הערוך. Edited by Salomo Gottlieb Stern. Pressburg, 1844. Reprinted, Jerusalem, 1970.

מחזור ויטרי לרבינו שמחה, אחד מתלמידי רש"י ז"ל. מהדורת שמעון הלוי הורוויץ. נירנבערג, תרפ"ג.

אזולאי, חיים יוסף דוד (חיד"א). ספר מחזיק ברכה. ליוורנו, תקל"ז.

אייעש, יהודה. ספר מטה יהודה. ליוורנו, תקמ"ג; ד"ח, ירושלים תשל"א.

ספר מנורת המאור לרבי ישראל בן יוסף בן אלנקאוה. מהדורת הלל גרשום המכונה הימן ענעלאו. ניו־יורק: בלוך, תרצ"א.

מסכת סופרים. מהדורת מיכאל היגער. נויארק: דבי רבנן, תרצ"ז.

אליהו מווילנא (גר"א). ספר מעשה רב עם פירוש פעולת שכיר. בתוך ספרי הגר"א. ירושלים, n.d.

ספר מצודת דוד, טעמי המצות לרדב"ז. זאלקווא, תרכ"ב; ד"ח ישראל, תשכ"ד.

שלום מקאידינאוו. ספר משמרת שלום. ווארשא, n.d.

נמוקי יוסף, מסכת ברכות. בני ברק: אור הגנוז, 1985.

נמוקי יוסף על מסכתות מגילה ופסחים. מהדורת משה יהודה הכהן בלוי. ניו־יורק, תש"ך.

סדור רב סעדיה גאון. מהדורת ישראל דודזון, שמחה אסף, ויששכר יואל. ירושלים: מקיצי נרדמים, ראובן מס, הדפסה חמישית, תשמ"ה.

סדור רנת ישראל, נוסח אשכנז. בעריכת שלמה טל. מהדורה שלישית. ירושלים: מורשת בע"מ, תשל"ז.

סדור רש"י. מהדורת שלמה באבער ויעקב פריימאנן. ברלין: חברת מקיצי נרדמים, תרע"ב.

בער, יצחק בן אריה יוסף דוב. סדר עבודת ישראל. רעדעלהיים, תשכ"ח. דפוס חדש, תל אביב, תשי"ז.

סדר רב עמרם גאון. מהדורת דניאל גולדשמידט. ירושלים: מוסד הרב קוק, 1971.

סידור רבנו שלמה מיוחס לרבנו שלמה ב"ר שמשון מגרמייזא וסידור חסידי אשכנז מבית מדרשם של ר"י החסיד ור"א מגרמייזא בעל הרוקח. מהדורת משה הרשלר. ירושלים, תשל"ב.

ר' אלעזר מגרמיזא. ספר סודי רזייא. ירושלים: שערי זיו, 1988.

אזולאי, חיים יוסף דוד (חיד"א). ספר עבודת הקדש. בני ברק: הוצאת ספרים "מישור," תשמ"ו.

אזולאי, חיים יוסף דוד (חיד"א). ספר עין זוכר. בתוך ספר יעיר אזן. למבורג, תרכ"ה.

מנחם עזריה מפאנו. ספר עשרה מאמרות עם פירוש יד יהודה מהור"ר יהודה ליב ב"ר שמעון... למבורג, 1858; ד"ח 1973?.

ר' יצחק לאמפרונטי. פחד יצחק. דפוס צילום, בני־ברק, 1980?. ממהדורת מקיצי נרדמים.

פירוש הרא"ה על הלכות הרי"ף מסכת ברכות. מהדורת משה יהודה הכהן בלוי. ניו־יורק, תשי"ז.

פירוש הרשב"ץ על ברכות. מהדורת דוד צבי הילמן. בני ברק, 1971.

ר' יהודה ב"ר יקר. פירוש התפלות והברכות. מהדורת שמואל ירושלמי. ירושלים: מאורי ישראל, תשכ"ט.

פירושי סידור התפילה לרוקח. מהדורת משה הרשלר ויהודה אלתר הרשלר. ב' כרכים. ירושלים: מכון הרב הרשלר למחקר ולהוצאה של ספרות תורנית והלכתית, תשנ"ב.

פירושי רבינו חננאל בר חושיאל לתלמוד. מהדורת דוד מצגר. ירושלים: מכון לב שמחה, תש"ן.

פירושי רבנו אליהו מלונדריש ופסקיו. מהדורת מרדכי יהודה ליב זק"ש. ירושלים: מוסד הרב קוק, תשט"ז.

פרקי דרבי אליעזר. ווארשא, תרי"ב. דפוס חדש, ניו יורק: אום, תש"ו.

מנחם בן אהרן בן זרח. צדה לדרך. ווארשא, תר"מ. דפוס חדש, ישראל, 1960?.

אברהם בן אריה ליב (Lowenstamm). ספר צרור החיים. באוהעלי, תרכ"ט.

ר' חיים ב"ר שמואל בן דוד מטודילו. צרור החיים. מהדורת שמואל חגי ירושלמי. ירושלים, תשכ"ו.

ספר ראבי"ה. כרך א'. מהדורת אביגדור אפטוביצר. מהדורה שניה. ירושלים: מקיצי נרדמים, מכון הרי פישל, תשכ"ד.
רבנו אברהם בן דוד תשובות ופסקים. מהדורת יוסף קאפח. ירושלים: מוסד הרב קוק, תשכ"ד.
ר' יצחק בר ששת. שאלות ותשובות בר ששת. ניו יורק: מפיצי תורה, תשי"ד.
דוד בן שלמה נ' אבי זמרא. שו"ת הרדב"ז. ז' כרכים בב'. ניו־דזערסיא: הרצים, 1963?.
ספר שו"ת הרדב"ז מכתב יד. חלק שמיני. מהדורת יצחק צב"י בן נפתלי חיים סופר. בני ברק: עט סופר, n.d.
שאלות ותשובות הרשב"א. בני־ברק, תשמ"ב.
אדאדי, אברהם חיים. ספר שאלות ותשובות ויקרא אברהם. ירושלים, תשמ"ג.
ר' עובדיה יוסף. שאלות ותשובות יביע אומר. חלק ראשון. ירושלים, תשי"ד. מהדורה שניה, תשל"ד.
ר' עובדיה יוסף. שאלות ותשובות יחוה דעת. חלק רביעי. ירושלים, תשמ"א.
שאלות ותשובות להרב רבינו אשר ז"ל. ווילנא, תרמ"א. דפוס חדש, ירושלים, תשכ"ד.
שאלות ותשובות מהרי"ט צהלון החדשות. מהדורת יוסף בוקסבוים, מסעוד בן שמעון, ומשה רובינשטיין. ירושלים: מכון אור המזרח, תש"מ.
שו"ת מהרי"ל החדשות לרבינו יעקב מולין. מהדורת יצחק סץ. ירושלים: מפעל תורת חכמי אשכנז, תשל"ז; תשנ"א.
שאלות ותשובות מהרשד"ם. שאלוניקי, 1862. דפוס חדש, ישראל.
ספר שאלות ותשובות מהרש"ל. ירושלים, תשכ"ט.
שאלות ותשובות מן השמים. מהדורת ראובן מרגליות. ירושלים: מוסד הרב קוק, תשי"ז.
שאלות ותשובות מן השמים לרבינו יעקב ממרויש, מבעלי התוספות. ירושלים, תשל"ב.
ספר שאלות ותשובות רבנו יוסף הלוי אבן מיגאש. מהדורת שמחה חסידה. ירושלים: מכון לב שמח, תשנ"א.
שאלות ותשובות רבינו משה מינץ. מהדורת יונתן שרגא דומב. ירושלים: מפעל תורת חכמי אשכנז, תשנ"א.
שאלות ותשובות ריב"ש. ירושלים, תשכ"ח.
ספר שאלות ותשובות שחבר...ר' שלמה בן אדרת. כרך א'. בני ברק, תשי"ח.
ספר שאלות ותשובות שחבר רבנו שלמה בן אדרת. הלק ראשון. בני ברק, תשמ"ב.
שבלי הלקט השלם לרבינו צדקיה ב"ר אברהם הרופא. מהדורת שמואל קלמן מירסקי. ירושלים: סורא, תשכ"ו.
ורדיגר, יעקב. "שירותא דצלותא." בתוך סדור תפלה צלותא דאברהם. מהדורה שניה. ישראל: וועד להוצאת הסידור צלותא דאברהם, 198?.
שירי הקודש של אברהם אבן עזרא. מהדורת ישראל לוין. ירושלים: האקדמיה הלאומית הישראלית למדעים, תש"ם.
אלגאזי, ישראל יעקב. ספר שלמי צבור. שאלוניקי, תרנ"ה; ד"ח, ישראל, n.d.; מהדורה אחרת: ירושלים: אהבת שלום, תשמ"ז.
חיים ויטל. שער הכוונות עם הגהות רבותינו גאוני הקבלה הרב שאול דוויק הכהן, הרב שלמה ב"ר חייקל. ירושלים: ישיבת החיים והשלום וכולל עטרת צבי, [198?].
אליהו מווילנא (גר"א). ספר שערי רחמים. בתוך ספרי הגר"א. ירושלים, n.d.
רי"ץ גיאת. ספר שערי שמחה. פירטה, תרכ"א.
ספר שערי תשובה. מהדורת ירוחם פישל בן צבי הירש הלוי. לייפציג, תרי"ח. דפוס חדש בתוך קובץ ספרי הגאונים, תשובות ופסקים. חלק ראשון. בני ברק, תשמ"ה.
אברהם אבן עזרא. שפה ברורה. מהדורת גבריאל הירש ליפמאן. פיורדא, תקצ"ט. דפוס חדש, ירושלים, תשכ"ז.
אברהם אבן עזרא. ספר שפת יתר. מהדורת גבריאל הירש ליפמאן. פראנקפורט על נהר מיין, תר"ג.
ר' ירוחם. ספר תולדות אדם וחוה. ויניציאה, 1553. דפוס חדש, n.d.
ר' מאיר אבן גבאי. ספר תולעת יעקב. ירושלים: מקור חיים, תשכ"ז.
תוספות הרא"ש לרבינו אשר ב"ר יחיאל, מסכת ברכות. מהדורת שמואל אדוין. מלבורן, תשנ"א.
תוספות רבנו יהודה שירליאון. מהדורת ניסן זק"ש. ירושלים: האקדמיה האמריקנית למדעי היהדות, תשכ"ט.
רבנו פרץ ב"ר אליהו מקורביל. תוספות רבנו פרץ למסכת ברכות. מהדורת משה הרשלר. ירושלים: מכון שלם – צפונות קדמונים, תשד"ם.
תורתן של ראשונים. מהדורת חיים הורוויץ. פראנקפורט על נהר מיין, 1881.

יהודה אלחריזי. תחכמוני. בעריכת י. טופורובסקי. תל אביב: מחברות לספרות, תשי"ב.

ספר תניא רבתי. ווארשא, 1879. דפוס חדש, ירושלים, תשכ"ג.

ישראל איסרלאן. ספר תרומת הדשן. חלק ראשון: שאלות ותשובות. מהדורת שמואל אביטן. ירושלים, תשנ"א.

ר' שמעון בר צמח. ספר תשב"ץ. לעמבערק, 1891.

רבינו שמשון ב"ר צדוק. ספר תשב"ץ, מנהגים פסקים ודינים של מהר"ם מרוטנבורג...עם הגהות רבינו פרץ זצ"ל. ניו יורק, 1970.

תשובות הגאונים החדשות ועמן תשובות, פסקים ופירושים מאת חכמי פרובאנס הראשונים. מהדורת שמחה עמנואל. ירושלים: מכון אופק, ספריית פרידברג, תשנ"ה.

תשובות הגאונים מתוך ה"גניזה". מהדורת שמחה אסף. ירושלים: דרום, תרפ"ט. דפוס חדש, ירושלים: ח. וגשל, תשמ"ו.

תשובות הגאונים עם תשובות ופסקים מחכמי פרובינציה. מהדורת אלעזר הורביץ. ניו־יורק, תשנ"ה.

תשובות הגאונים: שערי תשובה. Edited by Wolf Leiter. New York: Philipp Feldheim, 1946.

תשובות הגאונים, הרכבי. ראה: זכרון לראשונים וגם ואחרונים.

תשובות הרמב"ם. מהדורת יהושע בלאו. ד' כרכים. ירושלים: מקיצי נרדמים, תשי"ח–תשמ"ו.

"תשובות ופסקים לר"י הזקן." בתוך שיטת הקדמונים על מסכת עבודה זרה. חלק שלישי. מהדורת משה יהודה הכהן בלוי. ניו־יורק, תשנ"א.

רבי מאיר ב"ר ברוך (מהר"ם) מרוטנבורג. תשובות פסקים ומנהגים. מהדורת יצחק זאב כהנא. חלק ראשון. ירושלים: מוסד הרב קוק, תש"ז.

תשובות רבנו אברהם בן הרמב"ם. מהדורת אברהם חיים פריימן ושלמה דב גויטיין. ירושלים: מקיצי נרדמים, תרצ"ח.

תשובות רבנו גרשום מאור הגולה. מהדורת שלמה אידלברג. ניו יורק: ישיבה אוניברסיטה, תשט"ז.

ספר תשלום אבודרהם והוא ספר עבודת יום הכפורים המיוחס ליוסי בן יוסי וגם פיוטים שונים של הפייטנים הגדולים עם פירוש גדול המפרשים רבינו דוד בר' יוסף בר' דוד אבודרהם. מהדורת אליעזר ליפמן בן רפאל פרינץ. ברלין, תר"ס.


## B. Hebrew Secondary Sources


אבערלאנדער, גדלי'. ספר פדיון־הבן כהלכתו. ירושלים, תשנ"ג.

אברמסון, שרגא. "להקים שם." קרית ספר סא (תשמ"ו–תשמ"ז): 171–174.

———. "על ברכת התרת נדרים ושבועות." סיני נ (תשכ"ב): קפה–קפו.

———. "פסקים קדומים, א. ברכה על התרת נדרים ושבועות." סיני מט (תשכ"א): רי–ריד.

———. רב נסים גאון. ירושלים, תשכ"ה.

אידל, משה. "התפילה בקבלת פרובנס." תרביץ סב (תשנ"ג): 265–286.

אורבך, אפרים א. בעלי התוספות, תולדותם, חיבוריהם, שיטתם. מהדורת חמישית מורחבת ומתוקנת. ירושלים: מוסד ביאליק, תשמ"ו.

———. ערוגת הבושם. ד' כרכים. ירושלים: מקיצי נרדמים, תרצ"ט–תשכ"ז.

אליצור, שולמית. "קהל המתפלל והקדושתא הקדומה." בתוך כנסת עזרא: ספרות וחיים בבית הכנסת, אסופת מאמרים מוגשת לעזרא פליישר. בעריכת שולמית אליצור, משה דוד הר, אביגדור שנאן, גרשון שקד, 171–190. ירושלים: יד יצחק בן־צבי ומכון בן־צבי לחקר קהילות ישראל במזרח, תשנ"ה.

אסף, שמחה. ספר המקצועות. ירושלים: מוסד הרב קוק, תש"ז.

———. "קטע מחבורו של אבן אלגסוס (או אלגסום) בעניני תפלה." קרית ספר כח (תשי"ב–תשי"ג): 101–109.

בית־אריה, מלאכי. "ברכות האברים." תרביץ נו (תשמ"ז): 265–272.

בלידשטיין, יעקב. התפילה במשנתו ההלכתית של הרמב"ם. ירושלים: מוסד ביאליק ואוניברסיטת בן גוריון בנגב, תשנ"ד.

בן־שמאי, חגי. "היצירה הפייטנית וסדרי הקינות של אבלי ציון הקראים – המסגרת והתכנים." בתוך כנסת עזרא: ספרות וחיים בבית הכנסת, אסופת מאמרים מוגשת לעזרא פליישר. בעריכת שולמית אליצור, משה דוד הר, אביגדור שנאן, גרשון שקד, 191–234. ירושלים: יד יצחק בן־צבי ומכון בן־צבי לחקר קהילות ישראל במזרח, 1994.

בר־אילן, מאיר. סתרי תפילה והיכלות. רמת גן: אוניברסיטת בר־אילן, 1987.

———. "קווי יסוד להתהוותה של הקדושה וגיבושה." דעת 25 (תש"ן): 5–20.

ברודי, ירחמיאל. "לחידת עריכתו של סדר רב עמרם גאון." בתוך כנסת עזרא: ספרות וחיים בבית הכנסת, אסופת מאמרים מוגשת לעזרא פליישר. בעריכת שולמית אליצור, משה דוד הר, אביגדור שנאן, גרשון שקד, 21–34. ירושלים: יד יצחק בן־צבי ומכון בן־צבי לחקר קהילות ישראל במזרח, 1994.

גוטליב, אפרים. "משמעותה של התפילה בקבלה הספרדית." בתוך תהפילה היהודית - המשך וחידוש, בעריכת גבריאל חיים כהן. 168–189. ישראל: המכון ליהדות ולמחשבה בת זמננו, 1978.

גויטיין, שלמה דוב. סדרי חינוך בימי הגאונים ובית הרמב"ם: מקורות חדשים מן הגניזה. ירושלים: מכון בן צבי, האוניברסיטה העברית, תשכ"ב.

גולדשמידט, דניאל. מחזור לימים נוראים. כרך ב, יום כפור. ירושלים: ח' קורן, תש"ל

———. "מחזורים כמנהג קהילות יוון." בתוך מחקרי תפילה ופיוט, 272–288. ירושלים: מאגנס, תש"ם. מספונות יג (תשל"א–תשל"ח): קג–קצ.

———. מחקרי תפילה ופיוט. ירושלים: מאגנס, תש"ם.

———. "סדור תפלות כתב־יד מן המאה החמש עשרה." בתוך מחקרי תפילה ופיוט, 289–296. ירושלים: מאגנס, תש"ם. מקרית ספר כ (תש"ג–תש"ד): 171–176.

———. "סדר התפלה של הרמב"ם ע"פ כ"י אוקספורד." בתוך מחקרי תפילה ופיוט, 187–216. ירושלים: מאגנס, תש"ם. מידיעות המכון לחקר השירה העברית בירושלים ז (תשי"ח): 183–213.

———. "על דפוס קדום של מחזור ספרדי." בתוך מחקרי תפילה ופיוט, 303–314. ירושלים: מאגנס, תש"ם. מקרית ספר מז (תשל"ב): 711–719.

———. "קטעי דפוס קדום של סידור ספרדי." בתוך מחקרי תפילה ופיוט, 297–302. ירושלים: מאגנס, תש"ם. מאוצר יהודי ספרד ספר ד (תשכ"א): 108–113.

גינצבורג, לוי. גנזי שעכטער. ספר ב: קטעים מכתבי הגאונים מן הגניזה שבמצרים. ניו־יורק, בית מדרש הרבנים אשר באמעריקא, תרפ"ט.

———. פירושים וחידושים בירושלמי. ד' כרכים. ניו־יורק, בית המדרש לרבנים באמריקה, תש"א–תשכ"א. דפוס חדש, תשל"א.

גפני, ישעיהו. יהודי בבל בתקופת התלמוד. ירושלים: מרכז זלמן שזר לתולדות ישראל, תשנ"א.

גראסבערג, מנשה. ספר גבול מנשה. פראנקפורט דמין, תרנ"ט.

גרונר, צבי. ברכות שנשתקעו. עבודת גמר לקראת קבלת התאר השני, האוניברסיטה העברית, ירושלים, תשכ"ד.

———. "הברכה על הווידוי וגלגוליה." בר אילן יג (תשל"ו): 158–168.

גרוסמן, אברהם. חכמי אשכנז הראשונים. ירושלים: מאגנס, תשמ"ט.

———. חכמי צרפת הראשונים. ירושלים: מאגנס, תשנ"ה.

———. "יצירתם ההלכתית של חכמי ספרד." בתוך מורשת ספרד. בעריכת חיים ביינארט, 150–173. ירושלים: מאגנס, תשנ"ב.

———. "על דרכו של הקליר בעשיית פשרה בדברי אגדה." נספח ב' לפרק ב של מנהגי ישראל של דניאל שפרבר, כרך ב, עב–עה. ירושלים: מוסד הרב קוק, 1991.

———. "הקשרים בין יהדות ספרד ליהדות אשכנז בימי־הביניים." בתוך מורשת ספרד. בעריכת חיים ביינארט, 174–189. ירושלים: מאגנס, תשנ"ב.

———. "הרקע לצמיחת פרשנות הפיוט בגרמניה ובצרפת במאה הי"א." בתוך ספר היובל לשלמה סימונסון: קובץ מחקרים לתולדות היהודים בימי הביניים ובתקופה הרנסנס, נה–עב. תל אביב: אוניברסיטת תל אביב, תשנ"ג.

גרינולד, איתמר. "פיוטי יניי וספרות יורדי מרכבה." תרביץ לו (תשכ"ז): 257–277.

———. "שירת המלאכים, ה'קדושה' ובעיית חיבורה של ספרות ההיכלות." בתוך פרקים בתולדות ירושלים בימי בית שני, ספר זכרון לאברהם שליט. בעריכת אהרן אופנהיימר, אוריאל רפפורט, מנחם שטרן, 459–481. ירושלים: יד יצחק בן־צבי, תשמ"א.

דינרי, ידידיה. "המנהג וההלכה בתשובות חכמי אשכנז במאה הט"ו." בתוך ספר הזכרון לבנימין דה פריס. בעריכת א. צ. מלמד, 168–198. ירושלים, 1968.

———. חכמי אשכנז בשלהי ימי הביניים. ירושלים: מוסד ביאליק, 1984.

דן, יוסף. תורת הסוד של חסידות אשכנז. ירושלים: מוסד ביאליק, תשכ"ח.

דנציג, נחמן. מבוא לספר הלכות פסוקות עם תשלום הלכות פסוקות. ניו־יורק וירושלים: בית המדרש לרבנים באמריקה, תשנ"ג.

———. "תשובות הגאונים 'שערי תשובה' ושו"ת מן השמים." תרביץ נח (תשמ"ט): 21–48.

דשן, שלמה. "חידת 'כל נדרי': בירור אנתרופולוגי והיסטורי." פרקים בתולדות החברה היהודית בימי הביניים ובעת החדשה מוקדשים לפרופסור יעקב כ"ץ..., 144–146. ירושלים: מאגנס, תש"ם.

הברמן, אברהם מאיר. תולדות הפיוט והשירה. ב' כרכים. רמת גן: מסדה, 1970.

היינימן, יוסף. "יחסו של רס"ג לשינוי מטבע התפלה." בתוך עיוני תפילה. בעריכת אביגדור שנאן, 110–123. ירושלים: מאגנס, תשמ"א. מבר אילן א (תשכ"ג): 220–233.

———. "שרידים מיצירתם הפיוטית של המתורגמנים הקדומים." בתוך עיוני תפילה. בעריכת אביגדור שנאן, 148–167. ירושלים: מאגנס, תשמ"א. מהספרות ד (תשל"ג): 362–375.

———. תפילה בתקופת התנאים והאמוראים: טיבה ודפוסיה. ירושלים: מאגנס, תשכ"ד; מהדורה שלישית, תשל"ח. Translated by Richard S. Sarason as *Prayer in the Talmud: Forms and Patterns.* Berlin, New York: Walter de Gruyter, 1977.

הקר, יוסף. "גאון ודיכאון – קטעים בהווייתם הרוחנית והחברתית של יוצאי ספרד ופורטוגאל באמפירה ועות'מאנית." בתוך תרבות וחברה בתולדות ישראל בימי־הביניים (ספר זכרון לחיים הלל בן ששון). בעריכת רואבן בונפיל, מנחם בן ששון, ויוסף הקר, 541–586. ירושלים: מרכז זלמן שזר, תשמ"ט.

———. "יוצאי ספרד באמפירה העות'מנית במאה הט"ז – קהלה וחברה." בתוך מורשת ספרד. בעריכת חיים ביינארט, 460–478. ירושלים: מאגנס, תשנ"ב.

הרכבי, אברהם אליהו. ספר המצות לענן: לתולדות הקראים וספרותה. ס"ט פטרסבורג, 1903. הדפסה שניה: בתוך מספרי המצות הראשונים לבני מקרא. ירושלים: מקור, תשכ"ט.

וידר, נפתלי. השפעות אסלאמיות על הפולחן היהודי. אוקספורד: ספרית־מזרח ומערב, תש"ז.

———. "לחקר מנהג בבל הקדמון." תרביץ לז (תשכ"ח): 135–157, 240–264.

———. "לחקר נוסח העמידה במנהג בבל הקדמון." סיני עח (תשל"ו): צז–קכב, רעט–רפד.

———. "פרקים בתולדות התפילה והברכות." סיני עז (תשל"ה): קטז–קלח.

זהרי, מנחם. דברי משה הדרשן ופיוטי אלעזר הקלירי בפירושי רש"י. ירושלים: כרמל, תשנ"ו.

זולאי, מנחם. האסכולה הפייטנית של רב סעדיה גאון. ירושלים: מכון שוקן למחקר היהדות, תשכ"ד.

ז"ק, ברכה. "התפילה במשנתו של ר' משה קורדובירו." דעת 9 (תשמ"ב): 5–12.

חלמיש, משה. "ברכת המגביה שפלים – ברכה שנשתכחה." אסופות ב (תשמ"ח): קצא–ר.

———. "ברכת 'הנותן ליעף כח'." אסופות א (תשמ"ז): שסא–שעז.

טובי, יוסף. "השירה העברית בארצות־המזרח לאחר הגירוש." פעמים 26 (תשמ"ו): 29–45.

———. "יחסו של רב סעדיה גאון לפיוט." בתוך כנסת עזרא: ספרות וחיים בבית הכנסת, אסופת מאמרים מוגשת לעזרא פליישר. בעריכת שולמית אליצור, משה דוד הר, אביגדור שנאן, גרשון שקד, 235–250. ירושלים: יד יצחק בן־צבי ומכון בן־צבי לחקר קהילות ישראל במזרח, 1994.

יהלום, יוסף. שפת השיר של הפיוט הארץ־ישראלי הקדום. ירושלים: מאגנס, תשמ"ה.

יערי, אברהם. תולדות חג שמחת תורה: השתלשלות מנהגיו בתפוצות ישראל לדורותיהן. ירושלים: מוסד הרב קוק, תשכ"ד; תשמ"ט.

כ"ץ, יעקב. "יחסי הלכה וקבלה בדורות 'התגלות' הזוהר." בתוך הלכה וקבלה: מחקרים בתולדות דת ישראל על מדוריה וזיקתה החברתית, 52–69. ירושלים: מאגנס, תשמ"ו. מדעת ד (תש"מ): 57–74.

———. "מעריב בזמנו ושלא בזמנו – דוגמא לזיקה בין מנהג, הלכה וחברה." בתוך הלכה וקבלה: מחקרים בתולדות דת ישראל על מדוריה וזיקתה החברתית, 175–200. ירושלים: מאגנס, תשמ"ו.

לוין, ב.מ. "משרידי הגניזה." תרביץ ב (תרצ"א): 383–410.

ליברמן, שאול. תוספתא כפשוטה. חלקים א–ה. מהדורה שניה. ירושלים: בית המדרש לרבנים שבאמריקה, תשנ"ג. חלקים ו–י. ניוארק: בית המדרש לרבנים שבאמריקה, תשכ"ז–תשמ"ח.

מירסקי, אהרן. הפיוט: התפתחותו בארץ־ישראל ובגולה. ירושלים: מאגנס, תש"ן.

———. "יצירתם של יהודי ספרד בפיוט ובשירה." בתוך מורשת ספרד. בעריכת חיים ביינארט, 118–149. ירושלים: מאגנס, תשנ"ב.

———. ראשית הפיוט. ירושלים: הסוכנות היהודית לארץ־ישראל, תשכ"ה.

———. "שירת ספרד – תכניה וסוגיה." בתוך הפיוט: התפתחותו בארץ-ישראל ובגולה, 617–652. ירושלים: מאגנס, תש"ן.

מרגליות, מרדכי. הלכות ארץ ישראל מן הגניזה. ירושלים: מוסד הרב קוק, תשל"ד.

מרטארה, מרדכי. "ספר שער השמים לר' יעקב בר' ששת..." אוצר נחמד ג (תר"ך): 153–165.

ספר קול יעקב ובני יעקב. ג'רבה: עידאן כהן צבאן הדאד, תש"ה.

ספראי, שמואל. "בית הכנסת." בתוך בית הכנסת בתקופת המשנה והתלמוד. בעריכת זאב ספראי, 15–42. ירושלים: מרכז זלמן שזר, תשמ"ו. מתוך בשלהי הבית השני ובתקופת המשנה, 143–170. ירושלים: מרכז זלמן שזר, תשמ"ג.

———. "הערות היסטוריות למשנת פסחים, פרק עשירי." בתוך המקרא ותולדות ישראל (מחקרים לזכרו של יעקב ליוור), 297–306. תל אביב: אוניברסיטת תל אביב, תשל"ב.

פאור, יוסף. "ספק ברכות להקל – כלל שטבעו הרמב"ם." אסופות א (תשמ"ז): שמג–שנט.

פליישר, עזרא. "בחינות בשירת פייטני איטליה הקדמונים." הספרות 30–31 (1981): 131–167.

———. "בין ארעי לקבע בתפלת הרבים בארץ־ישראל הקדומה." ספר הזכרון להרב נסים גאון - הלק השירה והפיוט. בעריכת מאיר בניהו. כרך ה', ז–לג. ירושלים: יד הרב נסים, 1958.

———. היוצרות בהתהוותם והתפתחותם. ירושלים: מאגנס, תשמ"ד.

———. "לוח מועדי השנה בפיוט לר' אלעזר בירבי קיליר." תרביץ נב (תשמ"ג): 223–272.

———. "לליבון ענין ה'פורס על שמע'." תרביץ 41 (תשל"ב): 133–144.

———. "לנוסחה הקדום של ברכת היום בעמידות השבת." בר אילן כו–כז (1995): 249–258.

———. "לקדמוניות תפילות החובה בישראל." תרביץ נט (תש"ן): 397–441.

———. "לתפוצתן של קדושות העמידה והיוצר במנהגות התפילה של בני ארץ ישראל." תרביץ 38 (תשכ"ט): 255–284.

———. "קריאה חד־שנתית ותלת־שנתית בתורה בבית הכנסת הקדום." תרביץ סא (תשנ"ב): 25–45.

———. שירת-הקודש העברית בימי-הביניים. ירושלים: כתר, 1975.

———. תפילה ומנהגי תפילה ארץ-ישראליים בתקופת הגניזה. ירושלים: מאגנס, תשמ"ח.

———. "תפילת שמונה עשרה – עיונים באופיה, סִדרהּ, תוכנהּ ומגמותיה," תרביץ סב (תשנ"ג): 179–223.

פרי (פלאום), חירם. "התפלה והפיוט בלשון־לעז בימי־הביניים." תרביץ 24 (1955): 426–440.

רבינוביץ, רפאל. דיקדוקי סופרים. ב' כרכים. ניו־יורק: M. P. Press, Inc., תשל"ז. מט"ז כרכים. מינכען, תרכ"ג–תרנ"ו.

רות, אברהם נפתלי צבי. "מבית מדרשם של הגאונים מגנ' קויפמן." סורא ב (תשט"ז): 276–312.

רצהבי, יהודה. מגנזי שירת הקדם (פיוט וחקרי פיוט). ירושלים: משגב ירושלים – המכון לחקר מורשת יהדות ספרד והמזרח, 1991.

שירמן, ח. "הרמב"ם והשירה העברית." מאזנים ג, סידרא ב (תרצ"ה): 433–436.

שלום, גרשום. "פרקים מתולדות ספרות הקבלה." קרית ספר ד (1928): 286–327.

———. ראשית הקבלה (1150–1250). ירושלים: שוקן, תשי"ח.

———. "שרידים חדשים מכתבי ר' עזריאל מגירונה." ספר זכרון לאשר גולאק ולשמואל קליין, 201–222. ירושלים: המכון למדעי־היהדות של האוניברסיטה העברית, תשי"ב.

שפייגל, שלום. "לפרשת הפולמוס של פירקוי בן באבוי." בתוך ספר היובל לכבוד צבי וולפסון, רמג–רעד. ירושלים: *AAJR*, תשכ"ה.

שפרבר, דניאל. מנהגי ישראל: מקורות ותולדות. ד' כרכים. ירושלים: מוסד הרב קוק, 1990–1995.

תא־שמע, ישראל מ. "ברכות המילה על הכוס בט' באב – כיצד?" בתוך מנהג אשכנז הקדמון - חקר ועיון, 335–327. ירושלים: מאגנס, תשנ"ב. מ"הברכה על היין בטכס ברית המילה." אסופות ד (תש"ן): מט–נו.

———. "הלכה מנהג ומסורת ביהדות אשכנז במאות הי"א – י"ב." בתוך מנהג אשכנז הקדמון - חקר ועיון, 105–13. ירושלים: מאגנס, תשנ"ב. מסידרא ג (תשמ"ז): 161–85.

———. "הפורס סוכת שלום – ברכה וגלגוליה." בתוך מנהג אשכנז הקדמון, חקר ועיון, 156–142. ירושלים: מאגנס, תשנ"ב. מאסופות ב (תשמ"ח): קעז–קפט.

———. מנהג אשכנז הקדמון, חקר ועיון. ירושלים: מאגנס, תשנ"ב.

———. "'מקדש מעט' – הסמל והממשות." בתוך כנסת עזרא: ספרות וחיים בבית הכנסת, אסופת מאמרים מוגשת לעזרא פליישר. בעריכת שולמית אליצור, משה דוד הר, אביגדור שנאן, גרשון שקד, 364–351. ירושלים: יד יצחק בן צבי ומכון בן־צבי לחקר קהילות ישראל במזרח, תשנ"ה.

———. נספח למרדכי מרגליות. הלכות ארץ ישראל מן הגניזה, לב–לז. ירושלים: מוסד הרב קוק, תשל"ד.

———. "'עיון תפילה' וראשית מעשה הפיוט." תרביץ נג (תשמ"ד): 288–285.

———. "קליטתם של ספרי הרי"ף, הר"ח, ו"הלכות גדולות" בצרפת ובאשכנז במאות הי"א–י"ב." קרית ספר 55 (תש"ם): 201–191.

———. "קריאת שמע 'על המיטה' – מה היא?" בתוך מנהג אשכנז הקדמון, חקר ועיון, 326–311. ירושלים: מאגנס, תשנ"ב.

———. רבי זרחיה הלוי בעל המאור ובני חוגו: לתולדות הספרות הרבנית בפרובאנס. ירושלים: מוסד הרב קוק, תשנ"ג.

———. "רבי יוסף קארו בין אשכנז לספרד – לחקר התפשטות ספר הזוהר." תרביץ נט (תש"ן): 158–153.

———. "רבנו אשר ובנו ר' יעקב בעל הטורים: בין אשכנז לספרד." פעמים 46–47 (תשנ"א): 91–75.

———. "תשובת הרמב"ם בענין ברכת־בתולים." In *Maimonidean Studies.* Volume 2. Edited by Arthur Hyman, 9-15. New York: The Michael Scharf Publication Trust of Yeshiva University Press, 1991.


## C. Non-Hebrew Sources


Alexander, Philip. "Prayer in the Heikhalot Literature." In *Prière, mystique et judaïsme.* Edited by Roland Goetschel, 43-64. Presses Universitaires de France, 1987.

Alon, Gedaliah. *The Jews in their Land in the Talmudic Age (70-640 C.E.).* Translated by Gershon Levi. Cambridge, Massachusetts: Cambridge University Press, 1989. Reprinted from Jerusalem: Magnes Press, 1980, 1984.

Altmann, Alexander. "Eleazar of Worms' *Ḥokhmath Ha-'Egoz.*" *JJS* 11 (1960): 101-113.

Ankori, Zvi. *Karaites in Byzantium: The Formative Years 970-1100.* New York: Columbia University Press, 1959.

Austin, J.L. *How To Do Things With Words.* New York: Oxford University Press, 1962.

Baer, Yitzhak. *A History of the Jews in Christian Spain.* 2 volumes. Philadelphia: The Jewish Publication Society, 1961. Reprinted 1971.

Baron, Salo W. *A Social and Religious History of the Jews.* Volumes 5 and 7. 2nd edition. New York and London: Columbia University Press; and Philadelphia: The Jewish Publication Society of America, 1957-1958.

Bauer, Erich. *Ethnologie der jemenitischen Juden.* Heidelberg, 1934.

Bauman, Richard. "Verbal Art as Performance." *American Anthropologist* 77 (1975): 290-311.

Benor, Ehud. *Worship of the Heart: A Study in Maimonides' Philosophy of Religion.* Albany: SUNY, 1995.

Berkovits, Eliezer. *Jewish Women in Time and Torah.* Hoboken, New Jersey: Ktav Publishing House, 1990.

Bloch, Maurice. "Symbols, Song, Dance and Features of Articulation: Is Religion an Extreme Form of Traditional Authority?" *Archiv. europ. sociol.* 15 (1974): 55-81.

Bodenschatz, Johann Christoph Georg. *Kirchliche Verfassung der heutigen Juden, sonderlich derer in Deutschland.* Erlangen, Coburg, 1748-49; 2nd edition with corrected transliterations, Frankfort, 1756.

Bowman, Steven B. *The Jews of Byzantium 1204-1453.* University of Alabama Press, 1985.

Joan R. Branham, "Sacred Space Under Erasure in Ancient Synagogues and Churches." *Art Bulletin* 74 (1992): 375-394.

——. "Vicarious Sacrality: Temple Space in Ancient Synagogues." In *Ancient Synagogues: Historical Analysis and Archaeological Discovery.* Edited by Dan Urman and Paul V.M. Flesher, 319-345. Leiden: E.J.Brill, 1995.

Brody, Robert. *The Geonim of Babylonia and the Shaping of Medieval Jewish Culture.* New Haven: Yale University Press, 1998.

——. "Saadya Gaon on the Limits of Liturgical Flexibility." In *Geniza Research after Ninety Years: The Case of Judaeo-Arabic.* Edited by Joshua Blau and Stefan C. Reif, 40-46. Cambridge: University Press, 1992.

Brody, Seth Lance. *Human Hands Dwell in Heavenly Heights: Worship and Mystical Experience in Thirteenth Century Kabbalah.* Ph.D. diss. University of Pennsylvania, 1991.

Buechler, A. "La Kedouscha du «Yocêr» chez les Gueonim." *REJ* 53 (1907): 220-230.

Cohen, Shaye J.D. *From the Maccabees to the Mishnah.* Philadelphia: Westminster Press, 1987.

——. "The Significance of Yavneh: Pharisees, Rabbis, and the End of Jewish Sectarianism." *HUCA* 55 (1984): 27-53.

Dan, Joseph, ed. *The Early Kabbalah.* New York, Mahwah, Toronto: Paulist Press, 1986.

——. "The Emergence of Mystical Prayer." In *Studies in Jewish Mysticism.* Edited by Joseph Dan and Frank Talmadge, 85-120. Cambridge, Massachusetts: Association for Jewish Studies, 1982.

——. "Ḥokhmath Ha-'Egoz, Its Origin and Development." *JJS* 17 (1966): 73-82.

——. "Prayer as Text and Prayer as Mystical Experience." In *Torah and Wisdom: Studies in Jewish Philosophy, Kabbalah, and Halacha, Essays in Honor of Arthur Hyman.* Edited by Ruth Link-Salinger, 33-47. New York: Shengold Publishers, Inc., 1992.

——. "The Religious Experience of the *Merkavah.*" In *Jewish Spirituality from the Bible through the Middle Ages.* Edited by Arthur Green, 289-307. New York: Crossroad, 1989.

Elbogen, Ismar. *Jewish Liturgy: A Comprehensive History.* Translated by Raymond P. Scheindlin from the 1913 German edition and the 1972 Hebrew edition. Philadelphia: The Jewish Publication Society; New York: The Jewish Theological Seminary of America, 1993.

Elon, Menahem. *Jewish Law: History, Sources, Principles.* Translated by Bernard Auerbach and Melvin J. Sykes. Philadelphia: The Jewish Publication Society of America, 1994.

Enelow, H. G. "Kawwana: the Struggle for Inwardness in Judaism." In *Studies in Jewish Literature Issued in Honor of Professor Kaufmann Kohler,* 82-107. Berlin, 1913.

Epstein, Isadore. *The Responsa of Rabbi Simon b. Ẓemaḥ Duran as a Source of the History of the Jews in North Africa.* New York: Ktav, 1968. Reprint of 1930 edition.

Epstein, J.N. "Sur les "Chapitres" de Ben Baboi." *REJ* 75 (1922): 179-186.

Feldman, Leon A. "Nissim ben Reuben Gerondi." *Encyclopedia Judaica.* XII: 1185-1186.

Fiensy, David A. *Prayers Alleged to be Jewish: An Examination of the* Constitutiones Apostolorum. Chico, CA: Scholars Press, 1985.

Fine, Steven. *This Holy Place: On the Sanctity of the Synagogue during the Greco-Roman Period.* Notre Dame University Press, 1997.

Finkelstein, Louis. *Jewish Self-Government in the Middle Ages.* New York: Phillip Feldheim, Inc., 1964.

Fox, Marvin. *Interpreting Maimonides: Studies in Methodology, Metaphysics, and Moral Philosophy.* Chicago: University of Chicago Press, 1990.

Freimann, Alfred. "Die Ascheriden (1267-1391)." *JJLG* 13 (1920): 142-254.

Gil, Moshe. "The Babylonian Yeshivot and the Maghrib in the Early Middle Ages." *PAAJR* 57 (1990/91): 60-126.

Ginzberg, Louis. *Geonica.* 2 volumes in 1. New York: The Jewish Theological Seminary of America, 1909. Reprinted, n.d.

——. "Saadia's Siddur." *JQR* 33 (1942): 315-363.

Goetschel, Roland. *Meir Ibn Gabbay: Le Discours de la Kabbala Espagnole.* Leuven: Peeters, 1981.

Goitein, S. D. *A Mediterranean Society.* Volume 2: The Community. Berkeley: University of California Press, 1971.

——. *A Mediterranean Society.* Volume 3: The Family. Berkeley: University of California Press, 1978.

Goldberg, Arnold. "Service of the Heart: Liturgical Aspects of Synagogue Worship." In *Standing Before God: Studies on Prayer in Scriptures and in Traditions with Essays in Honor of John M. Oesterreicher.* Edited by Asher Finkel and Lawrence Frizzell, 195-211. New York: Ktav Publishing House, Inc., 1981.

Goldman, Edward A. "A Critical Edition of the Palestinian Talmud, Tractate Rosh Hashanah, Chapter Four." *HUCA* 49 (1978): 205-226.

Goldman, Israel M. *The Life and Times of Rabbi David ibn Abi Zimra.* New York: The Jewish Theological Seminary of America, 1970.

Goldwurm, Hersh. *The Rishonim...* Brooklyn: Mesorah Publications, Ltd., 1982.

Goodblatt, David. *The Monarchic Principle: Studies in Jewish Self-Government in Antiquity.* Tübingen: J.C.B.Mohr (Paul Siebeck), 1994.

Goodman, Martin. *State and Society in Roman Galilee, A.D. 132-212.* Totowa, New Jersey: Rowman and Allanheld, Publishers, 1983.

Granqvist, Hilma. *Marriage Conditions in a Palestinian Village.* Volume Two. Helsingfors, 1935.

Gruenwald, Ithamar. *Apocalyptic and Merkavah Mysticism.* Leiden/Köln: E.J. Brill, 1980.

Hallevi, Judah. *Book of Kuzari.* Translated by Hartwig Hirschfeld. New York: Pardes Publishing House, 1946.

Halperin, David J. *Faces of the Chariot: Early Jewish Responses to Ezekiel's Vision.* Tübingen: JCB Mohr (Paul Siebeck), 1988.

Hammer, Reuven. *Entering Jewish Prayer: A Guide to Personal Devotion and the Worship Service.* New York: Schocken Books, 1994.

Haran, Menahem. *Temples and Temple-Service in Ancient Israel: An Inquiry into Biblical Cult Phenomena and the Historical Setting of the Priestly School.* Winona Lake, Indiana: Eisenbrauns, 1985.

Heinemann, Joseph. "The Formula Melekh Ha-'Olam." *JJS* 11 (1960): 177-179.

——. "Once Again Melekh Ha-'Olam." *JJS* 15 (1964): 149-164.

——. *Prayer in the Talmud: Forms and Patterns.* Translated by Richard S. Sarason. Berlin, New York: Walter de Gruyter, 1977.

Hengel, Martin. "Proseuche und Synagogue: Jüdische Gemeinde, Gotteshaus und Gottesdienst in der Diaspora und in Palästina." In *Tradition und Glaube: Das frühe Christentum in seiner Umwelt, Festgabe für Karl Georg Kuhn.* Edited by Gert Jeremias, Heinz-Wolfgang Kuhn, Hartmut Stegemann, 157-184. Göttingen: Vandenhoeck & Ruprecht, 1971.

Hoffman, Lawrence A. *The Canonization of the Synagogue Service.* Notre Dame and London: University of Notre Dame Press, 1979. Reprint, 1986.

——. *Covenant of Blood: Circumcision and Gender in Rabbinic Judaism.* Chicago: University of Chicago Press, 1996.

——. *Liturgical Responses Suppressed by the Geonim in their Attempt to Fix the Liturgy.* Ph.D dissertation. Hebrew Union College - Jewish Institute of Religion, Cincinnati, 1973.

Idel, Moshe. *Kabbalah, New Perspectives.* New Haven and London: Yale University Press, 1988.

Jacobs, Louis. *Hasidic Prayer.* London: The Littman Library of Jewish Civilization, 1972, rpt. 1993.

Kadushin, Max. *Worship and Ethics: A Study in Rabbinic Judaism.* Northwestern University Press, 1964.

Kayserling, M. "Das Castilianische Gemeinde-Status." *Jahrbuch für die Geschichte der Juden und des Judenthums* 4 (1869): 263-334.

Kimelman, Reuven. "The Literary Structure of the Amidah and the Rhetoric of Redemption." In *The Echoes of Many Texts: Reflections on Jewish and Christian Traditions. Essays in honor of Lou Silberman.* Edited by W. Dever and J. Wright, 171-218. Atlanta: Scholars Press, 1997.

——. "The Shema' and its Rhetoric: The Case for the Shema' Being More than Creation, Revelation, and Redemption." *Journal of Jewish Thought and Philosophy* 2 (1992): 111-156.

Klein, Michael L. *Genizah Manuscripts of Palestinian Targum to the Pentateuch.* Cincinnati: Hebrew Union College Press, 1986.

Knohl, Israel. "Between Voice and Silence: The Relationship Between Prayer and Temple Cult." *JBL* 115 (1996): 17-30.

Kraut, Benny. *German-Jewish Orthodoxy in an Immigrant Synagogue: Cincinnati's New Hope Congregation and the Ambiguities of Ethnic Religion.* New York: Markus Wiener Publishing, 1988.

Langer, Ruth. "The Birkat Betulim: A Study of the Jewish Celebration of Bridal Virginity." *PAAJR* LXI (1995): 53-94.

——. "From Study of Scripture to a Reenactment of Sinai: The Emergence of the Synagogue Torah Service." *Worship* 72 (1998): 43-67.

——. *Harm Through the Spoken Word: לשון הרע* and Related Concepts in Rabbinic Literature. Unpublished Rabbinic Thesis. Hebrew Union College - Jewish Institute of Religion, Cincinnati, 1986.

——. "Kalir Was A Tanna: Rabbenu Tam's Invocation of Antiquity in Defense of the Ashkenazi Payyetanic Tradition." *HUCA* LXVII (1996): 95-106.

Lerner, M.B. "The External Tractates." In *The Literature of the Sages,* Part I, 397-400. Edited by Shmuel Safrai. Van Gorcum, Assen/Maastricht; Philadelphia: Fortress Press, 1987.

Levine, Lee I., editor. *The Galilee in Late Antiquity.* New York and Jerusalem: The Jewish Theological Seminary of America, 1992.

——. *The Rabbinic Class of Roman Palestine in Late Antiquity.* Jerusalem: Yad Itzhak Ben-Zvi, The Jewish Theological Seminary of America, 1985. English edition, 1989.

Lewis, Bernard. *History Remembered, Recovered, Invented.* Princeton, N.J.: Princeton University Press, 1975; reprinted, New York: Touchstone Book (Simon and Schuster), 1987.

Mann, Jacob. "Changes in the Divine Service of the Synagogue due to Religious Persecutions." *HUCA* 4 (1927): 241-311.

Marcus, Ivan G. "The Devotional Ideals of Ashkenazic Pietism." In *Jewish Spirituality from the Bible through the Middle Ages.* Edited by Arthur Green, 356-366. New York: Crossroad, 1989.

——. *Piety and Society: The Jewish Pietists of Medieval Germany.* Leiden: E.J. Brill, 1981.

Matt, Daniel C. "The Mystic and the Mizwot." In *Jewish Spirituality from the Bible through the Middle Ages.* Edited by Arthur Green, 367-404. New York: Crossroad, 1989.

Meiselman, Moshe. *Jewish Women in Jewish Law.* New York: Ktav Publishing House, Yeshiva University Press, 1978.

*Migdal Chananel ueber Leben und Schriften R. Chananel's in Kairuan.* Festschrift for Azriel Hildesheimer. Leipzig, 1876.

Millar, Fergus. *The Roman Near East 31 BC–AD 337.* Cambridge, MA: Harvard University Press, 1993.

Neusner, Jacob. *First Century Judaism in Crisis: Yoḥanan ben Zakkai and the Renaissance of Torah.* Nashville: Abingdon Press, 1975.

——. "Rabbis and Community in Third-Century Babylonia." In *Religions in Antiquity: Essays in Memory of Erwin Ramsdell Goodenough.* Edited by Jacob Neusner, 438-459. Leiden: E.J. Brill, 1968.

Newsom, Carol. *Songs of the Sabbath Sacrifice: A Critical Edition.* Atlanta: Scholars Press, 1985.

Nitzan, Bilhah. *Qumran Prayer and Religious Poetry.* Translated by Jonathan Chipman. Leiden: E.J. Brill, 1994.

Perkins, Carl M. "The Evening *Shema*: A Study in Rabbinic Consolation." *Judaism* 43 (1994): 27-36.

Petuchowski, Jakob J. "The Liturgy of the Synagogue: History, Structure and Contents." In *Approaches to Ancient Judaism, Vol. 4: Studies in Liturgy, Exegesis, and Talmudic Narrative.* Edited by William Scott Green, 1-64. Chico, California: Scholars Press, 1983.

——. *Prayerbook Reform in Europe: The Liturgy of European Liberal and Reform Judaism.* New York: The World Union for Progressive Judaism, 1968.

——. "Some Laws of Jewish Liturgical Development." *Judaism* 34 (1985): 312-326.

——. *Theology and Poetry: Studies in the Medieval Piyyut.* The Littman Library of Jewish Civilization. London, Henley and Boston: Routledge & Kegan Paul, 1978.

Rappaport, Roy A. "The Obvious Aspects of Ritual." In *Ecology, Meaning, and Religion,* 173-221. Richmond, California: North Atlantic Books, c. 1979.

Redfield, Robert. *Peasant Society and Culture.* 1956. Reprint, Chicago: University of Chicago Press, 1971.

Reichert, Victor Emanuel. *The Tahkemoni of Judah Al-Harizi.* 2 volumes. Jerusalem: Raphael Haim Cohen's Ltd. Publishers, 1973.

Reif, Stefan C. *Judaism and Hebrew Prayer: New Perspectives on Jewish Liturgical History.* Cambridge: University Press, 1993.

Roth, C. "Melekh Ha-'Olam: Zealot Influence in the Liturgy." *JJS* 11 (1960): 173-176.

Rubin, Nissan. "Birkat Avelim - The Blessing of Mourners." In *Approaches to Ancient Judaism*, N.S., Volume 5. Edited by Herbert W. Basser and Simcha Fishbane, 119-141. Atlanta: Scholars Press, 1993.

Safrai, S. *The Jewish People in the First Century: Historical Geography, Political History, Social, Cultural and Religious Life and Institutions.* Philadelphia: Fortress Press, 1976.

Sarna, N.M. "The Chirotonic Motif on the Lachish Altar." In *Investigations at Lachish* by Y. Aharoni. Tel Aviv, 1975: 44-46.

Schäfer, Peter. *The Hidden and Manifest God: Some Major Themes in Early Jewish Mysticism.* Translated by Aubrey Pomerance. Albany: State University of New York Press, 1992.

——. *Hekhalot Studien.* Tübingen: JCB Mohr (Paul Siebeck), 1988.

——. *Synopse zur Hekhalot Literatur.* Tübingen: J.C.B. Mohr (Paul Siebeck), 1981.

Scholem, Gershom. *Kabbalah.* N.P.: The Jewish Publication Society of America, Quadrangle/The New York Times Book Co., 1974.

Schreiner, Martin. "Samau'al b. Jaḥjâ al-Magribî und seine Schrift 'Ifḥâm al-Jahûd'." *MGWJ* 42 (1898): 123-133, 214-223, 253-261.

Schwartz, Seth. *Josephus and Judaean Politics.* Leiden: E.J. Brill, 1990.

Septimus, Bernard. "Piety and Power in Thirteenth-Century Catalonia." In *Studies in Medieval Jewish History and Literature.* Edited by Isadore Twersky, 195-230. Cambridge, Massachusetts and London: Harvard University Press, 1979.

Shiloah, Amnon. *Jewish Musical Traditions.* Detroit: Wayne State University Press, 1992.

Swartz, Michael. *Mystical Prayer in Ancient Judaism: An Analysis of Ma'aseh Merkavah.* Tübingen: JCB Mohr (Paul Siebeck), 1992.

Tabory, Joseph. "The Conflict of Halakhah and Prayer." *Tradition* 25 (1989): 17-30.

Talmon, S. "The Emergence of Institutionalized Prayer in Israel in the Light of the Qumran Literature." *Qumran: Sa piété, sa theólogie et son milieu.* Edited by M. Delior, 265-284. Paris: Duculot, 1978.

Tambiah, Stanley Jeyaraja. "A Performative Approach to Ritual." In *Culture, Thought and Social Action: An Anthropological Perspective*, 123-166. Cambridge, MA and London, England: Harvard University Press, 1985.

Tishby, Isaiah. *The Wisdom of the Zohar.* Translated by David Goldstein. London: Oxford University Press, Littman Library, 1989; rpt., 1991.

Uffenheimer, Rivka Schatz. *Hasidism as Mysticism: Quietistic Elements in Eighteenth Century Hasidic Thought.* Translated by Jonathan Chipman. Princeton: Princeton University Press; Jerusalem: Magnes, 1993.

Verman, Mark. "The Development of Yiḥudim in Spanish Kabbalah." *Jerusalem Studies in Jewish Thought* 8 (1989): 25*-41*.

Washofsky, Mark. "Minhag and Halakhah: Toward a Model of Shared Authority on Matters of Ritual." In *Rabbinic-Lay Relations in Jewish Law.* Edited by Walter Jacob and Moshe Zemer, 103-107. Tel Aviv and Pittsburgh: Rodef Shalom Press, 1993.

Weinberger, Leon J. *Jewish Hymnography: A Literary History.* London: The Litmann Library of Jewish Civilization, 1998.

Weiss, J.G. "On the Formula Melekh Ha-'olam as an Anti-Gnostic Protest." *JJS* 10 (1959): 169-172.

Werner, Eric. "The Doxology in Synagogue and Church, A Liturgico-Musical Study." *HUCA* 19 (1945-46): 275-351.

——. *A Voice Still Heard...: The Sacred Songs of the Ashkenazi Jews.* University Park: The Pennsylvania State University Press, 1976.

Wheelock, Wade T. "The Problem of Ritual Language: From Information to Situation." *JAAR* 50 (1982): 49-71.

Wieder, Naphtali. *The Judean Scrolls and Karaism.* London: East and West Library, 1962.

Wiesenberg, E.J. "The Liturgical Term Melekh Ha-'Olam." *JJS* 15 (1964): 1-56.

——. "Gleanings of the Liturgical Term Melekh Ha-'Olam." *JJS* 17 (1966): 47-72.

Wolff, A. A. עתרת שלום ואמת, *Die Stimmen der ältesten glaubwürdigsten Rabbinen über die Pijutim.* Leipzig, 1857.

Wolfson, Elliot. *The Book of the Pomegranate: Moses de Leon's Sefer Ha-Rimmon.* Atlanta: Scholar's Press, 1988.

——. "Mystical-Theurgical Dimensions of Prayer in *Sefer Ha-Rimmon.*" In *Approaches to Judaism in Medieval Times,* Volume III. Edited by David R. Blumenthal, 41-79. Atlanta: Scholars Press, 1988.

Wolowelsky, Joel B. *Women, Jewish Law, and Modernity: New Opportunities in a Post-Feminist Age.* Ktav, 1997.

Yahalom, J. "The Poetics of Spanish Piyyut in Light of Abraham Ibn Ezra's Critique of its Pre-Spanish Precedents." In *Abraham Ibn Ezra and His Age, Proceedings of the International Symposium, Madrid 1989.* Edited by Fernando Díaz Esteban, 387-392. Madrid: Asosiacíon España de Orientalistas, 1990.

Zahavy, Tzvee. "*Kavvanah* for Prayer in the Mishnah and Talmud." In *New Perspectives on Ancient Judaism.* Volume 1: Religion, Literature and Society in Ancient Israel, Formative Christianity and Judaism. Edited by J. Neusner et. al., 37-48. Atlanta: Scholars Press, 1990. Reprint of *Studies in Judaism.* Lanham, MD, 1987.

——. *Studies in Jewish Prayer.* Lanham: University Press of America, 1990.

Zimmels, H.J. *Ashkenazim and Sephardim: Their Relations, Differences, and Problems as Reflected in the Rabbinical Responsa.* London: Marla Publications, 1976.

Zunz, Leopold. *Die Ritus des synagogalen Gottesdienstes geschichtlich entwickelt.* 2nd edition. Berlin, 1919.

# *Index of Sources*

## I. Rabbinic Sources

MIDRASH



OTHERS



## II. Geonic Sources

## III. Rishonim

## IV. Aḥaronim

## V. Siddurim and Maḥzorim

### GENIZAH MANUSCRIPTS



### MANUSCRIPTS AND EDITIONS

# General Index